CW00870984

POLYDORE VERGIL'S ENGLISH HISTORY,

POLYDORE VERGIL'S ENGLISH HISTORY,

FROM AN EARLY TRANSLATION

PRESERVED AMONG THE MSS. OF THE OLD ROYAL LIBRARY
IN THE BRITISH MUSEUM.

VOL. I.

CONTAINING THE FIRST EIGHT BOOKS,

COMPRISING

THE PERIOD PRIOR TO THE NORMAN CONQUEST.

EDITED BY

SIR HENRY ELLIS, K.H.

"Ornatissime Polydore, Opera tua sunt eleganter et feliciter excusa."
Erasmi Epist. fol. Lugd. Bat. 1706, *Ep.* DCCLX. 5 *Sept.* 1525.

FACSIMILE REPRINT, 1996, BY
LLANERCH PUBLISHERS, FELINFACH.

ISBN 1 86143 015 9

PRINTED FOR THE CAMDEN SOCIETY,
BY JOHN BOWYER NICHOLS AND SON, PARLIAMENT STREET.

M.DCCC.XLVI.

ALSO PUBLISHED BY
LLANERCH

SIMEON OF DURHAM:
A HISTORY OF THE CHURCH OF DURHAM
Translated by Joseph Stevenson

SIMEON OF DURHAM:
A HISTORY OF THE KINGS OF ENGLAND
Translated by Joseph Stevenson

JOHN OF FORDUN'S
CHRONICLE OF THE SCOTTISH NATION
Edited by W. F. Skene

WILLIAM OF MALMSBURY:
A HISTORY OF THE NORMAN KINGS
Translated by Joseph Stevenson

MALMSBURY:
THE KINGS BEFORE THE NORMAN CONQUEST
Translated by Joseph Stevenson

THE ANNALS OF CLONMACNOISE
BEING THE HISTORY OF IRELAND
From the earliest period to 1408
Edited by Denis Murphy

THE ANNALS OF TIGERNACH
Facsimile from the pages of Revue Celtique
Edited with intercolated translations by Whitley Stokes

THE CHRONICLE OF
HENRY OF HUNTINGDON
Translated by J. Forester

THE CHRONICLE OF
ROBERT DE MONTE
Translated by Joseph Stevenson

FLORENCE OF WORCESTER:
A HISTORY OF THE KINGS OF ENGLAND
Translated by Joseph Stevenson

For a complete list
Please write to:

LLANERCH PUBLISHERS
FELINFACH, LAMPETER
DYFED, WALES
SA48 8PJ

COUNCIL

OF

THE CAMDEN SOCIETY

FOR THE YEAR 1846.

PREFACE.

The Three last Reigns in this Translation of Polydore Vergil's History have already formed a separate Volume of the Camden Society's Publications. The interest they created led the Council to believe that an edition of the whole was desirable; not only as affording a faithful version of a work hitherto confined to the Latin tongue, but as preserving a beautiful Translation, made at a period when our language was beginning to assume the character of modern elegance.

The present Volume extends from the earliest traditions of our History to the close of the Anglo-Saxon period. A second, to be published after an interval, will carry it on to the end of the reign of Henry the Third. And a third Volume will take it to the close of the reign of Henry the Fifth, at which the Volume of the Three Reigns, already published, commences.

Since the Preface to that volume was written, two or three further incidents of Polydore Vergil's personal history have been ascertained. There can be no doubt now that he arrived in England in 1501; the date is fixed by the contents of a letter from Henry the Eighth to Pope Leo the Tenth in 1513, in which, recommending Polydore, who was about to pay a visit to his parents in Italy, to the Pope's gracious notice, it expressly states that he had been in England twelve years. The Letter will be found in the Appendix, Number I., copied from one of the volumes of the Vatican Transcripts made for the Commissioners upon the Public Records, and lately deposited in the British Museum.

From a passage, before over-looked, in the Register of Bishop Smyth of Lincoln, it appears that the patron who presented Polydore Vergil to the rectory of Church Langton in Leicestershire, Nov. 6, 1503, was Sir Nicholas Griffin, knt.

Another incident of Polydore's life, mentioned in Ruddiman's Preface to Gawin Douglas's Translation of Virgil, was also overlooked. In 1509, intent upon the production of his History, which he had then begun under the auspices of Henry the Seventh, he wrote a letter to James the Fourth of Scotland, wherein he requested that his Majesty would be pleased to send him a Catalogue of the Scots Kings, and memoirs of their most remarkable actions, especially where interwoven with the English history, in which he promised to do all honour and justice to the Scots nation. The letter was printed by Ruddiman in 1722 and 1724 :* a more perfect copy, however, from the original, still remaining in the Advocates' Library at Edinburgh, has been obtained through the kind assistance of David Laing, Esq., and will be found in the Appendix, Number II.

Ruddiman, however, says, "We incline to believe that he met with little encouragement, and that his Majesty could not expect an impartial account of our affairs from a Foreigner, addicted to the interest of his enemies; so he would not be obliged to him for what might be done more for his and the nation's honour, and to better advantage, by one of his own subjects. And for this perhaps it was that Hector Boetius shortly after set about the writing of our history."

What James the Fourth declined to do, the Bishop of Dunkeld supplied to Polydore at a later day.†

In the Preface to the Volume already published, a fragment of a note to Wolsey is mentioned,‡ in which the writer advises him to caution the King against Polydore as well as against the Cardinal S. Chrysogoni, otherwise named Hadrian de Castello, and recommending the interception of their letters. From whom it came did not then appear;

* Epistolæ Jacobi Quarti, Jacobi Quinti, et Mariæ Regum Scotorum, eorumque Tutorum et Regni Gubernatorum—ab anno 1505 ad annum 1545. Edinb. in ædibus Thomæ Ruddimanni, 1722, 1724. 2 vols. 8vo.

† See the Preface to the volume containing the Three Reigns, p. vii., and pp. 105, 106, 107 of the present volume.

‡ Pag. ix.

but a letter in the State Paper Office, in the same handwriting, and upon the same subject, shows it to have come from Andreas Ammonius, the king's Latin-Secretary, who, subsequently, upon Polydore's imprisonment, succeeded him as Sub-collector of the Peter-Pence. Henry the Eighth's letter to Pope Leo X., recommending Ammonius for the appointment to the Sub-collectorship, is remaining in the same repository, and will be found in the Appendix, Num. III. Ammonius succeeded to the office; but at no great distance of time, in 1517, died of the Sweating Sickness.*

Polydore Vergil, as has been stated in the former Preface, and as Henry the Eighth's letter shows, was imprisoned. He had written to his relation the Cardinal S. Chrysogoni "pessima quæque" both as related to Wolsey and to the King. What the slander was, appears no where; but a letter from Polydore to Wolsey, which he wrote from his prison, and which is still remaining among the papers of the latter, is a curious specimen at once of his fright on this occasion: and of the adulation, almost blasphemous, with which he sought to soften Wolsey's resentment. He seized the moment when Wolsey was made Cardinal, at once to compliment him,

* His death is thus noticed in a letter from Joannes Sixtinus to Erasmus—"Hodie amicus noster Andreas Ammonius sepultus est, sudaria peste (qua plerique magni nominis viri periêre) sublatus; sit felix bonusque ipsius animæ Deus, quo die concessit naturæ."

and to entreat for his own release. This also is given in the Appendix, Num. IV.

That Polydore had recovered favour before 1522 is evidenced in a passage of Collier's Ecclesiastical History, in which the subsidy granted by the clergy in Cardinal Wolsey's Convocation in that year is mentioned. He says, "By this grant, all Foreigners benefic'd in England were double charged: that is, they were to pay the full of their annual revenue in five years' time. The Bishop of Worcester and Landaff, POLYDORE VERGIL, Peter the Carmelite, Erasmus of Rotterdam, Silvester Darius, and Peter Vannes had the benefit of an exception, and were obliged to pay no higher than the natives."*

That Polydore Vergil's History is entirely without mistakes cannot be asserted, but they are very few. In p. 17 of the present volume, he mixes the history of Anglesey with that of the Isle of Man, only in consequence of both being called, in Latin, Mona. At p. 56 he considers the Trinobantes as Essex men; and elsewhere, p. 73, denies that Trinovant meant London. He places it at Colchester.

The Objections of his contemporaries to his History, as well as of some who followed them, have been already sufficiently refuted in the former Preface. His contemplating the exploits of Arthur, of Brennus, and of

* Collier, Eccl. Hist. ii. 18.

Brutus as fabulous, raised a loud cry against his work in his own day; and for the repudiation of Geoffrey of Monmouth's history, Polydore Vergil was considered almost as a man deprived of reason. Such were the prejudices of the Time.

Nevertheless, the reader who has leisure to go through the present Volume will find that his long and earnest endeavour was to write what he himself terms "a sincere History." His delineations in local description, his care in weighing facts and testimonies, the good sense of his remarks, all show him to have been a Historian beyond his Age, both in his power of discrimination and in his acquirements.

APPENDIX.

Num. I.

Henrici Octavi Regis Angliæ ad Leonem X. Commendatitia, pro Polydoro Vergilio Urbinate redeunte in Patriam parentes invisuro.
Ann. 1513.

[Ex Litteris autographis Henrici, Arm. xiv. caps. 11. nº 8.]

Beatissime Pater, post humillimam commendationem, et devotissima pedum oscula beatorum. Fuit in hoc nostro regno, plurimos jam annos, venerabilis vir Dominus Polydorus Vergillius, Urbinas, Wellen. Ecclesiæ archidiaconus, et vestræ Apostolicæ Cameræ in hoc regno Vice-collector, quem eximia eruditione, tum vero modestia, circumspectione, et gravitate preditus, ut quamquam quibusdam de causis haud mediocriter optaremus, Collectorem, sicuti non multos ante annos moris fuit, hic apud nos presentem habere; ipse tamen licet vicarius et substitutus huic nostro desiderio maxima ex parte satisfecerit, nec minori ornamento utilitatique tam Domino Collectori quam ipsi officio Collectoriæ fuerit.

Quare et claræ memoriæ olim nostro patri, et nobis, percarus semper extitit. Is vero nuper nobis significavit, post annos xij. quos in hoc nostro Regno, et quidem uti nos testes sumus, haud ex qua sua cum laude egit patriam, parentes, ac res suas, nostra cum venia et commeatu revisere; atque inde ad vestram Beatitudinem se conferre, ejusque sanctissimos pedes deosculari se cupere. Cujus justissimo voto nos ita annuimus, ut sine nostra commendatione discedere noluerimus. Ideoque vestram sanctitatem impense rogamus, ut dictum D. Polydorum ad se venientem, tum nostra tum suarum virtutum gratia, benigne admittere, sibique præcipue commendatum habere dignetur, quod erit nobis plurimum gratum. Ex Regia nostra apud Westmonasterium, die xxvj. Februarii, M.D.XII.

E. V. S[tis]

devotissimus atque obsequentissimus filius, Dei gratia Rex Angliæ et Franciæ ac Dominus Hiberniæ,

Henricus.

Num. II.

Polydorus Vergilius, Jacobo Quarto Scotorum Regi.

Sacra Regia Majestas, humillimam commendationem. Cum nullo sim neque servitio neque officio cognitus Majestati vestræ, paucis propterea perstringam qui sim, et simul quæ in presenti fuerit ad eandem Majestatem vestram scribendi causa. Cum enim superioribus annis, dum Patavii agerem, in primo nostri ingenioli tyrocinio scripserim libellum unum Adagiorum, et deinde tres libellos de Inventoribus rerum, et illos rogatu Ducis mei Urbinatis, viri tam Græcè quam Latinè docti, ediderim, qui nunc (qualescunque sunt) in manibus hominum versantur, leguntur que passim; et mox Quæsturæ Pontificiæ cura mihi demandata, in Angliam venerim, ut cupidus novarum rerum cœpi diligentissime situm terræ amœnissimum, opes innumeras, hominum mores spectatissimos contemplari, item Annales Britannorum atque Anglorum antiquissimos versare manu, lectitare, ac scripta scriptis conferre: ubi tot et tanta tum Regum, tum aliorum illustrium virorum Gesta memoratu digna reperi, ut non potuerim non valde mirari auctores Græcos veteresque Latinos, et præsertim Cæsarem et Cornelium Tacitum, qui hic quandoque fuerunt, tam pauca de hujusmodi inclyta Insula prodidisse. Simul quoque dolui, quod ipsi Annales ita varii, confusi, ambigui, sine ordine (quæ in primis abhorret Historia) sunt, ut non modo ea præclara facinora exteros homines, sed ipsos juxta incolas laterent. Quare ego, quem ubi per negotia licuit literario otio frui semper ab ineunte ætate (ut dictum est) plurimum juvit, sum arbitratus me esse operæ pretium facturum, in res tum Britannorum tum Anglorum gestas carptim perscriberem. Itaque opus etsi nostris viribus impar aggressus, jam prope consumavi. Caeterum cum una sit Insula, pari studio curavi de rebus quoque Scotorum, quæ etiam præclara sunt, obiter suo loco memorare: sed illud non servato ordine feci, cum nullum habuerim quem sequeremur scriptorem. Super qua re sum sæpius Dominum Gilbertum capellanum Majestatis vestræ allocutus, hortatusque ut curaret saltem nomina Regum Scotiæ edocere, [quo de illis suus in nostra historia locus (prout cupimus) meminisse dignosceretur:] quod tamen hactenus desideravimus. Nunc igitur Majestatem vestram, quæ nequaquam minus benefacere quam dicere novit, oro, uti dignatur, aut Annales (si qui sint) aut Nomina Regum suo ordine scripta ad me mittere, et imprimis quæ tua sunt, seu tuorum inclyta facta fuerint, nos edocere, qui in recognitione operis de rebus hujusmodi memorabilibus transsumpter mentionem faciemus. Et quamquam non eo sumus ingenio aut doctrina præditi, qui valeamus res regni Majestatis vestræ illustrare, id tamen haud dubie præstabimus, quod nihil honoris vel decoris per inscitiam aut incuriam nostram amittent, quæ. ubi supremam manum operi imposuerimus, Majestas vestra perspicue dignoscet: quæ diu bene valeat. Londini, die xiij Decembris M.D. nono.

E. M. V.

Servulus POLYDORUS VIRGILIUS *Urbinas*, Archidiaconus Vellen.

Sacræ Regiæ Majestati Scotiæ.

NUM. III.

King Henry VIII. to Pope Leo X. recommending Ammonius to be the successor of Polydore Vergil as Sub-Collector of the Peter Pence.

[From the Orig. in the State Paper Office, *Misc. Corresp.* 3 *Ser.* vol. VII. 5.]

Beatissime Pater, post humillimam commendationem ac devotissima pedum oscula beatorum. Etsi magno affectu semper et cura Magistrum Andream Ammonium, nostrum a Latinis Secretarium, vestræ S^{ti} commendaverimus, eamque studiosissime rogaverimus ut Collectoriæ Officium in hoc nostro Regno, præcipue nostro rogatu, a se eidem nostro Secretario promissum et datum, ac nonnullis suis ad nos Brevibus, ut putavimus, confirmatum ab omnibus litibus et controversiis explicare dignaretur, id nobis multo obnixius faciendum nunc esse censemus quum tam de conservanda nostræ apud vestram S^{tem} Gratiæ existimatione agi videamus. Cui haud dubie plurimum detraheretur si Cardinalis Hadrianus uti conatur seu quispiam alius beneficium singulari nostra gratia a vestra S^{te} concessum et datum infirmaret seu immutaret, quamquam dictum Cardinalem Hadrianum magis decebat binis presertim nostris Literis instanter rogatum nostro desiderio ac postulationi se accommodare, eo magis quam alias R^{do} D. Petro Grypho episcopo nunc (ut audivimus) Forolivien. cupidissime cessit, quum nihilo minus juris quam nunc sibi vendicat haberet, verum de predicto Cardinale olim viderimus. Interim ejus instigatorem Polydorum Vergilium ob hanc atque alias causas, sed inprimis quia conjunctionem inter vestram S^{tem} et nos, cujus maxime sumus zelotipi, verbis suis labefactare ac minuere contendebat, in carcere conjectum suæ illic temeritatis penas luere cogemus. De dicta autem Collectoria finem rogandi vestram S^{tem} nullum sumus facturi, donec ipsam pro solita et eadem summa sua erga nos benignitate paternaque indulgentia predictum officium in nostram specialem gratiam eidem nostro Secretario promissum datum, et ut diximus confirmatum, suæ potestatis plenitudine corroboraverit, et ab omnibus litibus controversiisque expediverit, quod ut vestra S^{tas} efficere aliisque maximis innumerisque suis in nos benificiis accumulare dignetur etiam atque etiam vehementissime rogamus. Quæ fæliciss. ac diutiss. valeat. Ex Palatio nostro Grenwici die xxij. Maij, M.D.xv.

E. V. Sanctitatis devotissimus atque obsequentissimus filius, Dei Gratia Rex Angliæ et Franciæ ac Dominus Hiberniæ.

Sanctissimo Clementissimoque Domino nostro Papæ.

Num. IV.

Polydore Vergil to Cardinal Wolsey, from his Prison.

[State Paper Office, Wolsey's Corresp. vol. I. 201.]

yħs

Maxime ac reverendissime Pontifex, et Columna Ecclesiæ Dei firmissima, humillimam commendationem. Audivi et ego Servus tuus, qui in umbra mortis adhuc jaceo, de ingenti gloria tua, et quanto mortalium omnium favore in excelso Cardinalis throno D. tua R^ma^ elevata sit, quæ huic supremo Ordini plus fere dignitatis præbet quam accipit ab eo, tanta .n. est virtus tua. Ego inter alios quoque gaudeo et gratulor, et quando licebit tuam M^tem^ coram adorare et contemplari, tunc profecto exultabit spiritus meus in te deo salutari meo. R^me^ domine Deus indulgentiæ, Deus pietatis, fac eandem misericordiam tuam cum humili servo tuo. Remisit nuper mihi tua benignitas culpam, per viscera misericordiæ Dei remittere et pœnam, ut perfecta sint munera tua, sicut et D. tua R^ma^ perfecta est. Jam adventat tempus quo Salvator noster Christus de cælo in terram descendit ad reconciliandum peccatores Deo patri, sic tu Presul maxime dignaris in hoc tempore gratiæ me ab ista umbra mortis dextera tuæ clementiæ extrahere, et in lucem sanctam restituere, ut nascenti Domino nostro, per te, ego quoque renatus gratias agere, ac pro tua D. R^ma^ mente quieta et spiritu leto simul eundem D. Jhesum Christum orare valeam, quod dum spiritus hos reget artus perpetuo faciam.

Igitur bone R^me^ Domine miserere cito mei, qui afflictus sum et humiliatus sum valde; et salvum me fac, qui salvare in perpetuum potes. Miserere inquam quia miserandi ac salvandi quia venit Tempus. Amen.

E. V. R^me^ D.

Humilis creatura

R. Domino Deo meo D. Car^li^ Eboracen. dig^mo^. Polydorus.

THE CRONICLE

OF

POLYDORE VIRGIL.

THE FIRST BOOKE OF POLIDORE VIRGILL OF THE HISTORY OF ENGLAND.

THE whole countrie of Britaine (which at this daie, as it were in dowble name, is called Englande and Scotlande), beinge an Ilonde in the ocean sea buttinge over agaynste the Frenche shore, is divided into iiij. partes; whereof the one is inhabited of Englishmen, the other of Scottes, the third of Wallshemen, the fowerthe of Cornishe people. Which all differ emonge them selves, either in tongue, either in manners, or ells in lawes and ordinaunces. Englond, so called of Englishmen the inhabitauntes, beinge farre the greateste parte, is divided into xxxix. Shiers, which commonlie men call cownties: of the which x., that is to weete Kente, Sussex, Surrey, Southehamton, Bareckshier, Wilshire, Dorsetshire, Somersetshier, Devonshire, and Cornewall, conteine the firste parte of the ilond, which enclininge towarde the sowthe liethe betwene the Sea and the river Thames; then even unto the river of Trente, which ronneth throughe the middeste of Englonde, there are sixetene other counties; whereof vj. (beinge in the formeste frontiers) are bente towardes the easte, namelie Estesexe, Middelsex, Hertfordshiere, Sowthfolk, Norffolke, Cambridgeshire; the latter, beinge x, which are more neare

Britaine devyded into iiij. partes.

England devyded into xxxix. Sheiers.

to the middell of the soyle, are these, Bedfordshiere, Huntingtonshiere, Buckinghamshire, Oxefordshire (albeit parte thereof ronnethe in lenghte one this side Thames), Northehamtonshire, Rotlandshire, Lecestershire, Nottingamshire, Warwickeshire, and Lincolneshire: behinde these are vj., which bownde towardes Walles and the weste partes, Glocestershire, Herefordshire, Woorcestershire, Shropshire, Staffordshire, and Chesseshire. Aboute the middell, and as it were the navell of the riolme, followethe Darbey, Yorcke, Lancastre, and Cumberlande (on the lefte hande towarde the weste), and Westhumberlande; but on the other side Durham and Northehumberlande, decllininge towards the northe, seemethe more to be apperteining to the Scottishe teritorie. These counties are proporcionallie distributed into the jurisdiction of xvij. busshopps, usuallie called diocesse, and that in this manner: The bisshopricke of Canterburie and Rochester contenith the frutefull province of Kente; the diocesse of London comprehendith Estesexe, Middelsaxe, and parte of Hertfordshire; the sea of Chichester conteineth Sowthsaxe; Winchester diocesse hath Sowthehamton, Surrey, and the Ile of Weyghte; Saresburie hathe in it Dorcester, Barckshire, and Willshire; Exceter bisshopricke hathe Devonshire and Cornewall; the bisshopricke of Bathe and Wells, united as one, conteineth Somersette; Worciter diocesse comprehendethe Glocestershire, Woorcitershire, and parte of Warwickshire; the diocesse of Hereforde hathe parte of Shropshire and Hereforde; the bisshopricke of Coventree and Lichefielde united, conteineth Chesshiere, Staffordshire, Derbieshier, with the partes remayninge of Warwicke and Shropshire, and so mutche of Lancaster as apperteineth to the river of Repill.[a] In the diocesse of Lincolne, beinge farre the biggeste, are comprised those viij. shieres which lie betweene the river of Thames and Humber, that is to saye Lincolne, Northehampton, Lecester, Rutland, Huntington, Bedforde, Buckingham, Oxeforde, and the remnante of Hertfordshire. In the busshopricke of Eley is included Cambridgeshire and the Ile of Eley. In the diocesse of Norwige

xvij. Diocesse.

[a] Ribble.

is conteined Suffolke and Norffolke. And this is the Province of the Archebusshoppe of Canterburie, which is metropolitane of Englande: adjoininge there unto Walles, which hath iiij. dioceses, as hereafter we shall make mĕntion. The bisshopricke of Yorck hath semblablie Notinghamshire, Yorkeshire, with the remainder of Lancashire. Durham diocesse hathe the cowntie of Durham and Northehumberlande. Finallie Carleyl diocesse hathe Cumberlande and Westmerlande: and this is the other Province or Circuit of the archbusshope of Yorcke, which is also metropolitane of Englonde, yea, and of longe season was allso primate of Scotlande, as ellswhere we shall make rehersall. Those dioceses are named of their cities, wherein the sea it selfe of the busshopps consistethe. Wherefore London of right is cheefe, wheare, indeed, furste of all was ordeyned the sea of the archbusshoppe; but as towchinge the transposinge thereof to Canterburie, a citie of Kente, in place conveniente we minde to make demonstration; for the famous citie of London is situate in the cowntie of Middelsaxe, on the north bancke of the river Thames.

The sea of the Archbusshoppe fyrst at London.

This moste pleasant fludde hath his hedd and originall risinge at the village named Winchecombe, and echewhere gatheringe encrease of his flowe and streame, first runnethe in length bie Oxeforde, and afterwarde, havinge full course bie London, hath issue into the Frenche ocean sea, where beinge receaved in wonderfull gowlfe, doth twise ebbe and flowe more then lx. miles in the space of foure and twentie howers, to the excedinge great commoditie of all men, bie cause that bie the meanes thereof merchandise hathe recourse and accesse to the citie.

Thames.

In this moste renowned citie is there a bridge of stone of wonderous artificiall woorkmanshippe, for therein are conteyned xx. piles of square stone, lx. foote of height, xxx. of bredthe, the one beinge distante from the other abowte xx. foote, yet knitte and joyned together with arches, in the toppe whereof howses one bothe sides are soe subtilye builded, that it rather representith a streete of great lenghte then a bridge.

The dyscription of London Brydge.

The description of England.

And this Englonde, beinge the chefest parte of Britaine, on the easte and sowthe side is limited of the ocean sea, on the weste parte with the bowndes of Cornewall and Walls, on the northe with the river Twede, which devideth the Englishe men from Scottes. At this Twede endethe the whole lenghte of the region, whiche havinge beginninge at the uttermoste bancke lienge sowthward is extended even thether bie computation the space of cccxx. miles. This cowntrie is of all places moste frutefull on this side of the river of Humber, for on the other side it somewhat to muche abowndethe with mountaynes; for, notwithstandinge to the beholder afarre of it appearethe verie champion and plaine, nevertheless it hathe manye hills, and such as for the moste parte are voyde of trees, with most delectable valleys, wherein the moste parte of the inhabitantes, especiallie the nobles, have placed their manners and dwellinge-howses; whoe, accordinge to their aunciente usage, do not so greatlie affecte citties as the commodious nearenes of dales and brookes, there dwellinge somewhate neere together, mindinge (as I suppose) therebie more easilie to eschewe the tempesteous blastes of boisterous windes, bie cause the Ilande itself is naturallie subjecte to greate windes, wherebie it comethe to passe that theruralls and common people, bie the entercourse and daylye conference which they have with the nobilitie, confuselie dwellinge emonge them, are made verie civill, and so consequentlie their citties nothinge famous. This river, which before I named Humber, havinge beginninge on this side Yorcke, and streightweye turninge towarde the sowthe, takethe forthewith his course into the easte, and so hath issue into the ocean sea, beinge firste augmented bie the rivers Dune and Trente. This Trente hathe his originall founteyne not farre from Stafforde, whiche, passinge thoroughe Darbie and Lecestre, and flowinge nighe unto Lichefielde and Nothingham, declinethe towardes the right hande; but the other, that is to witte Dunne, bendethe unto the lefte hande, soe that Dunne and Trente betwene them make the flow now called Axolme; and not farre from thence united a litle on this side the towne in aunciente time named Kyngstone, but now called Hull (well knowen bie reason of the assemble marte of biers and sellers) theye runne into Humber, throwghe the which owt of Fraunce, Germanie, and Denmarcke, there bothe commodious and safe passage. The grownde is marvelous fruitefull, and aboundantlie replenished with cattayle, wherebie it commethe to passe that of Englishe men moe are grasiers and masters of cattayle then howsbande men or laborers in tilling of the fielde, so that allmoste the third parte of the grownde is lefte unmanured, either for their hertes, or falowe deere, or their conies or their gotes (for of them allso are in the northe partes no small number); for allmoste everie where a man maye se clausures and parckes paled and enclosed, fraughte with suche venerie, which, as they minister greate cause of huntinge, so the nobilitie is muche delited and exercised therein. Thus muche for the firste parte of Britaine, leste I shall peradventure seeme tedious, seinge that as towchinge the situation thereof hereafter, and eche where through all this worcke, I meane to entreate in places convenient.

The description of Scotland.

Scotland is the other parte of Brytaine, whereof I will somewhat at large entreate in this place, to the entente I maie have no occasion hereafter to declare the situation thereof. In aunciente memorie it appearethe to have had beginninge at the mountaine called Grampius, beinge continued in lenght on the uttermoste bownde towarde the northe: but, after the distruction of Pictland, it did extende even to the ryver Twede, yea sumetyme unto Tine, the uncerteyne chaunce of battayle shewinge like mutabilitie in that pointe as it dothe in all other thinges; wherefore the length thereof from the ryver Twede to the fordeste bowndes is accownted to conteyne cccclxxx. miles; but bie howe much it is more longe than the realme of Englande, so much it is lesse in bredthe, for yt endethe like a wedge, that is to saye, small and sclender in the extremest parte, for the mountayne Grampius, beinge huge and rowghe (whereof Tacitus makethe mention in the Life of Julius Agricola), dothe runne throughe the middell of Scotland from the shore lienge over agaynste Germanie, that is to weete from the entree of the ryver Dee, it hathe excourse to the Irish seas, even unto the greate meere or lake called Lomund, which liethe betweene that border and this forenamed mountayne. Nexte unto the river Twede (which, springinge oute of a little hill somwhat beyonde Roxburrow, runnethe into the

The marshe.

Germanian ocean sea), sowthwarde enseweth that region which men call Marchelande, which is nothinge ells but the verie borders and marches of Englisshemen and Scotts: which is dissevered bie the river Twede from Northehumberland, the fardeste cowntie of Englande; the chefest towne thereof is Berwicke, which in owre time is subjecte to Englishemen. I suppose the same in times paste to have bene the cheef citie of the inhabitantes of the hills Cheviot. Scotland on the weste sometime bordered on Cumberland,

The river of Solway.

which is separated from the vale of Anandia bie the river Solve. Betweene these twooe regions Cheviot hills shewethe it selfe som-

Pickland, now cawlyd Lowdian.

what secretelie. On this Marcheland borderethe Picklande, at this time termed Laudonia, enclininge towarde the easte, havinge as greate scarsitie of trees, as to muche abowndinge in mountaynes. The townes therein of greateste names are these: Dunbar, Haddington, Leethe, Northe Berwicke, and Edenborrowe, the kynges cheefe pallaice wherein is a towre of no smalle

The river of Forth.

strengthe, called the Castil of Maidens, envirroned with the river Forthee, which as yet runneth into the ocean sea of Germanie. It makethe a wonderous greate mere called the Scottish Sea, wherein (omitting the rest) there is an isle dedicated to Sainte Colummbe, commonle named Aemonia, and that also is divided from Laudonia with a river. The region adjoyninge beinge

Fyfe.

plentifull in all thinges of the common people is named Fife, wherein are divers civill townes, as Dumfermile and Cypres; but of all others most excellente and notorious is thowght Sainte Andrewes, the more renowned bie reason of the universitie, and sea of the archebisshoppe, beinge there residente and metropolitane of all Scotland. On the other side, towarde the Irishe coste northewarde, it hathe Nithesdale, so called of the river running bie, whereas are twoo stronge and well fensed townes, Dunfreye and Dunglasse. On the sowthe side Gallowey is adjoininge, Galloway. a province more commodious for the forrage of cattayle then the tilthe of corne, wherein is the splendent howse and aunciente churche of Sainte Ninian, adorned especiallie bie the sea of the Called bysshoppe. Candida In this discourse or space nere unto the towne Casa. named Wigton, is there a poole of wonderous nature. For notwithstandinge throughe the rigor of winter parte thereof be never soe stifflie congeled with froste, yet parte remaynethe unfrosen. Next unto this is Caricta, in times paste notable bie reason of the towne Carleis, or Caricton, whereof paradventure it hathe the name derived. Above this Crea or Caricta is Aer, or rather Caricta Elgovea, for soe it is termed of Ptolemei, on the weste side border- is there termed inge on the ocean sea, wherein is that poole which beefore I Crea. named Lomund, of exceadinge greatnes, for therein are conteyned divers littell iles at the roote of the mounteyne Grampius, from the which the castell of Dunbriton is vii. miles distante; whereas the river Bodotria, nowe called Levnie, entrith into Clote, whereof The river hereafter we shall entreate in more ample wise. of Levin. A greate way on this side Grampius the greatest river of all Scotland, named Taus, The river hathe his hedd and springe owte of a lake of the same name, Tay. which, passinge bie Atholia and Calidon or Calendar and divers other places, runnethe bie the towne in fore time named Perthe, and now Saint Ihons; and finallie havinge his course bie Dondey, in auntient memorie called Alectum, it burstethe forthe into the Germanian sea, making an exceadinge greate flowe at the verie entrie, whereof Tacitus also maketh rehersall. Right over agaynste the bancke of Taus liethe Anguise, with whose streames this plea- Anguise. sant province is refresshed and watered, and is dissevered from Fife. The countrie Atholia lienge northwarde, as it is, is not farre Athole. from these three beinge moste delectable soyles of Scotland, soe is it not of all others most unfrutefull or barraine.

Arguile.

On the other side liethe Argatelia, which in that it aboundethe with mores, it yeldes more plenteouslie fodder than corne. The uttermoste border thereof approcheth so neere unto Irelonde that there are scarselie sixteene miles between them, in the which place is that promontorie which they call the hedd of their grownde. Plinie in his treatie of Irelonde, and iiij. booke, witnessethe that the Silurians in olde time were lordes thereof, whose wordes are these in effecte. This Irelond is placed a little above, verie nere to the people of Siluria, namelie within xx. miles, betweene the which and Elgovia westwarde there is the teritorie of Sterlinge, so named of a towne therin conteined. In this place the foreste Calidon, usuallie termed Calendar, had his originall, beinge greatlie spredde in bredthe and length towardes the inward partes of the riolme. In this woodde there are bredd white oxen havinge manes like liones, naturallie so wilde and savage that bie no meanes they can be tamed; nevertthelesse, after experience hadd once taught that there fleshe was saverie and pleasaunte in taste, there continuallie followed suche wracke and slaughter that bie reporte theie are allmoste all exhauste and consumed. There is also there the castell of Caledon, situate on the bancke of the river Taus called Dunchell. Owt of a litle hill apperteyninge to this foreste the river Glote hathe his springe, and havinge broade chanell towcheth it selfe in the Irishe ocean sea; for, havinge as it were reflection agaynste the botom of the mountayne Grampius, and turninge southward, it is receyved with suche wonderfull sourge of the sea, that (as Tacitus dothe write) it semed to the Romaines that there was besides it an other ilond beyonde.

Sterling.

Of this river the valey throughe the which it hathe passage is called Glotesvale, wherein is allso the citie Glasquen, a renowned universitie. Moreover towardes the easte is annexed the province called Anguise, and Merina, borderinge on the sea; in it is the towne which they calle Fordune, of a wonderfull fortified situacion, and well knowne bie reason of the reliques of Sainte

The universitie of Glasco.

Pallad, an apostle of no smalle credit emonge the Scotts. On the same side is the cowntie Marria, notable throughe the citie Aberdon, planted betweene twooe rivers, Don and Dea, sufficientlie enoughe knowen throughe the scholes and artes there professed. Next after these succedeth Morrovia, which is environed with twooe fluddes, Nesse and Spea: at the verie entrie standethe the towne named Elgis; abowte the banckes there is greate store of woodde, replenished with all sortes of wilde beastes, and a lake allso called Spina, abowndinge in the multitude of swannes. And within the midst hearof is the cowntie of Rossa, stretchinge forthe even to the uttermost corner: for on bothe sides it towcheth the ocean sea, beinge beste husbanded and tilled in partes neere to the easte. There is in it a porte so commodious to those saylinge, that commonlie it is called the Haven of Healthe or Safetie; the name of the toune is Thane. The uttermoste bownde of the ile is verie shorte, for the end is so narrow that it is scarselie xxx. miles broade, and, being fensed with iij. promontories, as it were arches, it firmelie resisteth the violent assawtes of the ocean sea, and, havinge in it two torninges enclosed of these mountaines, it hathe certen receptacles whereinto it receiveth the water quietlie. This daie men call that streightness of the earthe Cathanesia, windinge towards the Dewcalian sea. Thus muche of the partes particularelie.

Marre.

Murrey.

Rosse.

Cathness.

The Scottishe land hathe eche where havens of greate safetie, and entraunces bie sea, with pooles, fennes, fluddes, and fownteines well stored with fyshe, mounteynes also having levell grownde in the toppes of them plenteouslie yeldinge forrage for cattall, with wooddes runninge full of wilde beastes, throwghe the opportunitie of which places theie have bene allwaies so releved that as yet alltogether the cowntrie never had the overthrowe. For firste the fennes and wooddes have ministred refuge; the wilde beaste and fyshes have armed them againste famin. Abowt Scotlande in the Irishe sea there are extante more than fortie ilondes of Plinie, comprised under the titill of Britaine; of others theie were named as to them

The Iland, Hebrides more then xl.

semed convenient; of some Mevaniæ, of others Hebrides; wherof verie manie at the least are xxx. miles in length xij. in bredthe; emonge these there is one called Iona, greter of fame throwghe the Scottishe kinges there buried. All the inhabitantes speke the Irishe speehe, which argueth that of them thei had their beginninge.

The Ilondes Orchades xxx.

Beyonde Scotland toward the Northe Pole are the Iles Orcades (accordinge to the authoritie of Ptolomei), xxx. in number, part of them consistinge in the Deucalion parte in the Germanian ocean sea; the cheefe of them men call Panonia, bie cause the bishoppe therein is resident, beinge under the Scottis jurisdiction. The people use the tongue of the Gothes, which maie be a proof that their discent is derived from the Germanians; theie are taule in stature, sounde as well as in the disposition of minde as constitution of bodie, and, notwithstandinge their cheefe meate is fishe, yet are they longe lived, for the earthe continuallie allmoste being hardened with cowlde, doth hardlie beare corne, and trees not at all.

The ile Thule is behinde the ilondes called Orchades, the which now they caule Ila, from the which (accordinge to Plinie) the ysee and frosen seas are distant the saylinge of one daye, wherein is Iselande, unto the which in sommer season yearlie our marchaunde men doe repaire to bie their fisshes; and for because it liethe farre northe under the sterre called Arctos men suppose it to be Thule. Thus mutche I thought good to speake of the proportion and placinge of Scotlonde; neither will I altogether use silence as towchinge the nature and behavior of the people. Those Scotts which inhabit the southe, beinge farre the beste parte, are well manured and somewhate of more gentle condicion, using the Englishe tongue, and in steade of woodde, whereof there they have smalle store, they make fire of a certeyne kinde of blackstone which they digge owt of the grounde. The other parte thereof, beinge mutche under the northe and full of hills, a moste harde and roughe kinde of men dothe possede, which are not without good cause called wilde and savage; they have theire soulgiars

The nature and behavior of the Scotts.

clokes and inner garmentes died with saffron accordinge to the Irishe fasshion, and goe with their legges bare unto the knees : theire cheefe weapons are bowes and arrowes, and a brode slawght swerde and a dager sharpe onelie on the one side. Theie all have the Irish speache, and the sustenaunce of their boddie consistethe in fish, milke, cheese, and flesh, for the which cause thei mainteyne a greate number of cattaylle : they differ all generalli from Englishmen in laws and decrees, for they have in use the civill lawe as allmoste all other nations doe, as hereafter shalbe declared ; but the Englishe people usethe propre and municipall lawes. In some thinges there is no difference or dissimilitude : for there tongues are all one, the features and attire of bodies like, like hautnes and corage in battayle, and equall desire of huntinge to the nobilitie, even from their childhode. Their howses in the countrie are verie narrowe, and covered either with strawe or with reedes, wherein bothe theye and their cattayle do harborowe all together. Besides Saint Ihones towne, there is not one enclosed with walles, which a man maye ascribe to the valiaunce of their minde, seinge that all their tuition and saftie theie referre to the strenghte of theyr bodies. As towchinge the sharpnesse of their witt, nature semethe nothinge to have fayled them, as theire erudition and literature dothe well declare ; for to what arte soever they applie them selfe, they profite therein withowte difficultie. But of them suche as yelde themselves to eas, to slewthe and unscillfulness, theie, in all that theie maye avoydinge travayle even in their extreme penurie, boste of their nobilite, as whoe shoulde saye better it weare that a man in gentil bloode shoulde wante, then bie crafte [a] or science to gather for his livinge ; nevertheless they are cownted devowte and sownde as towchinge relligion.

Walles is the thirde parte of this Ilonde, beinge one the lefte hande, nere to the middell of Englonde, and in similitude somewhate like to a towrning downe :[b] it runnethe forthe within the ocean sea like to an half ilonde, wherewith it is environed on all sides, savinge on the easte parte, and there it boundethe on the river

The discription of Wales.

[a] arte. *interlin.*

[b] bending or compasing bancke, for *interlin.*

Severne. called Severne, which disseverithe the Welche and Englishe people (albeit there are manie writers of late time which limite Walles and Englonde at the citie Hereforde), adjudging that the beginninge of Walles is at the towne called Cheepstowe, where the river named Vey, beinge encreaside with the river Logus or Luggus, and flowing bie Hereforde, towchethe it selfe in the sea. This river hathe his springe in the middeste of Walles, owte of the same hill which Severne springethe (I dowbte whether it arise owte of the same founteyne). Cornelius Tacitus thinketh the same to bee called Anton, as in another place yow shall heare. For even thether dothe extende a greate arme of the sea, which, entringe into the soyle on the weste side, dothe on the right hande runne bie Cornwall, on the left hande throughe Walles. The which description, notwithstandinge it savorethe of late yeares, yet I am not agreeved to followe it. Wherefore Walles as it were with a streight line is extended from Chiepstow where it beginnethe a little above Shropshire unto Chester towardes the northe. It is crediblie lefte in writinge that those Britons which wear survivors and safe after the spoyles and destruction of their contreye, in conclusion to have commen into Walles, usinge the opportunitie of the mountaynes, wooddes, and fennes (whereof that countrie is full) for their refuge and saftie, in the which place as yet they continewe. This lond afterwardes the Englishe people named

Welshmen. Walles, and the Britons inhabitantes Walshman, for in the Saxon speeche Wallseman is nothinge ells but an aliente or straunger, even as to us the Italien or Frenchemen are. Wherefore the

Inglyshmen. Englishmen, a people of Germanie or Saxonie, beinge seased in the realme of Britayne did calle the Britons that were the remaynders of their ruined contrie accordinge to their accostomed use Wallshemen, bie cause they hadd a diverse language, and the Countrie Walles: which names remayned as well to the nation as to the londe, so that the Britons loste bothe name and contrie together.

The derivation of the Welshe name. This is the trewe forme and derivation of their name, which (for as mutche as I knowe) noe man hath fownde owt heretofore, so that who so thinketh that they have their name ether of kinge or quene of like appellation no doubte thei are deceived. The fieldes of the countrie are for the moste parte barraine, yet so mutche the lesse fruitefull in that they lacke husbandinge and tilthe; wherebie it cometh to passe that the ruralles ([a]) live hardelie, eatinge oaten breade, and drinckinge ther milke ether meddeled with water or ells whaye; and the younger sorte, rovinge abroade and wanderinge, moleste as well their owne natives as also other with their thefte and roberies. There are manie townes with Castles verie well embateled, and iiij Dioceses of Busshoppes, if Hereford bee accownted in Englond, accordinge to the newe descriptions. The firste is the bisshoppricke of Meneve, at this daye called the bisshopricke of Saint Davides, an auanciente citie, and placed on that shore which liethe agaynste Ireland westwarde; the second is the bisshopricke of Landafe; the third is the bisshopricke of Bangore; the fourth is the bisshopricke of Saynte Assaves; which all are under the jurisdiction of the Archebusshoppe of Canterburie. Whereas the Welche speeche differethe from the Englishe, they which derive their race and stemme from the Troian stocke affirme that their tongue is compounded and intermedlied partlie with Greeke, partlie with the Troian antiquitie; but, howesoever the case standethe, they speake not soe smothelie nor pleasantlie as the Englishe people. For Welchemen as I suppose speak more in the throate; but contrariewise Englishmen, resemblinge more the Latinistes, drawe theire voice onelie a litle within their lippes, which sounde is pleasaunte and likinge to the hearer. And thus much I mynded to entreate of Walles, beinge the thirde parte of Englonde; ther remayneth the fourthe, which men call Cornewall.

Foure bisshoprikes in Wales.

This province hath his beginninge westwarde, on that side the ile which boundethe toward Spaine; towardes the easte the bredthe thereof conteineth lxxx. miles, extending a little beyonde Saint Germaines, the which towne, being not altogether obscure, is planted on the right hande, where the greatest breadthe sur-

The dyscription of Cornwall.

([a]) contrye people. *interlin.*

mountethe not xx miles; for this litle plotte of the soyle on the right hand is limited with the ocean shore; on the lefte hand with that arme of the sea which (as above we rehearced) enterethe the lande even unto Chiepstow, and somewhat in fasshion like an horne. At the first fronte is narrow, afterward in more ample wise it runnethe beyonde Sainte Germaines. On the easte side it borderithe on Englande; on the southe, weste, and northe it is compassed of the ocean sea. The earthe thereof is verie barraine, yielding fruites rather throughe the industrie and travayle of the tillers thereof, then of the owne goodness. Yet therein is greate plentie of blacke and white leade, or otherwise tinne, in the digginge whereof the cheefe living of those contrimen consistethe. In that onelie part of this ilonde even unto this presente continueth the nation of Britons, which in the beginning, havinge thether excourse owt of Fraunce, did occupie the ilonde (if they are to be credited which firmelie assevere that the firste inhabitantes of Britaine came owte of Armoricke, that is to say litle Britayne, as hereafter wee will make rehersall). This maye seme a good token thereof, that the Cornishe men use the same speeche which those men have that they comonlie call Brittishe Britons; that also is a good testimonie which I have redde in an ancient booke of monumentes, wherein I have founde for Cornewall not Cornubia, but Cornugallia, whoe showlde saye the name were fourmed of an horne, whose figure it representithe, and of Fraunce, of which it receaved the firste inhabitantes, the derivacion of which name canne in no wise mislike mee. This is for a certaintie, that their tongue greatlie differethe from the Englishe, and in manie thinges agreethe with the Welche, for divers thinges are common to theim bothe; yet this is the difference, that when the Welchman speakethe the Cornishe man doth not so well understand the whole sence and sentence as certeyne woords therein, so that wee maie easilie perceave that these three kindes of people do no more understand one the other then the Scotts, of whome the inhabitauntes of the sowthe are discrepante in language from the northe parties, a thinge somewhat to be woondered at that in one ilond there shoulde bee suche diversitie of tongues. Cornewall is under the diocesse of Excitre.

Hetherto have I spoken severallie of the division of Britaine, that, in disclosinge the nature of the whole bie his members, wee mighte the easier make true demonstration thereof, which is this in effecte.

The discription of whole Brytane.

It is moste evident that the proportion of the whole contrie of Britaine is triangular or three-squared, for it hathe three corners and three sides, one towards the easte, an other boundinge westwarde, and theie bothe runninge in lenght towardes the northe are one bothe sides muche the longeste. The third side, beinge southwarde, is a great deale shorter then the other two, because the ilonde it self is much more longe then broade: so that the other twayne are proportionall to the lenght thereof, and this laste to the breadthe. I meane there whereas ether the Ile beginneth most broade or otherwise endeth moste narrow, that is to weete northewarde. The firste corner thereof estward is at Dovor and Sandwich in Kente, from whence the passage into Fraunce couteinethe xxx. miles to Callice or Bononie, that is to saye, townes on the Frenche shore, the one beinge xx. miles distant from the other, whereunto allmoste all shippes are wonte to repaire. At this Callice, or as the common people saye Bononie, is the porte Icius, whose name is allmoste nothinge differing from the towne, for now beinge termed Callice haven it semeth to have encreased the name throughe the towne adjoyninge. From this nooke, which buttethe over agaynste Fraunce, that ende of the ilonde runneth forthe to the third corner northewarde, beinge in Scotland; which, albeit it somewhat enclineth towards Germanie, yet hathe it no lande juste againste it, but is as it weare restreigned into a narrowe streight and corner. The shore of this side is wonderuslie voied of havens, beinge in lengthe DCC. miles; but the other side, which is next to this lienge sowtheward, havinge his excourse from the firste corner in Kente againste the weste partes, even unto the other corner on the lefte hande, endeth on the uttermost shore in Cornewall. This side is at it were the froonte and face of the whole Ilonde, which in all this space, as a man woulde saie spreddinge the armes to ether of the corners, showeth forthe a broade breste, beinge here in deede moste broade, for from Dovor to Saincte Michaell's promontorie, which is on the uttermoste frontiers of Cornewall, it is supposed to be CCC. miles, on which side are havens of greate fame, and shippes moste safelie doe there stande at rode. Finallie, from this corner on the lefte hande, the other and thirde side takethe his beginninge (which goinge toward Spaine westward, on the which side Irelond hathe place between Spaine and Britaine), and so with manie windinges of the shore passinge bie Walles (which is placed betwene) tournethe towardes the northe, even juste to the thirde corner; in which discourse, conteininge the space of D.CCC. miles, it knitteth uppe and endethe the Ilonde, for beyonde it there is nothinge but the mayne ocean sea.

On that side allso there are havens of greate safetie, from whence yee maie saile to Irelonde in one daie: but somewhat lesse if yow pass out of Walles thither, for if you saile to Waterforde, the borderinge towne of Irelonde, it is like to the passage betweene Calice and Dovor, or litle more; but of all other the passage betweene Scotland and Irelonde is leste, as we have sayd before. From this the laste corner even to Antowne, being the uttermoste towne toward the sea southward, whereof it seemeth to be called Southehamtoune, between the other two corners of Kent and Cornwall, as it were with a streight line, menne measure the whole lenght of the Ilonde, affirminge it to conteyne D.CCC. miles, even as the bredthe from Saynt Davides to the towne called Hyermouthe, which is the uttermoste parte of the ile estewardes, amountethe to the somme of CC. miles. For, as it was declared before, it is broade on the southe side, which we have accounted the firste froonte thereof, and exceadinge narrowe in the ende, soe that the whole compasse of this Ilonde rownde about comprehendith no more then xviij. hundred miles, and bie that meanes ij. hundred lesse then Cæsar surmised. There are manie litle iles adjacent to Brytayne, and ij. of indifferent fame disjoyned from it with a narrow sea, in quantitie not unlike: the one called the Isle of Wighte, lienge agaynst the sowth bancke of Englonde, from whence, in the neareste place, it is distant but iiij. miles, in somme other places vij., in others xij. miles. The writers of most auncient yeares doe reporte it in portrature to be like an egge, for from the este westward it is longe, conteyninge xxx. miles; the bredthe, extendinge from the sowthe northewarde, is scarselie xij. miles. It is well furnished with inhabitantes, beinge Englishemen, and is annexed to Winchester dioces. Vespasiane, in times paste, beinge sente into Britayne bie the emperour Claudius, is thowght to be the firste which brought it under the Romayne empire. The other Ilond, beinge somewhat famous, is the Isle of Mone, or Man bie the exchaunge of one letter, which one the northe side enclinethe towarde Scotlande, sowthe-esteward towardes Englond, on the weste towardes Irelonde. In olde time, whensoever there appeared decrease or ebbe in the ocean, which at all times dothe rage and swell, it was divided with so small a sea, and was so neare unto the lande, that a man might have gonne thereunto without shippinge, which thinge (as Cornelius Tacitus recordethe) was donne of the Romaines, who, in the xiiij[th]. booke of his histories, and in the life of Julius Agricola, affirmethe, that first Paulinus Suetonius, and after that himselfe, Julius Agricola, embassadors of Britayne, did bie force of armes and marciall prowes vanquishe the Ile of Mone, beinge of greate puissaunce, throughe the inhabitantes, and a redie refuge for roges and ronnawayes; neverthelesse when thei minded to geve their firste assaut they, laienge aside all burdens (which might hinder suche an enterprise), sente before the moste likelie men of their armie, who bothe beste knewe the shalloe places and were moste experienced in swimminge, that thei might succor and guide the reste of the hoste swimminge in the deper places of the water, at the which feate the men of the ile being astonished, which missed the navie and looked for the munition of there sea, of a sodeyne required truce of Agricola. But, as the same man

The Ile of Wyght.

The Ile of Mone or Man.

writethe, Paulinus finished not there his exploitures with such facilitie or like expedition, who when he had passed over there sea, sodainlie beefore the shore apeared divers bandes of the inhabitantes, well addressed with their weapons, the women runninge emong the men in terrible attire like ghostes with their heare spredde abroade, with fire brandes in their hands, and theire preestes, beinge Druides, that is to say, of hethen religion, sainge their accursed prayers, and holdinge uppe their handes towardes heaven. This straunge sight soe apalled the coradge of the Romishe souldiers, that at the firste, as thowgh their limmes had beene starcke, they weare not able to withdrawe them or to save their bodies unwounded; yet at the lenght, partlie of their owne motion, partlie through the encoraginge of their captayne Paulinus, beinge perswaded not to feare a madde and effeminate companie, they hoysed their standardes, and joyninge in battayle destroyed all that they mette. Thus the people of the ile beinge overcomme, Paulinus ordeyned there a garison, at whose commandement their wooddes were cut downe, beinge dedicated to monstrous superstitions, for in them the people of the ile thought it lawful and acceptable to God to make their altars smell of the bloode of their captives, and to aske oracles of their goddes with the entralles of men.

But nowe we will retourne to our former purpose. The Scottes were lordes of this ile in the beginninge; the space lienge betweene them is lesse then xxvj. miles, in our memorie; it is inhabited bothe of Irishemen and Englishe, which have in use both there languages; but the Earle of Darbie, a worthie lorde of the Englishe nobilitie, hathe it in his jurisdiction, well knowne throughe the residence of his busshop. But see what the tracte and continuance of tyme maye doe; the ile is nowe more then xxv. mile from anie land, which in times paste was scarselie one mile distante. Where it commeth to passe that there ar some which dare affirme that yt is the Ile of Mone which men call Anglesea, beinge neare unto Walles and in the diocesse of Bangore; the nature of which place even at this daye is suche (accordinge to Tacitus) as wee declared that shore to bee, which is betweene the Ile Mone and that which is adjoined.

He retorneth to the discription of Inglond.

But let us make digression to that Brittayne, which we call England, that we may declare what the nature and qualities thereof was in our time. The wether commonlie cloudie intermedeled with showers and so mutche the lesse cowlde; the night season verie bright and in the uttermoste northe partes so shorte that there is smalle distance betweene the ende of the former daye and beginninge of the daye succeedinge; the dayes in sommer are verie longe, and this is the reason thereof, bie cause the iland lieth farre under the northe poincte, about the which the sonne, taking a longe race under the erth estward throughe the north parte, most neades tarie longe therein, even as in winter it is longe hidden while it runneth into the este through the south.

I have diligentlie noted at London, a cittie in the south partes of the riolme, that the nighte is scarslie v. houres in lenghthe in soommer when as the sonne is at his highest reache. The contrie it selfe at all times of the yeare verie temperat, noe sowernes or evell savor of the aire, insomuche that diseases raine seldom, and consequentlie lesse use of phisicke then in other places. Whearebie it commeth to passe that manie men live in divers places an hondred and tenne years, yea some sixe skore, albeit emonge artificers and husband men it is receaved as a prescripte that thei should sweate bie noe meanes. Never are there erthequakes, and lightening verie seldom. The grownde is luxurient and frutefull; besides corne and pulse, of the owne accorde bringing forthe all kinde of matter, saving firre and (as Cæsar saithe) beeche trees, with diverse other, as olives, which are woonte to growe in whotter soyles; but yt is well knowne that nowe there are beeches eche where in the londe. Thei plante vines in there gardins, rather for covert and commoditee of shaddowe then for the fruite, for the grape seldom commeth to ripenes excepte an hotte summer ensewe. They sowe rye, wheate, barlie, and oates, in theire dewe season, for they have noe other kinde of graine nor other pulses then beaens and peason; the corne shootethe soone uppe, but nothinge soe soone ripeth, the abowndance of moisture bothe in the earthe and wether is cause of them bothe. There corne and pulse as soone as it is ripe is carried forthwith in to the barne with eare and huske, and are so preserved till they thincke goodde to thresshe it or breake it accordinge to there exigence. The earthe, as wee have reherced, is not apte for wines, but instede thereof thei use ale or beare made of barley, beinge a drincke bothe commodius and pleasaunt to them which are accustomed thereunto; nevertheles thei have wines owte of France, Spaine, and Candie. Theire pleasaunt woodds are well replenished with apples and acornes or maste; thei have plenti of delicius rivers, pleasauntlie wateringe there feldes. It is straunge to bee towlde, yet verie trewe, that these floodds, Thamis, Humber, and divers other, are not easlie augmented with rayne; it maye wellbe for this cause, bie reason the erthe is verie sandie it drinkethe mutche water. There are manie hills cleane voide of treese and springges, bringing forthe thinne and shorte grasse, yeat suche as exceedinge well feadeth there sheepe, abowte the which in white flockes they wander day and night; and whether it bee throwghe the mildnes of the aire or goodnes of the grownde they of all other beare the moste softe and finest fleeces, but that is to bee asscribed to the barraines of there downes, as Virgil witnessethe in the iij. booke of his Georgicks, in this wise:

Avoyd all sharpe and thornie wooddis,
If care thow take of wooll,
With cleving burrs and briers rowghe,
And grown des with fodder full.

And, notwithstanding that of all others Englishe wooll is the beste, yet the olde writers make noe mention thereof, for Virgil dothe honor Miletus, a citte in Asia, as cheefe in that poincte, in the iiij. booke allso of his Georgickes, after this manner:

Within the chamber of deepe floodde the mother harde a sowne,
Whome rownde abowte the Nimphes did tose wooll of Miletus towne.

Miletus is a citte of Asia.

And likewise Columella, whoe flowrished under thempire of Claudius, aboute the liij. yeare of our salvation, in his vij. booke of howsbandrie, speaketh thus of sheepe then being of greatest price and estimation. The sheepe (saiethe he) of Miletus, of Apulia and Calabrie weare reputed of our men to be of excellent kinde, and of all other the beste are abowte Tarent: nowe the Frenche sheepe are thowghte more precius, the cheefe of theim being folded in the bare feeldes abowte Altina, Parma, and Mutina. This is his sentence, and surelie Plini in his viij. booke of the nature of cattaile is all moste of the same judgement, wherebie wee maye easilie gather that the auncient Brittons and Englishemenn tooke noe regarde of suche bestes as beare fleece, but ether verie latelie, or at leaste wise after the time of Plinie, transportinge theire wooll bie Frenchemen (being there nexte neighbowrs) to other nations, bie the which meanes it commethe to passe that even as yeat the Italians call the Englishe wooll French, as whoe shoulde saye Fraunce did bringe forth the same, and thus bie litel and littell men becam more industrius, for the like desier of wooll beegane to encrease emong the Scotts; albeit their fleese is muche cowrser. But I will retire to me former purpose.

Trulie this is woorthie the admiration, that thes sheepe receave noe drinke besides the dewe of the aire, insomutche that experience teaching how hurtfull drincking is for them thei are for the nonce kepte of theire shepherds from water. This fleece maie justlie bee alluded to the golden fleece wherin the chefe richis of the people consistithe; for great plentie of gollde and silver is yearlie of occupiers brought in to the realme, especiallie for suche merchandise which there perpetuallie remaneth, bie cause all men are forbedden to carrie it into enie other lande. Soe that I suppose there is in noe nation greater riches, for, besides the exceading sommes of monnie which eche wheare runneth throughe the handes of biers and sellers, and the plate dedicated to theire churches, the valeue whereof is incredible, there is allmoste noe man so neadie but for the dailie furniture of his table hathe his saltesillers, cuppes, and spones of silver, with manie and divers kindes of vessells, eche manne accordinge to his estate. England is well stored with all kinde of beastes, besides asses, mules, cammels, and elephants, but there is engendered nether enie venemus beastes nor raveninge, excepte foxes, and in old time woolves (as another place shall suffice to reherce), bie the which meanes there cattayle dothe freelie stray with oute harme all moste with oute attendant keeper; for a man maye see heardes of oxen and horses, yea flockes of sheepe, daylie wanderinge and nightlie, throwghe hills and vales, throughe common feeldes lefte open for pasture, and throughe suche severall grownde as everie neyghboure maye take the commoditee therof in feeding his cattayle after the corne is gathered in; and for this cause have their horses there stones cutte oute, that being made geldings, thoughe thei grase abrode, yet they maye contente them selves with lesse rowme or rovinge; a great companie of theire horses doe not trott, but aumble, and yet neither trotters nor aumblers are strongeste, as strengthe is not allwaie incident to that which is more jentil or lesse coragius. Their oxen are of like nature, wherefore manie of them at once are yoked in one plowe or carte (for bothe the earthe is tilled and carres drawen aswel with oxen as horses), which allso stande men in noe small steede as towchinge the bearinge of burdens. Their oxen and wethers are beasts as it weare of nature ordayned for feastinge, whose fleshe allmost in noe place is of more plesaunt taste, but beafe is peereles, especiallie being a fewe dayse poudered with salte; nether is it enie mervayle, for that beaste once releaced from laboringe is kepte uppe for there common feadinge; in fine, the cheefe foode of the Englisheman consisteth in fleshe; nether emong them doe those oxen lacke there commendacion which after longe travayle are killed in theire age, albeit there fleshe is harder then the other. They have an infinite nomber of birdes, as well fostered in the howse as breeding in their woodds.

The Kentishe hennes are the greateste; greene geese beefore they have caste there downie fethers are reputed as a daintee banqueting disshe, butt afterward not soe goodd. Of wilde burdes these are moste delicate, partriches, phesaunts, quayles, owsels, thrusshes, and larckes. This laste burde in winter season, the wether not being to owtragios, dothe waxe wonderus fatte, at which time a wonderfull nombre of them is caughte, soe that of all others they chefle garnishe menns tables: there are allso swannes in there lakes and rivers, not soe small a pleasure to the beeholder as a great greefe of minde. Crowes and chowghes are everie daye in the morning earlie harde clattering in theire kinde. In noe cuntrie is there a greater multitude of crowse; being soe harmefull a kinde of birdes, yet are thie spared in that lande, bie cause thei eate woormes and other vermin, whereof the contrey is the fuller in that it is verie moyste; but in other respectes thei are muche more hurtful, for thei doe not onlie devoure corne when it is ripe, but even as it groweth they pull up the sead with there bill, soe that at suche times the housbonde menn are compelled to apoynt boyse to drive them awaye with bowe and arrowse, when with showtinge and clamore thei will not bee feared. And for as mutch as herons are wonte afterwarde to builde in there neastes, therefore, these unhappie wretches are permitted to breede about the mannures of noble men, which delighte in the game of haukinge for herons, and thus crowse have free accesse to there highe trees, where with moste commonlie there houses are beesett the better to avoide tempestuos blastes; bie these means thei endure to the greate damage of the husbondemen. In consideration whereof, within our remembrance, an acte of parliament was promulged that suche crowes bie all meanse showld bea destroyed, a rewarde beinge assigned to the destroier. There aboundethe likewise all sortes of fishe, the names of the moste of them dissenting from the Latine (for these fisshes which in Latine and Italion are farre otherwise termed), are commonlie in use with them, as gornards, whitings, mullets, turbots, bremes, macharels (somwhat the lesse esteemed for theire naturall driness), schaddes, allso being veri base bothe in relishe and estimation; finallie, sturgion and pike, which fishe, as in times paste, it hathe ben taken for an abjecte, soe now thought verie precius emonge Englishemen, for, being taken owte of the fennie waters, and transposed into store pondes, and ther purged of the muddie savor, and being fedde with littell eales and other frie, groweth into a great fattnes, and after that peradventure being broughte into the market to be sowld, if for the sale neade shall require, hathe his bellie opened with a knife to shewe the fatte; but if it soe fall owte that hee bee nott sowlde (that which is most to be wondered at) hee dieth not of the wownde, butt hathe it sowed upp with threade, and within shorte space is healed with the slime touchinge of littell fresshe water fisshes. Osheters in noe place are ether more plentuos or better. More, this region bringethe forthe gowlde, silver, blacke leade and white, that is to saie, tinne and copper. Iron allso growethe in the costes bordering on the sea, thowghe nothing plentuoslie. Finallie, it hathe allso margarites and jeate. Thus muche breefelie of the goodd temperature of the aire and grounde. Now I purpose sumwhat to disclose the fourme and disposition of the menne.

The natur and maners of the Inglishmen.

Englishe menn are highe and taule in stature, of welfavored and faire face, for the more parte greye eied; and as thei resemble the Italian in theire tongue, soe doe thei allmost nothinge differ in lineaments of theire boddies; thei are verie civile, thei take counsell with deliberation, knowinge none to bee soe great an enemie to wisdom as rashnes; thei are prone of theire oune nature to all dewties of humanitee, yea, even towarde straungers; the nobilitee is exceadinge curteus; peradventure with the baser sorte of menn it is not soe, especiallie with the common sorte of citizens. They will bedde theire frindes to there howses, receaving them with all jentelnes, and in theire dinners and suppers thei are no lesse merrie, full of conceites, and exquisite, then sumtuus and liberall, accounting it a great pointe of jentilnes; allbeit (as Tacitus saieth) it is noe small servillite to feed deyntelie, to another manns soe great truble and lothesomnes. In battayle noe doubte they are valiant, and voyde of all feare; they surmounte all others in shootinge; in noe wise cann thei abide enie delaye in warfare, insomutche that when they joyne battayle, thei strive bie and bie as it weare for all the whole substance and goodds of the one parte, for all foloweth the good successe of the conqueror; but thei nether builde fortes and castels, nether do they repaire them, which, being builded longe since, throgh time are becomme olde and ruinus; yeat if in foraine countries they have to doe with theire adversarie, in all respectes thei observe the science and prescripts of warfare. The other sorte of them which applie there minde to learninge and studie of knowledge doe excell therin with great facilitee, of whome at this daye there flourisheth an infinite nomber. There attire is not muche unlike to Frenchemenn. Theire woomen are of excellent beutie, in whitenes not muche inferior to snowe, sumwhat beautified with the decencie of there apparell. There citties are princelie, theire townes famus; there villages populus and of great number; there manners and mansions curius and magnificent everie wheare. But, bie cause in an other place I minde to make rehersal, as wel of the situation of theire places as of the manners of the people, as touchinge this laboure at this presence I will use silence; wherefore as concerninge the religion of the nation I will saie somwhat. Brittaine (accordinge to the authoritee of Gildas) even from the first springe and divulgation of the hollie Gospell did ernestlie embrace the loove and woorshipping of Christe, observinge surelie, and holding faste the same, even emonge the tyrannicall persecutions of the Roman Emperours. At that time, albeit they did not openlie professe Christe, bie cause beinge vanquished of the Romaines and Saxons they weare compelled to sacrifise to straunge godds; nevertheles privatlie manie woulde not forsake there hevenlie dewtie, soe that the Christian relligion (as elswhere wee shall declare) was alwayse extante in som parte of the Ilond, untill that at the lengthe bie Saint Gregory it was

Bryten hathe ernestly imbrased the love and worshipping of Christ ever sens the fyrst spring of the Gospell.

cleane delivered from confusion, soe that I thincke there is noe people at this present which dothe more sincerelie and diligentlie observe all thinges that appartaine to the trew service and glorie of Godde. A goodd testimonie in this case is there noble Churches, which abownde everie where; the great assemble of menn repairinge daylie unto them; and to conclude, soe manie sumptuos tumbes of heroicall aunciters. Wherefore the cheefe commendacion of Englishemen consisteth in this, that of all other thei are moste Christian and relligius. I thought good to put these things in the former parte of mie woorcke, beefore I entered into the entreatie of battailes, to thentent the reader mighte understande what and howe greate a peoples valiant actes he had in hande, and allso what manners and contrie he showlde afterwarde here of; but Godd grannte that wee maye well finishe owre attempted woorcke.

The fyrst inhabiters of Brytane.

What kinde of people were the first inhabitants of Brittaine, whether thei that were bredde in the contrie or otherwise straungers, it was never yet sufficientlie knowne or determined; wherebie it commethe to passe that of longe season authors have not agreed thereof; as towching which thinge, leste I showlde ether over rashelie plighte mie trouthe in affirminge, or on the other side gette envie bie refutinge or falsifieinge, I thought good in this place to repete there sentences in order, and to laye them beefore the ieys of the reader, to the intent that all things maie stande to the arbitrement of other menn (as it is requisite those thinggs showlde which are incertaine), bie cause an Historie is a full rehersall and declaration of things don, not a gesse or divination. C. Julius Cæsar, the moste auncient writer of suche matters, in the v. booke of his Commentaries and entreatie of the Frenche battayle, dothe affirme that the inner partes of Britaine was inhabited of those whoe, as it is lefte in minde, were borne in the Ile; but the uttermost costes bee possessed of them which, issueng owte of Beauvosine and Gaules Belgique, camme to spoyle and make warre, where, beinge seased after battayle was ended, there thei remained and beganne to till and laboure the grownde. Cornelius Tacitus, in the life of Julius Agricola (which obteined Brittiaine under the empire of Domitian) is allmoste of the same opinion; whoe supposinge, yea contendinge bie reason to prove the lande to bee inhabited of nations adjacent, saieth thus in effecte. 'There grate limmes dothe confirme theire discent from the Germanians, the peincted faces and curled or writhen heare of the Pictes, allso their situation right over against Spaine, is a token that the olde Iberians or Spaniards did passe the seas and seasoned on those places. Thei are neighbours to the Frenchemen, and somwhat like,' and soe foorthe. But Bedas, an Englishman, (then whome I have seene nothing more sounde, sincere, or trewe,) who flourished abowte the DCC. yeare of our salvation, thinking farre otherwise of the originall of this nation, writeth thus in the firste booke of his Ecclesiasticall Historie, that those Britons which are environed of the ocean sea betweene Fraunce and Spaine, beinge browghte owt of Armoricke or littel Brittaine, didd bie force keepe this Ilond, gevinge it the name of Brittaine, whereas in deede beefore it was named Albion, as I will here after make relacion. The which opinion, that is to saye, appellation of the Ile, Pomponius Lætus allso, the moste authorised of late writers, dothe well alowe, even as allso hee dothe condiscende unto Cæsar as towchinge the originall inhabitants thereof, who, being borne in it, hadde the first possession and rule. But before Bede, Gildas, a Brittaine borne, of whome wee have made mention in our preface, (who, exilinge all fables, most ernestlie embraceth truthe,) hathe browght some lighte to theire firste beginninge, for as towchinge his description of Brittaine this is his saienge: 'This nation (saiethe he), stiffe necked and highe minded sithe it was first a people, doothe somtimes stubbernelie rise againe Godd, somtime ther owne citizens, and somtimes foraine princes.' Here Gildas geevethe us a watchwoorde that the firste inhabitantes of the region hadd the knowlege of Godd, of which sorte thei were which, after Noe's fludde, being great in nomber, replenished the erthe, and soe from

Gildas.

the beginninge it hathe not wanted inhabitantes, as herafter shall apeare more largelie. He saieth moreover that affaires somtime weare ordered bie theire owne citizens, somtime bie the Romanes, whome in divers places hee termethe kinges of parties beyonde sea, callinge Brittaine unthankefull in that it didd often as well breake there vowe to Godd the Father, as loialtee to theire owne princes.

This godlie manne hathe written an Epistel in fourme of a littell booke, wherin he hathe firste declared the situation of the Ilond, secondarilie he hathe towched in few wordes the historie of his time, laste of all hee hathe bewailed the iniquite of his Brittishe contrimen and times, alleging manie textes of hollie scriptures, wherbie he mighte as well traine them to goodnes, as cause them to abandon evell deedes; whose booke, bie reason it is somwhat obscure and knottie, it is allsoe rare and geison. I have fownde onnlie two bookes, owt of the which I have gathered butt fewe things, yet suche as are trewe and sincere. There is allso an other booke (that I may in time admonishe the reader of wicked subtilitee) which is falselie entituled the Commentarie of Gildas, being made noe doubte of some craftie compasser to fortifie an erroneus fable of a certaine newe writer. Trulie this moste shameles varlet, grating often on Brutus, hathe renewed that with the opinion of some new author wheron Gildas did not once dreame; and to the intent he might with more sleyght deceave the reader, he hathe interlaced som things of his owne, to the end that ether men showld conjecture there were two sondrie of the name of Gildas, or at the leste that woorke to be some compendius pamphlett of the former Gildas: whereof bothe are soe incredible to learned men, that everie man but indifferentlie skilfull maye perceave the crafte and rejecte it as a deceyte. But to the entente that no mann hereafter should continew in suche error, I have procured the right woorcke of Gildas him selfe to bee set foorthe. Now it is time I showlde retowrne thether from whence I have strayed. These are the verdicts and judgements

The Commentaries of Gildas falsly intyteled.

of auncient writers as towching the originall of the people of Brittain, which I thowght goode to sett beefore the ies of all menn, which I thincke I have done sufficientlie; nevertheles, divers other authors, which are of greter fame emong the common sorte of menne then ether theyre diligence or there credite in writinge dothe deserve, hathe founde an other original of the people, the which thinge trewlie of what force it hathe ben, even sithe the beginninge, William Newberie, an Englisheman, and not inferior to those authors, is a sufficient wittnes, whoe lived in the MCXCV yeare of our Salvation, in the dayes of King Richard the firste, who in the preface of the historie of his time, when he speaketh of the authoritee of Gildas, writeth in this manner: It is noe smalle argumente of his synceritee that in uttering the trewthe he spareth not his owne nation, and, wheare as he speakethe littell good of his contriemenne, he beewailethe manie eevels in them, nether dothe he feare in revealinge the troth thoughe he were a Britton, to write of Brittons that thei nether weare stoute in battayle nor faithefull in peace. But on the other side there hathe appeared a writer in owre time which, to purge these defaultes of Brittains, feininge of them thinges to be laughed at, hathe extolled them aboove the noblenes of Romains and Macedonians, enhauncinge them with moste impudent lyeing. This man is cauled Geffray, surnamed Arthure, bie cause that oute of the olde lesings of Brittons, being somwhat augmented bie him, hee hathe recited manie things of this King Arthure, taking unto him bothe the coloure of Latin speeche and the honest pretext of an Historie: more over, taking in hande a greater enterprice, he hathe published the sowthesaiengs of one Merlin, as prophesies of most assuered and approved trewthe, allways addinge somwhat of his own while he translatehe them into Latine. This saithe he, and Gildas before him; but not I, which write nothing but that which hathe ben written beefore, wherefore there is noe man which justlie can be angrie with mee for this sainge (that thei were nether valiaunte in battaile nether true in leage), which was

Polidor's excuse for his saiengs tochynge the old Brytons.

a reproche to the owld Britons. Nether was Saluste reprehended of the Romaines bie cause he writte that filthie deade don to the cittie of Rome bie Jugurtha, not with owt a cause, when he saied the citte wolde bee sowlde and speedelie perishe if there were ever a biar; for it is a lawe in historie that the writer shoulde never be soe bolde as to open enie fallse thinge, nor soe demisse as not to utter enie trewthe.

It is mencioned in that booke (whoe soe ever it is) that Brutus the sonne of Silvius, whoe (as it is wel knowne) was begotten of Askanius the sonne of Aeneas, after his passage throughe Greece, and conquest of Aquitaine, arrived at Brittaine, according to the admonition of the goddesse Diana; where at his first entrie, vanquishing those gyaunts which at that time possessed the Ilond and ranne to repelle the force of foriners, did himselfe occupie the contrie, callinge it according to his own name Brittaine: and soe to conclude that Brutus was the author of the Brittishe nation, whoe, begetting sonnes, inhaunced them and enlarged his dominion wonderuslie. But yet nether Livie, nether Dionisius Halicarnaseus, who writt diligentlie of the Romane antiquities, nor divers other writers, did ever once make rehersall of this Brutus, neither could that bee notified bie the cronicles of the Brittons, sithe that longe agoe thei loste all the bookes of their monuments, as Gildas wittnesseth, whoe flourished aboute the DLXXX. yeare of our salvation, for he, in the beginning of his epistel, maketh this protestacion: 'I will goe aboute to bringe forthe those things ownlie which Brittaine ether susteined in the time of the Romaine emperours, and dide to other cittizens and other wise to those which are farre distante, yet as neare as I canne, not so muche owt of the writinges of mine owne contreye or monumentes of writers, which (if there were enie) are not now extante, beinge ether burnde of our enemies, or farre hence caried away in the banishement of our citizens; as rather bie the testimonie of externe and foraine nations, which allso cannot bee verie evident, being discontinued and interrupted bie the great discours of time,' and soe forthe.

But in olde time theie did presume on this fraunchise and libertie that manie nations weare so bowlde as to derive the beginninge of theire stocke from the Goddes (as especiallie the Romaines did), to thentent the originall of there people and citties mighte bee the more princelie and prosperus, which things, albeit thei sownded more like fabels then the sincere witnesses of noble acts, yet weare thei receaved for trewthe; for the which cause even those things which last of all were committed to writinge of the antiquities of Britaines, were with soe easye credit receaved of the common sorte that thei have ascribid the fownteine of theire genialogie to Brutus; and lest bie enie meanse throwghe the iniquitee of time, forgetfullnes shoulde in that poinct prevayle, two excellent historiographers have provided for the continuance thereof bie writinge and letters, the one of them having to name Henrie Huntington, an arche deacon, the other which hathe named his historie Polichronicon; and these are the thinges which from late writers have discended to there posteritee concerninge the firste beginning of the people of Brittaine.

Now as touching mie selfe, albeit I have stedfastlie promised that I will nether affirme as trew, nether reproove as false, the judgement of one or other as concerning the originall of soe auncient a people, referring all things, as wee have don hertofore, to the consideracion of the reader; nevertheles the lesse[a] after the matter shalbe committed to conjecture, I shall utter in this place that which shall not alltogether seeme abhorrent from treuthe, that in soe great diversitee of owlde writers as towching the first inhabitants of this londe, wee maye, at the leste with som probabilitee, declare a certayntee, proovinge that (which as farr as I perceave) is not as yet evident in the testimonie of enie auncient writer: thinckinge it to be nothing honorable to leave a matter of it selfe cleere inoughe as uncomprised, in the middest therof using silence and taciturnitee. Wherefore, seing that the Ilond, on brighte dayse, maye easlie bee seene from the Frenche shore, and hathe a farre

[a] *Sic in orig.*

Polidor's opinion toching the fyrst inhabitors of this lond.

of geven prospect unto the saylers bie reason of the white rockes abowte the bancke (whereof it was called Albion), surelie it coulde never bee obscure or unknowne to the regions lieng rounde aboute it. Wherefore it is not to bee thought that at enie time it lacked inhabitants, which might then receave them when all other londes didd, not awayghting or intertaining the exiled or hurtfull roge runninge awaye owt of Spaine, Germanie, Fraunce, or Italie, as late Historiens make reporte.

Wherbie wee maye well bee persuaded that allmost, even fro the beginninge of the worlde, the Ilond hathe ben inhabited, and that, accordinge to other contries, after Noes fludd it receaved inhabitants, which Cæsar calleth the natives or people bredd in the soyle; wherin Gildas agreeth with mee, as I reherced aboove. Nevertheles I cannot denie but that Germanians, Frenchemen, and Spaniards, being the next people, and mingeled with those natives, did inhabit the same, (as thei doe Brittaines at this daye emonge them,) of whome, as theire first straungers and greater in multitude, Bede reporteth that the name of the Ilonde was chaunged. But Plinie, speaking in his iiij booke, of Brittaine, seemethe to assent that it receaved the name of those littel Iles betweene this and Irelonde, whoe saythe thus: 'This one had to name Albion, wheare as all the rest were comprehended under the name of Brittaine, wherof we wyll intreat sumwhat hereafter. Wherfore this is the trew beginninge, which dothe not diminishe or abase the renowne of the Brittishe nation, but dothe greatlie augment, establishe, and adorne the same; for if (as wee are wont) wee do measure woorthines and nobilitee bie the continuance of time (levinge to speake of the other giftes and fœlicitees thereof) canne there bee enie thinge more auncient or honorable then even from the beginning to be borne in good and honeste place, and in the same to multiplie householde, stocke, and dominion allmoste for an infinite nombre of yeares? For this cause the firste inhabitants of the auncient Latin estemed it a moste excellent commendation to them that beeing there begotten, they reigned there soe long season. The same maiestie of domesticall praies may bee an eternall monument of glorie to the first borne people of Brittaine. But wee will retorne to the matter it selfe, thinckinge wee have gonne as farre as the necessitee of our busines dothe require.

But whether shall we goe, seing that all things are full of darcknes. Trulie ther is nothinge more obscure, more uncertaine, or unknowne then the affaires of the Brittons from the beginninge; partlie bicause the Cronicles, if there were enie, were clene destroied (as wee sayd before), according to the testimoniall of Gildas; partelie bie cause the nation, as it is placed far from all others, soe was it longe unknowne to the Romaines and Grecians. This silence was the cause whie good authors have not lefte in memorie verie manie thinges of the originall of this contriemenne; and manie on the other side have ben bolde to speake so largelie, and to make suche a straünge historie thereof, that in the admiration of the common people (who allwais more regarde novelties then trewthe) theye seme to bee in heaven, whear with a good will I will leave them, thincking it not goodd to debate the matter with them as towchinge those feined trifls. But, bie cause it is wisdom, and time allso requireth the same, that in convenient places wee should couche those thinges together with our historie which Cæsar, Tacitus, and Gildas have picked forthe in there writinge of the affaires of Brittaine, wee will, therefor, brefelie passe through the life of those kinges whome this newe historie of a sodaine, and as it weare at one boorden, hathe browght forthe and placed in the lighte. The which thinge (albeit not altogether without indignation) yet will wee doe it, bothe havinge regarde to the time and the avoydinge of evel will; mindinge bie the way, as nere as wee cann, to amend the defaultes therein (which are infinite), to the ende that neither thei maye moleste the readers, nether thei fawle hedlonge into them. And this we purpose so farre till wee comm to the Romaine and Englishe empire, for then shall wee have more perfecte lodesmen, whome, as assured, wee will afterward followe;

Brito had the fyrst possession and impery of this Ilond and was the fyrst author of the Brytishe nation.

but let us speedelie enter the way that wee may the sooner attaine thether, as wee doe endevor. Wherfore that same Brutus or Brito, for soe he shoulde have been termed (if bie enie meanes Brittaine should soe have ben called bie his name,) is reported to have had the first possession and emperie of this Ilond, and to bee the first author of the Brittishe nation, and not longe after to have benne seene on the earthe. After whome his three sonnes, Locrinus, Camber, and Albanactus divided the kingdom betweene them; but within litle space Locrinus obteined the rule of the whole Ilond bie the deathe of his breetherne, whome his wife Guindelon, the doughter of Corineus, one of the companions of Brutus, did slea; for that with him selfe hee had refused her for the loove of an harlot.

Brut. Locrinus. Camber. Albanactus.

Madan. Mempricius. Manlius.

Madan succeeded his father, and beegat Mempricius and Manlius, betweene whome, after the deathe of theire father, didd chaunce a moste filthee and wicked contencion for the kingedom, in the which Manlius was slaine. Mempricius didde nothing in his life time wherebie his deathe might seeme the more honorable; for on a time as he went a hunting, departing farr from his companie, he was torne in peeces of woolves, whereof the contrie was full at that time. Next unto him reigned his sonne Ebrancke, whoe (as menne saye) builded the famus citte of Yorcke, betweene the rivers Vsa and Fossa,* which runne bie the cittee, and, meetinge to gether a littell way of, convay themselves into Humber. Hee is reported, more over, to have builded the towne of Maidens, now named Edenbroughe Castell, being planted in the uttermoste part of Brittaine, now called Scotlande. After Ebraucke folowed his son Brute Greenshield, whoe was greatlie renowned nether at home nor in warfare. Next unto him succeeded his sonne Leile, whoe menn say builded the towne Carleile, in the lefte parte of the Ile neare unto Scotlonde, not farre from the river Eden. The cittee of Carleil† at this daye is famos throwghe the residence of the bisshoppe thereof. Of this citte Roger Hovedene, an hystorien

*Thei are called Isis and Vrus of Leland, whearof he calleth Yorkeshire, Surovicana provincia.

Ebranck builded Yorke and Edenbroughe.

Brut Grenshelde.

Leile buiided Carleil.

†It is cauled Luguballia of Leland.

after Bede, writethe thus: 'Carliele in the Britton speeche is called Lugubalia in Latin. Leyle being dead, Rudibras obteined the kingdom, whoe is thoughte to have builded these two citteis, Cantuarburie in Kente, which of Englishemenn in times past was called Dorovernia, lienge xii. miles from the sea, and Winchester; and the towne called Septon, beinge in the southe partes, which in our time of the inhabitants is named Shaftesburie; and Winchester is a cittee on the sea coste sowtheward, placed betweene two hills, and is of good fame. Badude was substitute in the place of Rudibras being dedd, whoe menn suppose to have builded the towne of Bathe, at this daye notorious throughe the bisshopricke of Bathe and Wells; whereas the saing is hee made baines flowing with whote waters, the which woorcke som erroneuslie attribute to Julius Cæsar; whereas indeade it is evident that Julius Cæsar came not so farre as this place. The bathes are there as yet extant, whereas warme waters doe springe foorthe and boyle, wherin, for wantonnes, childerne moste of all others washe them selves; and there have I seene boyes swimminge and bringing up monnie in there teethe, which hathe for pastime benne throwne in to the bathes of the standers bie. At the lengthe this Badude, trusting to his magicall artes which hee towght everie wheare, and being sterred upp throughe the delusion and enchauntmentes of devels, waded soe farr in madnes that he made himme winges to flie, and indeade being lifted upp on highe he soddainelie fell downe, with the which fall hee died, and of likeliehoode discended into hell; thus his wicked sciens becamme an evell mishappe unto himme. Then ensewed his son Leir after him, whoe reygned manie years noe lesse worthelie then wiselie. Hee erected Leicester, a towne in the inner partes of the Ilonde, and hadd noe issue besides three daughters, the which hee, being verie aged, appointed to bee maried to three of his noble menne, and his gooddes to bee equallie distributed beetweene them, which notwithstandinge hee assigned to the elder twaine bie cause thei seemed more deerlie to loove him, whereas afterward he founde as well them as theire husbondes

Rudibras builded Canterbury and Winchester and Shaftebury.

Badud builded Bathe and made the baynes ther and not Julius Cæsar.

And trusting to his magicall arte, by makyng hym wynges to fly, fled downe and dyed.

Leir builded Leicester.

unkinde, crewell, and unreverent; but the yongest, whose name was Cordill, having noe dowrie besides her goodd demainor and beautie, was geeven in marriage to a certaine French prince. Shee (whome nature hadd endowed with a ripe and sharpe witte) beinge demaunded whether she didde exceedinglie loove her father, made this aunswer, 'That shee didd allwayse carrie her father in her ies, and showlde doe while she lived, albeit afterward it mighte chaunce her to loove an other more ardentlie,' meaninge therin her housbond; with the which aunswere (albeit it was sharpe and wittee) Leir was soe angree that, as I have sayd, with owte dowrie he maried her to a certaine prince of Fraunce then entangeled with the bewtie of the virgin; but within shorte space hee was beereeved and dispossessed of his kingdom bie his sonnes in lawe, thincking it to longe a season to tarrie untyll his deathe, and consequentlie was driven to flie unto Cordill, of whome (after she hadde distroed his monstruus sonns in lawe) hee was restored into his kingdom and princelie diademe, and reigned three years. In this season Cordill, havinge loste her howsebonde, retorned into the realme, and bie the assente of the people enjoyed her father's kingdom. In the meane while Morgan and Conedag, the sonnes of her sisters, didd with great greefe yealde homage and feaultie to a woman, and weare ashamed enie longer to susteine soe unseemelie a yoke of slaverie. In consideracion wherof thei, gatheringe a bonde of soldiers, began feirslie to destroe with slaughters, burninges, and roberis, the easlier to provoke this woman to battayle, whome not longe after thei tooke with a small hoste and committed her to prison. This noble woman (who wanted nothinge but the kinde and nature of a manne to surmownt the whole renowne of our former kinges), attainted with extreme sorowe for her kingdom, which shee had loste in the fifth yeare after she beganne her dominion, with unvanquished corage vanquished and slewe her selfe. The conquerors at the first departed the Ilond betweene them, but in showrte season there entred into them soe fervent a desire of rule bearinge, that finallie, Morgann being overthrowne and killed, Conedag becamme lord of all. In processe of time successivelie reigned all these :—Rivallo, Gurgustius or Gurguntius, Silius, Jagus, Chinemarchus, and Gorbodion. After the deathe of Gorbodion, his sonnes Ferrex and Porrex beganne to fight for the kingedom, in the which contention Ferrex was slaine, whose death strake soe greate doloure into his mother (who looved him entirelie) that, being incended with sodaine rage, bie the helpe of her waytinge jentilwoomen didd most owtragiouslie murder the other while hee slepte; a thinge surelie within the memorie of manne moste straunge and seldom to be harde. There ensued after this a time moste feerce in battayle, more seditius then dissention it selfe, verie crewel in the middest of truce and peace. For when as eche manne as hee was moste stronge so did he moste vehementlie affect the kingdom, thei foughte soe longe to gether, till the whole rule of the riolme was divided betweene v kinges. Necessitee urgethe in this place a littel to streye from mie purpose, warninge the reader of an error, which is noe small blemmishe to the bewtie of the new Historie if there bee enie in it; for after those v kinges, or rather tyrantes, which are not counted in the nomber of kings, is placed Dunwallo Molmicius, the father of Bellinus and Brennus; who beinge deade, wee reade that these sonnes divided the kingedom betweene them, and, apeasing the sedition which rose bie the partition of the realme, and joynenge there powers to gether, did first over comme Fraunce, then tooke and set on fire Rome; and that Brennus still continued in Italie after his conquest. Here cann bee fownde noe such agreement in the time of the comming of Brutus in to the Ilond, and the invasion of Rome bie Brennus, that streight next unto those v tyrants Dunwallo Molmicius, the father of Brennus, showlde be placed in suche order of the kinges; for Brutus is thought to have entred the Ilond the xth yeare after the deathe of his father Silvius, the fower thowsand and hundreth yeare from the beginninge of the worlde. But the DCCX. yeare after the arrivall of Brutus, the citte of Rome (as it appeareth as well bie the breviarie of Eusebius as in the Latin and

Greeke histories) was taken of the Frenche menn of the contrie of Lions, under the conduite of Brennus.

This Brennus (if wee beleeve the newe Historie and make the computation of years according to it, wherein thei have skarslie a goode beginninge), hee flourished in chivalrie abowte the cccc. yeare after the entrie of Brute into this londe. Wherefore, it is moste evident that that Brennus, whom the historie maketh mention to have invaded the cittie, lived ccc. and x. yeares beefore the battayle was taken in honde. Wherfore, leste this error doe cause moe errors to ensewe, wee will necessarilie chaunge the order, disposing the other kinges in this place untill wee comm to that time wherin reason itselfe shall minister to us occasion to have in remembrance Bellinus and Brennus. But let us retorne home againe. These v. tyrants, being ernestlie pricked with the desier of dominion, and burning in extreeme hatred, rushed hedlonge in battayle: the rage of sedition dothe noe lesse enter the hartes of the cittizens then grevuslie torment them. But soe it camme to passe, that the tyrants, beinge wasted in theire owne broyles, and, as it weare, wownded with theire proper swerdes, the common welthe was restored againe, and the estate thereof reduced into the jurisdiction of one manne; wherefore, at the instance and Gintoline. assente of the people, Gintoline was proclaimed kinge, whoe, as he was himselfe verie sage and wise, soe hadd he one Martia to wife, a wooman aboove all others moste fayre and wittye. Men surelie supposed that bie the verie providence of God it camme to passe that Gintolin should aspire to this kinglie estate, and that, wheareas the reallme was raced and weakened with civill dissention, he showld againe restore the same to the former condition; which thinge, with grete industrie, he perfourmed, for as sone as he was seased in the same, with lawes, ordinances, and custommes, he endevored to make new and furnishe the Brittishe common wealthe, which of others beefore hadd receaved som forme and furniture. But aboove all things he repressed and extinguished civill dissention, which as yet remayned as the reliques of the old factions; yet the envie of Deathe, whose stinge sparethe no manne, preventid his finall purpose, being vehementlie busied in these affairs. Of his wife Martia he hadd ingendered onlie one sonne named Sicilius, whoe, yet in that he was not ripe for imperie, Martia, having good experience in manie things, tooke in handde the charge and care of the kingedom, and thincking that all things was fittinge to her concerninge the availe of the common wealthe, she promulged lawes which of the posteritee were called Martian Lawes. After Sicilius, whose life endeured not longe, reigned Chimarius, Danius, and Morvidius, whoe, beinge of haute corage, yet of suche notable creweltie that wheras he was never satisfied with the torture of menne, whome partlie with his own hands he strake, partlie he committed to dredfull torments; at the lengthe, having conflicte with wilde beastes, made a beastlie ende, and thus (as the old saieng is) to miche stoutenes beecamme his owne confusion. His sonne Gorbonian, a mann muche unlike his father, succeeded in kingdom, a mann of exceading gooddnes and great parsimonie, allwayse preferring peace beefore battayle. After himme his brother Archigallo was crowned king, whoe, being malicious towards the nobilitee, minded to putt the cheefe of them to execution, and, having in feare their mighte and power, didd preposteruslie exalte and honor the moste obscure and servile persons; for the which causes the piers and lordes, impacient in soe great crueltie, dispossessed himm of his rioll authoritee. Into whose rome was exalted his brother Eliodorus, a mann of great justice and sinceritee, whoe, thinckinge it as a greate treason towards himme selfe if he hadd not especiall regard of all suche thinggs as mighte benefitt his broother, it is not credible to be towlde how ernestlie he entreated with his princes that Archigallo might bee restored to his kingdomm; which thing in processe tooke effect when he hadde assuaged theire mindes with continuall entreatie; noe doubte a rare example of pietee, if a mann shall deeplie way with himme selfe howe great desier of rule-bearinge is incident to mankind. Eliodorus, for this exceadinge pietee towards his

Eliodorus.

A rare example of pietee in Eliodorus.

brother, was surnamed afterward Pius, that is to say, godlie, piteus, or naturall. This Archigallo being towghte bie troubles and daungers that hee coulde not enjoye his kingdome without som exchaunge of demainor, passed som parte of his years voyde of all vice, and lived x. years after the second receipte of his reigne and crowne.

Thus calamitee sometimes dothe not onlie noe harme, but is rather a feate instrument to prays and commendation. Eliodorus was againe created kinge, whome his younger brothers Peridorus and Vigenius, throughe disceyte, toke prisoner at London, committinge him to prison in that place which is now called the Towre, as yeat there remaininge; the which being well embateled with manie turrets, whereof it hathe the name, the vulgars surmise to have been erected by Julius Cæsar, whoe, indeed, made noe mention of London, bie cause he cam not thither. Vigenius and Peridorus forthewith departed the riolme betweene them; yet, within a littell while, being bie sickenes browght to their laste daye, Eliodorus (having binne sufficientlie tossed with the frailtee of fortune, continuallie deludinge the minde of manne,) was yet once againe made kinge, a manne surlie woorthie eternall prayse, whoe, howe moche the more studiouslie he eschewed rule and imperie, soe muche the more was he accited and required for the vertewes at the which all menn wondered in himme. Hee reigned after this iiij. years.

The Toure of London, at this tyme, and not erected by Julius Cæsar, who came not ther.

There succeded a time cleane voyde of warlike valiaunce, but not of other vertewse, in the which these weare kings: Reginus, Morganus, Ennanus, Idwallo, Ryno, Geruntius, Catellus, Coillus, Porrex of that name the seconde, Cherinus, Fulgentius, Eldalus, Androgeus, Vrianus, and Eliud; after whome followed Dunwallo Molmicius (for this is his place if keapinge the order of their acts, wee have allso a respecte to the time), whome aboove wee declared, throughe negligence, to be nombered owte of order. This manne, even from the beginning, beeganne to take care for those thinges which hee thowghte to concerne the utilitee of the commonwelthe, renewing with the auncient usage the sciens of warfare sore

Dunwallo Molmicius.

decaied with discontinuance: hee sacred newe lawes, and those verie profitable, which afterwarde deservid to bee called Molmician Lawes. Hee appointed that the temples of the Godds showld bee a sanctuarie to all that would flie thereuntoe; hee was the first that wore a crowne of gowlde; hee releeved, as well with riches as favor, all those which applied themselves to laudable artes, to the end that bothe the cheefe of the reolme might doe the same bie his president, and yowthe mighte the better bee animated to the embracinge of vertewse; he ordeined measures and weights for the bieng and sale of things; hee punished theeves and noisom or harmefull creatures with severitee; he founded manie highe wayes, prescribing their bredthe, apointing terrible penalties as wel to the breaker of their immunities and rightes as to those which committed enie haynus offence in them. Furthermore, leaste the grownde showlde lie waste and the people bee ether oppressed or diminished for the wante of graine, if ownlie cattayle showlde feed in the fieldes which showlde bee tilled bie menn, hee appointed how manie plowse everie cowntie showlde have, enjoyning a punishement to those bie whome the nomber showlde bee made lesse, and forbiddinge that suche steares as showlde searve for tilthe to bee caried awaye bie enie magistrate, or otherwise to bee surrendrid to creditors for the debte of monnie, if otherwise the goodds of the debtor wowld suffise. This was thus ordered leaste the grasiers for advauntage showlde cause the fieldes of the housbondmenn to be untilled, the which lawe groweth owte of ure in theise our dayse, to noe small hinderance of the whole commonaltee. But finallie (that I maie retorne to mi matter), this Dunwallo lefte the kingdom in commune to his sonnes Bellinus and Brennus. Thei bie and bie beganne to contende for the superioritee and pre-eminence, but afterward, being reconciled bie the exhortations of their friendes, thei divided the kingdom betweene them. The woorse parte of the realme chaunced to Brennus, as to the yonger brother, whoe, having haute corage throughe the great confidence in his vertewse, did not take in good parte that his brother

Molmician lawes.

Bellinus. Brennus.

Bellinus showlde have the better portion; and, mistrusting that the matter was compassed bie deceite, entended to acquite him selfe of this injurie bie weapon and armes.

Wherfore, assembling an armie, as well of Britons as alients, he raysed battayle against his brother. Bellinus with like celeritie, being furnished of armoure and fightingemenn, mette with his brother; butt soe the chaunce when thei showld even presentlie joyne in fighte, their mother camm betweene them, bie whose praiers and instance they, being overcommed, were enforced sodainlie to departe from theire armowre, ether of them detestinge so fowle and unseemelie a contention. Brennus, after that time, havinge nothinge at home wherin he mighte take reste and delectation, settinge first all things in order at home, leste he showld waxe dulle throwghe laysie sluggishnes, passed the seas into France, mindinge emonge fighting people to passe the time in warres, and was had in great honor and estimation emonge the Frenchemenn of Lions (as I finde more trulie then emonge the people of Savoy, called *Allobroges*). At which time the people of Lions, whether it weare to unburden the companie of the noysom multitude, or that they weare sente for of the Italiens to make battaile, thei passed over into Italie, Brennus being theire capitaine, with a great multitude of men; and after thei hadd overcomme the Alpes passing into Tuscanie, and sodainlie setting on the cittie called Clusium, they destroyd the territories rownd abowt. The Clusians, astonied at the sodaine daunger, sent embassadours to Rome, requiering that thei wowlde send aide against this straunge nation. The Romaines, albeit at that presence thei were not confedered in societee with the Clusians, yet ponderinge that daungers might more nearlie aproche them if the other hadde the overthrowe, did at the first time send likewise three ambassadoures, the sonnes of M. Fabius Ambustus; whoe, in the beehoufe of the senators and people of Rome, pleated with the Frenchemen that they shoulde not assaulte the frindes and fiers of the Romaines; whereunto Brennus aunswered that

Brennus.

peace in noe wise he wold simplie reject, if the Clusians wold be contente to surrender parte of their growende (where of they had more then thei did occupie) to the indigent Frenchemenn; other weyse peace nether could nor should bee attained. On the other side, the legates of Rome, being enchafed with such woords, demaunded what the Frenchemenn hadd to do in Hetruria. With these and such like prowde saiengs, there mindes beinge set on fire on bothe sides, thei ranne to theire weapons. The legats, that thei might declare of what valiance and vertew the Romains were in battaile, contrarie to the lawe of armes, armed them selves speedelie againste the Frenchemenn. The Frenchemenn, on the other side, conceaving just ire against the Romaines, and raysinge theire siege, made an outcrie throughte all there tentes that thei moste neades hast to Rome with their weapons, which pretended deadlie hatred. Brennus, neverthelesse, thought good firste to sende embassadours to Rome, which mighte exacte dewe punishemente for suche breakers of the lawe; which thinge forthewith toke effect. But whearas woorde was brought againe, that the three Fabians, woorckers of this injurie, were not onlie not amerced, but allso assigned Tribunes for the yeare insewinge, thei all stormed more vehementlie; and, seing that of theire willfull enimie theire was nothing to be looked for besides warre, unrighteus dealinge, and treason, thei towrned all the force of that battayle on the Romaines, and toke their viage toward Rome, destroyeng all thinges on everie side. There was soe great speede of ther enemies, that thei could scarslie bee mette with all at the xj[th] mile. The Tribunes, taking thether there jornie, with an unadvised armie (conteininge about the number of fortie thowsande fightinge menn) founde theire enemies abowte the river Allia, which springeth out of the hills called Crustinium, and a littell benethe the highe way is receaved of the river Tybris. In this place the Romaines, encountring with the Frenchemenn, were in verie shorte space disconfited. Brennus cowld hardelie beeleeve that bee hadd soe soone geeven the overthrowe; wherefore a while he stoode as suspens with feare; but, when he perceaved all things to bee in saftie, first gatheringe the spoiles of suche as weare slaine, he proceadeth in his jornie towards Rome, wheare (at the firste discrienge of the enimies which approched) there was great clamor and no lesse feare on all hands. And, bie cause in soe great dispaire there was noe hope to preserve the citee, the senators with a garison of yowthe entered the capitol and towne, bringinge thether corne and armowre, that therebie at the leste the name of the Romaines might bee defended; but the elder sorte of senatours remained with a weake companie in the cittee, mindinge to die with their contrie if neads it muste perishe.

The Frenchemenn in the meanewhile drewe neare unto the cittee, and, enteringe at the gate called Collina porta, tooke the streight wey into the merkate plaee, musinge not a litell that the howses of the citizens were shutt, and the mansions of noblemen wide open. Fearing therefore to bee assaulted by somme treason, thie proceaded more warelie. But afterwarde, perceavinge suche aunciente fathers of suche antiquitie sittinge in their chairs, thei intentivelie beehelde them as the images of Godds. In the meane season M. Papirius did smite one of the Frenchemen on the hedd with a sticke, for that unreverentlie he stroked his bearde, wherewith hee was soe moved that he roved the olde man throughe with his swerde, which slaughter beginninge at this one mann gave suche occasion that other menn weare semblablie destroied sittinge in theire seates as triumphant. From thens theye sleaing with owt daunger suche as thei founde in the cittie, som houses they over threw, som they set on fire; and thus was Rome taken of the Frenchemen under the conducte of Brennus the CCCLX. and v. yeare after the biledinge thereof. After this in the night time thei privilie entred the capitoll, and beeinge at a verie neare poincte to have taken it (see the fortune thereof) they were sodainlie beeurayed bie the noise and crie of geese, and weare throune downe hedlong fro the toppe to the bottom of the rocke. The Romains as it weare for theire extreeme refuge chose one

Rome taken under the conduct of Brennus.

Camillus Dictator, which sojorned at Ardea, beinge theire banished from Rome, most earnestlie requiering him that hee wolde aide them and his unthankful contrie; who, nothing bearing in minde the injurie which he hadd receaved, but waieng more his dewtie toward his contrie which privile hee beewailed, tooke mooster forthwith of a warlike companie. In the meane time thei which fledde into the capitoll, beeing neare sterved with famine, did make covenant with Brennus, that for a thowsand pownde in golde the people showld be redeemed, and hee and his armie clene departe bothe owte of the citte and teritoris of Rome. Nevertheles it soe fell owte that the people of Rome was nott cleane distained with that ignominie. For the Frenchemen, not being contented with the dew somme of gowlde, did put one of their swerds into the weghtes: on the other side the Romaines denied to adde more goulde into unequall balance. And whilest with this debatinge and altercacion the time was prolonged and the gowld as yet not wayed, Camillus was present, and commanded the gould to bee taken away, sayinge that noe bargaine or covenant should be made of an inferior magistrate withowte the countermaunde of the dictator: and finallie he commaundeth the Frenchemenn to prepare themselves to theire laste conflicte. Thus they joyninge in battayle, the Frenchemen, which looked for gowlde and not to fight at that verie instance, weare verie easlie overcommed. Afterward thei departing owt of the cittee throwghe the way called Gabina uia, at the viijth mile were overthrowne with muche more crewel slaughter; thei were beereeved of their tents, and suche sleaing thear was on all sides that if wee beeleeve Livie there scarslie was remaining one messenger in this mortalitee. But Polibius recordeth that the Frenchemen retired from the beseeging of the cittee bie reason of domesticall warrs, makinge league with the Romaines and restoringe libertie to the cittie. But, howsoever the case standeth, it is evident that Brennus (the moste valiant and renowned captain that ever was, for whose sake wee nowe deflected from our purpose) never returned againe into Britaine,

Camillus delivered the cittie of Rome.

being either slaine at the overthrow geven at Gabina via, or otherwise passing the residue of his life in Fraunce. But, wheresoever he was, his deathe muste neades be honorable and famus after so manie and worthie exploits. An hundred and ten years after, there was another Brennus borne in Fraunce, under whose governance another trowpe of Frenchemen entered into Greece. Here I thowght goodd to speake of this other Brennus and capitane of the Gaulls, leste peradventure thei which are unscilful in the old histories, throwge the similitude of their names, shoulde thincke that it was all one man which tooke, burned, and sacked the cittee of Rome, and also which safeconducte the other armie, first into Greece, and then into Macedonia (for indeade thei being dissevered, at the lengthe streched forthe into Asia). But let us here retourne to Bellinus, who after he hadde established peace with his brother, nothing was more leefe unto himme then to garnishe the realme with newe and freshe woorckmanshippe; for he builded the cittee in Wallse named Caerleon, fownded noe doubte in a pleasant soile, and well beeset with houses, whereof there are sygnes and trackes at this daye; being afterward called the cittie of Legions, bie cause the Romaine armies weare woonte to winter in that place. Theire is allso an other towne of Legions builded in an other corner of the coste of Northe Walls, soe called likewise bie cause of soldiers did muche use here to harborowe: it is named Chester, being planted on the river Dea, which about six miles from thens ronnethe into the ocean sea. He did, moreover, at London ædefie a gate on the bancke of the river Thames, which, accordinge, to his name, of the posteritee, was called Belinsgate, which name it keepethe as yeat, adjoyning thereunto a littel haven into the which the lesser sorte of shipps have accesse, which bringe all things necessarie and profitable for the cittee. Finallie, being a mann noble and valiaunt bothe in peace and battaile, and in all felicities not unlike to his victorious brother Brennus, at the lengthe worthielie ending his life was kaste into the fier, (according to the usage of other landes, but) the first that was

Bellinus builded Carleon.

Belingsgate.

soe burned of Britton kinges. Next unto him succeeded his sonne Gurguntius, the second soe named, Merianus, Blandanus, Capenus, Ovinus, Silius, Bledgabredus, Archemalus, Eldolus, Rodianus, Redargius, Samulius, Peinsellus, Pyrrhus, Caporus, Dinellus, Helius, and Ludde. Of all these kings beesides Ludde, because they loved reste and ease, not having artes in theire dewe price and estimation, nothing is lefte in memorie worthie the writinge. But Ludd, as soon as he was created kinge, recognised and accounted the estate of his region; hee renewed certaine laws, hee rooted up divers abuses, and rejected manie thinges drawne to inconvenience bie evell example; and then, disposinge himselfe to the beutifienge of the cittee of London, redressed the walles, beinge ruinus throughe yeares, strengtheninge the same with divers turrets, by reason wheareof it was afterward called Luddstoune. Allso in the weste parte of the cittee he builded a portlie gate, at this daye called Luddegate. Ludds towne. Ludgate.

Of this cittie have I redde nothing more aunciente then that which is specified in Tacitus thereof, whoe termeth it Londinium; bie whose reporte it appearethe that in times paste it hathe ben a towne of noe great maiestie, in that he thus writeth thereof: London (saythe he) is a towne not soe famus throughe the surname of Cell, or the dwellinge places, as rather throughe the recours and convents of merchants. Peradventure it is the same cause whie Cæsar made noe mention thereof. Neverthelesse in oure time it is the moste princelie cittie of all others; the hedde of the nation; the pallace of kingges; moste abounding in riches. The river Thames rennethe bie that parte of the cittey which liethe sowtheward, over the which there is a bridge, as wee showed in the beginninge, towards Kente, conteininge xix. arches, with howses, verie sumpteuslie placed alonge on bothe sides.

But I will retourne to Ludde, whoe at his deathe leafte beehinde hime two sonnes, that is to weete, Androgeus and Theomantius; which, bie cause thei weare bothe yonge children, his brother Cassivellanus obteined the kingdom, whoe, leaste he shoulde alltogether seeme to defeate his nephews, he limited Cassivelanus.

to Androgeus the cittie of London and the province of Kent; and Cornewall to Theomantius. And thus muche, according to the new hystorie, these kings, unto Cassivellanus, reigned the space of MXL. years, if wee followe the times exactlie accounted of Eusebius, bie whose computation, from the time of the deathe of Silvius, the second kinge of Latines, (whom thei recken as the father of Brutus,) unto the time that Julius Cæsar mooved warres with the Brittons and vanquished Cassivelanus, are numbered ML. yeares; so that, abatinge X. yeares, (for soe much maye bee permitted to Brutus after his father's deathe, bothe to take viage into Britaine, and allso to sease the same into his handds,) MXL. yeares maye well bee reckened from the comming of Brutus into the Ilande to this saide Cassivellanus. But as concerning those which wee have hitherto mencioned, whether thei were kinges, or princes of the public weale, or tyrants, which I rather beleeve according to the sentence of Gildas which I have placed aboove, ther is noe certaine or determinate relacion; for nether enie old writer made records of them, (yea, as Cæsar witnessethe, manie citties used there owne dominions, as you shall hereafter heare more largelie,) neither are the names certainlie knowne of those townes which the newe historie makethe reporte to be builded of those kings.

The supputation of the tyme.

Here was an evident token of the negligence of writers, which, having noe regarde of times passed, affirmed the names of townes to be geaven of the ould British kings, which indeade were after invented bie the Englishemenne, Danes, and Normanns. For whoe hathe redde in Cæsar, Tacitus, Strabo, Ptolomei, or Plinie, Caunterburie, Bathe, Caerliel, Lecester, or enie such like names of townes, of which sorte if there hadd ben enie at that time, undowbtedlie thei cowlde not have ben obscure and unknowne to them. Whearfore thei made especiallie mention of those which were then extant, which are now soe entered into the blacke booke of oblivion that nowe wee are not able to say for a certayntee, whoe in olde time were called Brigantes, whoe Trinobantes, who Iceni, or whoe Silures, or what places they did inhabite.

And thus muche I hadde to entreate of the originall of the Brittains, of theire imperie and estate; but before wee enter enie farder, it shall not be greatlie owte of the waye if I speke somwhat as concerninge the fourme and composition of theire boddies, of the aunceant demanoure and decrees of the people, that it may plainlie be perceaved what manner of menn thei weare beefore the comminge of the Romaines into the Ilonde, whoe, as conquierors are accustomed, made exchange of all things, to the bettering of somm things, seeing that the Britons weare made more civill through them, as wee shall declare in convenient place.

What manner of people the Brytons wer, and of their auncient demenor before the conquest of the Romayns, throw whom they wer after made more civill.

The Britans differed emong them selves in features of boddie, as Tacitus witnessethe; some resembling in stature and visage the Germainans, some the Frenchemen, som the Spaniards, of whome longe sence thei hadd theire discent. Thei hade for the moste parte long heare, withowte wrest or curle; thei were of sterne countenance, but not without goodd semblaunt and favour, but that they smeered their face with an herbe called glastum that in fighte thei might bee the more terrible to beehoulde. This glastum being like unto plantaine, and causing a bleewe coloure, is thought to bee that which is in Italion called guadum, vulgarlie in Englishe wode, wherewith woollen clothe is much died. With this hearbe allso the wives and daughters in lawe of the Brittons weare coloured, and did soe goe in certain solempne ceremonies, according to Plinius authoritee in his xxii booke and firste chapitre. The menn used to shave all the partes of their boddie beesides theire hedds and upper lippes; they weare knottie and stronge in boddie, and in mind or corage invincible, cleane voide of all disceyte and guile. Thei which were fostered in wooddes ware the skinnes of beastes, and eatinge milke and fleshe, bie cause thei sowed not muche corne. The borderers on the sea weare more welthie and tractable, but the others weare not soe, bie cause it was forbidden bie lawe that noe merchanteman or forrainer showld comme to them, least the inner parts of the riolme should bee knowne unto them. Thei wear mervaylus conninge in the arte of

Wher the prayse of the Britons.

warfare, usinge divers kindes of fighte, whearat Cæsar graunteth that his soldiers wear afraide, bicause thei were not apte or prone thereunto. Thei hadde these weapons; swords, dartes, clubbs, bowes, helmet, and brigantine or cote of fense of linnen sowed faste with a great manie wrappings. There cheafe welthe consisted in cattayle, whereof thei hadd a great multitude. Thei trained up hares, hennes, and geese for pleasaunce, thinking it an hainus offence to taste of them. Thei used ether brasen monnie or else an iren ringe of a certaine wayght in steade of monnie. Afterwards in the time of the Prince Claudius thei beganne to coine gowlde and silver with the image of Cæsar, as Gildas witnesseth. There buildings weare like to the Frenchemenn, and theire attire allmost all one. They learned Greeke letters. Theire relligion and priestes, Druides, weare common to Frenchemen, and weare instructed of them with divers kindes of learninge; yet weare thei not written bie cause thei showld not be disparpeled emong the commons, and allso that the learners should have occasion more diligentlie to keep them in memorie. These Druides enformed youthe that sowles didd not perishe, but after deathe passe from one to an other, that soe they might allure them to vertue bie the contempte of deathe. Thei did more over teache and geeve forthe as towchinge the sterrs and motion of them, of the bignesse of the earthe and world, of the nature of things, and power of the godds. The which disciplines being first inventid in Brittaine the Druides are thoughte to have first caried into Fraunce. Cæsar is mine author in his vj. booke of the Frenche battaile.

The cause why Julius Cæsar dyd assaile Brytten, which was done in time of Cassivelanus: and thes kynges unto Cassivelanus rayned the

At those times C. Julius Cæsar, after he had conquered allmoste all Fraunce, did apoynt likewise to assaile Brittaine with weapon; even at that time being unknowne to the Romayns. The cause whie hee thus purposed was bie reason hee understoode that muche aide was ministered from thens to his adversaries in his Frenche battailes. And, not with standing that the cheefe time for warfare was allmoste passed, for summer was neare spente, yet he thowght it wolde redownde to his greate proffet, if he should goe unto the Ilande, and vewe the kinde of menne, and have some knowledge of the portes, the places, and entries. Wherefore he, callinge together travelers and making diligent inquierie of them, cowlde be satisfied in noe poincte whereof hee demaunded; for the which cause, to the entente hee mighte foresee all thinges which mighte bee conducible to this pretended conflicte, beefore enie farder triall, he thowghte convenient to send beefore C. Volusenus with a galley, geeving him in commaundement that after hee hadd diligentlie serched owte and espied all things hee showld with speede retire unto him. Hee himselfe with all his armie drewe towards the borders of Fraunce called Morini, buttinge right over against Brittaine, biecause that there is shortest passage in to the Ile. In this place was the haven Icius, able to comprehende a great navye in times paste, but nowe soe narrow that noe shippe canne enter but at suche time as the sea flowethe, which seemeth to bee donne for the nonce and of good purpose, bicause the towne Calice or Bononie (for there is a dowbte in it, as I sayde afore, emonge the common people) being there situat and kepte with suer garison mighte herebie bee the lesse indaungered to the injuries and assaultes of enemies. At this place Cæsar commaunded a navie to meete, bothe gathered of the bordering people, and allso that which he hadd addressed the yeare beefore againste his battaile at Venice (these Venecians are a people of Fraunce, and that of the firme lande of Brittaine dwellinge hard upon the ocean sea). These Morini, or people dwelling abowt Turwayne, in the mean time sent embassadors unto him, promising to doe all that he hadd commaunded, whom he verie willinglie receaved into his allegiance and faithe, being verie gladde that he showlde not bee constrained to leave an enemie at his backe. In the meane season, as sonne as his purpose was knowne and reveled to the Brittaynes throughe merchant menne, forthewith all that were of habilitee to weare harnesse made haste to the sea side to repelle there enemies. But Cæsar affirmethe that divers legates camme to himme out of sundrie citties of the Ilonde, and that hee after hee hadd exhorted them to presevere in that minde did sende them backe againe, not makinge enie mention of

space of 1040 years.

Cassevellaunus, but onlie in his seconde warres with the Brittons, to whome he saithe the chife prerogative of governinge and orderinge the battayle was committed bie the common consent of the Britons, yet not once doth hee name him kinge; but contrariewise in the newe historie wee reade that Cæsar in his letters demaunded tribute of kinge Cassivelaunus, and that he againe showld aunswere Cæsar, that hetherto he hadd learned not to serwe or obeye, but to defende libertie, yea even with weapon if neade showlde require, as he showlde well perceave, if beinge blinded with covetise hee durste disquiet and moleste the Brittons. Soe that in this poincte as in all other places all thinggs are diverslie written; wherefore, as I promised in the beginning, soe I thincke it mie parte severallie to open bothe the newe and oulde, that the more mie travaile is, the more plesure the reader maye conceave, when in readinge he shall note somme things worthie credite, somm worthie favor, and somme meete to be laughed at. But let us have recourse to owre purpose. In the meane time C. Volusenus, retorninge into France the v. day after he departed from Cæsar, made in good order relacion what places hee hadd serched owte. Then Cæsar, withowte delaye, chose soe manie of the shippes that weare assembled as wowlde suffise to transporte two legions, and, having gotte feate weather, hoysed sayle aboute the seconde wake of the night. The wether was not againste himme, soe that abowte the iiijth hower of the nexte daye hee hooved beefore Brittaine. The inhabitants of the Ilond, awaiting the arrivall of theire adversaries, swarmed abowte the shore in thicke rowtes; whome when they perceaved to bee as it weare over theire heddes thei addressed them selves bie and bie stoutlie to withstande, which thing when Cæsar understood hee abode at ancher till the hulckes approached which were laden with horsemen; then chaunginge his purpose, leaste at his verie firste unshippinge he showld bee driven to encownter with his enemies beefore his soldiers weare on drie londe, holdinge on his waye eight miles farder did there place his shippes on eeven shore. Nether were the Brittons at this time idle, but, sending beefore theire horsemen and chariot drivers to resiste the residue of the multitude, persewed to the place where the shipps weare at rode. Thus, while the Romaines passed forthe and the Brittons resisted, somtimes makinge excourse even to there shipps, there was a sore conflicte and longe contention. Nevertheles, biecause the egle of the standerd bearer was once sett on the bancke, the Romaines, more for feare of shame and foile then for enie saftie thei cowlde perceave, issuinge owt of there shipps, did a littell put abacke there enemies. The fighte was for a season dowghtfull, till the Romaines one in anothers necke russhinge to the shore did putt the Brittons to flighte, whoe as soone as ever thei eskaped into safetie, they bie and bie sent embassadours to Cæsar to treàte of peace, whoe graunted there unto uppon the receipte of hostages and pledges, whereof parte of them were owt of hand performed, parte wowld comme within shorte season. But sodainlie there arose such a boysterus tempest that the whole navie of Cæsar receaved greate skathe therbie, especiallie the laden hulckes which were fixed at anchore; for somme of them being battered and frusshed together, some having loste theire engines of warre and takles, coulde serve to noe use in the worlde. These troubles did not smallie endamage the Romains, for nether hadd thei stuffe to repaire and renew theire shipps, nether were they beefore hande purvayed of victualls for the winter season. The chiefetaines of the Brittons, perceavinge this grate distresse, and hoping that the Romaine capitaine wolde be eslie entrapped and indaungered, with this small number of men, did privilie conspire emonge themselves. Cæsar, conceavinge suspicion and fearing the woorste, bothe for the losse of his shippes and allso for that the Brittons ceased to perform thaire hostages, with celeritee provided all thinges, prepared victualls and redressed his navie. The Brittons did not greatlie reste, but of a sodaine invaded the seventhe parte of the legion which was sente for the purveyance of corne, on whome noe doughte thai hadd committeed notable slaughter if

Cæsar had not with speede comme to the succoure and rescewes of his soldiers bie reason of the duste which hee spied to be raysed rownde abowte them; thus the armie, bienge compassed of the Britons, and the raye broken throughe the drivers of chariots, and allmost oppressed on all handes, was preserved throwghe the comminge of theire capitan at the uttermoste instance. The Brittons used chariots in there fightes, which with the noise of theire horses and wheeles at the first copinge did greatlie greeve and astonishe the armie of their enemies; afterwarde alighting from theire wagons did mannefullie fighte on foote. There ensewed noisom tempests which manie dayes caused the Romaines to withdrawe from fightinge. The Brittons in the meane while with encrease of aide did swarme together, assalinge yeat againe the Romans with there weapons, whom they trusted easlie to subdewe. But in this fighte at the lenghthe thei weare putt to flighte, and consequentlie sent againe to Cæsar as touchinge trewce, whoe, takinge dooble nombre of pledges, condiscended to theire petition for a time, and thus returned conqueror into Fraunce a litle beefore winter, the æquinoctiall daye drawinge neare. These are agreeing to trewthe, but according to the newe historie Cæsar at the first conflicte was putt to flight and constreined to retire into Fraunce; and Cassivellanus, triumphing in his victorie, in solemne wise yealded manie sacrifices to the godds of his contrie. But I come to mie purpose.

Chariots in fyte.

Cæsar at the first conflicte put to flyghte.

Cæsar being desierus to bringe the Ile under the dominion of the people of Rome, passed the seas into Brittain the year folowinge, streyght after the beginning of sommer, with a navie well furnished in all poincts, and, plantinge his tents in convenient grounde, beeganne to assallte the inhabitants with warre. In the meane time Cassivellaunus tooke the shore beefore hand, whome the Britons, being constreined bie the comming of theire enemies, made cheefe ruler of all theire affaires (as Cæsar witnesseth), for beefore that time all the whole contrie was displeased with himme; yet, thinkinge that it shoulde be more availe unto himme to traine his enemie farder from the sea beefore they hurteled together in fighte, leaste aide might bee ministred of them which remained in the shipps, gave a littel growude, and pitchinge his tents verie neare kepte his menn all that daye in theire harnesse. The day followinge on bothe parties thie were boulde to fighte, and when they weare allmoste at hande strokes, tidinges were browghte to Cæsar in that verie instance that his whole navie was miserablie tossed rounde abowte the shore, wherefore hee commanded his armie to staye, and, reclaiminge his horsemen with blaste of retrayte to theire standerds, he retired to the shippes; and, convayenge awaye the residew of theim, assembled a great companie of woorckemenne to repaire the brused and torne vessels, and sente letters into France that spedelie theye showld sende moe unto him. And thus having sette all things in ordre he retourned to his enemies. In the meane time weare comme together greater garisons of the Brittaines, which moste ernestlie desiered to encounter with the Romanes, and not longe after the trowpe of the Cæsarian horsemen approchinge in the middest of the jornie there beganne sharpe assawtes; but yet theie being a littell driven backewarde, tooke privelie there carier abowte, and violentlie assailed the tents of there adversaries. Thei skermished stoutlie for the trenche; the contention was incertaine and painefull to the Romaines, wherin manie weare slaine, yeat the pavillions manfullie defended. The daye ensewinge the Brittons stoode peaceablie on hills a good way from theire tents, and from thens espienge the Romaines comminge to waste and destroye, with great showtes they sett uppon them; but, what with the raskalles folowinge the bende, what with the horsemen which camm to succours, theye weare caused to flie. After this flighte the Brittons] departinge did fullie apointe never after ward to geeve theire enemie battaile with soe huge and unrewlie companie; wherefore, passinge the river Thames, didde furnishe a newe multitude abowte the bancke theirof, drivinge into the same and the shallowe places sharpe stakes, therebie to restraine and hinder the passage of theire enemies. But Cæsar, undermining their counsels throughe his captives, went forward even unto the river, and there rested where verie hardlie a manne mighte eskape over on foote. This place (according to Cæsar) lieth lxxx. miles from the sea, soe that bie the probabilitee of the distance wee maye of right conjecture that this shallowe foorde of the river was a littell beyonde Windesore, which is xx. miles from London and boundethe weastwarde. Wherunto as soone as Cæsar drewe neare, albeit on the other side of the water hee sawe great multitude of menn, which Cassiuellaunus hadde sett in ordre, (for theire, as Cæsar reportethe, was his cheefe dominion.) albeit hee was privie to the depth of the channell and staking of the banckes, nevertheles he commaunded his menn to swimme over the fludde, whoe, corageuslie entringe the river, allbeeit their heddes wear skarslie above the water, yeat thei camme in suche thronge and violence to the other bancke that soone thei putte their enemies to flighte, wherebie it camme to passe that the Romanes more freelie didd straie in to ther feeldes, as well for bootie as to spoile; whome Cassiwellanus, with a picte sorte awaytinge the excursions and viages of his enemis, didd anoye and hurte bie sending forthe his menne of armes. At this time the people, then called Trinobantes, now Estesexmen, sent their legates to Cæsar, promising to yeald unto himme, and to doe what showld please himme, requiering that he wowld defend Mandubratius from the injurie of Cassivellaunus, restoringe him into their citte as guide and ruler; which Mandubratius, a yownge mann, minding rather to flie then to die, wente into Fraunce, trustinge to the goodnes of Cæsar, for that his father Immanuentius, king of theire cittie now called Coulchester, was slaine of Casswellaunus. To these menne Cæsar restored Mandubratius, but firste demaundinge hostages, which theye perfourmed.

The fyrst that yielded to Cæsar.

After these exploits an other parte of the Brittishe nation, then named Cenimagni, Segontiaci, Ancalites, Bibroci, and Cassi Trimobantes, folowing the example of the others, desiered to make leage with Cæsar; which thing beinge finished, Cæsar did assante, and bie assautinge did subverte the towne of Casswellaunus not farre distant from this aboove rehersed place, being on all sides beesett with wooddes and fenns and well stored with menne and cattayle. It was defended, moreover, with a forrest, a trenche, and a valley, and therefore the Brittons termed it a walled towne. In the meane while Casswellanus sent messengers into Kente (of the which these four were kings—Cingetorix, Carnilius, Taximagulus, and Segonax), commaundinge them of a sodaine to sette uppon the pavilions of Cæsar, planted for the munition of his navie, whoe executing diligentlie his commaundement, foughte manfullie but without luckie successe, for thei weare ether putt to flight or slaine. Then Cassiuellaunus being afflicted with soe manie adversitees was at the lengthe contented to geeve hostages, condiscending that Brittaine showlde becomm tributorie to the people of Rome; and Cæsar, charging his shippes with a great number of captives, abowte the æquinoctiall time of harveste, retourned into Fraunce with conqueste and saftie. Thus was accomplished the warre wherin Julius Cæsar annexed Brittaine to the Romaine imperie, that is to say, causinge the nearest partes thereof to yeald to the Romaines; wherefor it is not to be suspected that Cæsar hadd enie thing to doe with the northren menne, sithe he didd skarslie conquire, no, not see the first parte of this Region: and, whereas divers emperowrers have ernestlie desiered by weapons to chasten and subdew the same, refusinge to yeald homage, Cæsar maye rightlie bee thowghte rather to have shewed it to the vewe then to have made a gifte thereof to his posteritee. But as towchinge the casualties and consummation of this battayle, Gildas, a moste grave writer, dothe allmoste accorde in all poinctes with Cæsar, of whome for the more part wee tooke the drawght of owre former rehersall, whoe, accusinge the cowardise of his contriemenn Brittons, writeth thus: 'The Romaine princes havinge the highest type of imperie in the worlde, and having brought under theire yoke all realmes and iles adjoyninge; and estwarde confedering with the first froonte of the Parthians of Inde, didd allmost in all

Brytayne anexed to the Romayne imperie about sixty years befor the coming of Christ.

Gildas.

regions desist and cease from battailes, and had strengthened this quietnesse with a fame of more sownde strengthe, if a certaine armie, like to a flame of sharpe fier in the weast parts, with the surge and streame of the bleewe ocean sea, cowlde ether have beene repressed or extinguished; but the same passing over the sea browghte lawes of obeysaunce into the Ile, not so muche mined to vanquishe this weake people (as other nations) with weapons, fire, or engines, as with onlie threatenings, with thunderinge the judgements in theyre eares, and with superficiall sharpenes of the countenance berienge there greefes in the depthe of their hartes, and finallie denowncing there dewe obedience bie proclamation and injunctions.' This saythe Gildas. Brittaine was subdewed of Cæsar abowte the sixtie yeare beefore the comminge of Christ; Cassiuellaunus died the vij[th] yeare after his overthrowe, withowte children, but his nephew, Theomantius, succeeded, and next unto himme his sonne Cinbellinus, who is reported to have served in warres under Augustus Cæsar. I have nothing to saye of ether of them worthie the relation, but that even then the true and incomparable lighte shewed the glorius beames on the earthe, in as muche as in the reigne of Cimbeline Jhesus Christe was borne of the Virgin Marie.

Cimbelinus.

Christ his byrthe.

FINIS LIBRI PRIMI.

THE PREFACE OF THE IJ. BOOKE.

I HAVE with celeritee passed throughe that which I promised from the beginnige, that is to weete, the lives of LX. and VIII. kinges; for menn suppose that there were soe manie accordinge to the discowrs of the newe Historie, annexinge thereunto the life of Cassivellaunus: a littel moreover have I towched Theomantius and Cinbellinus, whoe succeeded Cassivellaunus in governinge and administration. This Cassivellaunus being prince, Brittaine became tributarie to the people of Rome, as wee showede beefore, and soe continued litell lesse then five hundred and three yeares after, untill suche time as the Brittons (being forsaken of Aetius, which in Fraunce was cheefe ruler of the armie of Theodosius the yonger) beganne to be soe overcharged with the longe battayles of the Pictes and Scottes beinge joyned in amitee, that of a great whiles they hadde hardelie susteined theire pilferinges and assaultes; in conclusion, misdoubtinge their power, weere constreined to sende for the Englishe Saxons, a warlike and stowte people of Germanie, for theire aide and succours; but it happened farre otherwise then thei misdeamed, for these Englishemenne reduced into there owne dominion that parte of the Ilonde which thei possessed: soe that howe mutche the renowne and glorie of the Brittishe nation did increase in a thowsande yeares, soe muche in this miserablie space it was apayred and extinguished, which was betweene the discease of Cassivellaunus and the entrie of the Englishemenn, whoe as wee have saide at the lenghthe obteined the imperie. But while wee endevowre to make all thinges plaine, beeholde there is suche diversitee emonge writers, suche negligence, or rather rashenes, that, beinge distract and troubled in minde, I knowe not what to affirme as true or false in manie thinges, especiallie as towchinge the order of the kinges which ensewed after Cassivellaunus to the time of the Englishemenne. For the Romaine writers, and especiallie Tacitus, maketh minde that in time paste the Brittons obeyed there kinges, and after that, being brought under even to the paieng of tribute, weare so diverslie draune bie the cheefe of their strife and factions, that to withstande or repell a common perill scarce two or three cittes woulde agree or assemble to gether; and thus while thei strived, particularlie thei weer universallie confounded and overthrowne. Bie this meanes menne saye that Brittaine was broughte into the fourme of a province of the Romaines, and that frome themme weare sente certayne to governe, called rulers or provostes, which should obteine the same. Yeat these selfe same authors made mention of certaine kinges which reigned in Brittaine, even then when the Cæsars weare lordes of the worlde. Gildas dothe wittnes the same, saing, Britaine hathe kinges, but, etc. Cæsar hathe lefte in memorie that in his time there weare iiij. kinges in Kente, beinge governors of those parties. Tacitus makethe rehersall of Prasutagus and Cogidunus, two kinges; Juvenall of Arviragus, and all late historiens of Lucius. Wherbie it appearethe that ether one or moe bare rule in the Ilond under the Romaines. Contrarie wise the common sorte of menne holde opinion that the cheefe dominion was all waise in the hands and power of the Brittons, and that the Senat of Rome, yearlie receavinge a pension, did of dewtie send there captaines in to the Ile, somtimes to apease the rage of sedition, somtime to defend the invasion of enemies, soe that the Brittons (say thei) did allwaies obey theire owne kinges, till at the lengthe they weare disturbed and dispossesed bie the Englishe menne. But whereas in the vulgar historie the order of the kinges was to bee observed, as often as it chaunced that there weare noe kinges to bee placed; somtime ther Romaine emperoures were convenientlie assigned, somtime theire cheefe rulers whoe weare reported to be made kings of the Brittons; as who showlde saye the Romaine emperoures weare inferior to these kinges, or at the least waye that the substitute rulers called Prefecti did not governe the province at the appoinctment and prescripte of the senat house or emperours, but at theire owne arbitrement and pleasure. But these thinges, as theye sownde and savor sumwhat to grosslie vulgarlie to be repeted in this place, soe will I clene lett them passe, seing that here after, purposelie and feetelye, wee will admonishe the reader of those thinges which are worthie the credit and written for trewthe. Nether will I leave undeclared howe divers and manifolde the fourme of administringe the Britishe common wealthe was beefore the comminge of the Romaines. Treulie, Cæsar writethe that Cassivellaunus had dominion in the Ilonde, the boundes wherof the river Thames didde dissever fromme the borderinge cittees, and that to him was geeven the title of governement bie reason of his comminge, for beefore that time hee had continuall warrs with the other cittees; moreover that theare weare fower kinges in Kente, that is to say, peeres, whome at this daye we calle dukes and earles; and allso that the people named Cenigmani, Segontiaci, Ancalites, Bibroci, and Cassi, didde send ambassadours, yealding themselves to himme. In the same place he hathe these woordes: 'The princes did assemble oute of all parties, and begann to committ themselves and cittes to Cæsar, etc.' Wherebie wee maie gather that suche was the fashion in those dayse of ruling in Brittain as it is at this presence in Italie and Germanie, (where somme cittees are reuled of one prince, somm of the nobilite, som of the people,) caulling them kinges which weare of moste puissaunce, as Cassivellaunus, whoe for that same cause was called kinge. These thinges have wee putt before the ieys of the readers that wee mighte make the historie verie easie in the understandinge.

But now let us follow our pretensed woorke, that at the length wee maye speake confuselie bothe of the end of the reign of the Brittons, and allsoe of the originall of the Englishe imperie.

THE SECONDE BOOKE

OF POLIDORUS VERGILIUS ON THE ENGLISHE HISTORIE.

In the time of the Emperoure Augustus, peace, which elsewhere flourished bie divine Providence, remained likewise sounde and inviolate in Brittaine, untill Guinderius, the sonne of Cimbelinus, brake the sacred lawes thereof; for hee, beeinge a stoute and boulde manne, and his bouldenes accompanied with rashenes, denied to paie the yearlie revennue dewe to the Romaines, and enkendeled the people unto newe tumultes; but houe soe ever hee was provoked, it soe fell oute that he made an open rebellion, as Gildas maketh rehersall. For the which cause Claudius Cæsar decreed to make warre with the Brittons; albeit Suetonius Tranq. seemeth to affirme, that the cause whie Claudius minded to moove battayle was, for that there beefell an exceadinge broile and uprore for not restoringe certaine run awayse, wherefore it is evident that Claudius was the firste of the Romaine emperoures which tooke voyage into the Ilande after the conqueste thereof bie the Dictator Cæsar, wherin he appeasid forthewith all thinges without fight, returninge into Italie within littel more then vj. monethes after his departure owt of the cittie. The which thing, according to the testimonie of Gildas, is most trew, whoe writeth in this wise of this sodaine defection, or breche of covenant, of the people: 'These thinges (saithe hee) being thus achieved, when suche newes were browght to the Senate, and that with speedie warriers thei minded to bee revenged, here was neither warlike navie in redines to

Guinderius.

Claudius Cæsar overcam the Brytons.

encounter for theire contrie, nether competent armie, nether politique disposinge of the righte winge, nether uther furniture of battaile planted on the shore, butt thei flieng turned there backes for bucklers and yealded ther neckes to the sworde: there bloodde for feare becamm cowld aboute their bones, and effeminatlie lifted up their handes to bee bownde, soe that it is farre spredde in proverbe and mockerie, the Brittons are nether stowte in battayle, nether faithful in peace; wherefore the Romaines, slainge manie of the recreants, and delivering manie into bondage, leste the lande shoulde becomme desolate, did returne againe into Italie owt of a contrie voyde of oyle and wine, levinge certaine cheefe rewlers of their owne companie, which showlde torment and afflicte this miserable people, not so mutche with the bende of soldiers as with stripes, and suche as showlde, if neade weare (according to the old sayd sawe,) lay the naked swoord to the side, that here after it might bee deamed not Brittaine butt Rome, commaunding all gowld and silver to bee figured and engraved with the image of Cæsar.' This saythe hee. But in the newe Historie a manne maie reade of great bickeringe and manlie conflictes betweene Claudius, and that Guinderius, being slaine bie treason, that his brother Arviragus renewed the warrs, not ceasinge to prosecute the same until Cæsar hadd geeven in mariage his dowghter Genissa, or Gemissa, to Arviragus, being chosen kinge in the rowme of his brother. But trulie, wheras Claudius, accordinge to Suetonius, of three wives had these doughters, Claudia, Octavia, and Antonia, commaundinge Claudia, not begotten bie him, to be caste beefore the dores of her mother Herculanilla, whome hee had devorced, mareinge Antonia to Cneius Pompeius the Great and successivelie to Faustus Silla, two noble yong menn, and his other doughter Octavia to his sonne in lawe Nero, surelie it is as unlikelie to bee beeleeved as unsemelie to bee saide that Claudius showld geeve his doughter Genissa in mariage to Arviragus. Yet, whether hee finished bie weapon or leage his exploytes, truthe it is that after hee hadd subdewed Orchades Iles, in the ocean sea beyonde

This spetch tochynge the Brytans was used by Gildas upon theyr being overcum so quietly by Claudius, who revenged the soden brech of covenant of the people after the conquest done by Cesar.

The new History.

Brittaine, at his returne to Rome hee triumphed in great pompe, and in remembrance thereof his sonne whome hee begatte on Messalina, firste caulled Germanicus, hee surnamed Brittanicus. While these thinges weare attempted, newes weare broughte that in Brittaine there sprange a newe insurrection: whereunto Cæsar as embassadowre promised Vespasian, which was an ominus beginninge of good fortune to comm, for at one battaile hee appeased all seditions, and browghte the Ile of Wighte, adjoyninge to Brittain, under the Romaine dominion. Arviragus. Arviragus, leste hereafter enie more hee shoulde bee mooved with vaine hope to rejecte and acquite him of the yoke of the Romaines, and sumwhat stirred with olde age (which drewe on), is reported to have confedered in peace with his enemie: but bie the authoritee of Cornelius Tacitus wee maye well gether that the Romaines being princes were wonte to ordayne certaine hedde rewlers, namelie, legats or solliciters in Brittaine, which bie there presence mighte the easlier bridell and keepe under the inhabitants, which thing allso Gildas affirmethe, as wee have saide before. Wherfore, after Vespasian being under the empire of Claudius, valiaunce and corage reentringe in to the hertes of Britons, it fortuned that firste of all consuls Aulus Plautius was legate, and next unto him Ostorius Scapula, whoe, at his verie first comminge, hadd great trowbles; for a stoute companie of the Britishe people, then named Iceni, accompanied with their borderers, taking lustilie their weapons in hande, pitched there pavilions in place moste likelie to anoye their adversaries, and eche whear chased the Romains. But the embassador, well experienced that mistruste or confidence depended on the first casualltie of the battaile, with all haste possible meetethe them, destroienge eche wheare suche as weare straienge, and afterwarde the rivers Anton and Severne hee minded to beesett with his tents, but these forenamed Iceni manfullie withstood him. Thus beinge frustrate of his hope, he proceaded to the tentes of his enemies, with whome when hee had encountered, he overcamme them manfullie, and, using the oportunitee of his victorie, ledde his armie in to the Welche people cauled Cangi, ingroching bootie echewhere plentifullie, and thus hasting towards his foes he was not farre fromme the sea which boundeth towards Ireland, wherebie it apeareth that that battiel was fought in the farthest partes westwarde, and that the people whome I called Iceni were dwellers abowte Severne and Anton, as the inhabitants at this daye of Wells, Excester, Worciter, Shrewsburie, and Hereforde; and that Anton is the river which menne call Veyus, which runnethe bie Hereford and joyneth with Severne not farre from the entrie thereof, even as it is semblablie well knowne that thei which were named Cangi did inhabite the inner partes of Walls westwarde. In the middest of these affaires the Romane capitane was withdraune bie reason of certaine discordes sodainlie enkendeled emonge the northen menn called Brigantes, which all hee did mitigate at his first cominge, puttinge to deathe the cheefe stirrers of the commotion. In this place allso, bie conjecture, Brigantes possessed that parte of the Ile which at this day hath on the northe parties the diocesse of Yorcke, on the weste the diocesse of Carleil, on the sea coste Lancastre and Kendall; which thinge allso is moste plaine in Tacitus, whoe reportethe there citte of all others to have benn most populus, as it is evident that Yorcke hathe heretofore beene, as maye well bee gathered bie the situacion thereof. In the meane season the Silurians, a moste feerce kinde of menne, chosethe an armie, trustinge to the noblesse and manhode of one Caratacus, a manne most politique in warfare, and of all others the cheefe, whoe was reported to have been kinge of them whiche were then called Ordoluces. To represse the force of this manne and others, a newe garison of owlde soldiers weare browght to the towne then named Camulodunum. And here wee maye a littell and commodiuslie streye from our race.

Cangi. Iceni. Brigantes. Silurians.

I thincke Camulodunum (sithe there maye doubte arise therein) was in times paste in that place whereas now is Dancaster, for the verie analogie of the woorde, representinge a certaine memorie of tentes and fortresses, seemethe to reteine the name of a place

Camulodunum.

Pountfreyt. chosen for refuge and succours in battalie. Likewise Pountfreyte, which is sumwhat nearer, xviii. miles on this side Yorcke, hathe a certaine probabilitee in this case, allbeit the place hathe more plea-saunce then naturall munitions. A castell is yeat there extante with somme signes and remainders of a temple, which was there dedicated to Claudius Cæsar, wherin weare two statues or images, the one of the Goddes Victorie, the other of himme selfe Claudius, unto which place it is to bee conjectured that his colonie and armie was browghte on all sides to minister aide and rescewse to his Romaines. This is the opinion of Tacitus, writinge thus in his xivth. booke: Moreover, saithe hee, there was a temple conse-crate to the heroicall Claudius, as an aulter testifienge perpetuall imperie. Nether was it hard to spoile or sacke this place of recepte and harborowe, beinge destitute of all defence, while our soldiers did more endevor to plesantnes then neade or opor-tunitee. This sayth hee. 'Certis, this place semed marvelowse goodd to defende the Romaine Province, which at that season was soe small that it extended not to the River Tine, which was within littel after the uttermoste bounde thereof, as the selfe same Tacitus wittenessethe, whereas he mencionethe the Romaine cheefetaines which weare sent into the Ilond after Vespasian, writing in this wise in the life of Agricola. The noble Claudius beinge founder of the woorckemanshipp, and transportinge his legions and aides, associating Vespasian in to parte of his affaires, which was a luckie principle of fortunate successe to comme; for the people was subdued, the kinges taken prisoners, and Vespa-sianus hereunto assigned bie destenie. Their firste governor emong the consuls was Aulus Plautius, and nexte unto him Ostorius Scapula, bothe justlie to be renowmed for their martiall prowesse, bie whome the nearer partes of the region was brought in to the fourme of a province, and a colonie or place of receite and retinue ordeined, etc.' Wherefore it seemethe the Romaine province at that time was not verie ample, sithe that onlie the first parte of the Ilonde (as Englonde in our dayse) was in theire jurisdiction. Nether was the towne which I called Camulodunum out of their circuite, seing that there was encamped the garrison of the olde grande warriers for the defence thereof; as it allso well agreeth with Ptolomei, who accountethe it not to bee farr distante from Yorcke, yea allmost in that verie place wheare wee bie likelie argument did make late demonstration. An other testimoniall that it consisted in the first soile of the Ilond is this, that Julius Agricola, whenne v. yeares withowte intermission hee chased with battell the Brittons lienge beyonde the river Tweede, and finallie conquered them, whereof Tacitus writethe diligentlie, Camulodinum is not once mencioned, which if it hadde benn situat in those costes, the Romaine legions noe doubte wolde have used the commoditee thereof ether in passage, retiringe, or sojorninge their. But now again to the matter. Thus Caratacus, a puissant manne emonge the inhabitants of Cheviot hills, chosinge suche place for the plantinge his artillerie, as throughe the mountaines might seeme more hard and greevos to his adversaries, encoraged his menne, surelie affirminge that that daye and that armie shoulde ether attaine æternall libertie or otherwise incurre perpetuall servilitee; severallie naminge the elders which hadd waged battell with Julius Cæsar, and soe conferring manie thinges, put them in assured hope of uncertaine victorie. Ostorius at this time used nether silence nor ydelnesse, but after like exhortations drewe towards his enimie and gave the onsett. Beefore handstrokes thei firste bickered with dartes and slinges, afterward pressinge together in thronge thei used the ministerie of ther swordes. The contention for a good season was noe lesse daungerous than doubtfull, till at lengthe the Brittons were constrened to forsake the toppes of the hills, wherunto the lighte harnesed menne ascendinge committed great slaughter. The wife of Caratacus, the dowghters and brothers, yealding themselves were receaved, and he himselfe imploringe the assistaunce and faithe of Carthumandua, queene of the Brigants or Yorckeshieremenn, was yealded uppe faste bownde to the overcommers. And thus Caratacus, the trumpe of whose fame was blowne throughe owt all Italie bie cause hee IX yeares maintayned warres with the Romains, was brought to Rome emonge other gregall captives, whoe, in presence of the Emperoure, with presente and bolde spirit, is reported to have spoken to Claudius Cæsar in this wise: 'Moste redowbted Cæsar, if prosperitee had benn other correspondent to mie will, or hadde accorded with mie fortune and condition, noe doubte I would have visited this cittie as a manne at free will and libertie, and trulie with all mie hart showlde I have seene it, seinge that I accompted it parte of mie felicitee, for I did allwayse so much abhorre the refusall of peace, that moste willinglie I wowlde have embraced the same beinge once offered; and, next to the fraunchise and freedom of mine owne contrie, I nothinge desired more ardentlie then the æquall amitte of the Romains. But now chaunce hathe soe served that I showlde fall into thie handes, to this intente (I suppose), that I, being in sundrie wise blessed and æsteeming mie selfe in heaven, might the better understande how miche affiance I owght to have in humaine casualties; and that thow beeng conqueror mightes purchase the more renowne, bothe that thow haste conquired, and allsoe spared and forgeeven, for soe I truste yt shall please the to doe accordinge to thie singular grace and clemencie.' With these woordes Cæsar beinge stirred to jentilnes, graunted life to himme, his wife, and breethren; soe that, accordinge to the olde proverbe, fortune is a friend to the valiant and coragius. After these exploits the Silurians (being the nexte people) of a sodaine set uppon the cheefe ruler of the tentes, with the hole bende and legion their lefte in garison and defence, whome thei hadd taken prisoner if aide had not speedelie benne ministered. Neverthelesse manie Romaines were slaine in that howrley burlei, for thei aboove all other did moste deadlie hate the Romaine name, being enkendeled therunto with the cruell saing of the captan, being echewheare spredd and blowne, which was this: 'Even as the Sicambers in auncient time were cleane extriped that thei mighte bee translated in to Fraunce, soe the verie name of the Silurians muste bee abolished.' Wherefore thei entrapped two companies of there garrison, foolishlie spoylinge throwghe the blinde covitise of there guides, and so bie their largesse in geeving bootie and releasing captives, thei allured others to slippe the coller; wherewith encumbered and with manie cares oppressed, Ostorius died, whose deathe beinge intimated to Claudius Cæsar, leste the province showld want a governor, he substituted Aulus Didius, whoe taking his jornie withoute delaye, fownde great broyles in all estates, perceavinge the legion whereof Manlius Valens was lodesmann to bee a littell beefore putt to flighte. Nevertheles in shorte space he appeased all thinges, reducinge the Silurians to conformitee, and defendinge the queene Carthumandua from the injuries of Venusius, who hadd wedded her, and minded to expulse her owte of the kingdom for the late sowne seade of sedition. At this season weare certaine cittes francklie geeven to Cogidunus, whoe remained faithefull untill the time of Domitian.

Avitus succeeded in embassage into this province under the Emperour Nero, at which time allso was receaved noe small overthrowe. Verannius beinge next unto him didd onlie preserve that which was gotton, and died within the revolucion of a yeare. Then Suetonius Paulinus (a mann whome fortune and vertue did contende moste to adorne) obteined Brittaine; whoe, gevinge assaulte to the Ile Mone, the verie refuge of runawais, subdued the same at his first arrivall, as wee shewed at the beginninge of this woorcke and description of the same Ilond. The Brittaines, having gotten the absence of Paulinus, debated amonge themselves the miseries of servage and villanie; thei conferred their wrongs and injuries; they murmured that noe availe cam bie sufferance, but a more open entrie to greater distresse; thei discoursed how the legate spente his dayse in their bluddeshed, and the solliciter in the procuringe their goodes used crueltie; in consideration whereof thei all enflamed mutuallie theire hertes to battaile, being somwhat more pricked forwarde with the knavishe dealinge

Igeni the inhabitors of Northumberland.

of the rascall soldiers towards them; for Prasutagus, kinge of the nation called Igeni, made Cæsar his heire and his two doughtors, supposinge bie suche obeisaunce to attaine the more saftie from injuries to his stemme and kingdom; but it fortuned himm farre otherwise then hee surmised, for his kingdom was wasted of the Centuriens, his wife called Vodicia banneshed of the owlde cancred soldiers, his doughtors disteined with lecherie, his piers cleane striped of their substance, his frindes and acquaintance numbered and recounted amonge bond slaves and peasants.

Camolodunum.

Moreover the olde servitors, being brought butt a littell before into the abode or harborow of Camolodunum, did echewhere disturbe manie owte of their houses and grownde, callinge all bie the reproche of slaves as if thei had ben captives. Besides this, in the temple erected to Claudius, preestes, under the pretext of relligion, distroied, spoiled, and consumed the goodes and wealthe of all menn. Then the terrible woonders and portentuus prognostications which at that time was fixed in the ieys of all men did not a littell provoke them; for the image of the goddesse Victorie at Camulodunum torned backe as thoughe it gave place to the enemies: the ocean sea flowed in appearance like bloodde, and the printe of menns boddies remained on the shore: the women, as it weare intoxicate with madnes, did prophesie in songes that their deathes day was comme: soe that the Britaines weare animated with hope, the olde Cæsarien warriars dismaied with dispaire. These and suche like things, whether thei were donn bie the illusion of menn or devells, or whether indeed there bee enie force in the nature of things, which the baser sorte doe som time superstitiouslie note as signes and woonders, I would gladlie have lett passe, lest wee showld seeme to bringe inconvenience to that relligion which, teachinge all thinges to be ordered bie the Divine providence of Godde, dothe rejecte suche vaine southesaings of thinges to comme, if the nature of an historie wowlde soe permitte, which will that all thinges trulie donne showld bee faythefullie written. Wherfore nothing shalbee opprobrius unto us, ether in this place or elsewheare, declaring suche thingges but to the follie of menne, whoe like olde wiches have gonne abowte with suche fore tokens to attaine the knowlege of things ensewinge; and this have I said partlie to thentent that noe manne should to farre welter in suche fanatike and fond observations; therefore even from the beginninge I thought goodd to speake of suche matters beefor hande, bi cause wee ernestlie minde that the reader shoulde incurre noe error: but now to the matter.

Voadicia emonge the reste didde chieflie exasperate their mindes with great plaintee of her wrongs which she hadd sustained at the Romaines, whoe, bie cause she burned of all others in greatest hatred, it was broughte abowght, herselfe beinge capitan, (for in rule-bearinge there was noe difference of kinde,) that a great parte of the people, persuadinge the menn called Trinobantes to refuse their dutie and homage, didde sodaynelie slide from the Romaines, in hedlong rage with weapon rising against them. On the other side, the auncient fightingmenn astonied at the first commotion of the Brittains, beetooke themselves to a certaine temple, wheras all were slaine from the first to the laste, and consequentlie a newe legion which at the guiding of Petus Cerealis, then embassadoure, camme to their succours, was driven to flie and slaine. Catus Decianus being at the same instance a solliciter for Brittaine, slinkinge in the middest of this feare, passed into Fraunce. This fiercenes of the Brittons streched even to the incorporate towne called Verulamium, throwghe the cittizens of Rome and their confederats, bie computation beinge slaine of the feeble multitude about seventie thowsand menne. Within short space Paulinus was present, and proceaded to London, dowbting whether hee showld chose that place for the perfourmance of his battayle: wherefore, departinge from hence, hee tooke a place with narrow entries, and behind soe beesett with woodde that hee might bee with owte guile or danger, knowinge for certeinte that he could not bee invaded but before his face.

Hee hadd abowte x. thousand soldiers with him, in whome having good confidence hee encountered with a mayne companie of enemies. The Britons farre surmounted in the multitude of fightinge menn, and therfore thei skirmished at the beginninge with sutch assured hope of victorie that the woomen stoode bie in cartes and waggons to beehoulde the combate. The place wherein thei foughte was verie streyght, and therfore commodius to the exilitee of the Romains; the contention from the first onsett was bluddie and terrible, but in fine the Brittains, whoe hindred one another's strokes throughe the narrownes of the place, not abell enie longer to withstande their adversaries, were putte to flighte, and eche where skattered in great slaughter, for almoste xxx. thousand were slaine. Voadicia, cheefe governes of the battale, lest shee shoulde fall into the hands of her enimies, ended her life bie empoysoninge her selfe. The estate of the Ile from that time forth was more quiet, being well maintained bie Petronius Turpilianus, whoe folowed Suetonius, and after that of Trebollius Maximus, whoe, in noe wise provokinge the Britains to wraithe, did tender and preserve

Igeni.

them. Here will I geeve sufficient warninge that Igeni, as thei differ in one letter from Iceni, soe weare theie a divers people, as wee maye wel perceave in Tacitus, and that thei inhabited the northe parties of the contrie, the which in these our daise hath to name Northumberland; nether was London the cittie called Trinobantum, as manie conjecture, as it well appearethe bie testimonie of the selfe same Tacitus; for Suetonius, having overcommed the Ile Mone, camm throughe an overthwarte waye to London as to a place of safetie, which hee wold never have donne if that towne hadde benne in the contrie of men named Trinobantes, which broke theire leage accordinge as others didde; wherebie allsoe it appeareth that the Trinobantes did not westewarde dwell on this side the towne named Watlingcester, which in time paste was righte over against the village nowe called Sancte Allbanns, xx miles from London, for even thether reached this furor of their adversaries. Trulie it hadde benne noe safe passage for Suetonius

Paulinus to have taken his jornie to London if that Trinobantes hadd possessed that parte of the Ilonde which wee call Essex, whose borders towche the teritorie of London, as Ptolomei writeth, whoe placethe the Trinobantes at the flowinge and ebbing of the river Thames, and termithe their auncient towne Camudola, which now hath to name Cowlchester; yeat are their somme which affirme that that was the cittey Trinobantum which at this daye hathe to name Northehamton, which is well declared bie the corruptinge of the name of the towne in the first two letters, for the ruralls in English call it Tranton, bie the which runnethe the river Nyne, which now hath the verie same name that the towne. But conjectures taken owte of divers opinions are woont bie reasoning and alltercation to make thinges dowbtfull, otherwise nothinge to bee dowbted in; which hathe chaunced in seaking the dwelling places of the Trinobantes: for at the lengthe their chaunced olde monuments in to mie handds whearin this was written, 'The Trinobantes allso, hearinge the terrible brute of the comminge of the Romains, did speedilie defend their cittee, furnished their shipps with armowre, to defende the borders of their contrie abowte the entries of the river Thames.' These woordes agree with Ptolomei, and plainlie shewe that wee ought to agree with them bothe, for bie these testimonies it is evident that London was never the towne Trinobantum, but that thei inhabited the este coste bounding on the sea, whose cheef towne is Coelchester. Now may I retire to mie purpose. Even as I thinke the people whereof Cæsar maketh mention to have ben in the middest of the ilonde, named then Cenigmani, Segontiaci, Ancalites, Bibroci, and Cassi, which places are now inhabited of the people of Coventrie, Lecester, Northingham, and Derbie, soe I doe gesse (if it be but a gesse) that besides London this onlie one cittie Ordovicum keepethe the primitive name, allbeit wee adding this letter N. to the beginninge call it Nordovicum or Norwiche. Trulie the posteritee, that is to weete, Pictes, Scottes, Englishemenn, Danes, and Normans, being lordes of the Ile, did voluntarilie chaunge all thinges, esteeming it as a monument to geeve newe appellation to the places which thei hadd conquered. At this time (as wee reherced aboove) was Arviragus cheefe kinge in Brittaine, in the dayse of the Emperour Nero. Juvenall, in his iiij. Satire, where hee flatterethe Nero (for it cannot bee referred to Domitian who reigned longe after) for the catching of a birte saith thus:

Arviragus chefe king of the Brytons in Neros tyme, in whos tym Joseph of Arimathea with his feloship cam thether and preched Christ, and optayned a lytell grond to inhabet about Wels wher Glasenberie monastery was built.

> Of greate triumphe a signe thou haste, some kinge thou shalt apall,
> Or from the Brittishe chariot Arviragus shall fall.

At which time that same Joseph, (as the Evangeliste Matheue witnessethe was borne in the cittey Arimathæa, and buried Christes boddie,) whether it weare bie chaunce, or of purpose, or at the apointment of Godd, with noe small companie cam into Brittaine, whearas bothe hee and his fellowshipp preaching the woord of Godd and sincere secte of Christe, manie were trained to the trewe piete, and being indewed with the right saving helthe wear baptized. These menn, surelie inspired with the hollie ghoste, obtaining of the kinge a littel grownde to inhabit, nere unto the towne named Wells, or not aboove iiij. miles distante, did sowe the seade of our new relligion, where at this daye is a gorgeus cherche, and faire monasterie of relligius menne of the order of Sainct Benet, called Glastenburie. These were the firste principles of Christian faythe in Brittaine, which in processe being againe allmoste extinguished, Kinge Lucius beinge baptized (as wee shall here after make rehersall) didde noe lesse woonderuslie lighten then devoute increase. For Gildas witnesseth, that from the verie first divulgation of the holie ghospell, Brittaine moste desieruslie embraced the same. Marius, next in discent from Arviragus, the LXXII. yeare of our Salvation was created kinge, whoe within shorte season hadd great warrs with the Pictes, whoe, as they weare a people of Scithia, and verie neare to the Gothes in contrie and manners, soe weare they a crewell nation and marvelus prone to fighte. Som men have lefte in memorie that thei weare called Pictes, ether of the blewe colours wherewith thei weare peincted, ether of their bluncket heres, ether of certaine marckes made with whot irons,

Maurius kyng.

Pictes and of theyr first aryvall in to Brytayn.

wherof hee that was more honorable had the most deepest and eminent printes, hee that was more abject and base had lesser and smaller. Somme supposed that they weare the people called Agathirsi, and therfor to be called Picts, biecause thei didd beesmeere theire limmes and visages that it cowlde not bee wasshed awaye. But whereof soe ever the name of Pictes was derived, most certaine it is that thei weare a people of Scithia. For thei on a time, with a goodd companie of shippes and there capitaine named Rodericus, roving abowte the ocean sea for spoyle and bootie, camme into the ile Ireland, desieringe this newe dwelling place of the Scotts, whoe (likewise having their originall of springe of the Scithians, albeit thei derive their discent another waye) weare then lordes of the Ilond. The Scottes, thincking it nothinge for their availe to entertaine a warlike and indigent people, dissembling and counterfeiting a certaine naturall remorse and loove, alleaged the tenuitee and streightnes of the soyle, enforminge them that Brittaine was not farre of, an Ile noe less plenteus then greate, and yet allmoste desolate, exhorting them to passe thither, promisinge there aide and industrie. The Pictes, whoe were more envegeled with the desier of praye then inflamed with the ambition of imperie, in noe wise abidinge, sayled towards the Ilonde, wheare at their first arrivall thei seasoned on a peace of the Northe parte, and their espienge fewe inhabitants, thei practised spoylinge; they used ofte invasions, and beganne to strey farther and farther; which thinge the Brittishe princes forthe with perceaving determined to meate them in armes, and hastelie setting on them which with owt all feare wandered in the fieldes, slewe their capitan, and overcommed at the first conflicte. The Pictes, which weare survivers after this overthrowe, conveyed themselves into the uttermoste partes of the Ile, which wee call Cathenesia in our dayse; whoe as men reporte longe after possessed all the grownde lienge betweene the wall erected bie the noble worckemanshippe of the Romains (whereof I will intreat in som other place) and the mowntaine Grampius, lienge somwhat estewarde; and bie these shiftes the Pictes becam great lordes in that parte of the Ilonde, whoe weare the seconde people which of straungers after the Romains entred Brittaine, obteininge dominion therein, which was the LXXXVIJ. yeare of our Sallvation. But after that thei hadde recovered some good successe after this unluckie overthrowe of their fellawshippe, thei rejoised that at the lengthe thei hadde established their seates and dwellings in Brittaine; yet did thei easlie foresee that neades it moste com to passe that their stocke showlde consume, and in noe wise surmounte the age of a mann, for wante of wooman kinde, (suche is the chaunce that continuallie there is some defect or obstacle to hinder or withstande the perfectnes and consummation of a mannes fælicitie,) for nether hadd they hope of propagation and children at home, nether as yet weare they joned in matrimonie with thir borderers: wherfore bie a common consent they sent embassadours to Brittains, requiering alliaunce and mariage for thes strangers. The embassage was hevelie harde, soe much was it contemned of all menn, soe lothe they weare to joyne bloodd and issewe with aliens and foriners; which thing notwithstandinge the Pictes tooke greevoslie, neverthelesse adjudging this injurie owght be revenged at an other time and means, sent unto them in Ireland, whoe were content to exhibite woomen on this condition, that as often as there chaunced altercation in chosinge the kinge, for default of lineall discent of heires male, then they shoulde apoint somme of the progenie of there women, which thinge as it is manifestlie knowne was allwayse observed of the Pictes.

But nowe let us enter into the Actes and Deedes of the Romaines doonne in the Ilond.

Next unto Trebellius Maximus (whoe departed not withowt ignominie, bie reason of a certaine tumulte ingendered of bestlie slugeshenes in the Oste,) Vectius Volanus was cheefe ruler in Brittaine. After him Petilius Cereales, whoe hadde to doe with a certaine sorte of disorderd men, whome hee vanquished and chastised for not obeieng his commaundements. Then Julius Frontinus, whoe allso subdued som others refusing to obeye. Finallie, under the empire of Vespasian, Julius Agricola obteined this province, even then trobelus and dowbtfull, bie whose prowesse and manwhode the Romaine armes beecamm muche more terrible to the Brittons, whoe founde the soldiers rechelus and laysie with ydelnesse, and the contrie it selfe wonderuslie hastinge to stirre uppe rebellion. For whearas the Norffolke menne hadd allmoste clene destroied one winge of the armie sojorninge in theire quarters, for the same cause the whole region conceaved allmoste assured confidence to récover libertie; which thinge Agricola understandinge, hasted with maturitee to resiste this eminent perrill; wherefore, crienge sodainlie to armes, after hee hadd gathered a small number, bie cause the Norfolke menn durste nott enter fighte if herin seemed to be enie æqualitee, hee therefore sett on them with weapon, bringinge a great sorte to confusion, and not mindinge thus to cease, as one that well knew how favorable fortune muste bee taken and prosecuted: in the same moment allmos thee tooke the Ile Mone, which beinge woonne a litel beefore by Paulinus, didd streyght rebell uppon his departure. After these thingges thus administred, hee, desieringe to roote owte the occasions of dissention, did neverthelesse exercise and travaile his menne in armes and watchinges, (as he was himme selfe moste prudentlie experienced in warfare,) leaste the vertue of ther mindes showld languishe and feynt throughe ydelnes of boddie. Moreover hee endevored to bewtifie the Brittons, being rewde for the moste parte, with manners and ordinances, encoraginge them to builde temples, marckett places, and howses, extollinge suche as weare prompte, reprovinge and chasteninge the sluggishe, that bie æmulation they might bee enflamed to more civilitee; for wheare as publicke honor is notte attributed to vertewe, their canne be noe zeale ether to vertewe or glorie, he especiallie admonished that the children of princes showlde bee fostered in good artes, preferringe their witts and inclination beefore the Frenchemenn, bie cause that to their power they affected the Romaine eloquence hee gave them lawes

Julius Agricola.

and broughte in ure certaine decrees of the Romanes, wherebie it camme to passe that in littell space the Brittains received excellencie in behaviour, their attire and fourme of life beeganne to bee much more delicate, soe that even then the magnificence of dinners and suppers didde passe throughe oute all honeste houses, beinge commonlie termed humanitee, wheras indeade, as Tacitus saithe, it is a certaine bondage and superfluitee. I might saye that the same exquisitenes in banquetinge did from thence discend unto our time [to] Englishe people. This was the diligence of Agricola in the winter, and his deads worthie memoriall the two firste years of his embassage. Afterwarde achiving manie and prosperus conflictes, and triumphing over manie unknowne people, he minded to geeve assault to that parte of Brittaine which wee call Scotlond, bounding towards Irelonde, whereunto noe small number of fugitives wear retiered, addressinge his armie and furnishinge a navie, that he might skirmishe bothe on sea and on lande; wherfore, entringe the river Forthe he passed it, notwithstandinge the bridge was broken, and assayth expugnation of divers castells, which thing after it was knowne, the Brittons gatheringe eche where menn of armes, ranne with speed, mindinge bie the demolition of the brige to entrappe their enemie beetweene the rivers Forthe and Taus. But Agricola turninge towards them without difficultie put them to flighte, chasing them to the flowe of the river Taus. And theise were the exploits of the iij. yeare. Agricola after this, minding to serche owte the extreemest borders of the Ilond, at the first race went to the river Glote and there pitched his tentes, where the river, in old time Bodotria, now called Levine, runneth into Glote. In this season the Britons environed him in thicke rowtes, on whome hee runninge in violent wise, he drave them to suche extremitee that they were clene beaten owte of the river in to an other Ile, as hee supposed, bie cause the river aboute the entries was verie deepe and brode; and these were the facts of his iiij. yeare. In the next sommer Agricola, sendinge for a navie, passed over Glote bie shippe, enforcinge straunge nations to yealde, and ordering garrisons about the sea costes bendinge towards Irelonde. He there harborowed for that winter; thus was the v. yeare of his embassage spente. After this, takinge deliberation bie all kinde of meanes howe to enter the inner parties of the ilonde, hee was greatlie discouraged with the difficultie of the fennes and mountains, which bothe nottwithstandinge in conclusion this invincible warrior overcamme, whoe, as juste rewarde of his labour and peines, toke noe small bootie in those quarters: for thether the savage people haunted with theire gooddes and cattailes as it weare to their laste refuge: and for bie cause hee understode bie espies that his adversaries satt bie the waies in sundrie rowtes, mindinge diverslie to bruste forthe on him, therefore he distributed his armie into iij. companies. While thes thinges were thus ordered, the Romaine navie, being assigned as it weare to glaunce alonge bie the Ile, didd ransacke all the havens, wherebie it camme to passe that the armie on lande and that which was on sea, to the great delectation of their minds, did often meate in one place, and there eche manne shewed and recorded his manlie gestes, extoilinge one an other to the heavens, even as it commeth to passe in prosperitie whereof everie most towarde will have himselfe partaker, but not of adversitee. The Brittons in the meane time, which hooved a farre of, as soone as they well knew the shippes which they hadd espied, thei weare greatlie agreeved, in that the secrets of there sea being disclosed and open to their enemie, thei accounted that their was noe safe receptacle for suche as were vanquished, and thinckinge with themselves that there was noe foyle or spotte of mischief unsuffered, retieringe desperatlie to their weapons, of a sodaine invaded the newe legion in the nighte season, as that which was of lesse strengthe and habilitee to resiste. The fighte was sharpe on bothe sides, untill suche time as Agricola issuenge owte of his tentes succored and refresshed his traveled soldiers. Nowe the Brittons beinge againe putte to flighte, and yeat beeleevenge that their enemies attayned not the superiorite soe muche bie theire peculier prowesse as bie the occasion and pollicie of their captaine, didd nothinge suppresse or abate their corages. But when sommer drewe towardes his uttermoste date, weapons for a while weare laied aside, bie reason of moste noysom tempestes then fallinge; and so the vj. yeare of his embassage browghte some quietnes. Nevertheles, when as the springe time was comme, Agricola entred into Calidonia, and pitched his pavilions bie the river Taus, the which as wee saide beefore runnithe into the ocean of Germanie, being receaved of the sea in trubelous gowlfe, more then two miles broade. Then the Brittons, perseavinge their laste daunger to hange over their hedds, were fullie in themselves resolved ether for their liberties to die honestlie, or for the victorie to contende manfullie. Wherefore first of all with sacrifice and solemne othe thei made and celebrated a common conspiracie of all their citties; secondarilie, thei browghte their wives and children to the mountaine Grampius, and, having a place feetlie selected for the plantinge of their tents, theye revestred* their yowthe in armowre; and, leaste discorde might springe throwghe the multitude of governors, which is the onlie plague and hinderance of the goodd ordering and success in battaile, the highest titell of imperie was committed to Calgacus, a mann of noe lesse prudence then valiance, conceavinge the better hope in that the Visipians, of whome an armie was browght to the verie shore, did slippe awaye from the Romains at that same instant, whoe being a people of Germaine, and dwellers on Rhene, whereas they weare sente in aide to the Romaines, they traitoruslie slewe theire Centurien, and, desierus to finde newe dwellinge places, were all most all utterlie perished and piened with famine. But when as Agricola hadd as it were undermined the purpose of his adversaries, hee forthewith passinge the river Taus placed his tentes in a level grounde as neare as hee coulde to the bottom of the mountaine Grampius; and thus their mindes being on bothe sides provoked, thei shortlie came to hande strokes. But Calgacus first gave instigation to his

* putte. *interlin.*

liege menn, in ample oration declaringe how woorthelie libertie was to bee reputed of all sortes, as then the which nothing coulde next unto the goddes bee more leefe or deare unto mankinde, upbroydinge the Romaines in mennie respectes for theyre avarice and pride, terminge them the robbers and theeves of the whole worlde. On the other side, Agricola exhorted his companie allso in manie woordes, with stowte stomacke to endewre this last labor of eight years, as the finall end of all warres, wherebie they might happelie bee repleneshed with the abowndant fruites of victorie. Thus the armie of ether partie beinge sett in order, the battayle was soe fearselie attempted as whoe shulde say eche mann thristed other's life, which being continued untill eeven tide, nothinge seemed more convenable to the Brittons then to encompasse their enemies on their backes; but Agricola preparing iiij. winggs of horsmen for their comminge, did cleane disapointe them, and constreine them to flie, of whome weire slaine more than x. thowsande, and of the Romaines allso a great numbre. Then Agricola taking hostages commaunded his shippes to retowrne, and the residewe of his legion to repaire to their winteringe places. These woorthie factes were doonne, Domitian beinge emperowre, which provoked him to hate and envie Agricola, (being him selfe a manne nothing favorable or frindlie to vertewe,) for in shorte space hee was called backe, to bee Leeve-tenant of Siria, now lienge voide bie reason of the dethe of Attilius Rufus. Next unto him succeeded Cneus Trebellius, whome Domitian apointed to bee Præsident of Brittaine. This was the estate of the Brittishe affaires when Marius was kinge, of whome Tacitus maketh noe mention.

This Marius reygned xlviij. years, levinge behinde himme his sonne Coyllus, whoe continued for a longe season at Rome, and contrived all his yowthe in the service of their warrs, and in other noble qualitees; whoe being crowned kinge after the deathe of his father, all the time of his reygne (which admounted to xlv. years), was greatlie beeloved of the Romaines, and confirminge peace

Coyllus kyng.

echewhere bie all meanes eschewed battaile; but the moste divine thinge and woorthie memoriall that ever hee didd to his stocke and posteritee was this, that hee broughte into this worlde his sonne Lucius, whoe of Brittaine kinges beecamme the first Christian; for hee in the clxxxij. yeare of our salvation and the xiij. yeare of his owne reygne, inspired with the loove of the trew and indeficient relligion, in his letters treated with Elewtherius, bisshoppe of Rome, that washinge him and his subjects in the celestiall fountaine hee wold adjoyne them to the numbre of Christians. Wherfore Fugatius and Damianus, menne of singular devotion, weare sent thether: who baptized the kinge, with all his familie and people, and, abolishinge the fantasticall woorshippinge of devills, did instructe the nation with the right fourme of sincere pietie and godlines. At that time weare theare in Brittaine xxviij. preestes accordinge to the usage of the Gentiles, and iij. highe preestes, in whose rowmes soe maynie bisshopps and iij. arche bishopps weare substitute, wherof one had his sea at London, the other at Yorke, and the thirde in the cittie of Legions, or Legicester, whearas weare builded churches as well sumpteus in ornamentes as magnificent in buildinge. Thus Brittaine, partlie throughe the industrie of Jhosephe of Aramathie (of whome wee made relacion a littell beefore), partlie throughe the hollie instructions of Fugatius and Damianus, of all provincies was the firste that openlie receyved the ghospell: the which pietee they stifflie observed untill the tyrannie of themperour Dioclesian, whoe aboove all other, nexte unto Nero, most cruellie persecuted the Cristians eeven allmoste to the verie deathe. For after that, as Gildas wittnessethe, relligion becamm soe cowlde through the severitee of persecutions, that unethes the cinders thereof apeared. Some there bee which ascribe the cherche of Saincte Peter a littell withowte London to Lucius, albeit divers other doe attribute it to Sigibert, as wee shall shewe hereafter; declaring allsoe how it camme to passe that these Saxons weare named Este Saxons, Middel Saxons, and Weste Saxons. This place, especiallie re-

Lucius the fyrst Christian king of the Brytons A°. D^{i}. 178, in whos time Brytayne was the first of all provinces that openly reseved the gospell.

nowned through the buriall of kings, is named Westminster, vulgarlie, bie cause it liethe weastwarde; but their are divers other causes allsoe wherebie it is greatlie adourned and garnished, as the highe street, the kinges pallace adjoininge an abbaye in times paste of moncks of the order of Sainct Benet, whereof it was named a monasterie; allsoe an auncient cherche dedicated to Sainct Stephen, the sanctuarie gevinge immunitee to guiltee persons, and the common place or barre for the administration of lawe and pleytinge of causes. I finde in a booke of great antiquitee, yeat withoute name of author, that this place in times past was on all sides environed with waters and called Thornie Ile; the which name surelie dothe verie well allude with the name which it hathe in our memorie, notwithstandinge that it is voide of thornes; for the great multitude of hurtfull and guiltie persons which weare wont to flie thether as to a sanctuarie, whilest menne demaunded causes and questioned with theim, they weare sufficientlie pricked with thornes, that is to saye, they hadd compunction of theire vices. But Lucius, striken with cœlestiall gladnes, that hee hadde trained his people to the perseverance of the true Godde, least thei might enie more bee envegeled with the sorceres and prestigiation of devels, he tooke awaye and inhibited to bee used all prophane service, and, consecratinge to Christe suche temples as weare erected for the idolls of the jentiles, largelie adorned them with his munificentie; finallie hee now moste gladlie and diligentlie referred all his actions to the encrease and fortifienge of relligion, in respect whearof he contemned all suche thinges as mortall menne are woonte to embrace with admiration. Wherefore this Lucius being emonge his menn the author of the æternall light wherin him selfe didde especiallie shine, did leave the kingdom to his posteritee (which he hadde receaved of his aunciters) not embrued with the bloodd of menne for vaine glorie, not puffed uppe with riches wrested owte of all costes, but firste havinge a noble principle of quiet and reste, secondarilie established in excellent orders and customs, finallie augmented in the divine relligion, and endewed with the moste sincere doctrine of Christe, exceadinge withoute controversie so muche all former princes, as things divine surmounte humaine affaires; he reigned xx. years, and dieng withowte issewe of his boddie, requiered the nobilitee to have singular regarde of the common wealthe, and that they would measure the utilitee of the vulgars bie the performance of their dewtie.

After the departure of Julius Agricola, the Brittons, especiallie suche as dwell beyonde Tweede, weare for a fewe yeares quiete, partlie bie reason their force was apaired, partlie beinge bounde bie the former surrender of their hostages. In which space Cneus Trebellius being legate; albeit he was of good forecaste, neverthelesse the Romaine soldiers beinge restie, beeganne to quarrell emonge them selves, and not esteeminge the wordes of the embassadoure, became no lesse harmefull then dispiteus to the Brittons, whoe on the other side perceaving themselves overcharged with slaverie, and eche daye to bring increase of mischeefe, they conceaved a great confidence of the recoverie of libertie and preservation of their contrie; wherefore with stowte stomacke they addressed themselves against the Romains and streight invaded them; yeat advisedli inoughe, soe that (accordinge to the usage of their contrie) when neade should require they might speedelie convay them selves into woodds and difficult places. There weare manie slaine on bothe parties, which ministred promptnes to the whole Ilonde to rebell; but Hadrianus, then emperoure, beinge certified of Trebellius as towching this commotion, at the firste utteringe passed the sea into Brittaine with an armie, whoe asswaged all the rage of the inhabitantes, and usinge curteos humanitie towards them made the Ile marvelus quiet; the bowndes and limites wheareof hee first of all prescribed and determined, if wee beeleeve Spartianus: for hee neglectinge the region beyond Tweede, which wee call Scotlond, ether for that it was more barraine or that hee thoughte it lesse commodius to bee kepte, hee commaunded the same to bee limited of the river Tine. Wherfore from the entrie thereof to an other river called Eske, hee made a wall eeven to the

Curteus humanyte used after Reformation, which made marvelus quietnes.

The first bonds and lymetes of this lond.

Irishe ocean sea, for Tine brustethe forthe into the Germanian ocean. Others attribute this limitation of the Ile to Severus. Yeat after this the Brittons, burninge as well in hatred toward the Romaine legion, as proposing ther owne servilitee beefore their ies, contended againe to freedom; which thinge being once knowne Antoninus Pius, Emperoure at that season, sent Lollius Urbicus as embassadour in to Brittaine, whoe after certaine conflictes caused them to continue their allegiaunce; yeat hee hadd not soe extinguished battaile, or cooled their corages, but that bie and bie they assaied ether to attaine their olde fraunchises, or to incurre farthere daunger. Wherfore M. Antoninus, who succeeded Pius, didd after Lollius sende Calphurnius Agricola legat into Brittaine, whoe, as Julius Capitolinus writeth, with facilitee vanquished and subdewed his foes. Afterward Pertinax beinge sente of Commodus in to the Ile, appeased all seditions rather bie wisdom then weapon.

Thus the province was quieted, and Pertinax beinge revoked to Roome, after the deathe of Commodus, was made emperowre. Then to Clodius Albinus was committed the rule of the armie in Brittaine, as Capitolinus in the treatie of his life bearethe wittnesse: after whome Junius Severus succeeded, beinge sent of Commodus, if wee beeleeve the same manne. But Herodianus writeth muche otherwise, whoe saithe that Clodius Albinus was longe conversant in the Iland after the deathe of Commodus, and that the Emperoure Severus, beinge verie desierus to procure the distruction of Albinus, transfreted into Fraunce; and againe, that Allbinus pickinge forthe the verie strengthe of the Brittishe armie departed owte of Brittaine to meete with him, and, joyninge in battayle at Lions, the warlike valiaunce of the Brittains was suche, that Severus was at the verie poinct to have benne overthrowne, yeat Albinus in the ende was slaine. Then Heraclitus, as legat, was sent for the governance of the province, whoe Spartianus reportethe to have benne promised thither of Severus. But the Romaine estate was suche in Brittaine abowte the cxcv. yeare of our salvation, that, the worthie prince Lucius beinge deade, the peeres of the realme by and bie entendinge there owne commoditee, while everie manne was busied in the aspiringe to imperie, thei began to sowe the sparckes of dissention; the which thing when it camme to the knowlege of the Emperour Severus, beinge then greatlie striken in years, hee tooke it nothinge heavelie, for hee beinge a manne of nature somwhat to propense to the desier of glorie, after his victories estwarde and in the northe partes, hee wowlde have benne passinge gladde to have benne surnamed Britannicus. Moreover for the discorde of his two sonnes, Bassianus Antoninus and Geta, wherewith he was marveluslie trobled, not being able to reconcile them bie enie meanes for the greate hatred which harteburned them, hee determined to leade them with him into Britaine, partlie that these yownge menne beinge disjoined fromme the delicius cittee, mighte cleave together in there troublesom tentes, partlie that their eares beinge shutt from the plausible tales of flatterers (which hee wrongefullie surmised to bee the cause of their strife) thei mighte the eeslier accorde and fall in favor. Wherefore, notwithstandinge his great age and that he was diseased with the gowte, taketh his voyage into the Ilonde, accompanied with his sonnes, whethre when hee was arrived, gatheringe soldiars to gather with increase of puissance, he was shortelie at the poincte to make warre. The Brittons being amazed at the sodaine arrivall of themperour, and feared allso with the great multitude in readines against them, sente embassadowrs as towchinge peace and their owne purgation to Severus; but he of purpose trifelinge with them and seekinge delayse, and to muche greadie of honor, rather condescended to battaile then peace: wherefore manie skirmishes were made with the Brittons, and those more harde to the Romaines then to themm, whoe beinge wel inured with the places, did often as necessitee urged use mockerie for fighte; and thus battaile beinge discontinued, Severus, what for greefe and sedition of his sonnes whearwith hee was vexed, and not a littell wasted with owlde age, hee died after hee hadd reigned XVIIJ. yeares;

whose bodie beinge burned and asshes put into a littell vessell of alabaster, was carried to Rome of his sonnes. But I am not aggreved to bee of their minde whoe have lefte in memorie that Severus at the firste pacifienge that parte of the Ile which was tributarie to the people of Rome, didd wage battayle with the Pictes, of whome wee made mention a littell beefore, whoe like theeves makinge ofte excursions sore annoyed the province. Herodianus dothe manifestlie shewe that they weare Pictes with whome Severus often hadde to doe, writinge thus of their demainor in thende of his thirde booke: 'They knewe not the use of garmentes, but gerded their weapons abowte their bellie and neckes, thinckinge that to bee an ornament and a token of riches, as other barbarus nations use gowlde; moreover thei peincte theyr boddies in sondrie wise, in all poincts representinge the shape of beastes.' Thus saithe hee. But Severus, leste his enimies farre driven awaye owte of the region beyonde Tweede showld doe skathe unto other Britons, accordinge to the guise of robbers, he is reported to have limited the Romaine province, bileding a wall like a trenche in that place: wheras, according to Spartianus, wee declared that Hadrianus didde bylde it: thus the doctors dissente. Somme there are which assevere that this walle was made of sownde and whole stone, the trackes whereof are at this daye permanent. But Gildas saithe that in the beeginninge it was not soe muche made of stone as of turffe, which was the cause whie it coulde not withstande the incursion of enemies; but afterwarde it was reædified onlie with stone, which at this time, althowghe not wholie, maye bee perceaved bie the littel embateled towers in æquall space distante. It was a righte princelie woorcke, as bie the which not onlie the rigoure of the Pictes but the Scottes allso was for a season repressed. But if wee geeve enie credite to this author, as moste assuredlie I beeleeve wee owght to doe, this wall was not erected by Severus, but more then two hundred yeare after bie Theodosius the sonne of Arcadius, and Valentinianus, the thride time possessinge the dominion of the weste partes, whearas it is evident that it was builded whan Aetius, being capitaine, warred on the Burgonions, as wee will teache in an other place. In this poincte allmoste all late writers have erred, bie all meanes fallslie attributing this woorcke to Severus. But now I will returne a littell to Severus and his sonnes.

The emperowre Severus disceassed in the Ilonde the ccxiij. yeare of mann's salvation; after whose deathe his sonne, Bassianus Antoninus, surnamed Caracalla, restored peace to the Brittons, and, receavinge pledges of them, sente them unto Rome to the Senate for the better preservation of quietnes, which was the occasion whie the Britons afterwarde the lesse desisted from their dewtie and loyaltie. Afterwarde hee, departing towards Rome, slewe his brother Geta and obteined the empire alone. From this time for the space of lxxvj. yeares the estate of the Ile was exceadinge peaceable and quiet, when Carausius, under the empire of Diocletianus, governed the same the ccxc. of our salvation, of whome wee will speake hereafter; and it is neadeful that wee satisfie theim which noe lesse undiscreetlie then unadvisedlie have dreamed that Bassianus Antoninus reigned over the Brittons xxx. yeares (whereas hee beinge but xliij. yeares of age, regned onlie vj. years), and that he didde fighte in Brittaine with Carausius, and finallie was slayne of himme, which one error dependinge on an other hathe caused manie to be deceaved. For Antoninus, accordinge to Herodianus and Aelius Spartianus, sojorning at Carris, a cittie of Mesopotamia, visited the temple consecrated to the moone as a goddesse, which being situate in that region but a littell from this cittie was hadde in great reverence of the inhabitantes; he brought thither with himme a small trowpe of horsemen, wherefore in the middeste of his jornie yt chaunced himme to goe aside accompanied with one manne onlie, to do the necessitee of nature or untrusse a poynte, to the which place Martialis, a centurien (partelie allured bie the fayre proffers of Macrinus, livetenent, partlie stirred up with a private grudge, for the emperoure hadde slaine his brother), ranne thether speedelie at the firste becke of his prince, and with his dagger thruste Antoninus throwghe as hee pulled downe his breeches: but wee will returne unto Carausius, whoe, beinge discended of base lineage, yet renomed throwghe his jolitee in warfare, when as Dioclesianus commaunded himme to fortifie the costes of the ocean environing the Belges of France agaynst such Saxon pyrats as infested the seas, he was thoughte of purpose not to have coped with his enemies untill hee understoode that they weare laden with prays, that hee might semblablie sacke them; nevertheles suche things as hee tooke didde hee not surrender to his provincialls; wherfore being guiltee of his offence, as soone as it was disclosed unto himme that Maximianus Herculeus (whome Dioclesian hadde chosen as his coequall in imperie then being in Frannce) hadd comaunded hime to bee slayne, he sodainlie slipped awaye into Brittaine, whome the Brittaines bie littell and littell, makinge a tyrante, abjecting the Romaine yoke, created him kinge. After which time there were manie conflictes made with him; but biecause hee coulde not bee overcomed he easlie obteined peace, and vij. yeares after possessed the Ile. But Alectus, one of his confederats in conclusion bie treason entred on him and slewe him; soe that, according to the olde proverbe, wickednes proceaded fromme the wicked. Hee also sett himselfe foorthe for the monarchie, whome forthewith the Brittons saluted as their kinge, who likewise within shorte space after was himselfe of one Asclepiodotus, a certaine cheefe Justiciarie, not onlie defeated of his present dominion, butt allso beerefte of his life. And thus this region after ccc. yeare of our salvation, in which time allso Brittaine was crewellie plagued with the creweltie of Dioclesian moste bitterlie afflictinge the Christians, for theyre churches weare overthrowne, and manie godlie persons, tormented with punishements, aspiered to the triumphe of martyrdome. In this raginge iniquitee of that recreaunt prince, admowntinge to the somme of xx. years (for soe longe he reigned), Albanus, a righte devoute manne, was put to deathe at his incorporat towne Werlamcester, right over againste the same place wheare at this

Carausius.

Alectus.

The Christians afflicted by Dioclesian.

daye is a village resoundinge the martyrdome of the hollie manne called Sainct Albans, of the churche dedicated to this saincte, and of late yeares a religious howse of monckes of thorder of Sainct Benedicte. This filthines, as Gildas witnessethe, dide so generallie plage the people and soe wasted the christian relligion, that in verie fewe it remained sownde and inviolate. Now to mie purpose.

Not longe affter, when the Brittisshe affaires beeganne to be in broyle and unstedfastnes, the inhabitants grevoslie bearinge the Romishe burdens, Constantius the nephew of Claudius bie his doughter, whome Diocletian with Galerius Maximianus prownownced with the title of Cæsar, camme into Brittaine, and forthewith revived quietnes in the same, espowsing in matrimonie Helena the dowghter of a certain prince Coill, a virgin of wonderus goodlie beawtie. I have not thowght goodd to agree with them which have lefte in memorie, that Helena was the concubine of one Constantius, of whom hee showlde begett one Constantinus, whoe nothinge more regarded then his favor towardes Christians, and the encrease of Godds trewe religion. After this Diocletianus and Maximianus Herculeus voluntarilie beetakinge theimselves to private life, Constantius and Galerius entred the imperiall throwne, the one beinge constreyned to devorce the dowghter of Dioclesian, the other Helena; Constantius married Theodora the dowghter in lawe of Herculeus, of whom he begat vj. sonnes and brothers unto Constantine. These above said, dividing the emperie betweene theim, Galerius chose the easte parties; Constantius tooke Italie with all Affricke, Spaine and Fraunce. Neverthelesse, in that he was a prince of great parsimonie, and in noe respecte ambitious, he lived onlie satisfied with the dominion of Fraunce and Spaine; finallie, xiij. yeares after the beginninge of his reigne in Brittaine, being a while attainted with diseases at Yorke, ended his life, being justelie numbered emonge the heroicall persons. Their was in himme as it weare in æquall balance, gravitee, measure, integritee of life, liberalitee of goodds; for he, greatlie

Constantinus.

Helena.

usinge bowntie and largesse, hadde a minde in no poincte yealdinge to riches, yea, forgettinge his peculiar commoditee, was woont to saye that welthe was muche better in the hand of privat men then in chestes of princes, where thei cowlde proffet or availe noe mann; bie the which humilitee and popularitee of the goodd prince his provinces florished in most convenable quietnes. Hee was most prudent and wise in the administration of all functions, and for his skille in warfare verie profitable to Romaines, wherebie his verie memoriall seemed in moste pleasant wise to affect his soldiers, insomuche that with the greate favor of all menne they forthewith saluted his sonne Constantinus, begotten of Helena in Brittaine, in the name of moste puissant emperowre; and in the meane time at Rome Maxentius the sonne of Herculeus of the Pretorian soldiers in sodaine uprore was salued in the titell of Augustus. Here must wee make deepe rehersall as towchinge Constantinus, of whome I thincke it better to use taciturnitee then to speake but littell, for hee, being begott of Brittishe mother, borne and made emperour in Brittaine, noe doubte made his native countrie paretaker of the greatnes of his glorie. Herculeus Maximianus, which surrendered the empire with Diocletian, lived then privatlie in Lucania, who when he harde that his sonne Maxentius was bie voyce denownced emperour, in all haste cam to Rome minding again to take on himme the empire, geeving bie his letters instigation to Diocletianus that hee wowlde revoke his owlde dignitee, which thinge Diocletianus, in this poincte wise and warie, refused and abhorred as a thinge moste pernicius and pestilent to manne; but the other in a great assemblee didd reason and debate the matter with his sonne, and beeganne to currie favour with the soldiers, moovinge them to disposses Maxentius, and restore the imperiall power to him. From the obteininge of this purpose he soe much fayled, that with great reproaches thei justlie upbroyded him, which thinge was bothe covertlie and craftilie donne, leaste the suspicion of enie suche guile as hee intended towardes Constantinus shoulde openlie apeare. Wherefore Herculeus bie all meanes having attempted the deprivation

Constantinus.

Lucania a coutrie perteininge to Naples.

of this younge man, he turned toward Constantinus his sonne in lawe (for to him hadd he married his dowghter Fausta), whoe havinge lefte rewlers in Brittaine, didde then leade his life in Fraunce. Constantinus jentilie interteyned Herculeus, but the olde manne greatlie sollicited in minde to hasten his distruction, trustinge to the loove of his dowghter Fausta, didde participate his whole councell with her, whoe, partelie fearinge deceyt and treason, partelie moved with the seemelie loove beetweene manne and wife, forthewith disclosed the same to her husband Constantinus, noe marvaile, thoughe hee desired to bee revenged; but Herculeus at Massilia, from whence hee minded to have fledde unto his sonne, was slaine by the commandement of the emperor. Galerius not longe departed this life, and a littell beefore hee died yealded to one Lucinius borne in Denmarcke the appellation of Cæsar. And soe all at one time Constantinus obteyned Fraunce, and the weste costes; Maxentius Italie, Affricke, and Ægypt; Maximian, whoe was a great while beefore created Cæsar of Galerius, helde the east partes; Licinius had under himme Illirium. But Constantinus, inflamed with the empire of the whole worlde, passed over into Italie, wheare, five years after the beginninge of his dominion, hee raysed warre againste Maxentius; which didd manifestlie proove that noe societie of kingedom canne longe endewre or abide a fellowe and coequall. After a fewe conflictes, Maxentius beinge put to flighte at the lengthe beefore the ende of the vj. yeare of his reigne, at the bridge called Milvius pons, neare unto the cittie of Rome, he with a certaine number of his menne were throwne hedlong into the river Tibris, to there utter confusion; and that fortune mighte in all respectes seeme to bee correspondent to the wille of Constantinus, it fell owte verie commoduslie not longe after that hee had taken possession of Italie that the yonger Maximian joyned in battaile with Licinius, whiche Licinius havinge married Constantia the sister of Constantinus for this alliaunce hee grewe in suspicion with Maximian: but deathe sodainelie prevented his intente at Tharsis, moste studiuslie endevoringe his warrs. Constantinus, Maximian beinge deadde, didde straighte waye warre upon Licinius, notwithstandinge that hee was joined in amitee and alliance unto himme: whome, when after much fightinge hee hadd bereft of all regalitee, he moreover, contrarie to his promise, procured himme to bee slaine at Thessalonica. Leadinge a private life, Licinius reigned under the appellation of Cæsar xv. yeares, which was the CCCXXVIJ. yeare of our salvation. Constantinus bie these meanes havinge engroched large dominion, entituled his sonnes Cæsars. This denomination of Cæsars (that wee maye in this place make commodius interpretation) was not so muche the reall dignitee of the empire, as a degree and steppe of preferment thereunto, to the end that (as it weare bie the handds of himme which was Augustus and Emperoure) those Cæsars mighte receave the government of the empire. This manne, as we have seyde beefore, after hee hadd geven the overthrowe to Maxentius and seased Italie into his handdes, proceaded to Rome, unto whome shortelie repaired Sylvester Bisshoppe, of singuler and ægregius holliness, and with facilitee perswaded himme to deserve well of the Christian religion, whoe of his owne accorde all readie hadd good affiaunce therein; farthermore, beefore that he went to Rome (as it is crediblie thought) hee was soe instructed of his own moother Helena, that goinge towards battayle he used the sygne of the crosse as a defence. There are which write thus: that the selfe same daye wherein he victoriuslie encountered with Maxentius, the wether beinge cleere, he aspied a crosse and worshiped the same, and harde a voice from above sayinge, 'O! Constantine, in this signe shallte thou vanquisshe;' nether didde this oracle lacke effecte. Wherefore this goddlie prince beegonne in all corners of the earthe greatlie to augemente and defende religion; for at Rome in the gardines of one Equitius hee builded a cherche, beawtifieng the same with bownteus giftes, offeringe a diademe or crowne of gowlde, richelie beeseene with precius stones, to the ende that Silvester and all the bisshopps succeedinge showlde wear it. But this man, replenished with modestie and verie temperat in ex-

The differens between the name Cæsar and Augustus.

What gyftes Constantyne gave to Sylvester.

pences, wowlde in noe wise receave it, as a thinge nothinge agreeing with relligion, being contented with a white Phrigian mitre. Moreover hee builded the howse called Constantia, at this day named Lateranensis, in the mownte Cælius, adjoyninge there bie a foonte of our sacred baptisme of redde marble; and neare unto that on the hill Vaticanus a cherche to Saincte Peeter prince of the Apostells, and an other to Sainct Paule, noe lesse resplendent in furniture, in the high waye called Ostiensis: allso in the theatre of Sessoria hee builded Hollie Crosse churche (for soe it is termed) beinge beefore in Jherusalem, there beestowinge a peece of our lordes crosse which hee browght from Hierusalem; for Helena, the mother of Constantine, a woman of unspeakable devotion, went unto Hierusalem to serche forthe this victorious banner of our Saviour, which thing trewlie seemed verie harde; for, to thentente that all monumentes of Christes passion (for soe our Divines doe name it) mighte cleane bee abolished, the picture of Venus was set up in the place where the crosse lay hidden of the mischevus enemies of the Christian name: nevertheless when the rubbishe was voyded owt of the place three crosses were fownde confuselie lienge together, the one was our Lordes, the other those whereon the two theeves weere put to execution; but that Christes mighte bee discried from the reste it was engraved with a triple titell: which was this, 'Jhesus of Nazarethe kinge of the Jewes,' all moste beinge worne owte with yeares. But a greater token ensewed, for the crosse beinge put unto a deade womanne restored life unto her. This noble prince Constantinus beinge mooved with those thinges didde forbedd in this wise to putt enie moe to deathe, to the ende that that thinge whiche beefore was a reproche and villanie emonge menn might now beecomme in estimation and honorable. Helene streyght after shee hadd fownde owte this crosse, ædefied a sumptuus temple, bearinge with her at her departure to her sonne the nayles wherewith Christes blessed corpes was fastened to the woodde, whearof the one Constantinus ware in the creste of his helmet, an other he bestowed as a munition on his horse

Helena.

for the fielde, the thirde he kaste into the sea to apeace the rage thereof, and to chaunge a stormie tempest. But that peece of the crosse which Helena browghte owte of Siria, garnishing the same with gowld and precius stones, he beestowed in his howse of Sessoria, which was allso exceddinglie resplendent throwghe his munificentie. Hee builded the churche of Saint Agnes with a christeninge foonte wheare his doughter and sister were baptized, greatlie settinge forthe the same with his riche giftes. He ædefied two other churches, the one in Tiburtina via to Sainct Laurence, the other in Lauicana to Sainct Marcelline, beetweene two baye trees, where he made a tumbe for his mother, includinge the same in a sepulchre of redde marble. To this churche, like as to the reste, weare geeven manie precius jewells; but what kinde of giftes these weare, and howe precius, which weare beestowed in suche holy places by the Emperoure, I minde not to expresse, least I showled incurre the envie of evel prelates, sithe that vj. hundred yeare since they weare taken owte of the churches. Withowte the cittee he buildid mani churches, one at the towne named Ostia to the two apostells, an other to Saincte Jhon Baptist in Alban, the thirde at Capua under the common name of the apostels, the fowrthe at Naples, the fifthe and sixte at Constantinople. Constantinus, biesides these godlie woorckes wherof wee have spoken, did banishe Arrius, prelate of Alexandria, with vj. other lewed ministers of wicked supersticions, bie the Nicene Councell, bie cause hee went abowte to skanne the Christian relligion with mischevus lies and glosinges. All temples of idolls, with the golden tables of Apollo at Delphus, bie the injunction of this prince, weare destroyed. Finallie, he founded noe relligus place but that francklie hee gave thereunto assuered giftes and certaine pensions.

Other gyftes of Constantine.

And these are the noble and godlie woorckes of the great prince Constantine and his mother Helen (whome the renomed parent Brittaine brought foorthe), worthie of all memorie, and easlie surmountinge all the actes of the former emperoures, allbeit I have towched them sleyghtlie; for others throwghe blooddshedd and manslaughter purchased their glorie emonge mortall menne, but these bie their godlines, there trewe relligion, their great liberalite, their justice, obteined of Godde (as it is justlie to bee thowght) everlastinge life, and on the earthe everlasting prayse and honor.

Constantyne is baptysed in Jordaine.

Constantine (according to the testimonie of Sainct Hierom) beinge verie oulde, or not longe beefore he departed this life, was baptized of Eusebius, Busshop of Nicomedia, and is reported to have deferred his baptisme unto that time, that accordinge to the example of Christe he might bee baptized in the river Jordan. But the notorius bathinge vessell, which he so sumpteuslie made at Rome, maketh a manne (not withoute cause) in that poincte to thincke noe otherwise than Sainct Hierom writethe. For marvaile it weare that a manne soe well deserving of Christes relligion, woold not at the verie firste broonte enter the gate of Christian pietie, that is to saye, bee baptized, seing that this oracle of our Saviour is well knowne to all menn, 'Whoe so ever beeleeveth and is baptized shall bee saved,' &c. But uppon these thingges, sithe thei are diverslie written, I will not greatlie tarrie. Constantinus was a mann as it weare ordayned to great perfection, as in whome within the remembrance of manne weare the greatest vertewse bothe of boddie and minde, conninge in the warlike sciens, fortunat in battaile it selfe, an ernest embracer of justice; finallie, borne to have praise and commendacion. Some laws hee made profitable to the common wealthe, som he abolished. He builded the Citte Constantinople as the counterfaite and like unto Rome, in the coste of Thracia, whearas Byzantium stoode. Hee repaired Drepana, in Bythinia, naminge it Helenople, bie his mother's name. There are somme, which, as concerninge his ende, doe write that as hee went owt of Byzantium towardes whote baines for the recovery of his helth that hee lefte his mortall life, wherebie peradventure hee maye seeme to have ben sicke of the leprie; but their are divers authors, and emonge the rest Sainct Hierom, which testifie that he, mindinge to warre with the Persians (or, as Eutropius saithe, with the Parthians, bie cause thei invaded Mesopotamia,) did die at a common village, called Aciron, bie Nicomedia, the CCCXL. yeare of our salvation. Hee was lxvj. years oulde, and reigned xxxi. But see how it ofte chauncethe that longe life is hurtfull to a man; trulie, Constantine, a great patron of Christes relligion, at the length, according to the authoritee of Sainct Hierom, was not cleane at defiance with the heresie of Arius. At that time that this emperoure chaunged life for deathe there appeared a great comete, or blasinge starre, of wonderous bignes.

But thus muche hetherto; now let us returne to the opposicion of those things which concerne the state of Brittaine.

THE THIRDE BOOKE

OF POLIDOR VERGILL ON THE ENGLISHE HISTORIE.

At what time the Emperoure Constantine departed owte of Brittaine into Fraunce, as wee made rehersall in our laste booke, hee lefte behinde him certaine cheefe officers to ordre the Ilond, and emonge the reste one Maximus, a manne of haute corage: he ledde with him a goodde parte of the youthe and princes, in whose valiaunce, faithe, and constancie he reposed his whole confidence: with whome he beinge accompanied and garded passed into Fraunce, and consequentlie into Italie, eche wheare suppressinge his adversaries. In the meane time the Brittishe contrie, at the lenghthe seeminge to have purchased libertie, biecause havinge Constantine, a Brytayn borne, theyr kinge and governoure, the lorde of the whole worlde, it surmounted all others in honor, dignitee, and authoritee, and moste plausiblie continued in this estate, so that if there were in foretimes enie hatred on their partes towards the Romaines, it was now cleane abolished, seinge that bothe bie the Providence of Godde and the benefit of the redoubted prince they enjoyed peace, and a luckie principle of suche honors as mighte redownde to their posteritee. Albeit the imperie remained not longe after in the stocke of Constantine (so sodaine is the fall of humaine treasures), neverthelesse the maiestie of the imperie coulde not perishe, sithe that even at this presente the kinges of Englonde, accordinge to the usage of their aunciters, doe weare the imperiall diademe as a gifte exhibited of Constantinus to his successors. Thus Brittaine was quiet, as Eutropius wittnessethe, at such time as Constantine departinge this life, lefte behinde himme three sonnes, Constantius, Constans, and Constantine, as heyres to the empire. To this laste was allotted Brittaine, Fraunce, Spaine, and the Iles Orchades; but within shorte space contention risinge betweene himme and Constantius, he joyned in fighte at Aquileya in Italie, and was slaine; so that Brittaine and the other provinces fell into the dominion of Constantius, whoe dieng laste of all his breetherne, more then xx[ti] yeares hadde the same in his jurisdiction; after which time the province littel lesse then xxiiij. yeares after didde not refuse dewtie and loyaltee, which was the vth yeare of the reigne of the two brothers, Gratianus and Valentinianus, which was the CCCLXXXVIJ. yeare of our salvation. At the same season Maximus, of whome wee made mention beefore, was made Emperoure in Brittaine throughe the suffrages of his soldiers, albeit som menn reported it to have benne donne in Spaine. This manne, enflamed with the desier of encreasinge his power, forthewith tooke mooster of his lustie younge menne, in whome hee perceaved sufficiencie of force and might to make battaile, and, limitinge a good quantitee of soldiers, departed into Fraunce. The Emperoure Gratianus goeng owte of the cittey to resiste and extinguishe this commotion, in the conduite of his armie into Fraunce gave preferment to the bende of the menne named Halani (whoe weare discended of Scithians), and entised unto hime bie goulden rewardes: which ministred suche great offence to his owlde warriers, that not longe after they cleane forsooke himme, and the Romaine trowpe betoke them selves to Maximus. Gratianus beinge amazed at the sodaine alienation and fleete of his menn, and endevoring to retire into Italie, beinge entrapped with disceite was slaine at Lions. Valentinianus, the brother of Gratian, runninge away for feare of hostilitee, went to Byzantium unto Theodosius, which at the commandment of Gratian had taken on himme the rewle of the easte partes. This Theodosius (as Saincte Hierom reportethe) was the sonn of that Theodosius which was murdered in Affrica at the instigation of Valens, for whome Gratianus sendinge owt of Spaine in those troblesom broyles made him copartener of the empire; wherefore Theodosius, not forgetful of good turnes, entertained Valentinian with fatherlie loove, mindinge beefore all thinges to preferre the revenginge of the deathe of Gratian, raysed warre against Maximus, whoe as then sojornied in Italie. But all thinges weare donne with suche celeritee that hee hadd allmost overcommed the difficultee of the Alpes beefore that it was reported that Theodosius was removed from Byzantium, and Maximus, not knowinge that then especiallie sinistre and evel fortune is to bee feared when it makethe moste frindelie and propice semblant towards us, did then securelie sojorne at Aquileia, wheare he sodainlie beinge beeseeged and apprehended hadd his hedde striken of: suche is the unstabilitee of worldlie matters, that bothe they florishe and perishe in one moment. Some writers doe affirme that three miles from thence Maximus was overcommed of Theodosius and Valentinianus, and so yealded quicke into the handes of his enemies, there receavinge his laste penaltie of the conquerors, one yeare being scarslie accomplished after the death of Gratian. Martin the Bisshopp of Towres, a mann of singuler integritee, is reported to have towlde beefore unto Maximus, then abidinge in Brittaine, that hee shoulde ende his life unfortunatlie: besides this, Victor, the sonn of Maximus, was slaine in Fraunce. Thus all the attemptes of Maximus came to small effecte and evel ende. From thencefoorthe the estate of the Ilond beegan sore to decaye, for in shorte space the Brittons, as wee shall hereafter declare, loste bothe libertie and empire. Fardermore, it is a common saieng that Maximus while he was in the pursuite and chase of Gratian, in the parte of Fraunce named Celtica, did appoint Conan a Britton borne as cheefe guide over the cittes bordering on the ocean called Armorieke. This Conan, after that with noe small rowte of his Brittons he hadd while made there abode and reigned, to the ende hee mighte there make

Now lytell Briten.

assewered continuance of his nation, eche wheare dispossessinge the Gaules, bestowed his Britons in all places, yea, and refusinge with contempte to joyne in matrimonie with the Frenchemen, sent to have wives out of Brittaine for his people, whearbie, as menn saye, it camme to passe that a plentuus assemble of virgins camme thether oute of the Ilond, and at one time, partlie bie shipwracke partlie bie slaughter, perished xi. thousand of bothe kindes, for the barbarus sorte slewe them and took them captives on the shore; emong whome it is thought that sainct Ursula was, the doughter of Dionotus kinge of Cornewall, which was espowsed to this Conanus. When the death of Maximus was knowen in Brittaine, one Gratianus, a man borne in the Ilonde, exercised rewle and tyrannie for a season, who being speedelie exempted from that function, the Romaine soldiers which as yeat weare lefte in garison did elect Constantin, a manne of whome noe accompte was made, nether in stocke noble, nether renowmed in warfare, in whom onlie they seemed to bee draune with the affection of his name. This manne with an armie passed owte of the Ilond into Fraunce, remaininge emonge the people called Veneti, and other while emonge those which were named Cenomani, and emong other borderers on the ocean sea, endeavoringe to solace quietnes in Fraunce; and beinge desierus with the Vandals, Suevians, and Halans, hee demaunded at the leaste wise trewse if thie would not condiscend unto peace; but hee obteined nether, which greatlie endamaged the common welthe: but not longe after Constantius, a man of politique wisdom, being of Honorius sent in to Fraunce with an armie to restore and defende the maiestie of the imperie, subdued and slew this usurper Constantine, aboute Orleance, being farre spente and weried with beeseeginge. But Constans (whome his father Constantine of a moonck hadde pronowneed Cæsar), at what time hee mooved warre agaynst Dyndimus and Severianus, easlie subdewing them which minded to repell Constantine, and the alients which folowed him from the entrie of Spaine, within a littell time after marchinge towards Vien, hee was there slaine of his companion Gerontius: thus at one instance Constantine the father and Constans the sonn did perishe, and Honorius, bie procurement of Constantius, a most valiaunt capitan, receaved in to his jurisdiction the Ilond and Brittishe armie. Paulus Diaconus and Bedas are mine authors, who bothe well and diligentlie wrote these thinges. The selfe same yeare whearin Constantine was denounced emperowre of the Romaine soldiars, Arcadius died at Constantinople, and the Rioltee of the empire openlie appaired. After the death of Constantine forthe with disceased his sonne. Then Honorius, retaininge the Brittishe armie, did againe derive and traine the Ilande to the empire. After this a fewe yeares ensewing, when as after the deathe of Honorius, and after that Theodosius the sonne of Arcadius had pronownced as Cæsar and Augustus, Valentinianus, the sonne of his aunte Placidia, an importunate number of the barbarus people beeganne to moleste the Romaine imperie, with whome the Romishe capitans hadd often conflictes. In the meane time Brittaine seemed as it weare subject to spoyles and made feete for the invasion of hostilitie, partlie having the cheefe strengthe of soldiers wasted with tyrants, partlie beeing carried forthe to warre on forraine nations, as it is commonlie seene. that one discomoditee beefallethe not without an other. Which thinge bie fame being once bloune abrode, the Scottes, whether for the hope of bootie or for the desier of novelties, as Gildas testifieth, hastilie issued owte of Ireland in to this Ile; and with owte delaye makinge conspiracie with the Pictes, and on all sides assemblinge the lostehopes and raskalls, beganne with the thefte and robberie of their gooddes, they proceaded to spoyle them of their cattalls, and finallie endevored to plete possession on the Ilond it selfe. This mischeefe daylie encreised, and the bowldnes of these too nations grewe farder then seemed easie to bee resisted in time to comme, soe that noe manne but shortli mistrusted the sackinge and distruction of the Ilonde withoute speedie resistance, aide, and remedie. Brittaine was then, as I shewed beefore, withoute garrison; for the which cause the selie multitude beinge afraide, as farre unable to decline this tempeste, sente embassadowres to desier succoure of Aetius, whome Honorius a little beefore in the roome of Constantius hadde made cheefe governor of the armies, a manne discended of the familie of a senator of Dorostana in Moesia. Aetius, beinge solicited and moved with the intercession of the Britons, which as yet remained in dew allegiance, didd for there defence sende them one legion owte of Fraunce, of whome the Scottes and Pictes weare plagued with divers overthrowes, and the Brittishe condition was well refourmed; and, leaste this tranquillitee showlde in processe bee disturbed of their enemies, it seemed goodd to the lodesmen of this armie that the walle wherof mention was made in the former booke shoulde bee ædefied beetweene the Romaine province and the borders of the Pictes, which was performed according to the testimonie of Gildas; but in that it was more bylded with turffe then with stone, it was not afterwarde of sufficiencie to withstande enemies; and thus at this season was this wall made bie the capitans sent of Aetius, not of the Emperours Hadrianus or Severus, as manie menne have lefte in memorie verie falselie, if wee beeleeve Gildas, a Brittyshe historiographer. Brittaine was quiet, throwghe the munition of this one legion, untill suche time as the Burgonions, bie molestinge of Fraunce, caused Aetius of necessitee to revoke his menn oute of the Ilande, and consequentlie disposinge one legion emong the Parisiens and Aurelians, and sendinge an other to their winteringe to Taracon, with the rest of his power hee marched towardes the Burgonions.

The Scottes and Pictes streyght after the departure of this legion or garison invaded the gooddes of the Brittons. They spoyled there herdes of neate, they robbed them of their sheepe, and, finallie, wasted their teritories with fier and sworde. Of these sparckes had flamed a newe and mightie fier of battayle, if at the commaundement of Valentinian (whoe of all things did moste desier to anticipate warres) the armie which harborowed at Parris hadd nott aided them at their entretie for succours. At this time allso was this forsayde wall fenced againe, and was fortified with stone that it might be more stronge to repell the power of the enemies, so that now the incursions of Scottes and Pictes beganne to doe lesse harme. Yet thei within a while, perceaving the Romaine puissaunce to bee greatlie appalled, and allmoste overthrowne, (for soe fickle are oure treasures that rather they decay then increase,) thei invaded them with muche more fearcenes then ever they didd beefore.

At this time Aetius sente noe aydes to the Brittons, notwithstandinge they ernestelie required the assistance of Romains; howbeit it maie be dowbted whether he wolde not sende in that hee was scarse frindlie affected towards Valentinian, or whether he cowlde not, beinge detained and vexed with greater cares of more pernicius warres; but how soe ever it was, it did ingenerat great mischeefe, bothe to the Romans and Brittons, yet the Brittishe nation in woordes plaintife miserablie lamented their chaunce, writing in this wise, as Gildas witnessethe. 'The mowrninge of the Brittons sent to Aetius three times, beeinge Consul: Wee implore and beeseeche thee that thow wilte vouchsafe to sende succours to us, the Romane province, oure contrie, our wives and children, being at this instant in extreme daunger. The barbarus people raginge, drivethe us to the verie seas; the sea repelleth us againe unto them. Thus are wee extinguished in doble funerall; ether the swoorde of savage creatures cuttethe our throtes, or otherwise wee are drenched in surge of water; nether have wee lefte enie succor or releefe in these mischeves; wherefore generallie wee are all thie peticioners that, accordinge to the singuler disposition of thie naturall clemencie, it shall please thee to assiste and releeve us.' Bie these woordes wee may well knowe that the Brittons in fine didd not forsake the Romaines but gretlie against their wills, for now, beinge accustomed to imperie, thei hadd them in estimation of whome they hadde learned civile and goodd manners, as Cornelius Tacitus makethe minde; for the sonnes of princes weare wholye fostered in liberall sciences; their wittes flourished, not so muche abhorringe the Romaine language as ærnestlie desierus of eloquence. Emonge other things the Romaine attire grew into reputation, and gownes weare commonlie worne; yea, if it bee trew that Gildas writethe, they learned the sciens of warfare. And thus Brittaine was loste of the Romaines allmoste five hundred yeare after the entrie thereunto of Julius Cæsar; and thus, allmoste in the same verie momente, havinge attained libertie, entered into moste truculent warrs, wherby he did lese both name and empire, as shall hereafter bee declared, and that was the xvj. yeare fro the beginning of the reigne of Theodosius with Valentinianus Augustus, the sonne of his aunte, the yeare of our Lord CCCCXLIIJ.

In the meane time, while the Britons contrived the time in sending embassadours about the treatie for succours, the Scottes possessed the uttermoste parte of the Ile which boundeth from the mountaine Grampius northewarde, which they have at this daye, naminge the same according to them selves, Scotlonde. And this is the thirde people which, after the Pictes, firste, as wee sayd beefore, camm owt of Scithia into Ierlond, next in Brittaine there placing them selves: The capitaine of the bende of the Scotts, as Beda testifieth, was Reuda. But the Scottishe coronographers make computation that long before Reuda one Fergusius camme into Brittaine, who gave to cognisance in his standerde the Redd Lion which the kinges doe now use, and that for his fortunate administration of all others he was first called kinge of his nation, after whome in deade succeeded his nephew Rewthere, in ample wise enlarging his dominion, whome Beda called Rewda. But paradventur there will bee somme which will not a littel bee aggreeved at these thinges, for of late one Gawine Dowglas, Bishop of Dunchell, a Scottishe manne, a manne as well noble in ligneage as vertewe, when he understoode that I was purposed to write this historie hee camme to commune with mee; in forthe with wee fell into friendshippe, and after he vehementlie requiered mee that in relation of the Scottishe affaires I showlde in no wise follow the president of an historie of a certaine contriman of his, promisinge within few dayse to sende mee of those matters not to be contemned, which in deade hee perfourmed, in the which there was a verie auncient originall of that people in this wise: Gathelus, the sonne of Neolus, king of the Atheniens, flienge from the harde servage of his father, departed into Ægipte to aide Pharao against the Æthiopians, unto whome Moses was sente from Godde, with the which benefit the Ægiptian kinge beinge stirred, gave his daughter named Scota in marriage to Gathelus, whoe forthewith serchinge new dwellinge places arrived in Spaine, and inhabited that coste which after him was called Portugallia, as who woulde saye the porte of Gathelus, terminge his subjects Scotts, accordinge to the name of the noble woman his wife, Scota. Thus havinge issew and propagation of discent, three hundred yeare after, the Scotts beinge brought into Irelond bie their kinge Simon Brechus, weare the beginninge of a newe kingdom, and finallie, before the comminge of Christe, camme into Albion. It followed consequentlie that the Pictes not longe after camme allso owte of Scithia in to Albion, and that these two externe nations had issewe of stemme and encrease of kingdom in that coste of the Ilond which is now called Scotlonde, from which time they allways mantayned warrs with the Brittons, with the Romains, and Julius Cæsar especiallie, the Scottes remayninge still inviolate, as not disturbed from their degree. Finallie this was there in written, that owlie theire Kinge Rewtheres havinge evel succes at home in his troubles with the Brittons, didde once avoyded his contrie and fledde into Irelonde; and that within a while after haveinge encreased his power with Irisshe menne retowrned to his former possessions; and that in this beehalfe Beda was nott of sufficient perseveraunce, which calleth this retorne the firste comminge of the Scottes in to Albion. All this was donne beefore the comminge of Our Savior.

As soone as I hadde redde these thinges, accordinge to the olde proverbe, I seemed to see the beare bringe foorthe her younglinges. Afterwarde, when for recreation wee mette together, as wee weare accustomed, this Gawine demaunded mie opinion. I aunswered, that as towchinge there originall I wowlde not greatlie contende, seinge that for the moste parte all contries weare woonte to drawe the principles of there pedegree ether from the Goddes or from heroicall nobles, to the ende that they which afterwarde beinge not easie of beeleefe minded to skanne and derive theim, when they showlde hardlie find enie thinge of more certeintee, they showld rather bee constreyned to beeleve it firmelie then enie farder to laboure vainelie. But to bee shorte, this in noe wise kanne agree that the Scottes and Pictes, two mightie people, showlde soe longe reigne in the Ilond, showlde performe so manie battailes, showlde soe often foyle the Britons and Romains, moleste them, and vanquisshe them, and yet noe antique or grave writer once make rehersall of theim; especiallie seeing that Cæsar, Tacitus, Ptolome, and Plinie (levinge to reherse the others) dœ eche wheare in there histories make mention of the people named Trinobantes, Cenigmani, Segontiaci, Ancalites, Bibroci, Brigantes, Silures, Iceni, Ordolucæ, Vicomagi, Elgouæ, with the other contries of Brittaine; but of the Scotts and Pictes not a woorde, bie cause as yeat they weare not in this region, which forsothe is to bee thoughte the verie cause whie late writers have soe slacklie used the memoriall of theim. Wherefore I towlde him, even as frindlie as trewlie, that as concerninge the Scottes and Pictes beefore there comminge into Brittaine, (which Bedas in his time hadd well assigned,) it showlde not bee lawful for me to intermeddell, bie reason of the prescrit which is incident to an historien, which is that hee showld nether abhorre the discooveringe of falsehoode, nether in anie case alowe the underminingе of veritee, nether to gyve suspition of favor nor yeat of envy.

The dutie of an historiographer.

This Gawine, noe doubte a sincere manne, didd the lesse dissent from this sentence, in that it plainelie appeared to him that reason and trewthe herin well agreaed, soe easlie is trewthe allwaise discolowred from feyned phansies. But I did not longe enjoy the fruicion of this mie frind, for in the yeare of our Lord

MDXXI. he died of the plague in London. After this ensewed these two kinges of Scotts, Eugenius the First and Fergusius the Second. Eugenius was slaine in battayle of the Pictes, being then under the Romaine allegiaunce; wherefore the Scottes, misdowbting their saftie, and mindinge to beestow them selves somme wheare, in sondrie ways fledd owte of the Ilonde. After xliij. yeares the bannished Scottes were reclamed, partlie owte of Ireloud, partlie owt of Norway, bie the Pictes, whoe feared the power of the Romains; and thei camm home under the conduite of their lodesmanne Fergusius. After Fergusius succeeded his sonne Eugenius, whoe, confederinge with the Pictes, beganne so sore to oppresse the Britons that at the verie firste encounter, as wee saide beefore, thei weare constrained to expostulat succors of the Romains. But Eugenius lived not longe, so that in his steede succeeded his brother Dongardus; and now I retorne to mie matter.

The Scottes havinge prosperus successe didd the more licentiuslie invade the inhabitants of this Ilonde, more like to raveninge spoylers then noble warriars, contumeliuslie egginge and provokinge their adversaries to fyghte. The Brittons being forsaken of Aetius, albeit they reposed more safetie in enie thinge then in fightinge, nevertheles, caulinge to minde there owlde valiaunce, and well perceavinge that in soe greate perturbation of all thinges they muste either geeve wowndes or suffer bloodshedde, they wolde noe longer bee of demisse spirits and abased corage; but beinge as it weare stirred up with the blaste of trumpe, or enraged with some furie, they sodainlie proceaded againste their enemies, which wandered more dissolutelie then they weare accustomed, as they which thought nothing was to bee misdowbted; they caused themme to forsake their grounde whome they firste mett with all, and russhinge into the middest of these miscreantes made great slaughter. The Brittaines wear superiors in this conflicte, most excellentlie conqueringe which were woonte to be conquered; yeat there enemies neverthelesse, assaienge their chaunce, did againe assaulte them. They tooke booties, they roved heere and there, they stroyed feeldes, they fiered howses, they slewe all those thei mette, with owte respecte of age; they didd all these kindes of injuries as thoughe them selves hadde beene voyde of all infirmite. With this feare manie weare so astonied that of there owne francke will they ministered all suche thinges as their enemies hadd neade of, which thinge seemed to bee of soe great force that it muche more amazed them then battayle it selfe. The Britons in these evels, bie necessitee constreined to doe that which seemed most expedient to keepe away hostilitee, tooke deliberation and councell, and forthewith renewed, restored, and enlarged that wall which wee saide beefore was erected bie the soldiers of Aetius. This woorcke for a time restrained the rude raginge of the frenetick Scotts, which notwithstandinge afterwarde burste foorthe, encresed with more beastlie feritee, for not long after they camm to skale the wall, whome the Britons hardelie and not warelie inowghe resistinge, they threwe the wall flatte on the grounde, puttinge there adversaries to flighte, and chasing them with the sworde; nether yet dide the Scottes enjoye this victorie withowte bloodshedde, for their king, Dongardus, was slaine in the fighte, after whome succeeded Constantine. In the necke of this mischeefe was sodaynelie annexed a great skarsetie of corne, wherebie manie sterved bie famine, for the continuance of warres caused the grownde to be desolate and unmanured; yeat was it a cause that, after overthrowes on both sides, the desier of warre sone waxed cowld on bothe parties, and that plentie more abundantlie ensewed bie the more diligent tilthe of their feeldes. This divine benefit was hurtefull to the Brittons, (as Gildas writeth,) for they beginninge to rejoyse, instead of abstinence and shamefacednes embraced pleasures and vice, wherebie it camme to passe that leaste this nation, which continuallie offended, showlde lacke feare and daungers, bie the juste judgement of Godde, there arose a great pestilence, wherbie (as the same manne purportethe) was exhauste and destroied an incredible companie of menne, which diseas was within a littel after annexed with another, for they weare miserablie oppressed with a sodaine invasion of the barbarus people, and brought to suche greate distresse, that to their utter undoeing (I thincke their destenie drawinge them) they weare enforced to sende for into the Ilon the Saxon Englishemen, noe dowte men of exceadinge stowtenes and valiance, but not soe faytheful, as they afterward hadd experience, not without there marvelus discommoditee. Moreover the Brittons, seinge soe great broyles hanginge over there hedds, bothe of Scottes and Pictes, most feerce and truculent enemies, and fearing least while they mayntained forinsecall battayles there mighte spring domesticall contention for the sufferaintee, sithe it is naturallie grafted in the disposition of all men bothe highe and low to thirste and affecte honors and lordeshipp, thei determined to electe somme one Kinge and sole monarche. Wherefore assembling a counsel, the more parte bie and bie adjudged that this title and dignitee showlde be bestowed on one Vortigerius, bie cause that of all men he was of greatest authoritee, nobilitee, and vertew; which sentence was not ownelie defined bie them, but approved of all others. Vortigerius is made their kinge, whoe, nothinge oblivius for what cause he was enhaunced to the kingdom in this trowblesom season, accounted nothing more better then to beestowe all his cogitations and care on the common wealthe, to provide, to foresee, to caste all meanes how the fatall ende of his contrie, which was now all moste comme, mighte bee kepte awaye, or at the leaste wise proroged. Yeat, leaste hee mighte seeme to take too muche uppon himme, he would attempte nothinge withoute the avisement of his wise councell, therefore everie firste daye hee tooke deliberation of his domesticalls and generallie all his princes, conferringe with themme and measuringe bothe there owne puissance and the strength of theire enemies, diligentlie discussinge, revoltinge, and contrivinge what remedie shoulde seeme convenable accordinge to the inclination of the time. In conclusion, the piers of the reallme, misdoubtinge their riches and wealthe, and especiallie the kinge himselfe, was fullie resolved to accite and send for the Saxon

Englishemen, a people verie notable throughe there renowne of chivalrie. Then were certaine speedelie sent in to Germanie, which with monnie, giftes, and promises, should tempte, exhorte, and allure theim to there succours, which if they denied not, they showld forthwith bring theim into Brittaine. The Saxons assone as they hadd harde these tidinges, as menn desierus to serve for stipende, chosing forthe a stowte bende of lustie yowthes, and committinge them to shippes, under the conduite of the two bretherne Hengistus and Horssus, forthewith tooke their race into the Ilonde the CCCCXLIX. yere of our Salvation. The kinge enterteyned them curteuslie, and assigned them Kente for there habitacion and dwellinge place, and from thence bie and bie brought theim to the Scottes and Pictes, distroyenge the contrie on all sides. For a while the skirmishe was manfullie perfowrmed on bothe sides, but the Englishe menne calling to minde that this was the day which showlde ether purchase to theim æternall fame and glorie emonge the Brittons, or otherwise perpetuall ignominie and repulse, doobled there force in suche violent wise that there enemies, not able to endure there vehement assautes, were put to flighte and eche wheare slayne. The kinge, obteyninge this victorie, regrated with woorthie rewarde these straungers, throwghe whose hardines hee hadd conquered his enymyes. Somme there are that write that the Saxons weare not sente for of the kinge, but bie casualtie arrived in the Ilonde, havinge this occasion of there voyage. Surelie emonge the Englishe Saxons, a moste warlike nation, it was the custom that when the multitude admownted to suche infinitee of numbre that the soyle coulde not easlie susteyne them, at the commaundement of their princes, bie lotte the cheefe of there yowthe showlde bee picked foorthe, and soo extermined their costes, bothe to serche new contries, and allso to make warrs; thus it fell owte that they arrived in Brittaine promisinge there service under the kinge.

Longistus, a manne of great witte and wisedom, fealinge the king's minde, who ownlie rested in the valiaunce of Englishemenn, and having goodd triall in the fertilitee of the contrie, beganne more profoundlie to waye with himselfe bie what crafte or subtilitee hee mighte bie littel and littel comprise a kingdom for hime and his in the Ilond. Wherfore firste bie stelthe he beganne with munition to fortefie the place which was geeven himme to inhabit, to enlarge the bowndes, to confirme it with garrisons, then hee goethe abowte to persuade the kinge that a greater numbre of menne showlde bee sente for owte of Germanie, that with there assistance the Ilond beinge corroberat, it mighte strike a certaine terror into the adverse parte, and yealde quietnes to himme and his. The kinge, not knowinge the iminent chaunce, wolde in noe wise contemne this device, which in deede was full of treason. It cam to passe, that in shorte time a huge number of people cam into Brittaine, and with them, as menne say, the dowghter of Hengistus was brought, called Ronix, a virgin of woonderfull bewtie, to tempte the minde of Vortigerius, for this Englishe manne didd allredie sufficientlie smell to what vice the kinge was prepense. Bede affirmethe that the Saxons, the Vites, and the Englishemenn, thee most feerce nations of Germanie, camm together into the Ilond, and that of the Vites discended the Kentishe men, and they which at this time inhabit the Ile of Weyghte, bein over againste the others; but of the Saxons camme they which are termed Est Saxons, Sowthe Saxons, and Weste Saxons; but of the Englishemen, ether of the place or of there queene so called, discended the Este Angles and they which inhabite the middell of the soyle, and the inhabitants of Northehumberland, whose capitaines weare Hengistus and Horssus. Cornelius Tacitus makethe especiall memorie of the Englishemen in that booke which hathe written of the situation of Germanie, yeat callethe them not Anglos, but Anglios, so that the name conteineth three silables, and this letter i is the laste saving one. But let us retorne to our former beginninge. Hengistus, perceavinge his people to bee verie well accepted of the kinge, beganne so like a foxe to deale with him, that hee mighte inflame his minde with loove, which is the thinge which aboove all others dothe blinde, bewitche with follie, and somtimes destroye men, yeat with suche pleasaunte poyson that they perishe withoute open greefe. Hengistus invited and entertayned the kinge at a sumptuus, pleasaunte, and well furnished supper; and it was soe ordered that when all thinges weare warmed with wines the dowghter of Hengistus was at hande, geevinge the cuppe looverlike to Vortiger, with all the grace and neatenes that might bee, accordinge to the fasshion of her contrie. The kinge, assone as hee hadd fixed his ies on the mayden, sodainlie was enravished with this bayte, being bothe delighted with her beawtie, and havinge taken vewe of her behavior, in so mutche that now not so wise as was fitting unto himme, hee divorcing within a littell while after his former wife, maried this trulle, geevinge therin the moste detestable example within the memorie of manne. This hainus deade of the kinge bredd offence in the mindes of his nobles, and hastened the distruction of the contrie, for the Saxons, understandinge the allienge of there stock with the kinge, gathering a great companie, camme in suche number into the Ilande, and as it weare strivinge whoe showlde bee firste, that it is not to be towlde in how shorte space they weare growne to an infinitee, soe that bothe bie reason of the multitude, and allso for there hardines in warfare, they beganne easlie to be a terror to the inhabitants, which at first accited them willinglie.

Now am I in writing cumme thether, as oftentimes elsewhere, wheras I finde manie thinges lefte dowbtefull, bothe of the Italian and Brittishe writers; wherefore, leste like those that wander wee shoulde seeme to follow uncertaintees, wee will particulerlie sett beefore yowre ies the sentence of everie writer as wee shall conceave that to farre it is not unlike to the trewthe, that bie this meanes wee may the better preserve the dewe faythe and assewrance of an historie. Gildas of the callinge hether of the Saxons writethe thus: 'Then (saythe he) all the councellers, with the insolent kinge, weare greatlie blinded, findinge owte this preposterus safegarde, or rather the overthrowe of their contrie, that the feerce Saxons, menn of evel name, hated bothe of Godd and manne, showlde be intertayned into the realme as wolves into a sheepecote, to withstande and represse the northern people, then the which thinge there was never enie thinge more bitterlie or daungeruslie perpetrated:' hee allegethe beesides this that they cam as champions for the contrie, but indeade warriers againste the contrie, for breakinge the covenante of societie they toorned ther perfidius weapons on the Britons. But Beda indeede dothe more largelie handle these thinges, who testefieth that the Saxons, after they beganne to bee feared of others, for a time thei made leage with the Pictes, with whome at that time they maintaned warr, and abruptlie torned there force on the Brittons, there frindes and entertayners, and menacinge them with deathe, commaunded them to surrender soe mutche corne as mighte yealde sustinance to theire importunate covente of alienes; which thinge beinge refused of the Britons, they slewe withowte respect of age or kinde all suche as they mett disperpeled in the feeldes; they sett fier on howses; they exercised moste truculent creweltie towardes the priestes as worshipers of idolls; so that in fine the Brittons, exanimate partelie with feare, partlie with the desier to avoyde slaughter, like madde creatures ranne here and there into divers wayse, ether hidinge them selves in thicke covertes, or putting there neckes under the yoke. But not longe after, according to the authoritee of Gildas, Beda, and Paulus Diaconus, Aurelius, or Aurelianus Ambrosius (for bothe wayse I finde it written), who onlie was remanent of the Romaine line, putting the purple robe on him, and proclamed emperoure or capitaine, beganne to warre with the Saxons. Here may a manne perceave that somme minde nothinge lesse then to tell the trewthe, who affirme that Aurelius Ambrosius was a Briton, wheras it appearethe most evidente that he camme of Romaine lineage. But now againe to the matter. Affter the alliaunce confirmed beetweene the kinge and the Englishe Saxons, his espouse sollicited himme to have her contriemenne in highe favor, causing them to aspire to great honors, and studiuslie endevoringe to exclude the Brittishe peeres owte of their domesticall Senat and preheminence, whearbie Vortigerius harde the evel murmur on all sides, to his great discommendation emonge all the nations adjacent; firste, that he was the fownteyne of one mischife in sendinge for, callinge, and allueringe the Englishe Saxons, a prowde, crewell, and wrothefull nation; and nowe the verie patrone of a muche greater evell, in that hee releeved and mayntained people againste himselfe, whome it wolde be to late to withstande, after the encrease of their authoritee, fame, and welthe.

Vortigerius, nevertheles, mindefull of there good toorne, not casting daungers to comme, could not but loove the Englishemen, throwghe whose mighte hee hadde quenched the furie of the Scotts and Pictes, throwghe whose factions hee cowlde not erste have enie fruition of tranquillitee; and thus, accordinge to his owne arbitrement, hee lived a fewe yeares after. The common sorte of menne as yet doe say that Vortigerius did entierlie loove a certaine soothesayer, called Merline, and that in his administeringe of thinges hee didde aske his advise as a prophet, bie cause hee knewe thinges to comme.

After Vortigerius succeaded his sonne Vortimerius, a yownge manne borne to honor, if continuance of life hadde served. After the deathe of Vortiger, the Englishemen, of whome there was an huge nomber in the Ilonde, (for this indigent and boysterus people like ants swarmed thether continuallie, not onlie engrochinge Kent, but allso somme of the weste partes, and a goode portion appertaininge to Scotlonde,) supposinge now to be tyme to assaye the fortune of battaille, didd make league with the Scottes and Pictes; and then at one verie poincte of time bente there weapons towardes the Brittons, and soe molestethe them with injuries as thowghe rather somme evell then goodd toorne they hadd receaved of them. The Britons, albeit they minded manfullie to have withstoode ther enemie, being before of noe suche puissaunce, neverthelesse, beinge beesette with soe greate stormes of battayle on all sides, they cowlde not cheuse but bee marveluslie dismayde; for first with Hengistus, a capitan of haute corage, secondarilie with the Pictes, finallie with the Scottes, ether at once they most fight or incurre servilitee. But in the ende the lothesomnes of servage revived their verteu, for sodainlie thei gathered their spirits together, and with bowlde stommache eche wheare they made resistance; yet as impotents in this harde case they were skattered, slaine, and put to flighte; and presentlie mistrusting the ministerie of armoure, as disperpeled sheepe, folowinge som one lodesmanne, som an other, they hidd them selve in solitarie places, wooddes, and fennes. What shall I saye with Gildas, how they lefte their citties and townes alltogether voyde of artillerie and munitions. Then the Saxons, as lords of all, didd now peculierlie converte there madnes and violence to the cheefe nobles, that after the maistree and confusion of them they mighte the easlier enter possession on the whole Ile, which ownlie thinge they thristed and longed for. But the miserable Britons weare not cleane destitute of the divine favor, for beeholde they hadde the presence of Aurelius Ambrosius, as wee shewed beefore, whoe assone as with trumpett hee hadd pronounced open warre, eche manne hasteth unto hime, eche mann humblie beesechethe him, eche sollicitethe him to defende them, and that it woolde please him, even the verie firste daye, to joyne with them in battayle againe there mortall foes. Thus a legion being soone gathered, Aurelius marcheth forth against them, and stowtelie setteth on them; within a fewe dayse there was three ernest conflictes, as well bie wrathe as power achieved: at the lengthe the Saxons were put to flight, and Horssus, the brother of Hengistus, slaine; yet was there corage soe farre from coolinge, that, within littel time receavinge a new bende owte of Germanie, they entred on the Britons with muche hope. Assone as Aurelius Ambrosius understoode that his enemie camm with stronge force against hime, in noe wise delayenge, proceaded into the higheway, minding to goe towards Yorcke, fro whence that tempest aproched; but being in this pretended jornie, hee was certified that Hengistus had taken a resting place xvij. myles from Yorcke, bie the bancke of the river which is now called Danne, wheare as is Dancastre: hee tooke the streyght way thither, and the next daye settinge on his enemie, hadde the victorie, sleyng Hengiste at the first encownter with a wonderus nomber of Germanians. The fame of that victorie is as yet in memorie emonge the inhabitantes of that place, which marveluslie apaired the mighte of the Saxons, insomuche that now they beganne to thincke it a more filthie matter to enjoye peace, then miserablie to accomplishe theire battayles. Hengistus lefte these two sonnes behinde himme, Osca and Otha, whoe as thei whome they whoe weare greatlie aggreeved at this late skorge, gathering a small companie, fleeted into the weste parties of the contrie, thincking that mutche better then to retorne into Kente, wheareas was lefte a garrison not well apoincted to resiste. There they rifled and depopulated the territories, they brente villages, they discharged there handdes from noe kinde of creweltie: which thinges being knowne, Ambrosius, leste there his enemies mighte resuscitate their strengthe, hastened thether, and in plaine fight once againe put them to flighte, but hee himselfe receaved a deadlie wounde, whearof hee died within fewe dayse. The Englishemenne after this hadd quietnes, nothinge againste there wills, within vj. monethes having vj. hundred discommoditees; the Britons, nevertheles, intentive to nothinge, and the lesse readie to annoye them throwghe there deathe of there kinge, for whome, in the meane time, in that hee hadde well deserved of the common wealthe, thei erected a rioll sepulcher in the fashion of a crowne of great square stones, even in that place wheare in skirmished hee receaved his fatall stroke. The tumbe is as yet extante in the diocesse of Sarisburie, neare to the village, called Aumsburie. In the meane time disceased Vortimerius; after whome succeeded Utherius, surnamed Pendraco, whoe did nothinge more fullie determine then clense his contrie from all feare of thes aliens, which hee cowlde not well comprise, bie reason of the discord of his citizens. At this time all citties neare to this contrie pitied the infelicitee of the miserable Brittaine, in that it hadde bothe forreyne and domesticall adversaries. But, aboove all others, this calamitee moved with compunction the Frenche busshopps, whoe harde saye that in this heape of miseries there chaunced noe small decaye of relligion in the Ile. For the xvij. yeare before the arrivall of the Englishe Saxons, the Pelagien heresie as a festering canker hadde crepte throwghe the Ilonde, which bie tyrannie of the Romaine Emperours was confirmed emonge Christians, to the greate endamaginge of the true Christian secte. For Pelagius a Briton, borne in the hether Brittaine, was persuaded that a manne of himme selfe didd attaine salvation, and bie his owne free will aspiered to righteousnes, that hee was borne withowt originall sinne, and therefore hadd noe neade to bee baptized, and bie this meanes this wicked creature intended to adnihilat Baptisme. Wherefore the Brittishe bisshops, bestood with weapons and enemies, when thei coulde not execute all functions, and perceaved that the prelates their neighbours weare prompte to assiste them, theye treted with the Frenche busshops bie letters and messengers, that in these times so daungerus to the Christian affayres they wowld vouchsafe to sende them succours; whoe callinge a Sinod of busshops didd sende into Brittaine Germanus Altisiodorensis and Lupus Tracasenus, menne of singuler integritee, learning, and innocencie, whoe, accordinge to the definitive sentence of this councill, shoulde doe there endevoure to withhoulde the inhabitants in their dewtie towardds Godd, whoe, as they sayled in the ocean, notwithstandinge they were strayed, yet partlie throwghe there hollines of livinge, partlie through miracles, weare easlie browghte into the righte waye. Celestinus, the Romaine bishoppe, for his parte assentethe to this busines, whoe not longe beefore hadd promised unto Scotlande, having allreadie receaved the right Christian religion, the bisshopp Palladius, whoe at the lenghth did there give the rightes of priesthoode, consecratinge one Servanus, a manne of sincere livinge and modestie, with the hollie rights of a busshope, whome after he sente into Iles Orchades to instructe the inhabitants with the trew relligion of

Christe, which thinge hee executed diligentlie. But Palladius, a goodde, godlie, thanckefull, and verie studius persone, the whiles he was in Scotland did bie all meanes diswade ther kinge Constantine that he wolde nott aide with armes those Englishe Saxons, a moste lewde generation, againste the Britons, beinge Christian menne, seeinge that hee might well perceave that their distresse wold in time to comme redownde to his owne undoeing, sithe it is evident that they minde nether the frindeshippe of Pictes nor of Scotts, but the imperie of the whole Ilond; and allso that hee wolde nott so often in other menns names and causes endanger him selfe and his nation with warre, the ende whereof, of all thinggs, is moste incertaine. This admonition tooke suche effect with Constantine that hee promised never hereafter to howlde with the Englishemen, which he perfourmed, for hee ministred divers aides afterwarde to the Britons; which thinge for a season greatlie releeved the Brittishe strenghth, preserving them from sodaine ruine. In the meane while, the Englishe Saxons renuenge frindshippe with the Pictes, (for they harde say that all readie the Scotts weare alienated from them,) thei assembled in more abundant manner, they invaded againe the gooddes of the Brittons, they russhed foorthe in to the middell of the soile, they bended there voyage towardes London, mindinge to goe into Kente; whoe, when they camme to the river Trente, (as probablie wee gesse) they pitched there pavilions on the other bancke: they sente there horsemen abrode, out of all corners, to espie if there were enie companie of theyre enemies abrode in the fildes. The Brittans being certified of removinge of there adversaries, did congregate the owlde beaten soldiers, and delibered as towchinge the meeting with them. There was no want of good will, but rather the lack of hope of fortunate successe, bie cause they hadde noe armie, nether hadd they taken enie mooster beefore; yeat, leaste their hertes showlde alltogether fayle, there were certaine named thei made on oste rather of suche as thei gathered newlie, then of suche as were owld approved. The feaste of Easter was at hande, wherof they weare all exceading gladde, mindinge to execute the solemnitee of there ceremonies and devotions beefore they wolde cope with their enimies, notwithstandinge that daunger honge over heddes, as whoe say they hadd more confidence in the divine helpe then in there owne substaunce. And sure these good mindes of theres were not destitute of goodd councell; for, whilest they weare intentive in the service of Godde, Germanus, a bisshoppe of inestimable sanctitee, not soe well fenced with armoure, as faythe, pietee, and innocentie, professed him selfe lodesmanne of there armie. Wonderful it is to be spoken how mutche the Brittons bie that message weare enhaunced both in strengthe and corage; wherfor, this feaste being finished, hee marched towards the Saxons, plantinge his tents as neare as might bee. The daye ensueng Germanus, capitan of the oste, executed the divine functions earlie in the morninge, beeseeching Godde of victorie, and, whilste all menn weare occupied in prayer, hee forthewith thrise gave them the watcheworde of fight, singinge with lowde voyce Alleluia: the whole armie didd likewise as often resownde the same voyce, uttering suche clamor that when the adverse partie sawe them comminge to joyne with theim thei forthwith weare vanquished with dispaire, and, throwing away there weapon, beetooke them selves to their legges, as thoughe being conquered with longe travaile, and in dispaire of saftie, there weare noe feater refuge then plaine ronninge awaye. Thus in victorie acchived bie divine grace there was nether slaughter nor prisoner, yeat manie of the enemies, as Beda testifieth, were missed after the passage over the water, whoe, beinge feared with this miracle of their owne swinge, weare quiet a while. The Britons did the like, so that, as it weare truce made between them, they ceased on bothe sides, untill the Britons bie civil discorde suffered the losse of their libertie. But the Saxons bie all meanes enkendled to dispossesse the Brittons of the Ilonde which they inhabited. Havinge citties and townes (as Gildas purporteth) as thinges lefte desert. Not longe after thei swarmed uppe into a verie highe hill in that part of the Ilond which butteth over againste Germanie, which at that time (as also Gildas saith) was called Badmicus. I suppose it to bee that which commonlie is called Blachamore, parteininge to the river Athesis, which dissevereth Yorckeshire from the busshopricke of Durisme, and hath an entrie into the which oute of Germanie menn doe commodiuslie direct their shippes, where the Englishemenne did everie daye looke for succors, for daylie they sent for some oute of there contrie. When these thingges weare revealed to the Britons, they made expedition thither, they beeseeged the hill, they placed garrisons on the sea coste, leaste they that camm might have free passage to enter the londe. The Saxons a fewe dayse with helde them selves in those difficult places, at the lengthe compelled with the defecte of victualls, of necessitee, with there ranckes sett in order, they discended into the next plaine grounde, and geevenge oportunitee of fighting they grasped with hande strokes. They fowghte fro the morneinge till the daye was farre spente with so greate occision of menn that the erthe was beespredd with redde bloodd; yet the muche greater skourge alighted on the Saxons, so that havinge loste there sufferaine guides Osca and Otha, they now seemed to bee shaken out of the neckes of the Brittons; but destinie could not be avoided, as shalbe shewed hereafter. Gildas maketh especiall memorie of this notable conflicte, whoe as himselfe affirmeth was borne the same yeare, which was the xliiij. after the comming of the Englishemenne, and the CCCCXCIJ. of our Salvation.

At this time Vtherius departed owte of this world, after whome succeded his sonne Arthur, being noe doubte suche a mann as, if hee hadd lived longe, hee surelie woulde have restored the whole somme beeing allmoste loste to his Britons. As concerninge this noble prince, for the marvelus force of his boddie, and the invincible valiaunce of his minde, his posteritee hathe allmoste vaunted and divulged suche gestes, as in our memorie emonge the Italiens ar commonlie noysed of Roland, the nephew of Charles the Great bie his sister, allbeit hee perished in the floure of his yowthe; for the common people is at this presence soe affectioned, that with woonderus admiration they extol Arthure unto the heavens, alleginge that hee daunted three capitans of the Saxons in plaine feelde; that hee subdewed Scotlande with the Iles adjoyninge; that in the teritorie of the Parisiens hee manfullie overthrew the Romaines, with there capitan Lucius; that hee didd depopulat Fraunce; that finallie hee slewe giauntes, and appalled the hartes of sterne and warlike menne. This redowbted conqueror, of so manifolde exploits, is reported to have ben sodainle retrayted from his jornay with domesticall contention, while hee minded to invade Rome, and consequentlie to have extinguished his tratorus nephew, Mordred, who usurped the regall power in his absence, in which conflict hee himselfe receaved a fatall stroke and baleful wounde, whereof hee died. Not manie years since in the abbey of Glastonburie was extructed for Arthur a magnificent sepulchre, that the posteritee might gather how worthie he was of all monuments, whearas in the dayse of Arthure this abbaye was not builded.

Next unto Arthure reigned Constantine, a dissolute manne, whome the hollie Gildas, which then lived, didd hate extreemelie, that is to saye, he cowld not but disallowe his corrupte demainor, yet loving him in that he was a manne; wherfore hee didde as humblie admonishe himme of his salvation as ernestlie reprehende his vices, for Constantine, who, contrarie to Divine and humaine lause, hadd rejected his wife, and was openlie forsworne, did eche daye commit six hundred haynus offences, with which example he didd moste harme in the depraving and corrupting his Brittons. This did Gildas reproove, this hee accused, this was the thinge which hee tooke so hevilie, whoe for the same purpose drawinge divers testimonies owt of treasurie of hollie scriptures, declared that Godd dide rewarde everie one accordinge to his facts, somtimes jentlie exorting them to goodnes and resipiscentie, somtime seducing by menacing like a severe and careful father. After Constantine ensewed Aurelius Conan, Vortiporius, Maglocimus,

Carentius, Cadvanus, and Cadvallo. These menn in those fewe years which they reygned had ynoughe to doe to proroge and defer the exitiall fall of their contrie, oftentime buckelinge in armes with the Saxons, somtimes using good administring, otherwhiles provident consultation; which things Cadwallo especiallie didde; whoe, when hee perceaved the fatall date to drawe neare, betoke himsellfe to the citte of Legions, which standethe on the west side; from whence hee makinge often excursions on his enemies, didd soe deface the Englishe power, that it seemed hee wold shortlie bring them to utter extremitee, if in the meane time hee had not been overcome and slayne of Oswalde King of Northumberlande, as wee will hereafter expresse. After these kings Cadwalladar, the sonne of Cadwallo, obteined the riall power of the kingedom, in all places raced with fier and murder. This prince in the beginninge of his imperie, as well bie good artes and politik councel as bie weapon and armes, defended his contrie, being now at verie poinct to comme to ruine, from the tyrannie of hostilitee; but not longe after (for that which is neare unto cinders muste neades fall and bee dissolved at the lengthe) hee fell into sharpe sickenes, whearwith hee beinge greavuslie tormented, the piers of the reallme, mistrustinge his life, beeganne to contende for the regalitee, which was the verie confusion of the nation; for as soone as the furie of hell discorde beganne to displaye her rayes, all feeldes laye as waste and voyde as it is woont to bee when the Goddes peace is exiled, and the whole multitude rashelie propensed to warre and seditions; whearbie it camme to passe that in a littel time a greate famine arose, and another evell more daungerus then that, for the pestilence, which is coosin germaine to famine, did in suche wise accompanie the same, that the live cowlde not burie the deadd, insomutche that the carkas of the dead lay in the sighte of men, which all way looked for the like deathe, soe that the dead made others sicke, the sicke infected the whole bothe with disease and feare. Wherfore Cadwallader recoveringe himselfe, wheras he was beeset with suche difficulties, hee passed over with a good companie into litle Britayne, whear in shorte time gatheringe noe small numbre, and being assertained that the plague was ceased in the Ilonde, he addressed himselfe to retorne, but beholde an image havinge somwhat more then earthlie shape is reported to have thus commoned with him as he reposed him to quietnes. 'O king, I saye unto thee, cease enie more to heape warre upon warre against them, whome if thou cowldst withstand, as thow kannest not, yet kannest thow not resist fatall destine. Thie contrie shall fall into the hands of thine enemies, which thie progenie longe hereafter shall recover.' Marvayle it is how mutch credit Cadwalladre gave to these woordes, whoe, accordinge to the olde sayd sawe, seeing silver to bee torned into drosse, layeng aside all weapons, commaunded the Britons which he ledde into Fraunce to retire home, and himm selfe departed to Rome, where he ended his life godlie, which was the xij yeare of the rayne of Cadwalladre, and the DC. of our Salvation. Thus at the lengthe the Englishe Saxons obteining the lordeshipp of the whole Ilonde, besides Scotlond, and that which the Pictes possessed, distributed the same emonge them, as wee shall hereafter make rehersall; which thing was not ordered bie common cowncell or assente, but as everie manne being moste of mighte woulde lay clame to enie parte, soe did hee institute his imperie. And to the Britons which hadd escaped the sackinge and demolition of their contrie was surrendred a portion of the Ilonde, bowndinge westeward, which the Englishemen afterwarde termed Wales, and the people Wallshemenn, bie reason the Germanians, as I sayd in the firste booke of this volume, doe call all foriners which have a divers language Walsmen, that is to say, aliens or straungers, of the which sorte thei, havin engroched the whole type of the region, accounted those Brittons which weare the survivers of the progenie. I will not alltogether use silence how David busshop of Meneva, a litell beefore the excision of the contrie, throughe the singuler sanctimonie of his livinge, as well alive as deadd was notorius in miracles, and as yet is. At this time Constantine, kinge of Scottes, whome we recited beefore as a fautor of the Brittishe affayres, died withowte issew; after whome succeeded Congallus, his nephew on his brother's side. These kinges ensewed, Goranus, a stowte manne, Eugenius the thirde, Convallus, Anitillus Aydanus, Chennethus, Eugenius the fowrthe, for the fowrthe, Donwaldus Maldvinus, Eugenius the fifte, Eugenius the vj. and Ambercletus. These menn did endevor nothing more then continuallie to make warre on the Pictes, and emonge the reste especiallie Ambercletus, whoe in the ende perished in those battayles. I suppose they didd forsee in there imagination how the one in conclusion wold destroye the other, as in the end indeade it camme to passe.

THE PREFACE OF THE IIIJ. BOOKE.

We have aboove expressed the deades and exploits of the Britons unto the comming of Cæsar into the Ilonde, written as indifferentlie worthie the credit; the residue allso, beeing serched forthe with no small travayle, I have hetherto layde abrode accordinge to truthe as thinggs which I have glened owte of goodd authors: and so bie writinge I am comme to the destruction of the Brittishe kingdom, founded on littell principels, yeat afterward, when it was growne to great perfection and maiestie, and established with artilerie, lawse, relligion, and councell, at the lengthe it came to ruine, even as in auncient times the mightie dominions of the Assirians, Medes, Persians, Macedonians, and Romans, camme to desolation; suche is the fickel nature, and propensitee to deathe, bothe of menne and humaine affayres. Yeat the force of nature, leaste it showlde apeare to injurius is this, that of how muche it beereeveth us in one place, soe muche is it woonte to yealde and repaye in an other, rendering like for like, or somtimes in more ample wise. Troye, as is well knowne, was raced and consumed, yeat the Troyans which escaped bylded Alba, of Alba sprange that puissant Rome. Even so, after the overthrowe of the Britons, leaste the riolme showlde seme destitute of fraunchise and imperie, the dominion of the Engleshemen, as a fresshe burden and ofspringe of nature, beeganne therin, and bie litel and littel aspired to great welthe and opulencie. But the Englishe princes from the beginninge partinge the kingdom beetweene them, and after that noe manne being contente with his owne limites and bowndes, whilest everie one was over careful for his owne kingdom, they fell into civile contention, which thinge indeade was not soe great a detrement as a wonderus good toorne unto them, a thing marvaylus to be tollde, in so miche that a manne wolde easlie beeleeve that the cheefe piers, while thei skowrged one an other with suche mutuall plagues, didd attempte nothinge ells but of a littell soe to enlarge the common welthe, and to derive it to suche absolute fourme as in conclusion most surelie it camme unto, for at the lengthe the monarchie was devoluted to one onlie, whoe encreased the same moste of all others, levinge it most safelie fenced to the successors. Of these thinges I must nowe especialie entreat, which I will earnestlie endeavor, and as trewlie I canne perfourme; but before that, I will particulerlie expownde and shewe the distribution of the Ilond beetweene the princes, and of the vij. kinges, (for somtimes so manie weare there at one season), strivinge and fightinge together, to the entent that the reader in suche an auncient matter may understande first of all what borders everie of their kingdoms hadde, albeit they never hadd certaine and determinat spaces or limites, bie cause the divers chance and ende of battayle, as hereafter shall bee shewed, did sometime farre enlarge theim, somtimes restraine them verie narrowlie.

THE FOURTH BOOKE

OF POLIDOR VERGILL ON THE ENGLISHE HISTORIE.

THE Kentishe kingdom was the firste of all others; for Hengistus, as beefore wee declared, possessed Kente, callinge him selfe kinge therof. This kingdom hadde on the east and sowthe side the ocean sea, on the northe the river Thames, on the weaste it was limited by the Sowthe Saxons, and finallie it conteined soe mutche grownde in circuite as the dioceses of the Busshopps of Cantwarburie and Rochestre comprehendethe at this daye. After Hengistus succeaded his sonnes Osca and Otha, Hunericus allso, and Ethelbertus, being the vth from Engistus, a manne noe lesse milde in innocentie, then noble in minde, and verie industrious as towchinge warfare, whoe, after he had once attained quietnes in forrein contries, in noe wise abiding the restines of ease, was the first that moved warrs againste the princes of his owne nation: wherebie he is reported to have enlarged his kingdome even to the river Humber: nether didd hee seeme to doe it contrarie to the lawe of armes, because the reallme newlie distracted from the Britons semed even as then to lie voyde for suche as cowlde enjoye it: and whoe soe cowlde defete others of enie portion semed to have as good titell as the beste. This goodd prince (like unto whome there were fewe in those dayse) to the perfect consumation of his glorie wanted nothinge but the divine knowlege of the trewe relligion, wherefore it happened bie the providence of Allmightie Godde that hee espowsed a wife of Frenche line named Bertha, a most Christian ladie, with whome emonge others camme an hollie bisshoppe called Lothardus, whoe bothe afterwarde usinge daylie the rightes of their relligion in the courte and pallace, did beegin noe doubte to lighten with the resplendent rayes and beames of celestiall lighte the minde of this prince being overwhelmed in profounde darcknes, and trayned him to the discipline of the Ghospell, which at the lengthe hee embraced. Sainct Gregorie aboute that time sent into Brittaine Augustine and Miletus, two monaches of sownde livinge, with divers others, who when they arrived in Kente, thei were verie jentlie entertayned of Ethelbertus, being now well instructed bie his wife and the hollie admonitions of Lethardus that he showlde not abhorr the Christian name, bie the preachinge and exhortations of the which menne hee first of all, and consequentlie all the Englishe menne, as wee will shewe in convenient place, didd wholie receave the opinion of our relligion. This was the DCIIJ. yeare from the birthe of Christe. Augustine was driven to the Ile in Kent called Tanet, which boundeth eastwarde, and is skarce ix. miles longe and ij. in breadthe lytle lesse, but a fewe yeares since a littel arme of the water was so overcommed wherebie it was disjoyned fro the next firme lande that now a good peece of it is united and woonne to the soyle. Ther is allso an other Ile at the entrie of the Thames not muche bigger termed Heppia. But as towching that poincte whie the Englishe people were cheefelie made Christian bie the helpe of Gregori Bisshop of Rome, it is lefte in memorie that this was the cause: it cam so to passe that certaine bond children of Englond of excellent bewtie wear browght to Rome to be sowlde, whome when Gregorius hadd seene, being then a secular preest, he is reported greatlie to have mervayled at their witte and welfaverdnes, and as hee was a manne of great sinceretee, soe did hee lament their chaunce that soe goodlie a kinde of menn was ignorant in the trew Godd; wherefore afterward aspiringe to the busshopricke, hee preferred nothing in the world beefore the winninge of Englishemenn to the societe of the Christian common welthe. Thus the relligion of Christe was at the lengthe restored againe in the Ilond, which, after that King Lucius hadde firste receaved the same, sometime it beinge oppressed bie the Romains, sometime bie the Saxons, didde onnlie remaine emonge the Brittons, that is to say, Wallsmen, albeit it was never but privatlie celebrated for feare of tyrants. Thus Augustine didde exceadinglie well deserve of relligion, as one whoe astemed all daungers and discommoditees as trifles in respecte of the salvation of manne, and being made an archebisshoppe, perswaded with Gregorius that the see of the archebusshopp, which from the firste receavinge of the Christian piete under the reigne of Lucius was allways at London, mighte from thence be translated to Cantaburie. Miletus, the companion of Augustine, was apointed Busshoppe of London dioces after the transposinge of the archebusshopricke. Augustine forthewith, after the disposition of this seat at Cantuarburie, dedicated unto Christe the sumptuous temple which, as the brute goethe, was there erected of the Romaines to their prophane goddes, there placinge the chayer of the busshop metropolitan. Likewise when hee hadde confirmed the foundacion of the Christian relligion emong the inhabitants of Kente, he consulted with Gregorius as towchinge the promulgation of lawse, whoe made these decrees: that suche things as weare geeven for howsold stuffe, parte therof showlde be contributed to the busshoppe, wheareof he shoulde maintaine an howse of hospitalitee, an other parte to the other preestes, the thirde to poore folke, the fourthe for the reparacion of churches, that divine service mighte be executed in the best wise; that sacrilege and churche robbers shoulde bee soe ernestlie punished that they might acknowlege their offence, and restore if it weare possible the stowllne gooddes: that in the contracting of matrimonie it shold bee lawfull for the Englishemenn to marie with the fowrthe degree of consanguinete and kinred, or at the leastwise within the fifte, for that is more certaine: that the Bushopps which weare ordeined of Augustine should be consecrated of three or fower Bisshopps; besides this, that Augustine him selfe showld clayme no jurisdiction over the Frenche Bisshops: finallie, that a woman great with childe, beinge noe Christian, showlde be baptized, and after her deliverie, according to the auncient usage, after xxxiij. or xlvj. dayes shoulde be pourged, or enter into the churche beefore if shee weare desierus. Not longe after this Gregorius wrote letters unto Ethelbertus the Kinge greatlie commendinge his sincere devotion in receavinge the woorde of Godde, exhorting him to persevere in that hollie trade of life, whearbie he mighte worthelie receive reward of Godde. But now to the former purpose.

Moreover this noble Prince Ethelbertus, at the request of Augustine, fownded a church to Sainct Peter and Powle the apostels, adorninge the same with large giftes, which after beecam the more of renowne throwghe the sepulture of Augustine himselfe and the Kinges of Kente; and another peculierlie to Saynct Powle at London (which cittie a littell beefore hee hadde broughte under his jurisdiction), and another hee dedicated to Sainct Andrew at Rochester, garnishinge them bothe with bounteus liberalitie. Besides these he dayle employed suche godlie woorckes, at the which time Augustine, whoe hadd as it weare alltogether devoted himselfe to the fortifieng and increase of relligion at home and abrode, foreseeinge that in shorte space hee shoulde bee unburdened of this life, and fering leaste the sheepe which bie divine power he hadde gathered in to the flocke shoulde straye into contagius and deadlie pastures, beinge destitute of a sheepeherd, hee chose his companion Laurentius, a manne of noe lesse profounde learninge than excellent demainor, and commended his sheepe to himme, sainge thus, or like to this: 'I praye thee, O deare Laurentius, that treadinge under thie feete all worldlie affaires, with prayenge and preachinge, as it behoovethe a goodd bishoppe, that thow wilte have singuler regarde to the salvation of those menn:' within shorte time after, this hollie father disseased, the xv. yeare after the beginninge of his residence there. His bodie restethe in the churche of Sainct Peter and Powle, allbeit it was not as yet finished. His soule joyfullie no doubte ascended to Godd the Father, to receave in heaven the reward of his travaile, as it is justle to bee thought of all men, seenge that for the sake of this Augustine, the veri apostel of the Englishe people (for soe is hee termed of Englishemenn), great woonders and grace is daylie shewed. Ethelbertus died the xxi. yeare after hee beecame Christian, and the lvi. yeare of his reigne, a manne surelie at all times and of all men greatlie to bee commended, especiallie of the better sorte, bothe for the receaving of Christes relligion and geevenge the same to his people, and allso in that hee was wholie inclined to pietee, for even to the verie laste houre of his life his merites weare singuler towarde the Christian common wealthe, of the which after his deathe hee was not unworthelie ascribed emonge the sainctes. His corps was caried to the churche of the apostells and there enterred, and at this daie is in miracles resplendent.

After that in this maturitee of years Ethelbertus was deceased, his sonne Edbaldus, being the vj. from Hengistus, was created kinge, being as then but a verie childe, whearbie, when he cam to his owne swinge, hee casting beehinde his backe the howlsom precepts of his father, gave him selfe wholie to all vicius behavior, and firste of all other thinges maried his steppe mother; secondarilie hee soe renownced the Christian relligion, so dispised and persecuted the same, that as a pestilence hee seemed to detest and abhorre it, insomutche that it camme to passe that manie, what for the feare of there prince, what for there owne madnes, they chaunged the vertuus institution of their life; notwithstandinge that the archebisshopp Laurentius didd not cease from his accustomed exhortations to the people as towchinge theire persisting in their former race, for the which cause the kinge was wonderuslie mooved at himme: but the good prelate did longe suffer injuries pacientlie, but in the ende, when he perceaved that hee did but leese his brethe and laboure in preachinge and admonishinge, sithe the ranckeure of this tyrante daylie encreased towardes the Christians, hee minded to fleete into Fraunce, folowinge Miletus and Justus, two busshops, whoe, as wee shall elswhear make rehersall, departed thither, beinge exiled bie the sonne of Sibertus Kinge of the Est

Saxons. But while hee addressed him selfe to this jornie, in his vision it seemed to him that Saint Peeter greatlie reprehended and punished him, in that hee, being unmindefull of the commandement of Augustine, wolde for the feare of penalltee leave his flocke to bee devoured of woolves; with which thinge he was soe feared that, sodainlie chaunginge his purpose, hee ceased from his enterprise; which thinge, when it was for certaintee intimated to Edbaldus, being stirred with this divine matter, hee asked pardon of Laurentius, and foorthewith disanullinge his filthie wedlocke, entred the trew saving helthe and was baptized; he revoked Miletus and Justus, and soe refourmed his life that it was evidentlie tried that his vitius yowthe was a pleasure unto him; but the Londiners, which served idowlls, wold in noe wise receave Miletus, and for that reeson he made his abode in Kent, and not longe after, Laurentius beinge deedd, he was consecrate archebusshop as third from Augustine, whoe when he hadd wrought manie thinggs worthie to be woondered at, the iiij. yeare after the beginninge of his residens, he passed from his mortall life into eternall. After Miletus succeaded Justus, worthie of that appellation for his justice. In the bisshopricke of London Cedas succeded Miletus, the brother of Sainct Cedda or Chadde; after Cedde, Winas; after Winas, Erchenwald, that righte hollie father, who to the ende hee mighte conferr all his substance to the communite and participation of the relligius, hee founded two abbayse, one of monaches of thorder of Sainct Benedicte, at Chertsey, a village in the countie of Surrye, an other of noonnes at Barchinge, a village standing on the bancke of the Thames estwarde vij. miles from London. But I will retire to mie matter. In the meane while Edbaldus, when he was becomm not muche inferior to his father in good deads and sanctitee, died the xxv. yeare after the beginninge of his reigne, whome everie mane bothe maye justlie and owghte to prayse and honor exceadinglie, for bie how muche it was longer ere ever he attained to the knowledge of the Scriptures, bie somuche didde hee the more ardentlie embrace the same, so that it was not easie to be discried whoe better deserved of our relligion, whether his father, in that he acknowleged and receaved it before him; or hee, in that hee redressed and renewed it being eche where explosed and contemned.

Next unto him reyned his sonne Ergombertus, not muche unlike to his father nether in loove towards his coontrie, nether in devotion towards Godd; for he, folowinge the example of his grandefather and father, made flatte with the grownde the chappels of the hethen goddes which as yet weare remaininge, that vaine superstition mighte bee clene eradicate and destroied, for as longe as their weare enie remainders of prophane temples dedicat to falls godds, it was not easie to withdrawe the hartes and mindes of men from the fanaticke worshippinge of idolls. Bie these goddlie factes it camme to passe that xxv. years he administred peaceablie the kingdom which he had regallie furnished with lawse and ordinances.

At this season died Justus the archebisshoppe of Canterburie, after manie his goodlie woorckes for the beawtifienge of the region, who a littell beefore hadd consecrated Paulinus Bushoppe of Yorcke, the companion of him and Miletus sente longe before into the Ilond bie Gregorius, unto whom he enjoyned this busines to enstructe the people of Northe Humberlande in the Ghospell, which, as it shallbee declared in an other place, hee didde verie well and diligentlie. Not long before, Boniface the Bisshopp of Rome hadde geeven power unto Justus to make Bisshops, as Bedas witnessethe, and within a little after that Honorius beinge Bishop of Rome sendinge his palle to Honorius Archebusshop of Canterburie confirminge the same, and grauntinge that as often as it showld happen the Archebisshopp of Canterburie or Yorcke to bee deade and the sea voyde, hee that was the surviver showlde consecrate him which was chosen in the other's place; least if that function shoulde be demaunded of the Busshoppe of Rome, or the Frenche Archebisshops, relligion newlie sprong emong the Englishemenne might percase suffer detrement. Next unto Justus succeded Honorius, after him Theodatus, after Theodatus Theodorus the vij. from Augustine, whoe at his verie first takinge his office called a congregation of busshops and preests, wherein weare made divers decrees to all orders of menn veri conducible to the blessed leadinge of their lives. The cheefe of theire acts and injunctions Bedas reciteth in the iiijth booke and vth chapiter of his Ecclesiasticall Historie, whereof it is the lesse requisite that I showlde entreat. After the death of Ercombertus, his sonne Egbertus attained the regall crowne, of whome there is noe notable deade in minde by reason of the shortnes of his time: somme there are that have lefte in writinge that bie the meanes and woorckinge of Egbertus, his uncles, two moste hollie menne, Ethelbertus and Ethelbrittus, were put to deathe, whose bodies weare buried in the abbaye of Ramsie. Notwithstandinge that it is crediblie thought that Egbertus didd sore fore thincke himme of this detestable facte, yeat veangeance was taken on his sonne Lotharius, accordinge to the divine oracle in Exodus, the 34 chapter: visiting the iniquitie of fathers on their sonnes to the thirde and fourthe generation. This manne havinge layde an evel foundacion in the governinge of the reallme, within shorte space, bie the procurement of Edricus, the sonne of Ethelbertus, (whoes restles rage pricked him to the revengement of his father's deathe,) he fell into civile dissention, in the which, emonge the Kentishemen, who in sodaine uprore rose agaynst himme, hee was sore wownded, and shortly died under the handes of the leches and surgeons. Under the reigne of Lotharius the Archbisshop Theodorus called another convent of mani busshops, wherin the estate of relligion and orders of priesthoode were newlie sifted and redressed, for not beefore that time hadd the Englishe churche receaved those former hollie sinods and counsels kepte amonge the Greekes, wherin manie hereses weare abolished owt of the Christian Churche.

After Lotharius, Edricus, the sonne of Ethelbertus, was made kinge, whoe being wrapped in domesticall contention, wherof himselfe was author, two years beinge skarcelie accomplished, hee was of his owne subjects stripped from the imperie, and beereeved of his life; which thinge beinge once blowne abrode, Cedowalla, kinge of the weste partes, beetweene whome and the Kentishe menn was ever deadlie hatred, accompanied with his brother Molo, sodaynlie invaded the Kentisshe territorie, and, without resistance, made great spoyle, wastinge all that hee coulde reache, burninge in rage againste all men. The Kentisshe menne, feeling themselves wownded with suche sodaine discommoditees, bie necessitee constrayned to abandon all feare, ranne upon theire enemies with suche a bande as thei coulde gather in that distresse. The westerne menne, not able to susteyne their violent incursion, but levinge behinde them a great parte of their bootie, ran awaye, forsaking Molo in the middest of his enemies. Molo, beinge destitute of his fellawshipp, fledd, and hidd himselfe in the next vile cotage, whome his enemies pursewing, caste fier into it and stifeled him. Thus the inhabitants of Kente beinge delivered from this present perill, makinge noe deliberation or provision for these things, strove emonge themselves for the creation of their kinge. Whilest manie were desierus of the kingdom, Vithredus, the other son of Egbertus, when bi diligence hee hadd extinguished envie, and hadd reconciled the next borderers with monnie, with the great hope of his cittizens he was made kinge, beinge the xi. from Hengistus. At this season Theodorus the Archebusshopp yealded upp his life, in whose place was instituted on Brithowaldus, first of the Englishe busshopps, (for the others wear all Italians.) beinge the eighte in order of the bisshopps. Withredus beinge an approoved good manne, and verie desierus of quietnes, when he understoode that Ina, the westerne kinge, prepared to make warre against himm, he procured his frindeshippe with a great somme of monnie. And when hee hadd thus obtened peace he fullie fixed his minde on godlines, havinge Godde's true relligion in great price, and furnishinge the realme with hollsomm decrees, and finallie, that nothing mighte bee wantinge to the unfeyned felicitee, (that which menne accounte noe small matter,) hee begott iij. sonnes, not unlike to himme selfe, Edbertus, Ethelbertus, and Alricus, whoe reigned most prosperuslie after himme. The kinges which folowed after these didde so degenerat from there predecessors, and weare soe drowned in sluggishenes and impudencie that this onlie worthie the memorie I have to say of them, that throughe their verie supine idelnes the Kentishe menn weare browght under the dominion of the westerne people. There names weare these which ensewe; first Edbertus, or Edelbertus, whoe, geevinge greater attemptes on the people named Mercij then was fittinge to his power, was apprehended and bownde of them, and, after beinge releaced, cowlde not bee receaved of his owne vassailes, they made so small accounte of himme; it is incertaine what was his finall ende: in all he reigned but ij. years. The next wear, Cuthredus, Baldredus, and Ethewelphus, whoe was the xviij. and laste in the discours of these kings, for, being taken prisoner of Egbertus, kinge of the weste partes, yealded uppe his large dominion to the conquerer. Somm have lefte in writinge that hee escaped, and after ledd a private life. Thus was the kingdom of Kente united to the west Saxons. The time of the reigne in Kente unto the losse of their libertie, from the time of Hengistus, was aboute cclxiij. years.

There names and dominions are hereafter expressed.

The second kingdom was of the Sowthe Saxons, which tooke the originall of the Saxon Ella the xxxi. yeare after the arrivall of the Englishemenn in the Ile; for hee, whilest the Britons weare tossed with divers and variable waves of battayle, bie littell and littell engroched on the sowthe partes of the Ile; there ordering his kingdom, and levinge it to his posteritee, who weare for this cause termed Sowthe Saxons, biecause the south winde, blowinge owt of the southe, hadde full recours throwghe there contrie. But there reigned verie fewe kinges, for as it beganne soone, soe it endewred not longe, for as muche as they, being trodden downe in civile dissention, did first of all enter under the dominion and appellation of the West Saxons. The greatest parte of men surmise that those weare the bowndes of their imperie, wherin at this day the dioceses of Winchestre and Chichester are limited. After

Ella ther ensewed but onlie iiij. kings, Sisca, Ethelvalchius, Berutius, and Aldinus, whome Inas, the westerne kinge, deprived bothe of life and kingdom, as herafter more plaine declaration shall bee made.

The third kingdom was of the Est Angles, or Englishmen, bie cause they inhabited that parte of the Ile which bowndeth estwarde; havinge therbi there denomination; which space at this daye is comprehended in the dioceses of Norwiche and Elye, beinge devided into three sheeres, that is to weete, Sowthefolke, Norffolke, and Cambrigeshier. Of these Uffa was the firste kinge, after whome shortele ensewed Titullus and Redovaldus; this mann being excellent in martiall prowes, achieved a luckie battayle againste Ethelfredus kinge of Northe Humberlande, as in an other place wee will declare in the life of Ethelfredus himselfe, (restoringe that kingdom to one Edwinus, a younge man of goodlye disposition,) and receaved the Christian relligion after his renowne gotten in warfare, that he mighte semblabie bee as well beloved of Godde as redowbted of menne. But, alas! hee profited not longe in this good purpose, for, beinge invegled with the wicked devises of his wife, a moste importunate and ungodlie creature, he renounced Christe, and so, within shorte time dienge, fell into the societee of the blacke Goddes. Next unto him succeeded his sonne Carpwaldus, by instinct of nature verie well disposed, for at the first, beinge baptised, hee beegan to leade an hollie lyfe; but the line thereof was soone cutte in sonder bie the unmercifull treason of malicius menne. Then didde Sigibertus obteine the kingdom, as brother unto Carpwaldus bie the mother's side, and fifte from Uffa, whoe with all celeritee embraced the Christian faythe, wonderuslie amplifienge the same in his dominion. This wise prince, knowing nothinge to bee so comlie an ornament to menne as learninge, and that there was great defecte and scarcitee thereof in his riolme, sumwhat the more bie the exortacions of Bisshoppe Felix, a Burgonion borne, and a verie skilfull manne, hee fownded schooles eche wheare in his kingdom, and especiallie at Cambrige, that children there from there verie childehoode mighte receave erudition, wherebie in shorte time theye becamme singuler learned menne; and from that time the universitee of Cambridge continuallie flowrished in the gooddlie knowlege of all disciplines and sciences; wherefore Englonde, in that it hathe allways hadd afterwarde learned menn, it is moste beholdinge and cheeflie it hathe to thanck Sigibertus, as himme whoe layde the first fowndacion of all goodd litterature, which was donne the DCXXX. yeare of our Salvation. Sigibertus beganne now to bee of greate yeares, and so mutche the more studiuslie still to muse with himselfe how harde a thinge it was soe to governe a common welthe as it beehooved a goodd prince; wherfor in fine he resolved to leade a private life in the residue of his dayse, wherfor, surrendringe the administration to his coosine Egricus, hee cowched him selfe in an abbay. But within shorte time after, when as Penda, a moste tyrannicall kinge of the Mercians, didde sore anoy Egricus in warrs, Sigibertus, to assiste and releeve his owlde people, was constreyned to com forthe of the relligius howse; yet, leaste hee might seeme unmindefull of relligion and former pretence, carienge a wande insteade of a scepter, and havinge noe other armor but his sworde, hee entred the skermish, there receavinge his deathe with Edricus, and allmoste the whole armie. Thus this sincere mann, incowntering with Godd's adversarie, semethe as a martir to have loste his life. The next king was Annas, being the vij. from Uffa, whome Penda likewise with weapons browght to his bale. Then ensewed Ethelberius, Ethelbaldus, Aldulphus, Elwoldus, Beornas, Ethelredus, and Ethelbertus, being the xiiij. in the order of kinges from Uffa. This manne from his tender age was soe fostered and trained of his father Ethelredus that, being at defiance with vicious demaynor, didd ownlie cleave to the ingenius exercise of goodd artes. Manie, as well his deades as saienges, may suffice for proofe, in that he was suche a prince that none coulde bee mor industrius, or more acceptable in all respects; none more indewed with humanitee or popular humilitee, whoe was accustomed to have this perpetuallie in his mowthe: that it beseemed all menn, the greater and mightier thei weare, to be so much the mor humble and affable, bie cause, quod hee, the Lorde hathe throwne doune the mightie, and hathe exalted the meeke harted. Beesides this hee exercised the studdie of wisdom, not so muche in woordes as in sobrietie of manners and continence of life. Bie these vertewse did he quicklie allure to him the benevolence and loove of all sortes, and for bie cause he hadd allreadie brideled his affections, he fullie determined not to make effeminat and weaken his boddie bie the companie of women, for the which cause hee ernestlie refused mariage. But contrarie wise hee hadde vehement instigation of his councellers to provide better for his posteritee, and the rather therefore to marrie. At the lengthe the matter being putt into the handdes of the cowncell, hee being but one, was dissuaded bie them all, in so mutche Alfreda, the dowghter of Offa, king of the Mercians, was empromised him to espouse. This moste jentil prince, who liked well the loove of all men, beinge desierus to comm in greater favor with his father in lawe, wente him selfe to bringe home this mayden, whoe as hee wente was feared with manie straunge things, and suche wonderus tokens as semed to portende som infortunate ende of his life; for when he tooke horsse the earthe in appearaunce trembled under his feete; and while he jornied in the middest of the day hee was soe beeset with a clowde that for a season hee sawe nothinge; and, finallie, in his dreame it appered to hime that the chefe toppe and pinnacle of his pallace fell sodaynlie to the earthe. With these portentius thinges albeit he was feared (for, indeed, well he might be astonied,) yeat, fearing noe deceite, as a manne that measured all menn's usage bie his owne, went forward on his waye. Offa entertayned this noble impe civilie, but his wife, whose name was Quendreda, a wight more wilie then piteus or goddlie, nothing moved with loove, but of audacitee sufficient to attempt enie hainus enterprise, wente abowte to persuade with her husbande that he showld murther Ethelbertus, and, consequentlie, season on the whole dominion of the Est Angles. The kinge at the first abhorred suche a crime, blaminge greatlie his wife; nevertheles at the lengthe, at the importunate sute and sterne behavior of this wooman, hee was clene turned, and agreethe to this blooddie facte. The busines of hasteninge the deathe was committed to one of a prompte and bowlde stomacke, which showlde espie time and place to accomplish this purpose, whoe accompanienge divers other with him, as though he hadde benne sent from Offa to call for Ethelbertus, camme to him in the nighte time, and strangled this innocent yownge manne, thinckinge on noe such matter; and forthewith Offa invaded bie force his realme, and possessed the same: but the good virgin Alfreda, knowinge the deathe of her espowse, accursinge her parents in all her praiers, and stirred sodainlie with divine inspiration, did longe beefore pronownce that it wold comm to passe that her mother showlde suffer iuste penaltie for soe develishe a deede, which in short time happened; and she herselfe vowinge herselfe to Godde in her virginitee, convayed herselfe into a place named Crolande, and lived there moste devowtlie; the which place beinge a marishe grownde, liethe betweene Elie and the river Nine, and in times past, abowte the DCXCV. yere of our Salvation, beganne to bee famus throwghe the memoriall of Saincte Guthlake, a monache, where he longe dwelled, and was buried. Whearebie, in processe throughe the miracles there shewed manie menn being browght thither, fownded there an monasterie of relligius persons of the order of Sainte Benedict, hard bie the river Nine, which even of late was extant; finallie, the corps of this martyr Ethelbertus was buried at Hereforde, wheare miraculuslie it resteth. After this the kingdom of the East Angles was somtime under the jurisdiction of the Mercians, somtime under the West Saxons, somtime under Kente, until Edmundus, an hollie man, laste of the Englishe line, obteined the same, whoe, when he aspired to the kingdom, governing with tranquillitee, and using piete and liberallitee towardes eche degree, being at the lengthe slaine, throughe the treason of barbarus people, attained martirdom, wherof this is reported to bee the occasion. Lothebricus, a Dane borne, the father of Agnerus and Hubo, (of whome wee shall hereafter have oportunitee to entreate,) beinge greatlie delighted in hawkinge, as menne saye, on a time, taking a littel barcke, while hee wandered abowte the shore persewend the water fowle, with sodaine blaste of the winde was driven into the maine sea, wheare, being tossed to and froe two dayse and two nightes, at the lengthe was blowne to the shore of the Est Angles, and forthewith, for his good skill in flieng with haukes, was entertayned into howsholde of Edmundus. Manie dayse weare not passed, but that a servant of the king's, being a fawkener, hadd slayne him for envie, that hee was conninger then himselfe in that qualitee: for the which offence, when he perceaved that he cowlde gett noe pardon of the kinge, hee fledd into Denmarcke, and there, burning in hatred againste Edmundus, in that he would nott release himme, bethoughte him of this develishe[a] devise. He certified for a trewthe Agnerus and Hubo (too verie sorefull orphans, for the mischaunce of their father Lothebricus) that he was slaine emonge the Este Englishemen, bie the commaundment of kinge Edmundus. Agnerus, as soone as hee understode of his father's murthering, is sayde owt of hande to have hasted into the Iland with noe small number of armed soldiers to revenge this injurie; and that as soone as hee camme to the Est Angles, that hee sente one of his men as espiall weare Edmundus sojornied, commaunding himme that hee showlde exacte monnie of the kinge, and other necessaries, as one all readie vanquished, declaring more over that hee showlde no longer reigne, excepte withowte delay he wowlde submitte himme selfe to the Danes; and hee him selfe all this while not in farre distance followed the espie as a manne professinge open hostilitee, and mindinge to make all thinges ether boorne with fier, or swimme in blodde. Edmundus, after hee harde the message, marvelinge not a littel at the unseemlie rashnes of this barbarus people, was marveluslie dismayde and appalled,

[a] Villainous, *marg.*

and makinge som delaye in musinge and cogitation, delibered with himselfe what might bee moste expedient in soe sodaine a terror; at the lengthe, this moste innocent creature, remembringe the saienge of Christe, hee that loesethe his life shall finde the same, settinge all feare aparte, made this aunswere to the messengere: Saye unto thie haute capitaine that Edmundus, a Christian kinge, shall never becomme servile to the Danes, abhorringe the ownelie savinge relligion of Christe, onlesse hee shall firste embrace the same allso. Hee hadde scarselie said these woordes, but Agnerus was sodainlie present, and russhing into the pallace, slewe divers menn, and apprehended Edmundus himselfe. Somm there are which write that this goodde prince at the firste avoided them, and afterward of purpose turned againe to them; and being demanded if hee knewe wheare the kinge was, made this aunswere: While I was in the court there was allso Edmundus, whome you seeke, and when I departed hee voyded likewise, whoe whither hee shall escape youre handds or nott onlie Godde knowethe. When the Danes, bie an exposition, understode that Godde was named, perceavinge verie well that this was the kinge, they tooke hime, they frushd him with clubbes all moste to deathe, they roved him throughe with arrowse, and finallie smote of his hedde, while hee called on the name of Godde; and thus this woorthie kinge receaved the noble victorie of martirdom. Yet these rude raskalls, not thus content, raged on the dead carkas, and hidde it emonge thicke shrubbes and briars, leaste the Christians showlde exhibit there accustomable ceremonies therto. But humane impietee prevayled nothinge against Divine providence; for while the Christen menn, which founde the boddie, made dilligent searche for the hedde, beeholde a voice was sodainlie hard in one corner of the woodde, wherunto all menn approched, findinge the hedd sownde and inviolate. There hooved faste bie it a woolfe, which wonderuslie kepte and preserved it; and (that which was to bee marveled at) this raveninge beaste didd not once taste of the bloode, which continuallie dropped from it. This begunn to bee notorius amonge the miracles of Saincte Edmunde. But on the other side divers other have lefte in memorie that sharpe battayles weare fowght beetweene him and the Danes, with great slaughter on bothe sides, beefore hee cam under the yoke of his enemies. This was the yeare of our Lorde DCCCLXXI. Edmundus lived xxxix. yeare, and reigned xvj. His boddie was enterred in a relligius howse of thordre of Sainct Benedicte, founded of an hollie bisshopp of that region called Alswinus, and dedicated unto him in a towne in the countie of Suffolke named Berie. These are the thinggs which certaine authors have alleged as the causes of Saincte Edmundes martirdom, whose opinion I will not affirme to bee alltogether trewe, for as much as it is evident that the Danes camme nott at that time oute of Denmarcke to revenge the death of the father of Agnerus and Hubo, but weare longe before in the Ile, whoe at the lenghth overcomming the people of Northumberlande at Yorcke, (as it shalbe mentioned in the life of Alured, the kinge of the Weste parte,) they invaded the Est Angles, wheare shortlie thei slainge Edmundus, reygned over them certaine years. The which thinge one Saxo Grammaticus maketh especiall mention to bee trewe, who writethe of the Danishe gestes. Trulie he affirmethe that in the beginninge, firste, one Frotho, and then Amlethus, subdued the Brittishe kinges and Scottishe, and in fine that the Englishe kings allso, whoe beefore vanquished the Britons, weare over commed of Frotho the thirde, Iverus and Regnerus, to [whom] at the lengthe was geven a valient ruler, called Agnerus, whoe sharpelie afflicted the people which weare unfaythefull unto himme. This man of the Englishe cronographers is unfytlie called Juguares, even as of this Saxo hathe evellie termed the Englishe kinges, I thincke throwghe the defaulte of the printer; but let us retorne to the purpose. The Danes, when they hadd geven the overthrow to the East Angles, they made kinge one of their capitains, called Guthorinus, whoe, as hee was a prowde mann, soe hee governed crewellie, mindinge to extirpe bothe the stocke and name of Englishemenne; but, beinge prevented with death, hee cowlde not fullfill his bloodie intente. After him succeded Ericus, likewise a Dane, whoe in that hee alltogether followed the stepps of Guthorinus, bie his insolent rewlinge, within littell after the beginninge of his reygne, the Englishemenn being browght to the utter desperinge of all thinggs, in a furie slewe him; which thing nevertheles proved noe great commoditee to them; for what with the Danes beinge desierus to revenge this murther, what with the westerne kinges desierus to enlarge there dominion, they weere so terriblie afflicted beetweene them, that in conclusion they weare faine (as I will shewe ellswheare) to submitt themselves to the westerne kinge, called Edwardus, surnamed Senior; so at the lengthe loste bothe their kingdom, which had leasted longest, and their name bothe at once.

The fowrthe kingdom was of the Este Saxons (if wee beeleeve Beda, who maketh a difference betweene Saxons and Englishemenne). There kingdom tooke his originall of kinge Erchenwinus; the head and regall majestie therof was at London, which cittie (as wee shewed beefore) the Kentissh kinge Ethelbertus afterward enjoyed; it was limited with those veri bowndes wherewith, in our memorie, the dioces of London is determined. But other writers (unto whome I rather assent) surmise that the kingedom of the Est Angles and Est Saxons was but all one in effecte, yeat to have somtimes benne administered of two princes, in that they are annexed; for it is well knowne that London was the cheefe and rioll seat of them both. The kinges, which in the beginninge succeaded Erchenwinus, wear theas, Sladda and Sibertus. This laste was baptized of Miletus, busshopp of London, to whome they ascribe the abbay of Westmonaster. Howbeit, som authors, to whome I easlie agree, do rather suppose the same to bee the worcke of kinge Lucius. Sibertus begatt iij. sonnes, Serredius, Sewardius, and Sigibertus, in whome shined nether sanctitee, nether the feare of Godd, nor enie sparcke of relligion; they soe dispised the Christian name, they ranne to suche wonderus maddnes, that havinge in contempte the eucharisticall sacrament, moste grosslie and dispituuslie they receaved the same, in so muche that Miletus, denienge that he could ministre it to suche as hadd not ben sprinckled with the celestiall dewe of helthefull baptisme, was commaunded bie them forthewith to departe owt of the kingdom. Miletus being thus exiled, made expedition towards Laurentius, archebisshopp of Canterburie, wheare, when the good prelates hadd a while consulted as menn ignorant what was best to bee done, and how they might sustaine the relligion, being now echewhear in extreeme distresse, in the ende they agreed rather to geeve place to this unbrideled tyrannie, then to bee afflicted with soe menie scathes, and nothing to availe the Christian common wealthe; wherefore, Miletus and Justus, the bisshop of Rochester, went with all speede into Fraunce, as Bedas is author. In the meane time, Serredius havinge warrs with the West Saxons, was slaine, bothe hee and his breethren; thus it was the pleasur of Allmightie Godd that cruell tyrants showlde bee regrated with juste penaltie for there great impietee.

After Sirredius succeded Sigibertus, surnamed Parvus, that is to saye, littell, the sonne of Sewardus, whoe, farre dissentinge from his father in judgement, willinglie receaved the Christian relligion; but suche is the worlde, that no mann knoweth whome hee maye safelie truste, for not longe aftere hee was of his one people prevelie murthered at home, bie cause hee was mercifull to his enemies, folowinge this precept of Christe, wheare he saithe, Doe well unto those which hate you. Next unto himme regned Suthelanus, Sigerius, and Sigehardus, of whome, saving that they weare baptized, I have no notable thinge to endite. After that these menn hadde runne the short race of their life ensewed Offa, the sonne of Sigerius, being the ixth. from Erchenwinus, in the ordre of the kinges, a yownge prince of exceadinge goodd nature, who moved with devocion, wente unto Rome to be absolved, wheare he yeelded uppe his ghoste unto Godde. Hee made Colredus his heire. After whome succeeded Suthredus the XI. and laste of the Este Saxon kings, of whome wee will speake more afterward, in our treatise of Egbertus kinge of the West Saxons, who, with this dominion of Est Saxons, joyned allso Kente and the kingdom of Northumberlande unto his power and jurisdiction.

The fifthe kingdom was of the Mercians or Middel Saxons, havinge originall of Crida the Saxon, which was farre the greatest and moste riche, bothe biecause they inhabited the moste plenteus soyle of the Ilonde, and allso that theye cheeflie flourished in the prosperus propagation of menne. Of the breadthe and lengthe thereof is noe certeyntee lefte in memorie, but menne doe well accounte that they inhabited those places wheare now are Lincolne, Coventree, Lichefielde, and Worciter diocesses, and that parte of Hereforde dioces was within the limits of this kingdom, as it is to be seen in oulde monuments, for in the moste auncient cronacles wee maye reade that it was distributed into v. dioceses, eeven as there are som that put a diversitee betwene the Mercians and the Middel Saxons, which weare on this side the river Trent, wheare as the others say thei, namelie the Mercians, weare placed more westwarde, albeit indeade I thincke them to bee all one people. Crida, beinge a manne bothe opulent in treasure and renowned in fame, in bickeringe with the Britons, bie littel and litel obteyned that kingdom, which at the lengthe hee surrendered to his sonne Vibbas; whoe, beinge in haute corage nothing inferior to his father, did not ounlie preserve the same, but allso augmented it, eche wheare over comminge the borderinge Britons. Then Cearlus seased on the kingdom; after whome succeaded Penda the sonne of Vibbas, the fourthe from Crida. Som write that this man was the author and beginner of the Mercians, which I am not able to saye. Hee was a man of great wisdom, witte in forecaste, easlie brideled with reason, yet in stoutenes of stomacke and warlike valiance passinge excellent: thease vertewse weare counterpeased with the equallitee of vices. He was verie sharpe in manners, sterne of nature, exceading crewell, verie fallse and deceytfull, wonderuslie dispiteus and envius towards the Christian name. With this trust and confidence of his vertewse and vices, the firste day that ever hee was crouned king, as

Whoe weare the Mercians, and what contries it doth conteine.

thoughe the whole Ilonde hadde ben dewe to himme, thinckinge noe occasion of battayle to be refused, hee beganne to provoke with warre as well his fiers and confederats as his enemies, soe that partelie bie force, partlie bie guile and deceyte, he overthrewe and slew with sworde Edwinus and Oswaldus, kinges of Northehumberland; and Sigibertus, Egricus, and Annas, moste noble princes of the East Angles. Nevertheles, it camme shortlie to passe that intollerable covetise to longe raging on his oune nation, at the length lighted uppon well deserved punishment, for Oswinus kinge of Northumberlande, more bie the provision of Godde then puissance of menne, did firste putt himm to flighte, and secondarilie with all his armie allmoste destroyed himme. Penda thus dienge lefte vij. children beehinde him bie his wiffe Chineswid, namelie, Peda, Wilferus, Ethelredus, Wedas, Merwaldus, and two others whose names are not extant. Merwaldus bie his wife Ermenburga begat iij. dowghters, Milburga, Mildreda, and Milwida. These moste continent virgins, partlie throughe the hollie leadinge of there life, partlie throughe there godlines in relligion, wherin continuallie they inured themselves, weare thowght worthie of our forfathers to bee numbered emong the Sainctes. Likewise Chineburga, and Chineswida, whoe, as mention is made, weare canonized. Peda, a verteus younge mann, succeaded next unto Penda: from whome Oswinus winning Mercia bie the right of battayle, graunted him againe the sowthe parte thereof, and his daughter Lluchefreda in mariage, uppon this condicion, that he would beecom Christian, the which thing with in a littell while after hee perfourmed bie the exhortation of Alfredus or Egfredus, the sonne of this forenamed kinge Oswinus, whoe had espowsed his sister Cunburga. This manne was the first of the Mercian kings that was christened, whose example the Mercians followinge, within the compasse of two yeares weare allmost all baptized; notwithstandinge there are somme which fallselie ascribe this facte to his brother Weda. In the meane while, after the deathe of Peda, the whole companie of the nobles beinge heevie and sadde, and soe mutche the rather in that three yeares, verie sore against there wills, they hadde obeyed not soe mutche there owne kinge as their conqueror, desiered bie all means to retorne againe into libertie: what showlde I say? they forsooke Oswinus, and pronounced kinge one Wilferus, another son of Penda, a man well knowne to bee of singuler godlines. The estate of Mercia beeganne well to amende, for Wilferus, endevoringe the generall commoditee of the whole people, firste made moste profitable lawes, secondarilie never ceased to persuade them to relligion till thei all hadde received baptisme. Hee mooved one battayle againste Cenovalchius, kinge of the West contrie, whome when hee hadde overthroune, hee ammerced himme with the surrender of the Ile of Wighte; which was in his jurisdiction, and not long after hee tooke leave of this mortall life. Hee begat of his wife Ermanilda, Chenredus and Wereburga. This mayden was browght bie her mother to the nonnerie at Elie, where being dedicated unto Godde, shee perpetuallie kepte her virginitee unspotted, and after her departure owte of this worlde, for her goodde life, was reckened emonge the sainctes. But as towchinge the foundacion of this college of Elie, we will heereafter make convenient declaration. Chenredus beinge now destitute of his father, and yet unripe to beare rewle, it pleased the nobilitee, that, till his nonage weare expired, his uncle Ethelredus, as protector, taking his tuicion, showlde governe. Thus Ethelredus beecam kinge as vij. from Crida, a temperate prince, and suche one as justelie mighte in righteusnes and relligion bee compared with the former kinges. Hee was of as honest dealinge in his riall maiestee as in his private condition, gentill towards all estates, soe excellinge in the sciens of warfare as one that rather desiered to defende his riollme then to enlarge it. He foughte in sundrie battailes for the exercise of his warlike knowlege; the one with the Kentishemen, leaste hee mighte bee noted of cowardise emong his borderers: the second with Egfredus king of Northumberlande, rashly invading Mercia, whome at the firste encounter he put to flighte; and afterwarde ceased from armes, mindinge to bee a soldier under Christe: wherfore hee renowncinge the life of a kinge the xxx. yeare after the beginninge of his reigne, restored the kingdom to his nephew Chenredus, and toke on himme the profession of a monache. Chenredus in all poinctes folowing the stepps of his uncle, at the last, the v^t^. yeare after, tooke his voyage towardes Rome with Offa kinge of the Est Saxons, wheare entringe a relligius hows with his companion died the DCCXI. year of our Salvation. As concerninge these kinges, which of devotion went to Rome, Platina maketh mention in the life of Bisshop Constantine. After him reygned Celredus, and then Ethelbaldus, whoe in the beginninge of his life enjoyed great tranquilitee, but not soe in the ende, for having noe troblesom tempestes did a great while rest peaceablie, which turned him to great displeasure, for the Mercians beginninge now to be wearie of their longe quietnes (for suche is nature of the common sorte to bee desierus of novelties), after hee hadd reigned xl. years, didd trayteruslie murther the goodd kinge, who in all menns opinion was accounted blessed. The author of the facte was one Beruredus, which usurped the regall dignitee: doeng noe feat worthie relation, saving that hee, beinge overcommed bie Offa, in recompence of his hainus offence was rewarded with crewel deathe. This Offa, after the overthrow of his enemie, possessed the kingdom.

In this manne was in his yowthe a certaine proportion, or rather contention, of vertewse and vices. Hee extreemelie thristed after riches and the amplifienge of his dominion, bie reason wherof hee somtimes vexed the princes adjacent with warres; somtime he entrapped them with deceits. On the other side, there was allmoste noe vertewe which hee didd nott ernestlie practise. He was industrius in the feates of armes; hee was of suche stowtenes of minde that who soe at that time was moste coragius was unethes able to countervayle him. Then, when maturitee of yeares drewe on, in commendable demaynor and modestee, yea, in inocentie of life, hee surmownted all menne. Yet in the beginninge of his reigne, when hee was fresshe from the slaughter of Beruredus, hee was of audacitee sufficient to adventure on all things; hee chased with warres the people of Northe-humberlande and Kente, miserablie afflictinge them; he maintayned a right mightie fighte with Cenewolphus, the westerne kinge, wherein of longe time the contention passed beetween them in equall balance. At the laste hee departed conquirer. Which thinges the more noblie hee achieved the more hee was puffed with pride; the more incended to wade farther in creweltie; for Ethelbertus, a moste innocent kinge of the East Angles, hee procured to bee murthered, bie treason entringe uppon his kingdom, as more openlie wee specified in the life of Ethelbertus. Emonge the reste hee conceaved this hawtines: he wolde neades translate the See of the Archebusshopp from Canterbwrie to Lychefielde, that his riolme might exceade all others, as well in the pontificall dignitee as regall maiestee, envieng not a littell the Kentishemenne the prerogative of their archebisshopricke. Nevertheles his successor Cenulphus made to them restitution of this preeminence, whearof they were unjustlie abredged. Bysides this hee founde oute manie covetus sleyghtes, wherebie hee might encroche as well the goodds of the prelates as allso the commonaltees; but the beste was that in the vices hee persevered not longe, for firste perswading with himselfe that hee ought to have somme feare of menn, he confirmed amitee and societee with the people adjoyninge, for he maried his dowghter Egburga to Bitricus kinge of the Weaste Saxons. Hee earnestlie procuered bie embassage the frindeshipp of Charles le Mayne, the kinge of Fraunce, not forgetting in the meane time to allure the benevolence of his owne liege menn. One of his legates is thought to have beene one Albinus, or Alchuinus, bie whose instigation Charles founded two universitees, or common schooles, as wee will shew in the life of Alured. But now againe to mie purpose. After this, for the feare of punishement, whearwith hee thowght hee showld be plagued, to the intente he mighte the better appeace Godde's wrathe, hee forgave the prelates, and all indigent persons, the xth parte of their goodes; hee beestowed large giftes on a magnificent churche, beinge then extant at Hereforde; he caused with great diligence to bee serched foorthe the reliques of the boddie of Sainct Alban, and to bee transposed into a golden shrine garnished with precius stones, and placed in the abbay which hee had erected to Saint Alban, enrichenge the same with large possessions, and in that place he edified an other relligius howse of thorder of Sainct Benedicte. Somme menne doe allso thincke that the monasterie at Bathe was his woorcke. Yeat Offa, whoe hadde trewe compunction of his sinnes, thincking that as yeat hee hadde not made full satisfaction for his offences, departed towardes Rome, that bie the sequestration of his worldle riches hee might the easlier obteine remission of his crimes. He made his riolme tributarie to the Romaine busshop Hadrianus. The tribute was this: that everie howse showld pay a peece of silver, usuallie called a pennie, which was the yeare of our Lord DCCLXXV. Of this yearlie pension I will speake more heereafter in the life of Ina, kinge of the weste partes, whoe at the same time, or littell beefore, gave the same gifte to the Bisshop of Rome. Offa, retieringe home from the cittee bie reason of age, which now drew on, when in all respectes hee hadde shewed him selfe a goodd prince, he, as it weare with his handes, yealded uppe his kingdom to his sonne Egfridus, and died shortlie after. Egfridus, being a yonge mann well enclined of nature, beeganne fro the beginninge of his rewle to followe the goodde doengs of his father, and to stirre greate expectation to all menn of his yeares ensewinge; but, peradventure Godd havinge conceaved displeasure with the stocke, it cowlde not be perdurable, as the virgin Alfreda, dowghter of Offa, didde divine, as I shewed beefore. For there were scarslie fower monethes passed when this yonge impe, skarse ripe for deathe, departed owte of this transitorie life. He ordeyned Cenulphus his heyr, who derived his stemme and line from Penda. This manne, beinge in magnamitee, in pollice, and sincere life able to bee compared of right with enie other prince, hadde one great conflicte with the Kentishe people, and tooke prisoner alive there kinge Edelbertus or Edburtus; but afterwarde, beinge moved with compassion, he graunted himme libertie. Hee allwayse hadde in greate honor his lordes and peeres of his riolme: he was allso a great patrone to the Christian relligion, for at the village named Winchecombe hee builded a sumptuus churche, with an howse of relligius menne, of the ordre of Sainct Benet, enrichinge the same with faire possessions. Thus he reigned xxiij. years. After this goodd father ensued a moste excellent sonne, named Chenelmus, but a verie childe, yeat of laudable demainor. Within fewe yeares, hee beinge growne to muche godlines, and onelie intentive to divine matters, bie the procurement of his sister Quendreda, a moste execrable viper, in his veri childehode was bocherlie mothered of his instructor and bringer uppe; and, leaste this horrible crime mighte at enie time comme to lighte, or bee prejudiciall to the develishe trespasser, the corpes of this innocent was prevelie buried in a place unhaunted. But according to the owlde saide sawe, nothinge is soe covertlie donn but at lengthe it will be knowne; so this was not soe closelie wrowght as after openlie perceaved, for when the childe was not accustomablie seene the suspicion might easlie arrise both of the slaughter, and of the slear and homicide; yeat, biecause miracles did well please antiquitee, they reported not longe after that a certaine skrowle of paper, entituled with gowlden letters, was layde bie an uncertaine author on the cheefe aulter in the churche of the prince of the Apostels at Rome, wherin were conteined divers thinges of the martirdom of this moste innocent Chenelmus, and in what place his boddie did lie; and that bie this meanes it was miraculuslie knowne of this hollie childe. The boddie was afterward fownde, and reverentlie and solemplie enterred in the abbay of Winchecombe, whereas at this daie that blessid martir is devoutlie worshipped, for manie miracles are donne there. But Quendreda, which had geeven noe small mayme to her stocke and contrie, bie the crewel distroienge of her naturall brother, was not admitted to bee governesse of the realme, as she hoped; but within shorte time, bie the juste plague of Godd, was striken with blindenes, and miserablie finishinge the date of her dayse, was tormented with manifolde and condigne afflictions. After this hollie Chenelmus, the kingdom of the Mercians beinge greatlie shaken and weakened, did manifestlie incline towards ruine, after whome folowed these kings: Cewolphus, Bernulphus, Ludicenus, and Uthelacus, menne neither notable in the integritee of life, nether deades of armes, for Bernulphus and Ludicenus weare ignominiouslie slaine of the East Angles; and Uthelacus, being conquered bie Egbertus, the westerne kinge, was yoked with servage. After these succeaded Bertulphus, who a few years governed well at home, yet nothinge prosperus in battaile. Once, at the beginning, hee fowght hand to hande with Egbertus, the prince of the weste parties; but finallie, beeinge overcommed of the Danes, and bereved of his kingdom, hee fleeted from thence into Fraunce, and there ledde a private life. The Danes at that time camme into the Ilonde, under the conduit of their capitan and king Regnerus; and, being noe lesse desierus of spoile then to inhabit the Ilonde, ceased not to annoye the inhabitants, and soe muche the more biecause they wear farr from home, thei lived of spoyle, embracinge all things with slaughter and bloodd, greatli fearinge nether weapon, nether violence, nor treason; insomutche that afterwarde, when they beganne to have the maystrie over the Mercians, whileste they weare to carefull to enlarge their dominion bie the subdueng of the whole Ile, and good abearing of the inhabitants, a certaine valiaunt manne, named Buthredus, whoe was noted of singuler industrie, for that bie the right of lawe the Mercian kingdom was apperteyninge to him, with great number of armed menn sodainlie entered the bowndes of Mercia, eche wheare afflicting his enemies, and bie so sodaine feare putting them to flight, proclaimed himselfe kinge; which thinge was not a littell acceptable to the Mercians, bothe for that thei wer accquitted of the yoke of alienes, and allso bie cause thei hadd gotten a kinge of their owne progenie. This Buthredus reygned xx. yeares, havinge manie rigorus conflictes with the Danes; but finallie hee receved so sharpe a plage that, beinge expelled owte of his contrie, for the perfourmance of his vowe hee wente to Rome, and within short space died a private manne. The Danes re-entering the riolme of Mercia, fell into great anxiete and dowbt whom thei showld make cheefe rewler of the Mercians, for they hadd them in great distruste, thinckinge it more for their avayle if thei sett up a kinge of their owne lineage; yet in fine, misdowbting that thei cowld not bothe withhoulde Mercia, and sufficientlie besides susteine the burden of suche warres as mighte happen one in another's necke, in a lande so eche wheare abownding in hostilitee, they ordeined for there kinge one Cevolphus, an olde servant to Buthredus, binding him bie his othe at their pleasure and will to be deposed. Cevolphus was the last kinge of the Mercians, and xxii[th] from Crida, the first kinge, a prince, trulie, under whome the realme cowld not possiblie but decline to ruine and utteraunce, for the fatall destruction of this monarchie well accorded with the prince, as well obscure in stemme as voyde of all vertewse. This manne was oppressed bie Aluredus with great facilitee, beinge kinge of the weste parties, who soe enjoied the kingdom of Mercia. This was the year of our Lord DCCCXI.

The vj. kingdom was of the Northe Humbrians, or people of Bernicia, which was allso divided into the kingdom of Deira. It hadd the beginninge of Ida, the first lorde of that soyle after the arrivall of the Englishemenn, which was the lxxxviij. yeare of the comminge of Englishe people, and the DVIIJ. of our Salvation. Som men conjecture that, at the first, Dukes weare the governors of Northumberland, who sufficientlie enlarged the bowndes thereof, and consequentlie Earles. Wee maie justlie surmise the largenes of this riolme to have ben of as ample wise as at this day the dioceses of Yorke, Carleyle, and Durisme. It was named Northumberlond, bie cause it bowndethe northwarde, and is full of shaddowe, throughe the heighte of the hills wherin it abowndethe, and is divided in two partes, that is to saye, Bernicia, which joineth upon Scotland, and Deira. It is thought that Alla or Ella did first possesse the same, reininge therein xxx. yeares. But Idas, which was a stowte and warlike manne, to the intent he might well deserve the name of a kinge, and that his kingdom might agree thereunto, soe bestirred him with weapon that he enlarged it from the river Humber to the Scottishe sea, vanquishinge Lothus, prince of the Pictes, and subdueng Coranus kinge of Scottes. Thus within the revolution of xij. yeares of his government their befell so great maiestee to this kingdom that to the confines and borderes it was noe lesse terror then in admiration. After Idas reigned his sonne Addas, Clappas, Theodulphus, Freodulphus, Theodoricus, Ethelricus, within the space of xxxij. yeare. After Ethelricus succeded his son Ethelfredus. With this Ethelfredus it is lefte in memorie that Ethelbertus the Kentishe kinge treated streyght after the beginninge of his reigne to confeder with him in battaile against the Britons (whoe betoke them selves in to that coste which we call Wales), and especiallie against the monaches of Bangor, which weare aboute two thowsand in nomber: whoe albeit thei receaved the Christian relligion, under the reigne of Lucius, yet being mindeful of their injuries, did not onlie not ædefie the Englishemen with Christian relligion but denied moreover to assiste eeven Augustine himselfe preaching the Ghospell. Trewlie the relligius persons, accountinge them there mortall enemies, did undowbtedlie beeleeve that, accordinge to the divine adage, it was not lawful to bestow that which was hollie uppon dogges. Nevertheles I surelie beleeve that Ethelfredus, partlie throwghe desire of rule, partelie bie reason of the owlde festered canker of hatred, did moove this new attempte towards the Brittons. The Britons at this time held the cittey of Legions, which the king mindinge to assaute endevored to plante a sige rownde abowte it. But the citizens, which preferred enie evell beefore beeseechinge, and in nothing misdoubtinge their power, issued forthwith scattering on thier enemies, whome Ethelredus entrapping bie deceite did easlie putt them to flight, usinge cheeflie extremitee towards the monaches of Bangor, which resorted in great rowtes into that place, mindinge to make supplication to Godd for the prosperus successe of their companie. Hee did moreover put the Scotts to flighte, whoe desierus bie warrs to abate his fælicite had ministered releefe to the Brittons. After these exploites, thus luckelie achieved, hee now having noe forayne enemie, to the ende he might at home likewise accquit himselfe of all daunger, hee beeganne to deliberat and kaste with himselfe how

That is Legiceste, now it is thought Chester.

he might dispatche owte of the waye Edwine the sonne of Alla king of Deira, whome his father hadde made heire and he hadde beerefte of his kingdom ; for well hee perceaved this yownge impe to bee indewed with singuler vertewes, and daylie occasions whie hee showlde more bee feared then that hee showlde feare : for in ridinge hee was noe lesse skillfull then stowte, the darte hee threwe artificiallie, he for exercise contended with his æqualls, hee gave himselfe to noe vice, nether sufferinge him selfe to be corrupted with riott nether with slouggishenes, to the ende hee might becomme worthie of a kingdom : this disposition to goodnes was a terror to the kinge, knowinge that eche mann as hee was most valiaunt so was hee naturallie moste desierus of imperie, yeat at the lengthe, judginge that it showlde not goe well with him if bie treason hee showlde destroye suche a yownge manne as was wel beeloved of all men, hee feynedlie pretended a great crime towardes himme, and in this coloure banished himme, thinckinge that hee bie this meanes beinge browght to miserie shoulde have the waye more open to offende, but it fell owt farr otherwise then hee surmised. Edwine fledd to Redovalldus kinge of the East Angles, of whome hee was gentlie intertayned and well estemed, for well perceavinge the vertews of the yownge man, hee cowlde not but embrace him as a father, for his parte purposinge to aide him with his advise, authoritee, yea and with weapon rather to protect him then bie enie injurie hee showlde bee hindered of his adversaries. These tidinges, as soon as they weare browght to Ethelfredus, he determined bie some meanes ether to make an ende of Edwine or of him selfe, wherfor in all haste he sent ambassadours to Redovaldus requiring him to send back Edwine, or otherwise to bedd himme to battayle. Redovaldus, when hee hadd harde the entent of the legats, denied ether to infringe the auncient rightes of hospitallitee or to surrender the nobel yownge mann to soe dispiteus an enemie. The legats having their aunswer departed home and pronownced warrs. Within few dayse after, there mindes were so enchafed on bothe sides that the kinge camme to handestrokes. After long contention Ethelfredus was slaine in fighte, with a great number of his men. Redovaldus after this conquest liberallie restored to Edwine his father's kingdom. In the meane space Oswaldus, Osmius, Enfredus, Osricus, and Offa, the sonnes of Ethelredus, hearing of the death of ther father, fledd speedelie into Scotlond, whome Eugenius the Forth jentellie entreated, causing them to be baptized, ministring to them for his time riches and succors, especiallie to kinge Oswaldus, against his enemies. The Virgin Ebba followed her brethren into Scotland, and was browghte to the entrie of the river Forthea, of whome the next promontorie toke the name, being at this day called Ebba. Edwine streyght after the entrie of his kingdom enlarged the limites thereof on all sides. For hee subdued the iles lieng abowte himme, which Bedas (as we sayd in the first Booke of this woorcke) callethe Mevaniæ, som others Hebrides: he overcam the Scotts, and compelled the Picts to abide in their allegiance; he overcamme in plaine field Cadwalle, a kinge of the Britons, a man naturallie crewell, and stowte bothe in boddie and in minde. These thinges when hee hadd abrode honorablie perfourmed, at home allsoe with like diligence he disposed all things, and browghte to passe that in his riolme and dominion ladie justice might bee the governesse in all thinggs: soe that to the obteining of the trewe glorie, this mann, no lesse valiaunt than wise, seemed onlie to lacke the knowledge of the Christian relligion: the which allso to the ende hee mighte embrace, firste he hadde occasion throughe an oracle, by the which (as he eschewed the raginge furie of Ethelfredus, as hereafter shall be shewed) he was admonished to have goodd hope: secondarilie, the societie and alliaunce which hee hadde confirmed with Edbaldus the Kentishe kinge; finallie, the moste helthefulle advertisments of Paulinus busshopp of Yorcke. For Paulinus, a manne of sincere livinge, abowte the DCXXV. yeare of our Salvation, was sente bie Justus archebusshopp of Cantuarburie, with Ethelberga the sister of Edbaldus, unto her husband Edwine, as yet not seene in the divine scriptures, that he mighte instructe the menn of Northumberlande in the Ghospel, and execute his hollie ministerie beefore the Virgine, for Justus thowghte that in shorte time it wowlde so growe in use, that bie thease meanes bothe the kinge and people wowlde the lesse abhorre the name of Christe; which forecast toke goodd effect, for Edwine willinglie promised that his wife showlde live accordinge to the Christian rightes, promising of his owne accorde to enter the felawship of the Christians, if so be that the Christian sect, being well examined of his menne, showld bee fownde more sownde and hollie than the reste. In the meane time Ceoloulphus the V. kinge of the West Saxons repined at the presente fælicitee of Edwine, for he sent a certaine villaine, ready for suche a purpose, forthewith to slaye himme. When the ruffian camm to the kinge he marched towardes himme as one that wolde have declared somme great matter, and, drawinge owt his dagger, strake att himme. The kinge, misdoubtinge some treason, went backwarde soe hastelie that one of his familiars entered betweene the stroke and himme, and was therewith thruste throwghe the boddie; neverthelesse, the stroke was so sore and vehement, that throughe the bodie of this friendlie manne the kinge was hurte, albeit verie little; but this varlet in the verie place was torne in peeces. The selfe same daye Ethelberga brought forthe a doughter named Ethanfreda; for bothe the which giftes Edwine thanked his fonde godds, whome Paulinus admonished to acknowledge these benefits as receaved of Christe, not of vaine godds. The kinge easilie herde the goode busshopp well enfourminge himme, and againe promised that in all haste hee wowlde receave the trewe relligion, if bie the goodd assistaunce of Christe, according to his minde, with his hande hee might well revenge the injuries which hee hadde receaved of the westren kinge: and to the ende he might shew assuered hope of keepinge his promise, hee delivered his late borne doughter to Paulinus to be consecrate unto Godde, whoe forthwith baptized her, being the firste christened of all the Northumbrians. Paulinus againe warned the kinge that he should not aske vengeaunce of Christe, shewing bie example that wee owghte to spare, yea and to loove our enemies. Edwine, as sone as he hadd receaved his wownde, prepared an armie, marched towards his enemie Ceoloulphus; he overcamme him and chastened him with crewell death; which busines being luckelie ended, Paulinus, who studiuslie endevored to winne the kinge unto Christian pietee, getting oportunitee, drewe neare, and shewed to Edwinus that the Allmightie hadd heard his praiers, requiring him not to contemne relligion, nether seeke delayse therin, but that he wowlde incontinent beecom Christian. The kinge, which ordered all thinges with prudence, alleginge himme selfe to bee a straunger in the case, caused all learned menn to bee sent for, that they mighte dispute with Paulinus of the Christian relligion, to thende that he might well perceave whether that weare better then his idolatree or nott. While these thinges of Paulinus weare in hande, the kinge receaved letters from Honorius, the Romaine busshop, wherin, bie divers reasons, he was moved to receave the worde of the eternall Godd. But the king's minde stickinge in the secte wherin it was fostered from his tender years, didd allmoste nothinge encline to enie new relligion; which thinge trulie I wowlde saye was don bie divine providence, for peradventure, Godd wolde that this prince, which at that time was accounted moste wise, showlde firste well ponder bie dowbtinge the relligion, as longe beefore Sainct Thomas the Apostell did in the firste beginninge in the encrease of the Ghospell, beefore he wowlde receave the same, to thentente that therbie others, nothing mistrustinge the trewthe therof, might most desieruslie affecte the same. Emonge these thinges, while learned menn wasted the time in disputation, Edwine remembred the former oracle, wherbie hee was the better induced to beeleefe, which revelacion was of this sorte: at suche time as hee beinge expelled his contrie, lived with Redovaldus, and was desiered bie the legats of Ethelfredus unto deathe, hee beganne to stande in great ambiguitee of his saftie, fearinge that if hee shoulde tarrie to incurre the handes of his enemies; if hee showlde preveli departe, hee showlde bee noted of unfaythefulnes for mistrustinge so thanckefull an entertainement. In this perplexitee [he] beehelde sodainelie at midnighte a certaine manne of strange countenance and attire approchinge unto himm, demaunded what rewarde hee wowlde geeve himme if hee should shewe him the thinge which shoulde clearlie dispatche him of all languor and sorrow: unto whome Edwine (allbeit hee finallie trusted the wordes of an unknowne person) made this aunswere, that what soever hee cowld lawfullie desier, or he himselfe justlie performe, willinglie hee wowlde graunte. Then streight hee opened how it showld comme to passe; firste, that hee showlde escape the traines of his enemies, and consequentlie recover the kingdom of his auncitors, enlarging the same on all parties bie the overthrowinge of his enemies. After this hee layde his hande on his hedde, sainge, 'O Edwine, when thow shalt beecomme conquiror, as often as enie mann shall come unto the, and shall laye his hande on thie hedde, then well remember to keepe this faythe and promisse.' After thease woordes this divine sowthesayer sodaynlie vanished owt of sight, that it might evidentlie apeare that it was noe mortall mannes prophecie whose minde is ignorante in the things to comme, but the verie messenger of Godde. The younge manne, beinge wonderuslie delighted with this oracle, revolvinge it longe in his minde, durste nott of a goodd season utter it unto enie manne. Wherefore, when as afterwarde of purpose hee delayed these affaires, nor was not flexible, bie the procurement of enie manne, Paulinus, whoe profited nothinge for a longe season in his advertisements, came unto himme, than beenge at Yorcke, and throughe hevenlie instillacion, as it is to bee thought, laide his godlie hande on his hedde, requiringe himm to call to minde what this acte showlde portende. Edwine, bie and bie, as one afraide with the wonderus successe of this oracle, withowte delaye fell prostrat beefore the feete of the bisshop, and lookinge uppe into heaven, is reported to have sayde in this wise,

'Yeat at the lengthe, O Allmightie Godde, this present daye doe I acknowlege thee, throughe the noble worcke of thie sonne Jhesus Christe, wherfore moste humblie I desier the of pardon for mie soe longe impietie, that beinge hetherto soe perverslie driven, I have not so mutche as yelded the thanckes of thie divine benefitts;' and successivelie turninge towarde Paulinus, sayed, 'And thee, allso, O reverend father, I desier, that first thow wilt vowchesafe to gieve mee a littell space to consulte with mie liegê people as towchinge this erneste matter of relligion; and then, with all speede, associat mee to the blessed number of Christians;' and for beecause there was noe convenient place for divine service in Yorke, beinge a cittie full of idowls, the kinge, bie necessitee, was compelled for the season to byld a churche of woodd, which he wolde have consecrated to Sainct Peter the Apostel; wherfor at the last, in this temple, after longe contention as concerning the Christian fayth, Edwin, the xi. yeare of his reigne, and the clxxx. yere after the comminge of the Englishe menne, which was the DCXXVIJ. of our Salvation, with a great number of his menn, was baptized of Paulinus; and after he was lifted owt of the fonte, he layed the foundacion of square stones, but beinge intercepted bie deathe, lefte this worcke to be accomplished to his successor Oswaldus. In this churche Paulinus placed the see of the archebusshopp. At this daye it is a sumptuus temple, and inferior to none in magnificence of the worke. Edwine having consecrate bothe churche and cittie to Godd, bie this example and diligence of Paulinus, Carpwaldus, kinge of East Angles, with all his people, were allured into the Christian common wealth; which things, as soone as they weare knowne, Honorius, bisshopp of Rome, being greatlie delited thearwith, did incontinent for a reward sende unto Paulinus the moste notable robe or mantell of the arche busshop, and unto Edwine and himme directed his letters, full of grace and humanitee, wherin especiallie hee commended the integritee, diligence, and pietie of the prelate, which hadd soe well deserved of the relligion: and the kinge, allso, even unto Heaven he extolled, that not onlie hee hadde embraced the Christian opinion, but allso hadd benne a president and example to others for the receavinge of the same; exhortinge him stoutelie and faythefullie to defende the same, even with patience, unto the deathe, in consideracion that of our Lorde hee showlde receave worthie rewarde. Thus it cam to passe that the North Humbrian kingdom especiallie flourished, and that, bie the industrie of the prince, peace in all costes was purchased untill the sodaine breche and uprore of Cadwallo disturbed the same; for soe daylie experience teacheth that nothinge is bie manns power donne, but commonlie bie the same it is undonne; for Penda, a moste cruelle tyrant of the Mercians, being to muche agreeved at the prosperus successe of Edwine, suborned Cadwallo to rebellion, whoe of his owne swinge didd hevelie beare the dominion of the Northe Humbrians, and they bothe togethers unitinge their force and gooddes, didd in great violence sett on the menn of Northe Humberlande. This fierce and coragius prince, on the other side, as sone as he herde of the comminge of his adversaries, hee camm forthe of the cittie with a small troupe of horsemenne, more to discrie the number of his enemies, and to knowe their purpose of his neighbours, then to joyne in handstrokes; neverthelesse, wheras his enemies weare not farre of, and in multitude seemed muche lesse then indead they weare, hee was nothing dismaide with the smallnes of his companie, but mannfullie invaded them: thei fowghte sharplie on both parties: nether weare the soldiers of Edwine appalled, biecause at the first fronte they perceaved the rowtes of the parte adverse to be augmented, but rather everie one beinge enkendeled with the example of the stowte and princelie capitaine, with great travaile endevored to withstande the sodaine irruption of the unwildey multitude, and beinge in the verie assured hope to attaine victorie, Edwine, in the middeste of his manful and worthie assault, was striken downe starcke dead. This rutheful deathe of the haute prince didd interrupt a moste noble victorie, for the fighte revowlted moste lamentablie to the Northe Humbrians, and the fightingemenn, astonished at the slaughter of their prince, weare miserablie putt to flight and slaine; and in the same moment Offredus, the kinges sonne, was slaine in the battayle. Edfredus, his other sonne, for the preservation of his life, yealded himselfe unto Penda, whome hee, breaking perjuriuslie his vow, afterwarde murthered. Ethelberga, the king's wife, for as mutche as thinges fell owte so infortunatelie, moste piteuslie lamentinge the deathe of her housbonde, accompanied with Paulinus and her two doughters, Enfreda and Ethelereda, fledde unto Edbaldus her brother, then kinge of Kente; and thus in one littel instance of time the estate of North Humberland was cleane defaced. This was the DCXXXIIJ. of our Salvation. Edwine lived xlviij. years. Paulinus, at his goinge to Cantarburie, was jentelie entreeted of the archebusshopp Honorius, and was endewed with the diocesse of Rochester, in the steede of the Romaine busshop, being latelie dead, wheare he liv'd moste continentlie. Trulie herebie wee maye see that in times paste other busshops hadde noe riches at all, as a thinge nothinge necessarie to preestehoode, or at the least wise that thei regarded them not, sithe that Paulinus, renouncinge the archebusshopricke of Yorcke, did take on him the meane bisshopricke of Rochester, being muche lesse in revenues. The diocesse of Yorcke a certaine years after, emonge the persecutions of tyrants, was administred bie the busshops of Lindisfarne; at the lengthe Ceddas, a right hollie busshop, toke the charge on him. Wilfredus succeded next after himme, who suffered manie discommoditees, in so mutche, that twise within the space of xlv. yeares, whearin hee was resident, hee was deprived. Hee and Ceddas allsoe, for that thei bothe well deserved of the religion, after their sownde and sincere life were ascribed emonge the sainctes. The fayre churche at the village named Ripon is the worke of this saincte Wilfride, where he erected a college or chantrie of priestes, in which place of late dayse his corps was reverentlie observed. Bosas succeded next, and after him Ihon, being v^{t}. from Paulinus. After that Edwine was slaine in fighte, it appeareth that the kingdom of Northe

Humberland was divided between Osricus, whoe hadde Deira, and Enfredus, who had Bernicia. These menne, albeit they weare Christians, yeat weare thei soe drawne of their vices wherin they weare notorius, that in shorte space they detested their relligion. But Godd would not longe suffer this impietie, or rather atheonisme, for scarslie one yeare hadd runne his race, that thei weare both with weapon slaine bie Cadwallo kinge of the Brittons. And for this cause their are som which, bothe for their uncleane life, and allso for the shortenes of their dayse, doe not accompte them emonge the Northehumbrian kinges. After this, Oswalldus, the thirde sonne of Ethelfredus, being the x. from Ida, was created kinge of Northumberlande, whoe, after the decease of his father, was longe banished in Scotlond, wheare beinge made a Christian, hee passed the flower of his yowthe in good artes emonge good menne, and especiallie throwghe travaylinge and exercise he learned the arte of warfare, which he estemed as certaine relligion, never mindinge to put the same in ure without great provocation; whearbie it camme to passe that Cadovallo the Brittishe kinge hadde him allmost in contempte, for in that not longe beefore hee hadde overthrowne two princes, he wasted and spoyled all things more freelie and crewellie, whearas noe manne was prompte to encounter or resiste his hedlonge temeritee, his stomacke was enhaunced, his minde becam orgulus, in comparison of him selfe; all Englishemenn he contemned, neglected, and dispraised, accusing them of cowardise, securitee, and sloggishenes, so that openlie hee bosted himselfe as borne to their utter distruction. While his minde was overwhelmed in this pride hee feared noe daunger: thus this lustie Britton chalenged Oswaldus in battayle, nothinge waienge how puissaunt his adversarie was in armes. The Englishe prince withoute delaye broughte his soldiers into the plaine feelde, whearas in times paste the menne of the Romaine Aetius hadde builded a wall to represse the incursion of the Pictes, and notwithstanding that of his adversarie hee was provoked to fighte the firste daye of his comminge, yet hee kepte him within his tents, and in the meane time caused the crosse of our Savior to bee carried rownde aboute the tentes, and the armed menn ernestlie to pray for the good perfourmance of their affayres, which beinge donne, the cross was there placed as a monument of the victorie to comme. The name of the place was afterwarde called the heavenlie campe. The nexte daye, after the execution of divine service, hee browght it forthe towards his enemie, desiering to skirmishe, and, after the onsett was blowne moste feercelie, he gave them battaile. The fight was stoutlie mainteined with æquall strengthe on bothe parties, until the force of the Britons beganne somwhat to bee abated and diminished, which as sone as Oswaldus apperceaved, hee renewinge the battayle, firste putt this his fierce enemie to flighte, and afterwarde apprehending himm, slewe bothe him and allmoste his whole retinue. This was the final ende of Cadovallo, a moste impatient adversarie of the Englishe name. Of nature and countenance he was mervaylus terrible, and for that cause menn say that the Britons made his portraiture and image, that it might bee a terrour to their enemies beeholdinge the same. After this mann succeded his sonne Cadowallader, whoe, in that the Brittishe estate semed to encline to the fatall daye, leving his kingdom went to Rome as we sayd before, and there died. After the fortunate accomplishinge of his battayle, the godlie prince Oswaldus endevored nothinge more intentivelie, to the ende he might seeme to regrate Allmightie Godd for his victorie and others his benefites, then moste studiuslie to encrease the Divine service and establishe relligion in all his reallme; for the which cause bye embassadours hee sollicited the bisshop Aidanus, a man moste excellent in all respectes, to comme unto hime, and caullinge to minde how well hee hadd instructed him with his hollie advertisements while hee lived in exile in Scotlonde, moste willinglie, livinglie, and jentillie he enterteyned hime at his comming into Northe Humberlande. Butt the goodd busshoppe streyght uppon his comminge did regarde nothinge more then to grave in the hertes of the North Humbrians the perfaiet foundacion of the eternall relligion, and for that cause requiered of the kinge a place convenable for the see of a busshop, and wheareas divers menne harped on divers places as expedient for soe godlie a ministerie, he thowght the Hollie Iland, then named Lindisfarnis, to bee moste feete, bie cause it lay farr from all concourse and haunt, so that therein, as in a certayne desert, hee might intende to the Divine function. In this soyle Aidanus placed the see, ordeyninge and providinge all things apperteininge to the dignitee of a busshop. This was the DCXL. yeare of our Salvation.

This place is aboute the borders of England and Scotland eastwarde, in the shore lieng on the right hand of the Ile, which everie daye twise bie the flowinge and swellinge of the sea in the space of xii. howers, is on all sides environed with waters, so that it is made a plaine Ilonde: nevertheles, when bie æquall time the waters departe, summe parte of the grounde remaining drie and annexed to this londe. The whole compass is aboute three miles. At this daye of the Englishe nation it is termed Hollie Ilond, bie cause there liethe enterred the bodies of Aydanus, Cuthbertus, and divers other saincts. The place as yet keepethe his nature, so that it appeareth howe they weare deceaved, which thought Lindisfarnis to be that Ile which is now called Farnem, being vij. miles distant, wherof wee will speake more hereafter. In this place when as Aydanus hadde established the Pontificall See, this sincere mann seased not to instructe the people with the hollie Ghospell; in all his preachinges there commonlie chaunced matter worthie the beeholding, for when as Aidanus declared the Christian faith, whoe as yeat was not skilled in the Englishe tongue, (which was then rude, alltogether intermedled with the Saxon phrase, not as yet garnished with trimme pronunciation, nor in noe poinct agreing with the Scottishe language,) the kinge, which was conninge in the Scottishe speach, receaving the wordes from the mouthe of this goodlie manne, didd evidentlie expounde them to the people, wheärbie it camme to passe that the kinge and the busshopp didde bothe at once preache the Ghospell, and that the vulgares, partlie throwghe the goodnes of the prelate, partlie throwghe the maiestie of the kinge, didd the more diligentlie attende, receave, and digeste the same. Bie this meanes relligion daylie more and more increased emonge thinhabitants of Northe Humberlande, cherches weare ædified, and especiallie in the cheef and celestiall fielde ther was erected a temple of magnificent worckmanshipp, whearin as soone as the devowte prince hadd made the crosse of our Lorde, the place becam notorius throwghe manie miracles, for in the whole contrie abowte Bernicia, before the erection of this crosse bie Oswaldus, there was nether churche nether enie monument of hollie things; nether didd the other affayres of North Humberland enie lesse increase then this piete, for Oswaldus, throughe his godlie love mixed with his noble corage (in the which as in æquall balance hee shined towards all menne), allmost withowte slaughter or bluddeshedde, the Brittons, Pictes, Scottes, and Englishemenn, being nations different in speeche, ether hee frindelie receaved into amitee, or stoutlie repressed with the yoke of servage. Thus Godd blessed with riches the good kinge, thus he directed him toward hevenlie rewardes who allredie hadd entered the jornie; but nether the greatnes of dominion nor the aboundance of treasure cowlde ever alienate or withdraw his minde from humanitee and mildenes. There was in this manne greate hollines, and marvelus affection towards mercifulnes; he never repayed to enie manne evell for evell, but accordinge to the example of our Savior Christ, the highe kinge of kings, he wisshed well and prayde for them of whome he hadde receaved injurie; he was not unmindefull of that owld texte, bie their fruites yee shall knowe them, desiering generallie to deserve well of all men, to visite the chambers of sicke persons, to releeve the diseased with woordes and giftes, to ransom the bonde and set at libertie the emprisoned, bie payeng dew debtes to the dispayring creditors, to norishe withe fatherlie pietie the selie widowse and orphans, defending them from the injuries of the deceyptful, and punishinge the deceavers. Emonge theese charitable deads one is especiallie worthie of memorie. On the daye when Jesus Christe had troden deathe under foote and resumed life, as he satte at dinner with Aidanus, he was certified bie his servaunts, that beefore the dores of his palace the pore people were assembled begginge for meate, whereat this charitable prince beinge moved, hee reched the silver vessel with meate which stode nexte to himme, and commaunded the same with the contents proportionallie to be distributed to his neadie Christian bretherne. Aidanus for so munificent and liberall a deade turned him towards the kinge, and takinge him bie the right hande sayd, Now Godde graunte that this handde never putrifie. Which thinge it is to bee thowght that this goddlie manne sayde not withoute the aspiration and assent of the Hollie Spirit, for trulie this hande, after the corruption of the boddie, didd allwayse remayne uncorrupte, being reverentlie preserved in a decent inclosure, in the kinges cittie and Saincte Peeter's church. We will in processe make mention in what place the kinge's cittie was. At the lengthe Oswaldus, when he hadde reconciled the mindes of the mene which inhabited Deira, and the people about Berwicke, (for in feretimes thei maynteyned contention as towchinge the Christian rightes, wherof he hadd exceadinglie well deserved,) hee nowe minded to move warres with his adversaries, not knowinge how neare his laste daye approched. It fortuned that one Penda, a moste cruel prince of the Mercians, did assaulte rigoruslie the Christians, spoyling there churches of their riche jewels, noe lesse desieringe then endevoringe to abolishe the verie appellation of Christianitee. On this tyrante, thus develishelie enraged, Oswaldus bente his force and weapons; but alas, in the verie beginninge of the fighte, he beinge on all sides beesett with the tracherie of these rude æthenickes, hee was sodainlie slayne, while hee ernestlie warred on these wicked persons. The Northe Humbrian armie, as all astonished at the deathe of their soveraine, torned their backes. Oswaldus reyned ix. yeares and lived xxxviij. whoe in that hee hadde passed this mortall life withowte mortall spot or crime (bie cause that above all things he worshiped and esteemed the maiestie of our Lorde, finallie in that for the behoofe of relligion he suffered deathe not unworthielie of our ancient fathers), he was accompted emonge the sainctes, whose memorie at this daye is not cleane voyde of miracles. His cheefe cittie in owlde time was named Sebba or Bebba (for I finde them bothe in writinge), soe named of a certaine queene, as testifiethe Bedas. After this, at suche time as other North Humbrian kings hadd possession therof, thei called it the pallace; it was situat eastward on the right side of the Ile against the Ile Farnis, lieng two miles from the same. At this day there is noe trackes or tokens of a cittee, onelie there is remnant a castell, which, whether it weare then byleded or afterward it is not surelie knoune, but of Englishemen it is termed Bamborowgh Castell: this littell Ile Farna or Farnis is continuallie environed with water, the circuit therof scarslie contening a mile; wherfore seeing that Lindisfarnis, which I called Hollie Ilonde, may twise in a daye on fote be safelie passed unto at the ebbe, and retire of the waters, as wee sayd right now, it is cleane divers from Farnis, albeit the similitude of name representethe noe difference; which in deade hathe beene the cause that manie have erred, thinckinge Farnis to bee that which in times paste was called Lindisfarnis, and surelie they bothe in the beginninge weare named Farnis; but the one afterward was cleped Lindisfarnis of the river Lindus, who having close passages under earthe unto that place dothe there burste forth into the ocean. There is allso a third Ile in the same discourse of the sea x. miles from Farnis, called Cochett.

After the receavinge of this miserable scourge, the kingdom of Northe Humberland was againe divided. Osuuius, the brother of Oswaldus, beinge the ix. from Ida, obtained Bernicia, or contries abowt Bernicia, and Osuvinus, the sonne of Osricus (whome beefore wee sayde to be slaine of Cadwallo), withhelde Deira, or parties abowte Deirham. These two at firste with great concorde beganne to communicate in cowncells to associat there power against their enemies, but not longe after the impacient desier of imperie did drive them to domesticall contention; insomutche that, after they hadde gatherid together armies on bothe sides, they minded shortlie to encounter; but when as this hotte rage of them bothe, which is wonte to blinde and perverte the mindes of menne, waxed somwhat cowlde on bothe sides, and that ether wayed the burden of present dawnger with greter circumspection, it pleased them of purpose to delay the daye appoyncted. In the meane while, Osuinus, being farre the lesser of habilitee, thincking it to bee more saftee for him to flie presentlie then to fighte, in the nighte time, being accompanied onlie with one servante, departed prevelie from his armie to the house of a certaine manne whome hee accounted his verie frinde; but hee being a covert traytor bewrayed this noble younge impe yealdinge unto slaughter to Oswus. By this means Osuinus, havinge obteined the whole kingdom, thinckinge therebie that it weare beste to attempte greater matters, in all speade mineded with fire and weapon to invade Penda kinge of the Mercians, whoe wee sayde aboove brought to their bale his brothers Edwinus and Oswaldus, except he cowlde firste happilie asswage so fierce an enimie bie giftes, as all menn stoode in great doubte of; this hee firste tried in vayne, and nott prevaylinge thought to use the oportunitee of armes, which battayle albeit it seemed exceadinge perilous, yeat havinge the Divine favor, not withstandinge that his feers and companie was moche lesse then semed to suffice for so huge an enterprise, hee settinge on them with owte tarienge, at the firste claspinge putt them to flighte, whose horsemen so bestirred them in the chase that emonge the reste himselfe Penda was slayne. Osuuius forthewith receaved the Mercians yeldinge them selves, thus preservinge his honor unsteined, and worthilie revenging the skathes of his brethren and frindes. This victorie moreover greatlie restored the wealthe of Northe Humberlande, and muche avayled the Christian faythe, which sustayned suche damage bie the deathe of Oswaldus that near hande it camme to distruction bie the crewell tyrannie of Penda. After thease affayres, Osuinus, being sufficientlie contented with the prosperus successe of his present estate, layde armoure aparte, and to wipe awaye the infamie, and allso to make satisfaction of his crime, whereof he was muche noted for the late murther of Oswinus, he beganne moste devowtlie to serve Godd, with muche lamentation to desier pardon of his sinnes, to geeve francklie to the poore, and finallie verie ernestlie to doe goodd to all menn; bie the which obsequies, as it is convenient that wee beeleve, hee became most leefe, bothe to Godd and manne; for beesides other his devowte doeings he was the occasion that the Mercians at the lengthe, abandoning their obstinate sturdines, entred into the Christian societee, for he noe doubte, streyght after the overthrowe of Penda, studiuslie procured that the people mighte be inured with Christian manners. Hee gave in mariage to Peda, the sonne of Penda, an ægregius yonge jentilmanne, his dowghter Aluchufreda, assigninge for her dowrie the sowthe parte of Mercia, as it is sayde beefore, on this condition that hee showlde embrace relligion; which thing this yonge impe executed with great maturitee, especiallie at the exhortation of the kinge; the like did the Mercians allso, accordinge to his president. Osuinus reygned over the Mercians onli three years, for they, beinge desierus of libertie, did sodaynelie slippe the coller rebelliuslie. This worthie prince builded an abbay at the village named Wittbie, and a nonnerie, assigninge for the cheefe governesse one Congilda, a verie hollie womanne, gevinge to her his doughter Edelfreda, to bee instructed, who becam a nonne. But within a goodwhiles after this relligius house was destroyed bie aliens and straungers, and was restored and inhabited bie monachs Benedictines. Owte of that place there sprange moste famus relligius persons, which afterward placed that notable abbay nere to the walls of Yorcke, and dedicated the same to the divine virgin Marie; albeit there are somm which ascribe the worcke to Alanus earle of Richemonde, but I knowe not how trulie they do it. But wee will beetake us againe to our matter. After this, the goodd kinge didd onlie endevor that which might profet Christes flocke. Hee was attaynted bie a disease, and therof quickelie consumed the DCC. yeare of our Lorde. He lived lvij. years; hee reigned xxviij. He engendered of his wife Enfreda, the doughter of Edwinus, two sonnes, Egfridus and Alvinus, and three doughters, Ositha, Aluchufreda, and Edelfreda. Hee made his sonn Egfredus heyre, as well of his kingdom as of his vertewse; whoe having attayned the realme, shewed himselfe in all poinctes a good prince, and worthie to howlde the sterne of a weale publique. Hee didd first of all thinges procure that Cuthbertus, a manne verie notable, bothe in leadinge his life, and allso in learninge, showlde be consecrate busshop of the Hollie Ilond, and consequentlie espowsed Etheldreda or Audrei, the dowghter of Annas, kinge of the East Angles, a virgin of no lesse corporall bowtie then endowed with heavenlie grace. This one mayden hathe shewed unto all ages an example of chastitee worthie the memoriall; for, notwithstanding she was twise maried, yeat didd she reserve her boddie untowched for the embracing of manns sensuall desiers, which thing was somwhat easie to bee donne with her former husbande, whoe died shortlie after the marriage; but in that she lived xii. years with Egfridus, a yonge manne of flowrishinge yeares, and never intermedeled with himme, that thinge truelie deservithe suche admiration that allmoste a manne cannot discrive whether more weare to bee commended the constancie of the virgine, or the intollerable continencie of the yonge manne soe extreemelie burning in loove; but noe dowbte æquall glorie is incident to them bothe. O how fewe are there which know like unto her how to withstand the tickeling pleasures of the frayle fleshe! Howbeit, in conclusion, the matter cam unto contention, yeat without all violence, for Egfridus havinge great remorse for the wante of issewe, sumtimes in the waye of flatterie, sumtimes in roughe and threatening speeche, incended his wife, that, accordinge to the rightes of lawful wedlocke, she woulde employe the honeste busines of procreation. But Audrie, on the other side, whoe hadd espoused her verginitee unto Godde, wold not reverse from her purpose, nether for the sweete poyson of pleasure, nether for the rigorus instigation of wordes. The kinge, which naturallie was of meeke disposicion, allbeit, the more his wife withstode, the more hee burned in affection, (for suche is our nature moste vehementlie to desier the things moste ernestlie denied us,) yeat he refrayned owtragius demaynor, and, to the end he mighte leave noe conclusion untried, he committed the charge of perswading with her to one Wilfredus, archebusshop of Yorcke, in whome this heavenlie creature hadd great affiance; but never a whitt hee profited in his travayle, so unmovablie persisted her minde: nether didd she sease in the meane time with continuall intreatie to sollicite her husbonde that voluntarilie hee wowlde vowchesafe to unknitte the sacred knotte of matrimonie, and that it might be lawful for her to leade a privat, single, and chaste life, which at the lengthe hee obteined, for hee cowlde nott but love virginitee in his wife, which he knew certainlie to bee vowed unto Christe. This virgin havinge purchased libertie, repayred to the noonne Ebba, the aunte of her husbande Egfredus, whoe was noted to bee of great sanctitee in livinge, and abbatesse of the nonnerie which stoode in the borders of Scotlonde, even there whereas in our time stode the village named Coldingham, and there beecamme a nonne. In processe of time this godlie creature, beinge zelus to encrease relligion, retorned to her owlde Est Angles, and with all speede in the Ile of Elie builded a relligius house, ordeyninge therein a college of noonnes, of whome herselfe was cheefe; but finallie, accordinge to the tenor of nature, she died, and was ascribed emonge the sainctes. It is lefte in memorie that this place of relligion at the firste was erected bie the meanes of Augustine archebisshop of Cantuarburie, in the honor of our Lady, at the charges of Ethelbertus, kinge of Kente; and that besides there was fownded an howse of Benedictines, aboute the DC. yeare of mannes Salvation. But after that time, when as Penda the Mercian tyrant did exceadinglie waste the Easte Angles, that abbaye was allso raced, which Audrie renewed, as wee sayde beefore; and not muche after, abowte the DCCCLXXX. yeare of our Lorde, at suche time as the Danes, having Agnerus to their capitan, raged on these East Englishe menne, the allters were throwne downe, the temples wear lamentablie defaced, the religius howse was made æquall with the grownde, which was yeat againe afterwards repayred of certaine good prelats, and a chauntrie of preestes therein ordeined. But finallie, aboute the DCCCCLXX. year of our Salvation, a monache, named Ethelwoldus, bisshop of Winchestre, soe pleted bothe with kinge Edgarus, and allso with John the xiij., busshop of Rome, that hee caused them to be displaced, and browght in his monachs, which even of late inhabited the same.

This Ile of Elie, encompassed on all sides with sweete waters, standethe sowtheward, within the limitts of Cambridgeshier; northeward, it buttethe on Northefolke; it bowndethe muche eastward, from whence the lengthe thereof westeward conteineth xxvj. miles, and the breadthe xiiij.; the whole compasse and circuite thereof exceadeth not lxxx. miles; and for that it abowndethe in fennes, especiallie in the wintre season, therfore somm menne surmise that yt was termed Elie, biecause ἕλος in Greeke signifiethe a fenne. There are somme famus townes therin, and cheeflie that which is named Elie, in auncient times a cittie, and now the residence of the busshop, as successivlie shall be declared.

Egfredus lived afterward whole iij. years, and all that season never accquited of warrs: first, hee encountered infortunatlie with the Mercians, then he transported his armie into Irelond, unmercifulli afflicting the Irishemenne, beinge unwares; after that hee molested in battayle Eugenius the vth. kinge of Scotts, notwithstandinge his nobles ernestlie required him not to hurte his frindes: finallie, mindinge of likeliehoode to sustaine juste penaltie of his defaultes, hee moved warre against Brudeus, kinge of the Pictes, albeit he hadd contrarie advertisement bie the goodd busshopp Cuthbertus; but, beinge shortlie entrapped with guiles, hee perished with no small portion of his complices. Egfredus reigned xv. yeares, and lived xl.

Alfredus, as menne say, the base sonne of Osuinus, was created kinge as the ixth. from Ida; whoe livinge in banishement all the reigne of his brother Egfride, throwghe his pregnante witte and continuall industrie in letters becam excedinglie well learned. Wherefore, as sone as hee was seased in this kingdom, which was raced throwghe the injuries of his adversaries, he procured the same to be restored with goodd artes, polishinge, and mainteninge it with singuler dilegence, and being contented with suche limites as withoute strife hee cowlde gette of the Pictes, usinge owtragiuslie the commoditee of victorie, after the overthrow of his brother, hee endevored honeste, tranquillitee, and peace, havinge intermission from forinsicall and externe broyles the whole xix. yeares which he reygned. At this presence Ihon, archebusshop of Yorcke, did greatlie florishe in the celestiall science of divine theologie; whoe beinge werie and at defiance with the publicke and politique life, renowncinge his archebishopricke, went into Beverlaye, where hee builded a churche and college of priestes, passinge most chastlie iiij. yeares as sequestred from all wordlie cares, where at this daye he is remembred with miraculus memorie, for longe since it is sithe he was canonized a saincte, after his residence of xxxiij. years. Beverlake is a towne in the northe east partes, standinge in a levell grownde well fenced. After this, Ihon succeded his disciple Wilfredus the second, who ended his life after he was resident xv. years; after whome ensewed Egbertus, being vij. from Paulinus, whoe deceasinge after accomplishement of xxxij. yeares, hadde these successors, Albertus, Embaldus the First, Emballdus the Second, Wilfius, Vimundus, and Wilferus, beinge xiii. from Paulinus; these continued the archebushopricke of Yorcke abowte an hundred and xx. years. After them succeaded Adelbaldus, Lodevardus, and Wulfstanus the xvj. from Paulinus, in the order of busshops, of whose hollie gestes I will make minde in the life of king Adelstanus as a place more convenient. After Alfredus, these were kinges, Osredus, Chenredus, Osrichus, and Celoulphus the xvij. from Ida: unto this manne did Bedas write the ecclesiasticall historie of the Englishe nation, who died allso at that season; moreover he writt a booke uppon the Acts of the Apostells, on the Ghospell of Marcke, and as concerning the variete of times, with certain homilies, which lacke not their use at this day emonge Englishemen; allso on the vij. canonicall Epistels, on the Apocalips, on Genesys, on Ezdras, on the bookes of Kinges, and many other things which are now wanting. Coloulphus, after hee hadd reygned vij. years, yealdinge the imperie to his uncle Egbertus, lived afterward a relligius life. This laste allso, after the xxi. yeare of his reygne, renowncinge his kingdom, beecam a monache. The affayres and estate of Northehumberland after this inclined to utterance and distruction bie the division of the people into factions. Next unto him succeeded Osoulphus, whome domesticall strife soone browght to his ende. Altredus folowed hime, who semblablie, after tenne yeare, bie civile discorde, was compelled to forsake the princelie diademe. In his rome entered Ethelbertus, who in shorte time being disturbed from the governance, had to his successor Aswaldus, who likewise with sinistrus fortune obteined the regall sceptre, for after xi. yeares hee was oppressed bie the intestine sedition of the people; bie whose example Osredus the Thirde, which succeeded him, gave himselfe to private life before one yeare weare clearli passed. Finallie Ethelbertus, or rather Adelredus, beinge the xxiiij. and laste from Ida, was bolde to take on him the charge of regalitee, which had benne hurtfull and exitiall to so manie his predicessors. Nether cowld hee avoyde the like destenie, for after the forthe yeare of his reigne he was semblabie murthered of his owne loyals. The regall dignitee laye vacant for a season, no manne daring to arrogate the same enie more, for like unto the owlde Seyans horsse they feared it. This thinge surelie deserved wondrus admiration, sithe noe imperie hathe benne erste so pernicius but that divers men with ambitius desier have affected the same. Thus Northe Humberlande beinge shaken with civil warrs aboove xxx. years, after laye open to the injuries as well of barbarus straungers as evill neighbowrs, for the Danes coming into the Ilond withhelde it, until at the lengthe thei being overcommed, Egbertus, kinge of the Weste Saxons, united it unto his dominion throughe the voluntarie yealdinge of the Northe Humbrians, extinguishinge all dissention, and extirpinge the foreine creweltie, as wee will shew hereafter. Thus the Northe Humbrians ceased to reigne the DCCCXXVIIJ. yeare of our Savior. But afterwarde Alured, as shall be specified in his life, made the Dane Gormon cheefe rewler, and bie that meanes the lande cam againe into the power of barbarus people, which at the lengthe Adelstanus delivered owt of their handds, annectinge it to his owne jurisdiction.

The vij. kingdom was of the West Saxons, which beginne abowte the seventie and one yeare after the arrival of the Englishemenn in this Ile, and the DXXI. yeare of Christe's nativitee, having the originall of Kinge Cerdicius. The bowndes of this kingedom fro the beginning weare not small, for, as wee may well gather bie conjecture, it conteyned so muche as dothe in our dayse the diocesses of Bathe and Wells, Sarisburie, and Excitre. Yet had it in processe greater amplifienge, for the westerne kinges, not satisfied with suche partes of the Ilond as at the first was allotted them, layde claime to the whole monarchie that beefore the Brittons possessed. Cerdicius cumming laste of all others into the Ile, with greate garrisons owte of Germanie, to succorre his confederates, was receaved with sharpe warre, butt with ease hee repressed and putte to flighte the unwildie multitude inordinatlie runninge on himme, which good primitive successe purchased him muche quietnes; for after that daye the beaten Britons weare of lesse corrage to stirre upp warrs; soe that Cerdicius bie littell and litell seasoned on the weaste partes of the Ile, there beginninge his government; and for the same reason was surnamed the westerne kinge; whoe enchroched to him and his posteritee farre the moste faire and ample riolme, well enriched bie himme. After this mann regned his son Cenricus, and consequentlie Ceawlinus, then Celricus, and Ceoloulphus, or Quichelmus, for I finde them bothe written in authors whome I follow, which doe not alltogether agree in the names of suche princes. These two are reported æquallie to have divided the kingdom, and bothe of them justlie and jentlie, with like will and pleasur, to have governed, which thinge is as rare to bee seene as to bee harde, and not easie to be donne; and to this there singuler integritee was adjoyned a Divine grace, for they bothe becam Christian; and, finallie, as they beganne to reyne at once, so they are thought to have ceased and have died aboute one time. Yet Celoulphus, as some others have thought, (whose sentence I refuse not,) did otherwise bothe dispose and end his lyfe, for at the verie beginninge, when as he lay in embushement, awaiting Edwinus, kinge of Northe Humberlande, (as it is specified in his life.) afterwarde encounteringe with him he was slaine. After whome succeded Cinigillus, under whose reigne the westerne people receaved the Christian faithe, throughe the industrie and advertisementes of Berinus, whome the bisshop Honorius at that season sente into the Ilond to preache the Ghospell. This Berinus was an Italian, and the moste hollie father that chaunced within the memorie of manne, who placed the pontificall see firste of all others at Dowrchester, which towne laye vij. miles from Oxforde, which was afterwarde, aboute foure hundred and three score years, bie king William Rufus, translated unto Lincolne. But let us prosecute the premisses. Next unto Cynigillus, Cenovalchius reygned, being vij. from Cerdicius, whoe, at the beginninge of his imperie, might have benne conferred with the baser sorte of princes, but in the ende he might justlie bee compared to the beste; for streyght after the entrie on his dominion hee entred allso a moste filthie trade of livinge; and being well pleased with nothing, least of all with quietnes, he foughte a battayle with Wilferus, the Mercian kinge, of whom being overcommed, he was tasked with the forfature of the Ile of Weighte. Hee neglected relligion; he made a lewde divorcement with his wife, being the sister of Penda, the Mercian kinge, which thinge so fell oute that it was bothe a calamitee and a saftie unto him, for Penda, for the injuries donne to his sister, forthewith assayled himm in fight, and deprived himm of his regall maiestie. Cenovalchius after this foyle fledde unto Annas, kinge of the East Angles. Annas first intertayned the younge manne jentelie, and afterwards blamed him, in that hee hadd so contemned relligion that hee hadd kaste of his wife, that so filthilie he hadd geven himselfe over to uncleanes. Then hee, repentinge his former life, it is not to bee thought how soone hee becamm goode, throwghe the holsome precepte and increpations of Annas. Suche is oure nature, sooner to acknowlege our defawltes in adversitee then in prosperitee. In all haste hee embraced the Evangelicall faythe; he reclaymed his wife; hee beecam more acceptable to Godd, and, consequentlie, soone recovered his whole kingdom: and again, not being unmindefull of suche benefits as hee hadd receaved, as one which dearli loved Godd's honor and glorie, hee builded the sumptuus churche at Winchester, wherin consistethe the see of the bisshop; but that was afterwarde divided, and from thence the busshopricke of Sarisburię was instituted. Thus the kinge, as a manne alltogether fixed on godlines, died, after the xxx. yeare of his reigne. His wife, named Sexburga, rewled allmoste a yeare after, who, allbeit shee was of corage sufficient for the rigiment, yet, being intercepted bie deathe, she cowlde not utter fullie her vertewse. There succeeded to yonge princes, Elcuinus and Centinnus, bothe notable in valiance and armes, for the former miserablie skirged the Mercians, the later afflicted the Brittans with warrs; but the shortnes of their life shadowed the continuance of there fælicitee, for thei hadde unethes reigned ix. years when they departed this life. I finde in somme authors that they reigned in commune, with whome Bedas consensethe not, but affirmeth that thei divided their kingdom. Cedovalla next obteined the realme, being x[th] in thorder of kings from Cerdicius, whoe from the beginninge, being desierus to bee avaunced for his nobel feats, thowght goodd to warre on his borderers, wherfor with speede hee sett on the Sowthe Saxons, and greatlie endamaged them. The Kentishe menne hee oppressed bie the gatheringe of bootie in their territories, howbeit in that conflicte hee loste his brother, named Molo. He entered the Ile of Wight with sharpe hostilitee, insomuche that hee hadd neare destroyed the same. Finallie hee soe bent himselfe towards liberalitee, and deserved soe well of all estates, that all moste a manne cowld nott desier more perfection in one which as yeat was not seasoned with owre relligion. Yet not longe after, desiering to comm into the Christian fowlde, he wente to Rome, whear he was baptized of Bisshop Sergius, and named Peter; and within shorte space he died, and was buried in the churche of Saincte Peeter, prince of the Apostells. Somme menne thincke that he was not baptized of Sergius, but he was beefore becomm Christian, and now, annoynted with the hollie chrisme, as the custom is, chaunged therebie his name; which sentence of divers others is fallsified.

After this mann Inas, as xi. from Cerdicius, was chosen kinge, a mann of great pollicie, and noe lesse valiaunce. Hee, as sone as he hadd aspired to highest type of the weale publique, as a stowt prince, mindinge to attain the commendation of warlike knowlege, with an armie riall hee bidde battayle to the Kentishe menne; but his enimie, all dismayde with this sodaine terror of warre, weare so abhorrent from joyninge hande strokes, that with a great somme of gowlde they rather desiered to fall to composition then to assaye the chaunce of battayle. After these his prosperus exploytes with the Kentishe people, he bent his force on Aldinius, the kinge of Southe Saxons, and enemie to the name of Weste Saxons, whome he easilie overcamme, and enjoyed the riolme of Sowthesax. At the lengthe, havinge wonne renowne bothe at home and abrode, applienge him selfe wholie unto learning, for that he loved in all respectes justice and righteusnes, whan he perceaved the administration of commone wealthes to bee wonderus troblesom, despisnge the porte of a prince, not longe after, accordinge to the precept of Christe, hee tooke upp his crosse and folowed himme. But before the execution of this purpose hee minded to have suffulted and releeved relligion with his goodds, for hee thowght it a moste lewde follie to permitte to an other man's curtisie suche goodds as hee himme selfe, which hadd gotten them, mighte franckelie contrive on suche uses as unto himme weare likinge; whearfore he builded the churche of Wells with great magnificence, and consecrated it to Saincte Andrewe the Apostel, assigninge therin to consiste the see of the busshop, supportinge the same with great possessions. In late memorie there florished a famus college of priestes, menne of honest beehavior, and well learned. Wherefore I accompte it noe small woorshipp that I mie selfe, xiiij. yeares since Archedeacon of Wells, was elected one of that college, and have suche jurisdiction in the dioces of Wells as makethe me muche the better sumtimes; for, having a charge to looke to the good livinge of others, I muste necessarilie prescribe mie selfe suche rule of life, being an overseer, that other menn maye the better measure theirs bie mine. The auncient cittie, Wells, is in the weaste partes of the Ilonde, and situat at the foote of the hill called Mendepius, which from the northe side, like a continuall wall, hangethe over it, verie commodius for the broode and feeding of cattayle; but now to the pretensed matter. This prince builded the churche of Glastenburie, with the abbaye of monachs Benedictines, geving great londes thereunto. But surelie this abbay, bothe for the singuler hospitalitee, and allso for dew observaunce of the monasticall function, excelled all others. Wee made mention in the second booke of this our woorcke that the common brute goethe that Josephe of Aramathie, whoe buried our Lordes boddie, didde founde therin a littel chappel, whearebie I conjecture, in memori therof, that Inas did erect this abbaye in that place. There are lefte in writinge infinite deades as concerninge the goddlie worckes of this kinge. Yeat will I not forgette that he made his realme tributarie to the Busshop of Rome, fininge everie howse at a certaine peece of monie called a pennie. Offa, the Mercian kinge, didde the like, beinge allured, as I thincke, bie his example, whoe reigned not longe after that time. This was the DCCXL. yeare of our Salvation. This tribute, as somme menne write, was encreased bie King Ethelwolphus or Atulphus, who, as shallbee specified in the next booke, obteined all most the monarchie of the whole Ilonde. The whole contrie at this time for devotion and zeal gave to the busshopp this pension of pietie, which was gathered of everie house, and the monie was termed Sainct Peter's pence, which was gathered bie the busshops questor, whoe of good reason was named the collector. I mie selfe bare that office of exaction a certaine years, and for the same cause was mie firste coming into Englonde. But to bee shorte, Inas beinge desierus to dispose in better order his reolme, to the ende he mighte [bring] his subjects to a more blessed trade of livinge, he promulged moste sincere lawes, which of his wicked posteritee weare bie littell and littell disannulled. Finally, partelie at the instigation of his wife Ethelberga, a verie discreete matrone, and partlie havinge tasted more then satietee of worldly things, he resigned the princelie power and diademe to his kinesman Ethellardus, noe doubtte a goodd manne, whome beefore hee hadde made his heyre, which beinge, as somm thincke, he wente to Rome, and there, beinge revestred with habit and orders of a monache, hee died. Queene Ethelburga did semblablie geeve upp the ghoste emong the noonnes of Berching, a village standinge on the bancke of the river Thames. I have nothinge worthie the relacion as towching Ethellardus. Next unto him succeeded Cuthredus, a manne of stowte corrage, whoe beinge endamaged with manie injuries by the Mercians in the beginninge of [his] reigne, insurged mannefullieagainste them, and noblie turned the foyle on their owne neckes; after which time hee was free from externall cares, usinge allwayse the commoditee of peaceable tranquillitee. In this verie time lived a virgin at Oxford named Frideswida, the dowghter of a certayne Duke named Didanus, whome it fortuned that a certaine prince Algarus soe ardentlie loved that he profered to deflowre her, yea, and that which is more, havinge deniall at her handes, he minded to use violence, but almightie Godd, the verie juste revenger of suche villanie, semed not to bee farre absente, for at such time as hee pursewed her, avoyding his temptacion and trecherie, as sone as she hadde recovered the towne, the gate was shutte againste himme, and the sighte of his ieys in the same moment taken from him. But forthewith this meeke virgin, in the beehoofe of Algarus, appeased our Lorde with her prayers, and hee in shorte season receaved againe his sence of seeinge. And for this cause the fame hathe benne that there grewe a certaine opinion in the headdes of suche kinggs as ensewed in soe muche that they feared to entre the cittie of Oxforde; soe easlie is the minde of manne drawne into the fowle lake of fonde superstition. But trewlie in our time Kinge Henrie the viij. rooted this scrupulositee owte of menns brayns, whoe being armed with the shield of goodd conscience marched stowtlie into Oxforde without enie detriment, to the great comforte and gladnes of the beehowlders. There was of late an howse of regular chanons at Oxforde (as menne say) consecrated to Frideswida: but mie pen shall returne fro whence it hath strayed.

Sigibertus did nexte obteyne the kingdom, a manne in domesticall affaires of muche asperitee and tirranie; in forayne matters full of cowardise and slowthe; whoe, beesides that hee wold not geeve eare to his sage counselers, hee did moreover brutishelie slaye one Cumbranus, geevinge to him even from bottom of his harte moste goodlie advertisements; at the which thinge the reste conceavinge woorthie indignation, assembled in conspiracie, and dejected him from his imperiall throne, the first yeare of his reygne. Then Sigibertus (as hee was of timorus disposition) fearinge worser matters bee tooke himselfe to wooddes and forestes, but not bie this meanes coulde hee eschewe the pursute of misfortune, for even there of a most abject slave of this saide Cumbranus was he murthered. Cinevolphus, a noble yowng impe, and discended of the regall stemme, was substitute in his roome, as xv^th^. from Cerdicius. Hee hadde one battayle with Offa, king of the Mercians, wherin hee was inferior, but not greatlie to his losse or damage.

Afterwarde, havinge attayned quietnes, he exiled Cineardus, the brother of Sigibertus, a jollie young manne of handds, for that he hadd him in distruste; whoe, on the other side, not being unmindeful of this injurie, intentive to revengement, not longe after privilie retiered into the contrie with noe small rowte of loste hopes, and findinge the kinge in the house of a certaine noble wooman whose companie he liked well, of a sodayne hee beeset himme rownd abowte. Cinevolphus, amazed at this unhoped danger, commanded the gates to bee shutte in all possible haste, hoping ether to mitigate his enemies with fayre language, or at the leastwise to feare them with his maiestie. But when he understode that nether of them wolde take effect, and that there was noe comforte to escape withowte fightinge, hee, foaming for anger, dasshed open the dores, and russhed on Cineardus, who stode formoste, and allmost wownded himme to the verie deathe.

Thus whiles he had allmoste revenged sufficientlie his deathe which honge over his hedde, hee died in manfull fighte. This heynus offense, when it was once knowne, his companie and servitors, which weare not farre of, hasted to these manquellers, and renewinge this broyle assayed to requite the slaughter of their soveraigne lorde. The contention was mayntayned for a season on the one side for theyr life, on the other for their honor, untill Cineardus, whoe in this calamitee at the leaste hoped for victorie, was slayne fightinge, at whose fall the residew became soe hartelesse and exanimate that fro the firste to the laste they were all slayne. Then was Britrichius created kinge, as xvi[th] in the ordre of kinges from Cerdicius, a quiet and modest manne, and more desierus of tranquillitie then to bee beholdinge to the goddesse Bellona, and for the same cause he marveluslie misdoubted the valiaunce of Egbertus, whoe succeeded him in regalitee, for the blood riall which hadd lineall descent from Cerdicius at that time was soe confuselie disparkeled, that eche manne as hee was moste of puissance and mighte, soe didd he thincke himselfe to have beste titell and clame to the westerne kingdom, in which number was Egbertus. Howbeit hee in deede was of the regall stemme and line; therefore this kinge, to the ende hee mighte live securelie, he banished this springehole as relagate in Fraunce, which thinge he accepted verie pacientlie, as a thinge which hee divined wowlde toorne himm to greate pleasure, as in deade it chaunced in processe of time. Thus Britrichius used securitee untill a certayne number of theevishe Danes arrived in the Ilond at the entrie of the river Humber, firste wastinge on the sea costes, and afterwarde spoylinge and robbinge the inner parties of the contrie. The kinge sente at the first tidinges a good companie of harnised menne to repelle the Danes from their recowrse to theire shippes; whoe when theye espyed the people runninge on all sides, levinge their bootie behinde them, they ranne with all speede to their navewe, and returned thether from whence they camme. But this thinge was the beginninge of a great mischeefe ensewing, for the Danes perceavinge the fertillitee of the soyle, within a litell while camme againe into 'the Ilonde, and waged so longe and sharpe battayle with the Englishe nation till they had possessed a goodd parte thereof, as shall bee made rehersall ellswheare. Britrichius in the xvj. yeare of his reigne, and DCCC. of manns salvation, ended his mortall life; whose deathe beinge in all places divulged, Egbertus coming speedelie into his contrie owte of Fraunce, bie a generall consent was made kinge.

But beefore I entreate of the reste, I thoughte goodd somwhat to say as towchinge the Scottishe estate at that instance of time. After that Ambercletus was slaine in the battayle of the Pictes (of whome wee spake in the ende of our thirde booke), these menne ensewed, Eugenius the vij. beinge his brother, Mordaius, the sonne of Ambercletus, Etfinus; menn as well in there owne nations as other landes perceaving quietnes, and well tried in politique administration: then Eugenius the viij. Fergusius the iij. whoe bothe continuallie weltered and turmoyled in fillthie vices, and bothe weare repaied with dewe penaltie, the one beinge slaine of his daylie wayters, the other of his citizens: after them governed Solvatius and Achaius the sonne of Etfinus. This prince, who merited eternall commendation, fearinge the wealthe and power of the Saxons, which daylie encreased, confedered in league with Charles the great, that they showld mutuallie helpe one an other. Truelie they boste that it was never donne withowte the Divine power of Godde, for as muche as at this presence amitee remaynethe unviolate betweene the Frenche menne and Scotts, soe that the one continuallie agreethe with the other. Som other impute it as remidee for the malice and hatred of there confines and neghbours, and to bee as well common to them bothe against the Englisheman as to the Englisheman against them bothe. Moreover, whearas Charles, mindinge to erecte new Universitees, didd sende for learned menne from all costes of the worlde, this kinge sente unto him Clemens and Ihon, exceading well learned menne, bie whose helpe Charles procured that at Tycinum and at Parris all men shoulde bee instructed in good letters. Then ensewed Convallus the seconde, Dungallus, and Alpinus; who valiantlie prosecuted suche warrs againste the Pictes as weare taken in hande bie Dungallus; but in the ende, infortunatlie bickeringe with them, he was taken prisoner, and withowte all respecte of the princelie maiestie hadde incontinent his hedd striken of with an hatchet, at the which facte his ij. sonne Chennethus takinge great indignation revived the warrs, and ceased not from his purpose beefore he hadd taken Druschenus the kinge of his adversaries, and hadd chastised him with the like severitee. Hee so used the oportunitee of his conquest, that bie litel and litell he hadd neare hande striped the whole stocke of the Pictes. And bie suche meanes the Scottes obteyned a greate while since suche kingdom as they have at this daye in Brittayne; this was the DCCCXL. yeare of our Salvation, and the dccliii. yeare of the reygne of the Pictes. Notwithstandinge, if wee beeleeve som Englishe cronicles, the estate of Pictlande hadd not this ende, for in them it is to be redde, that the Pictes weare not overcommed bie warrs, but bie male engine and treason, for, say thei, their cheefe menne and princes weare, under pretext of civilitee, invited to a sumptuus supper of the Scotts, and there perfidiuslie slayne. This thinge of others is esteemed as a fable, for as muche as it is uncredible that one supper coulde suppe uppe so manie bothe nobles and people. After Chennethus succeded his brother Donaldus; for cause that his sonne Ethus, bie reason of his age, was not meate for the regiment of a weale publique. This man, albeit hee weare dissolute, and for the same cause died of his owne hands when he had raigned vj. yeres, yet in foretime, beinge well helped bie his people, hee urged with battayle the remaynders of the Pictes, whoe beganne yet againe to shake their weapons, and cleane rooted them owte. After this Constantinus and Ethus wear made kings. This laste bie Gregorius was expelled owte of his kingdom, yeat mindinge to recompence this evell deade with goodd woorckes, hee wonderfullie augmented the Scottish welthe, bringinge Irelond under their dominion. Next to Gregorius succeded Donaldus the second, and after Donaldus, Constantinus the thirde, the sonne of Ethus, of whome wee will say more in the life of Edwarde kinge of Englond: but now lett us end this booke.

THE V. BOOKE

OF POLIDORUS VERGILIUS ON THE ENGLISHE HISTORIE.

In our former booke wee entreated of the beginninge of the vii. kingdoms, and of the finall end allso of vi. of them, namelie, of the kingdom of Kent, of Sowth Saxons, of Est Angles, of Este Saxons, of the Mercians, of the Northe Humbrians, allso of the battayles and contention of the kinges; now it remaynethe that we make treatise as touchinge of the Westerne realme, declaringe at what time the other regions weare adjoyned thereunto, that finallie bothe the order of the kinges and the discourse of matters incident may eche wheare bee correspondent. Egbertus, a man of great hope and singuler vertewe, as we mencioned erewhiles, bie the common assent havinge the suffrages of the people and princelie crowne, beganne moste prosperuslie to use this obteyned dominion as a mann well skilled in the warlike knowledge; for while in his exile he sojorned in Fraunce, hee labored that science, and employde the feates of warre, wherfore at the verie beginninge of his governinge he daunted the Brittons, that is, the Wallshemenn, whoe as yeat greatlie desierus of libertie, whense enie small occasion offred it selfe thie slipped from the Englishe nation and made daylie incursions on them, as they who albeit bie all meanes they weare vanquished yeat bie noe means wowlde they seeme to be overcomed; when with noe lesse fœlicitee then celeritee hee hadd achieved this exployte throwghe the fame of the facte, throwghe autorite and renowne, hee florished and was a terror to the borderinge princes; for thei perceaving him to bee suche an one in martial facultee had this conceit, that even allreadie in harte he was in the middeste of their treasurie. This thinge especiallie pricked the conscience of Bertulphus, a moste stoute kinge of the Mercians, whoe notwithstandinge he understode howe daungerus a matter it was to cope with so puissant a prince, and one that was soe skillful in fighte, yeat knowinge it to bee muche more honorable valiantlie to die then shamfullie to live, hee minded to have adoe with Egbertus, and indeade spedelie raunginge his armie, hee bidde himme battaylle. The westerne lustie prince made noe refusall, but speedelie leadinge his companie as it weare in a ringe, sett upon his adversaries: the fighte was continued sharpelie on bothe sides in doubtefull balance; at the lengthe the Mercians, who weare weried with their longe jornie and skirmishinge, beeganne a littell to geeve backe, which thinge as soone as the westerne menne perceaved, in greater thronge and violence thei pursewed the repulse and committed great slaughter. Egbertus, bie the gettinge of this victorie, gathered suche stomacke and hope that hee perswaded himselfe that verie easlie hee mighte subdewe his neighbor, well perceavinge their estate to encline towardes ruine; and beefore all others he minded to invade the Kentisshe kinge Ethelwolphus, a manne surelie of smalle name and lesse æstimation in Kente. Wherefore, enteringe his teritories with an armie riall, finding noe mann a great while that wowlde withstande, hee didd on all sides destroy the region, deliveringe all the villages to be spoyled and sacked to his soldiers. Ethelvolphus, whoe had small affiance in his owne power, astonished with the sodaine commotion of soe strange broyles, was soe farre from enie affection to fight, that (as somme menne wright) he fledde in haste, ever afterward banishinge himme selfe. Butt others have lefte in memorie (with whome I rather agree) that he with all celerite, gatheringe the beste rowte of menn that he coulde, didd righte manfullie encounter with his enimie, and was taken prisoner while hee skirmished valiauntlie; but, howsoever the game wente, soe it fell owte that Egbertus conquired, and possessed the

Kentishe kingdom. Thus the welthe of the Westerne people wonderuslie increased, and they beecam terrible to there confines, so that all menne the more easlie becam obeysaunt and servisable to Egbertus; who, to the intente he might allso abate the strengthe of the Mercians, he wiselie pricked forward the East Angles, (whose amitee and societie he hadde a littell beefor confirmed bie league,) that with an armie they showlde make irruption into Mercia, which thinge they weare nothing lothe to doe, bothe to thende thei mighte satisfie the expectation of the kinge, and allso bie cause they wolde revenge suche injuries as latelie they hadd susteined of the Mercians, whoe but a few dayes beefore hadd annoyed their borderes with incursions. In this skermishe, albeit it was exceadinge daungerus, yeat was Bernulphus, the Mercian kinge, slaine at the firste conflicte; within a littell space after, they beinge pricked on bothe sides with two stinggs, the one of wrathe the other of hatred, theye bickered againe, and in that conflicte Ludicennus the successor of Bernulphus was slayne. Thus, when the force of the Mercian realme was appaired, Egbertus in open field sett uppon Uthlacus who succeded Ludicenus and toke him prisoner, yokinge hime with captivitee. The Northe Humbrians, as menne all amazed at suche successe in all thes affayres, weare soone dejected from theyre estate, and weare more desierus to yeald them selves then ether to suffer or to prove the weapons and powre of their enemies; but rather ether expelling or sleaing their kinges and renowncinge the yoke of the Danes as menne weried and afflicted with domestical dissention, and tormented with the oppressions of aliens and straungers, they sent ambassadours to Egbertus concerning their voluntarie yealdinge, surrendering to his faythe and tuicion townes, citizens, lands, and goods, private and commune. Kinge Egbertus cureteuslie receaved this yealdinge, bidding them to have goodd hope, promising moreover that they shoulde never more bee tormented with the injuries of forreiners. Thus in fine the noble reame of Northe Humberland camme into the jurisdiction of the Westerne princes.

Yeat are there which write otherwise as touching the endinge of that kingdom, sayeng that the Westerne monarch chalenged in battayle Ethelbertus or Adelredus the laste North Humbrian kinge, and that hee being overthrowne, and his contrie cam bie that means in subjection, which I cannot thincke to bee muche untrewe if the computation of time were agreeable, for, as we mencioned in our laste book, it is evident that there weare thirtie years betweene the kinges and the time that Egbertus tooke possession of Northe Humberlande. At the same verie season Egbertus beerefte Juthredus kinge of East Saxons of his imperie. Bie this meanes the happie condition of the West Saxons soe daylie encreased bie the unitinge of three most riche and frutefull riolmes, that the residewe of the Ilond (allwayse exempting Scottelond), that is to saye, the monarchies of Mercia and the East Angles, weare of non accompt or valewe, but as thinges which, thretened with ruine, wold shortelie fall into handdes of Westerne menn; as indeade not longe after it chaunced, according to the expectation of Egbertus, whoe as a man whoe thowghte himme selfe all in all, partelie that bie the extinguishinge of the Brittishe name his fame mighte eternallie bee engraved in the region, partelie that all the people might have the use of one onlie name, and one kinde of lawe, hee firste termed Brittaine Englond, and the whole multitude Englishemenne, bie proclamation streightlie enjoyning that it showlde soe continuallie endure. After all these things, this wise prince, beinge nothinge the more puffed with pride for so fortunate successe, (which is wonte easlie to enhaunce menn's mindes,) was of equall clemencie, grace, liberalitee, towards all degrees, and moste studius of peace and tranquillitee, till in the lengthe the Danes did crewellie disturbe the godlie quietnes of this contrie (for suche are humaine affaires that in everie minute of an howre they are subjecte to sixe hundred casualtees). These menne, with a navie like pyrats abowte the sea, and being driven to the shores of the Englishe ocean, thei tooke the londe, and beeganne to season on botie; which thinge beinge once manifested, the kinge assemblinge a fewe soldiers, (as it is the guise in sodaine tumultes,) proceadeth to meate them as rovers, and, finding them withoute all order, sette uppon them. The fighte in the beeginning was more adverse and perilos to the Englishe menn; yet the kinge urged his people, bothe with remembraunce to fighte stoutelie, and allso used the rehersall howe fowle a shame it weare that they showlde be overcomme of theeves and robbers, who hadd overthrowne divers kinges. In the meane season, the Danes perceavinge howe harde it was to resiste, and that there was noe hope to werie their enemies, they lifted upp their corage, and dubbelled their force, and, sleainge on all sides, thei beesett Egbertus rownde abowt; but the night drewe on, wherefore the kinge, whoe was in great dispayre of his life, with a smalle number fownde the meanes, with mutche to doo, to flie. The Danes, albeit they understode them selves to bee superiors at that presence, yeat, fearinge close embushements in a londe so abownding in hostilitee, they ceased to chase enie farther. The Westerne kinge, beinge nothinge appalled with the detremente of that nighte, wherin he hardelie escaped daunger of deathe, forasmuche as divers remained unhurte at that conflicte, he gathered together and refresshed the relliques of the disparckeled armie; and manie beesides, heeringe of this unluckie conflicte, armed themselves forthe with, and voluntarilie drewe unto the kinge, wherfor, beinge furnished with a sufficient bande, he browghte them forthe into playne fielde, and geevinge them battayle againe, he putt them to flight with oute enie great travaile, being allredie spente with foraine contencions. Somme of the Danes weare there slayne; somm others escapinge to their shippes, didde adventure themselves to the windes. After this victorie Egbertus, whome the sownde glorie of vertewe made coequall with the Godds, whoe in moste ample wise hadde enlarged the seelie littell kingdom, which at the firste hee receaved, didde departe owt of his mortall life the xxxvij. yeare of his reigne, and the DCCCXXXVIIJ. of our Salvation. Hee lefte behinde him his young sonne Ethelwolphus, whoe succeaded himme. His father, well knowing how it beehoved a prince (that would deserve commendation) to be stowte, righteous, severe, grave, of haute courage, liberall and beneficent, did soe instructe him from a childe that righte well hee merited this prayse and honour, whoe, moreover, was from the beginning addicted to relligion, havinge the orders of a subdeacon; but shortlie after, bie the authorite of Leo the Romayne busshop, hee was losed of that bandde, and espoused a moste excellent virgin named Osburga.

Beefore wee proceade to write enie more of this mann, wee thincke it convenient to write of the originall of the Danes, whoe, issueinge owte of their contrie, somtimes like theves, bie wastinge of there teritories, and overthrowe of howses, somtime bie the verie rightes of warre, soe afflicted the Englishe nation that in conclusion they obteyned a kingdom in the Ilonde. But more of thease thinges in more convenient place. Now wee will make discourse of the principles of this so feerce a nation.

The Gothes, a most cruell kinde of Germanians or Scithians, (for in that poynct writers doe not agree emong them selves,) of auncient authors weare otherwiles termed Getes, otherwhiles Danes. Emonge the rest Strabo, in his vij[t] booke of Geographie, asseverethe the Danes to have a divers contrie from the Getes, and that the Danes possessed places more adjoininge to the middell of the soyle land bendinge towards Germanie, and nearer to the fownteines of the river Ister, in antique yeares being caulled Dawin; but the Getes to be more nerelie planted to the sea and east partes; wherfore the Getes and Danes seeme to bee all one nation, and onlie to bee dissevered in habitation, for as muche as according to his testimonie thei bothe hadde the use of one language. These menne hadde peace graunted them of Augustus, and weere prohibited in enie wise to passe the river Danubius, or Dunoise, who, not longe after, breakinge this inhibition, and exceading the prescribed limits, of two Romayne capitanes, first Oppius Sabinus, then in the time of Domitian of Cornelius Fuscus, being sent to acquite that trespase, weare, with all there garrisons, clerelie confounded and destroyed;

after that the Emperour Trajanus drave them owt of the Romaine bowndes into their owne costes, with noe small scathe and affliction. Then Antonius, surnamed Caracalla, conductinge an armie againste the Parthians, assayled of a sodaine and plagued the Danes, for that thei semed not contented with enie kinde of tranquillitee; and in processe Gordianus the younger abated their pride, while they endevored noveltees and immutation. After this there ensewed more troblesom tempestes with this generation of vipers, for under the empire of Philippus, whoe was the first christened of the Romaine emperors, manie wilde contries, transgressing the Romaine prescriptes, didd tumultuuslie annoye Thracia and Lysia, at the which time, or at the least not longe after, when as fatallitee drewe the pompe of the Romaine glorie towardes the laste date, these dregges and abjection of all menne burste forthe into all partes of the worlde in greate assembles; for the Gothes invaded Asia, having firste wasted Bithinia, with noe small portion of Macedonia and Thracia. At the lengthe Claudius the Seconde, Emperowre of Rome, browght allmoste to extremitee these slavishe rovers in Misia, sleainge and apprehendinge three thowsande of them. Yet weare they not greatlie quiet enie weare, butt afterward stirring in commotion, in mayne fighte weare vanquished of Aurelianus beeyonde Dunowe at the firste battayle. Thus in fine the Gothes, beinge tormented with so manie overthrowes, didd longe absteyne from bickering, till they weare conquered and put to flighte of the Hunnes, at suche time as the Emperowre Valens obteined the governement of the este partes. This people, notwithstandinge at the first thei weare called Gothes, yet, bie reason that of owlde historiens they weare som time called Getes, somtime Danes, it is not to be dowbted but that the Getes and Danes weare the cheefest people which, under the conduite of the Gothes, invaded the Romaine bowndes, under the reigne of Philippus; and, consequentlie, it is justlie thought that they beinge beaten out of their owne possessions, while thei serched newe places of abode, at the last rested in the northe partes of

Germanie, naming it Dacia, or Denmarcke, accordinge to their owne appellation. This parte beinge extended into the ocean, like a mann's arme, hathe the forme of Cheronesus, or of an halfe Ile. And, least the name of Getes and Danes shoulde bee dissevered from the Gothes, they are reported to have termed an Ile in the ocean sea (not far from Denmarcke, lienge towardes the sterre called the beare) bie there owlde name Gothia, which peradventure other then presentlie or after thei possessed: soe that as well this place as that same Cherronesus is inhabited of them; and, the olde name being cleane inveterate and exchaunged throughe their dominion, it is called Dacia, or Denmarcke. Trulie the Cumbrians, whome Caius Marius overcam longe since, withhelde this londe, which allmost was never inhabited of one onlie people, wherebie I suppose the auncient name to have perished, for the old contrie of Dacia was neare unto the Pannonians, now called Hungariens, and at this daye is termed Valachia, bie reason that the Danes, beinge expelled from thence to serche newe places, the Romaine colonie was sente thether as planted in theire roomes, for Valach in their speeche signifieth Italion. Of theis Valachians there were two contrarie factions, that 's to weete, beetweene the people called Dragulæ and the Danes; but the Dragulions beinge farre to weake for the Danes, within the remembraunce of our fathers, browghte in the Turckes into theier londe, whoe hadde allmoste overrunne the Danes, but they weare restored againe bie Ihon Huniades, the father of Matthias kinge of the Pannonians, whoe delivered them from the Turckes to their owne liberties and Christian name. Herebie wee maye easlie discerne whoe are the right Danes, and that wee oughte not to call them Danes which inhabite Cherronesus in Cimbria, consideringe that they as yeat remaine in Valachia, but rather those whoe, being tossed and disturbed owt of their contrie, didd finallie repaire in that forsayde peece of an Ilond; which thinge, even bie this example, may bee prooved, biecause that the lorde of that region in his title and charters pronowncethe himselfe not Danorum rex, but Dacorum, which thing noe doubt ministerethe error to those that intermeddell with the histories of the borderers of that ocean; and, amonge all other, Saxo Grammaticus, a coronographer of the gestes of that nation, is especiallie deceaved, if the booke which is sette forthe bee not mervayluslie fallse. Wherefore, lest wee semblablie showlde wander in the same erroneus shippe, I thowght not goodd in this point to followe suche authors. But now more of our purpose. This fierce people, which now borderethe on the Germian ocean, which in auncient years lived beyonde the river Ister, beinge dayle more and more overcharged with their owne multitude, soe longe with continuall warrs and incursions persecuted the Englisshemenne; for the ocean makethe noe great distance betweene England and Denmarcke; that in conclusion they gatte the better handde. Let this compendius brigement suffice as towchinge the originall of the Danes.

Now let us returne to Ethelwolphus. This moste redoubted prince, (who was comparable to his father,) as one whome nature did fabricate and bringe forthe as an image of humanitee and justice, did regarde nothinge in the world so mutche as without intermission to deserve well of his subjectes, allwaies preferring suche unto administration as were juste and equall dealers: a great peece of the occasion thereof weare Sainct Swithinus and Adelstanus, at that verie time menne of sincere livinge and grate wisdom, and of the kinges preevie councell, bie the meense wherof æquitee and tranquillitee flowrished echewhere, untill an huge number of Danes departinge owte of their contrie wandered for prayes abowte the Ilond, plaginge the inhabitants with a thowsand evels; for remedie of the which injuries, the kinge was necessarilie driven to use the ministerie of weapon, which naturallie hee abhorred, and oftentimes sharpelie persecuted themme; nevertheles, these wicked rascalls rinning hither and thether like the savage beaste, and exercising crueltie towards all sorts and contries, didd especiallie depopulate the fruitfull province of Kent. Howbeit, finallie they weare driven owte, laden with noe small store of bootie. The king, after his deliverie owte of trouble, for devotion wente to Roome, wheare, beinge jentellie entreated of Leo the forthe busshoppe of that name, hee made all that parte of the reallme tributarie to the see of Rome which his father Egbertus had annexed to his native inheritance, folowinge the example of Inas, as beefore we mencioned, and made a lawe that they whose possessions soever admounted to xxx[d]. or hadd divers howses, they showlde paye a pennie for everie one which they inhabited yearlie to the Romaine busshop at the feaste of Sainct Peter and Powle, or at the uttermost at Lammas, which lawe somme menn falselie do attribute to his sonne Alured; this was the yeare of our Lorde DCCCXLVII. He is reported to have re-edified a certaine schoole at Rome, which was nearlie consumed with fier a littell before his cominge to the cittie; the same was firste of all erected bie Offa kinge of the Mercians; but that schole at Rome, wherin onlie Englishemenn sojornied in their studdies and litterature, I suppose to have stoode even in that place wheare the hospitall dedicated to Sainct Thomas consistethe, whereunto the Englishe people have accesse and succoure. Kinge Ethelwolphus, after hee hadd made his abode at Rome the greatest parte of the yeare, he reversed homewarde, showinge him to all his not onlie a mercifull prince, but allso a verie patrone and father, referring all things to the supportinge of honestie and mayntayninge of modestie. Hee beegat bie his wife Osburga these sonnes, Ethelbaldus, Ethelbertus, Ethelredus, and Alfredus, or otherwise Aluredus, all yonge men of no lesse excellencie in disposicion then comlines in beawtie, whome hee procured to bee fostered in good arts, yeat nothinge he more endevored then that they showlde beecom bownteus and large in geevinge; for this most prudent prince well perceaved that there coulde none so fowle and unseemelie a vice beefall to a kinge as avarice, which commonlie goethe not unaccompanied, being the novice of all crimes, which, if it showlde be in a ruler, it most neades creape throughe and devowre the substance of manie. Wherefore thease rioll impes, being well informed of their parent, not unworthilie everie of them reigned after his decease. Ethelwolphus, temperinge all things with this sobrietee and integritee, was attainted with an easie sicknes, and nevertheles died therof the xx. yeare of his reign; his corpes was carried to Winchester, and there, with honorable buriall, intumiled. At that verie time there florished iij. virgins of moste pure and clene life, Modevena, in Ireland, Achea and Ositha in Englonde; this laste was tormented unto deathe of the Danes: the two others never felte the deadlie dartes of frowning fortune; yeat as well Modevena and Achea, as this innocent martir Osithe, weare in time enumered emonge the Saincts. Ethelbaldus bie succession hadde the monarchie as xix^t. from Cerdicius, wherin hee persisted onlie the space of v. monethes, for hee sodainlie falling into a fever died thereof, leving his diademe as dewe to Ethelbertus, a mann moste worthie of his father, grandfather, and suche his noble predecessors. Streyghte after the beginninge of his dominion, the Danes in greate rowtes made irruptions in the Ilond, and raunginge throwghe the province of Kente, they aggreeved the inhabitantes with infinite mischeves; with whome the kinge, not longe after, valiantlie encounteringe, did not leave to persecute them till after miserable occision he skoureged them all owte of this region; which thinges prosperuslie achieved this prince, revolving daylie with him selfe thinges of great importaunce, and conducible to the quiet estate of his contrie, hee was prevented of forecast bie the immaturitie of his deathe, skarcelie having accomplished the v^t. yeare of his reigne. Then was Ethelredus the brother of Ethelbertus created kinge as xxi. from Cerdicius, beinge a manne at home meake and affable, whoe bie his gracius behavior and renowne alluered the hartes of all menn to frindeship and benevolence; but abrode and in externall affayres hee was not soe, for, in that he was skilfull in the warlike sciens, hee executed all things with severitee, bie that meanes being noe lesse famus in quiet tranquillitee then tempestuus warrs; albeit bie the Divine power it was denied him to remaine longe ether in peace or in this life; for hee lived skarce vi. yeares, and all that space was tossed with the waves of continuall battayle; for the Danes, longe beefore having triall in the fertilitee of the Ilonde, didde often carrie greate store of bootie owt of the same, som times bie stelthe, somtimes bie open warrs: endevoringe soe to infringe and weaken the power thereof, that at the lengthe they might with facilitee obteyne dominion therein, insomutche that, daylie echewheare makinge troblesom invasions, they disturbed greevuslie the estate thereof. Wherfore Ethelfredus joyned oft in battayle with them, allbeit with variable and divers fortune; wherbie the Danes conceavinge victorie in their mindes, when they coulde perceave noe cause whie they showlde enie more use the matter like pickinge and tumultuus rovers, thei gatheringe a mayne armie minede to invade the Ilonde; wherefore within short time there kinge Inarus, with a great navie, arrived at the entrie of the river Humber, and, minding as it weare to contende for deathe and life, entred into the contrie with open profession of hostilitee. The kinge in the meane season beinge in noe poincte of lesse industrie, made expedition towards that place wheare hee understoode that his enemies weare encamped, and as soone as hee hadd them in sighte he sett forthe his menn, and thus placed them in order: In the lefte winge he assigned a parte of his trowpe of horssmenn, with all suche as weare ordeyned for succowrs, over whome he made governer his yonger brother Alured, a mann of singuler vertewe, at whose countermaunde he commaunded all the centuriens to bee readie; in the right winge he appoynted the residew of the horsemenne, with a likelie companie of archers, with the floure of the youthefullest footemenne, where himselfe was in riall presence. Whilest the Englishe armie thus marched towards the battaile, the Danes, in whome was noe lesse crooked corage then regarde of their doinges, after they weare in goodd araye thei approched nearer, and the onset bieng blowne at one time on ether side, they rushed feercelie to geether and exercised varietee of fighte. But when the Englishe people perceaved that there enimies camm on in greate thronge with there deadlie weapons, and in suche sorte that it was not easie for them to withstande in æquall condition, as warie warriors, and well inured in suche traine bie theire former fightes, thei didd a littell abate their force, standing stille even to middest of them, that bie the favoringe of their brethe and strengthe the reste mighte drawe neare, and that the heate of their enemies might waxe somwhat cowlde: thus ceasing for a season, thei reiterated the rase and ranne speedelie on their enemies. Nether didd the Danes wante this feate, whoe, keaping their order, sustained quietlie the violence of the Englishemen, and after while with brighte swordes thronged forwarde; the whole companie of the archers put them selves in the fore froonte, then hurtelinge rownde, was soe boysterus that unethes the Englishe soldiers cowlde abide it, but, geeving somwhat backe, beeganne to determine of flienge, which when the kinge perceaved, hee planted all his horsemen in convenient roome to breake this sharpe assaulte. The Danes not stirringe owte of their places, sumwhat repressed their rage, soe didd all the Engleshmen, for that the nighte drew faste on, which noe doubte was acceptable to both parties, for they hadd continued the fight from morening unto the eveninge, which departed the skirmishinge of the lefte winge, whereunto manie that were sore traveled and wearie did resorte; and the multitude of dead carkases did on eche parte hinder there fightinge; wherfore the retrayte, which was blowne on ether side, was easlie hardde, especialli of the Englishemenn, to whome it was verie commodius, for theye so hardlie resisted that alreadie it was bruted that they weare overcommed, soe that allmoste the Mercians, at the exhortacions of the Northhumbrians, weare readie to rebell. All that night the Danes were verie circumspecte and carefull, knowinge that in the contrie of an enemie they muste either vanquishe or die; they refresshed there traveled bodies with meate, they gathered the deadd corpses together, they cuered the woonded, and tooke reste themselves; the Englisshe people, on the other side, which that daye weare allmoste overthrowne, prepared freshe aides, for all men repayred on all sides to releeve there frindes, and the daye followinge, the wether waxing clere, when manie newe soldiers weare thrust in the place of suche as weare tyered, with haute corage they hasted to battayle; nether weare there adversaries behinde hand, albeit that they weare overlabored with forreine warrs, and nothing increased sithe the laste conflicte; wherfore, renewinge the olde contention, they bickered, but nothing in æquall sorte; for the deathe of Ivarus, whoe was slaine at the first encounter, so appalled the stomacks of the Danes, that forthewith they put them selfe to flighte, and a great number of them weare slaine beefore that they cowlde attayne to enie saftie; then immediatlie they assigned for their capitans the two brothers, Agnerus and Hubo, (of whome wee made mention beefore,) whoe greatlie indevored the renewinge and furniture of the armie. These thinges agree not with the opinion of Saxo Grammaticus, whoe affirmethe that Iuarus, when he cowlde nott obteine his purpose in a lion's skinne, he putte on the kase of a foxe, that is to saye, when with strength he cowlde not prevayle, with sublitee and disceyte hee assayled his enemie. Moreover, as the same mann purportethe, Iuarus, after peace made with the Englishe nation, obteined soe muche londe as hee cowlde compasse with an horsse skinne, and cuttinge the same into small thonges, semed to have encroched a place sufficient wherin hee mighte build a fayre cittee, and consequentlie fallinge againe to the owlde warrs, bie that meanes becamme a great lorde in the soyle; but within two yeares followinge hee was necessarilie driven to returne home for the appeasinge of certaine broyles and tumultes, leavinge Agnerus as a garrison for the Ilonde. Saxo recitethe noe name of this cittie soe sodaynlie erected bie Ivarus, but surelie the towne named Dongcaster semethe to have derived the name of som suche means, for caster in the owlde speeche signifiethe a cittee, and what a thonge is eche man knoweth; and for as muche as in our tongue, T is commonlie used for D, Dongcaster maye have the name thereof compounded, or at the leaste wise it shall bee lawfull for us soe to gesse. But againe to our matter: Ethelredus, notwithstandinge hee hadde obteyned so worthie a victorie, yeat nothinge contemninge or neglectinge the power of his adversaries, did omitte noe oportunitee of administringe the residewe of his affayres, and soe muche the rather, biecause hee was donne to understande that daylie an infinite nomber of people hadde recourse into the Ilond for to aide there natives. The Danes havinge restored there armie the xv[t]. daye after ther overthrow, coped againe with the Englishe people with suche assured hope that they so putte them to flighte that it was to bee feared leaste this weare the laste day that the Englishemenne showlde be able enie more to matche with them. The armie which hadde conquered bie and bie securlie beetoke them to spoyle, destroyeng all things rownde abowte them; and, while that freelie they raunged throughe the fieldes of their adversaries, they sodaynlie fell into an embushement which Ethelredus hadd layde for them, gathering to gather certaine of his disparckeled companie. There was noe small slaughter of the Danes, which ranne away; nether was the Englishe parte free from bloodeshedde, emong whome Ethelredus himselfe was wownded, with the torment whereof hee shortlie died. This was the vj[t]. yeare of the reigne of Ethelredus, whose noble gestes weare soe renowned that bie his unripe deathe hee seemed to have donne noe great harme, especiallie seing that in his dethe bedd hee resigned the charge of the realme to his brother Alured, a manne of æquall vertewse unto him, and one whome in fore times hee hadd made heir apparent. Aluredus, at the verie firste entringe on his dominion, for the performance of his vowe, wente to Rome, where he was againe crowned of Hadrianus the ij. Busshop of Rome, the DCCCLXXIJ. of our Salvation; wherfore it cannot agree that hee showlde receave this honor of Leo the iij. as som, mistaking the time, have left in writinge. The Danes rested not thus, but hastelie entered into Mercia, beereving kinge Bertulphus of his imperie; yet not longe after they wear expelled of

Burthredus, whome, not withstanding, in small time recoveringe, they dispossessed of his regalitee; and beinge nowe lorde of Mercia, thei made Ceovolphus kinge, as rehersall was made in our former booke, and, consequentlie, settinge on the Northe Humbrians, they overcamme them, beinge for feare enclosed in the citte Yorcke, sackinge and racinge allso the towne. With these fortunate exploytes they weare so puffed uppe that finallie thei subdewed the East Angles, sleainge there moste hollie prince Edmundus, apoyntinge as kinge one of their owne capitans, named Guthormus, after whome succeaded Ericus, whome for his crewel governinge in fine the Englishemenne didde slea. Thus all this season the Danes with held Mercia, and the Est Angles didde kast all kinde of wayse howe they might vanquishe the Weste Saxons, the encrease of whose power and welthe didd greatelie greeve them. Aluredus was a man as worthie to be praysed in forreyne affayres as to bee mervayled at for his domesticall ordinaunces, of great witte and highe wisdom: to himme all thinges weare full of difficultee at the beginning of his regiment, and afterward verie laborius, yeat full of prosperus successe.

The Danes, above all others, didd greatlie envie the manifolde vertewse of the prince, and ernestlie desiered in all haste to oppresse himme, for onne a time, he being in a certayne mansion of his, neare unto London, mindinge to recreate himselfe with huntinge, the Danes loyteringe in London weare certified that thei hadd oportunitee to destroye theire enemie, wherfore they hasted thither with a goodd companie of harnised menne, and sodainelie beeset the kinge within the walles of his manowre. The Englishe knightes, being sodainlie astonished at the chaunce, beinge few in number, woulde have perswaded the kinge to take flighte whilest that thei russhed foorthe; but hee, thinckinge that it wolde be opprobrius unto him, as a thinge scarslie feat, and unfittinge to the regall maiestie, delibered to withstande the adventure, and, indeede, metinge with them, whoe thronged in heddlonge, foughte righte noblie; but when he perceaved bothe himselfe and his menne to bee on all sides invironed, then at the laste, allbeeit sore against his wille, he put himselfe to escape; yeat didde hee not seeke dennes, or lurckinge places, but, like a rioll capitaine, levinge the rage of his adversaries beehinde his backe, with expedition hee gathered a bande of menne and mette with the Danes, who, hering of the assemblie of their enemies, not daring to comm abrode, retired againe to London, and, greatlie fearing the puissaunce of the kinge, beganne with embassage to treate of peace. The conditions weare, that with robberies, or hostile incursions, thei showlde never after moleste the westerne kingdom, and for the better perfowrmance of their bargaine they showlde geeve hostages. Somm write that the lawse of peace weare cheefelie that the Danes showlde departe owte of the Ilond, never more to retowrne, which indead was nether trewe, nether yeat perfowrmed, for havinge all readie incroched ample dominion, they wowlde not have soe donne, except verie extremitee hadd compelled. The king made noe refusall of thease conditions, as one that detested battaile in comparison of honeste quietnes, that, ceasing from martiall affayres, hee might noe lesse establishe with lawse then garnishe with letters his contrie, which as yeat weare verie geyson therein. Wherfore, takinge their pledges, he was willing to make composicion with his enemies: allbeit but for a littel season it tooke effect, for the Danes, which cownted allwais their commoditee to bee preferred beefore their relligion or promisse, shortelie after removing from London, in great jornies wente to Exciter, and bie force toke the citte. Exciter is a cittee in the countie of Devonshier, planted in an highe place, westwarde, havinge the river Exis ronninge bie, wherof it hathe the name, and is three miles distant from the sea; which horrible trespasse, as sone as Aluredus knewe, afflictinge the hostages with condigne punishment for the breche of the covenaunte, hee marched towardes his perfidius foes. The Danes weare not awares of the kinges cominge, and whether it weare that they minded to werie himme with persewing them, or that in deade they weare dismayde, leavinge

Excester, they retiered spedelie towardes London, and at xvij. miles of, at Chipenham, which is a village neare to Bristowe, they pitched their tentes, and there casting a trenche, thei fenced themselves. The towne of Bristow is situat at the flowinge place of the river Severne, westwarde, and hathe runninge neare unto it the river Havon, wherin the greater sorte of vessels have accesse thereto; which thing being intimated to the kinge, he turned owte of the waye, and plantinge his pavilions neare to his adversaries, with revilinge and reproches they weare provoked to fighte. The clamor waxed great on bothe sides that eche mann showlde to armowre. The Danes, who knewe that there was noe waye but ether to fyghte or to die, mad no tarienge in the case. The Englishemenn, without standerd, went hedlonge to the battayle, and, albeit, they weare owte of ordre, and fewer in nombre, yeat with suche impetuus violence they sett on there enemies that the verie animositee and corage was a terroure unto them; but afterwarde, being skattered emonge thicke rowtes of their adversaries, perceivinge that there was small succoures in soe small a nomber, thei beeganne to loke backe one on an other, and, beinge repelled on all sides, thei gathered into a rownde clustre, which, albeit it was the wisest councell, yeat the Danes being instante and feerce on all hands, they weare driven into suche a streyghte that scarcele they hadde enie roume to beestirr them with their weapons; yet, standing as it weare in this rownde globe, they browght to deathe manie of the Danes, and emong them was Hubo, the brother of Agnerus, and manie other capitains of approved magnanimitee. In conclusion, the Englishe warriers, whoe were compased with their adversaries as it weare with a garelonde or crowne, and smitten downe on all sides bie maine strengthe, burste forth and repayred to their tentes. This battayle was soe æquallie fowghte on bothe sides that noe mann cowlde discriee ether who departed conqueror, or whoe was vanquished. They committed the wownded persons to the leches, and suche as weare deade they buried; the Danes didd especiallie with honorable sepulture prosecute the corps of Hubo, which beinge finished, thei beganne to goe forwarde with their pretenced jornie, and camme to Abyndon, a village neare to Thames, distant xlv. miles from London, and there placed there pavilions: the Englishe menn weare allso immediatelie, and pitched there tents faste bie their enemies. In the meane season, the brute wente in eche coste that Aluredus was profliged of the Danes, for that bie littell and littell hee, coolinge the heate of the fighte, retrayted his menne to their pavilions: which thinge toorned to his great commoditee, for divers menne swarmed in the waye of succoure to the kinge. Aluredus, the nexte daye after his comminge thether, broughte his aydes into the maine campe; nether didd his enimies make delays, but manfullie susteyned the warres which sharpelie they hadde taken in hande, and, unitinge there whole assemble, did never fight with greter companie or bolder corage, for this contention was maintained with suche flaminge ire on bothe parties, that there was not a darte throwne on ether side; they beganne the battayle with brighte swordes, and worthile enduered the same, the condition thereof persevered soe doubtfull and uncertaine, that they semed not nowe to have adoe with the Danes whome they hadde eftesons foyled and overthrowne, but with som newe and straunge nation. There was not once thincking of flighte on ether parte, in so mutche that soone they drewe towardes the uttermoste poincte of their travell and daunger, for the horsemen on bothe sides leaving their horsses assayed to fighte on foote. Nowe didde the redde bloode flowe in stremes on the grownde. Now didde the huge heapes of dedd carckases hinder these undaunted warriors that allwayse fowght on æquall hande; now in there fierie mindes they often sighed that the daye was not perdurable accordinge to there stomaches. What showlde I saye? the night repressed necessarilie their rage, which never didd intercepte a more noble or glorious fight within the memorie of manne, and all this while was it unknowne which waye the victorie did encline, soe victoriuslie did ether armie supporte the warres on æquall balance: yea, it is lefte in writinge, that within the revolution of that yeare, beetweene the Engleshe people and the Danes, there weare vii suche battayles performed of like glorie and semblable ende on ether side. At the lengthe, when their force and puissaunce was indifferentlie abated on bothe partes, thei easlie drew to agreement and made these covenantes, that the Danes showlde cleane desiste from warre, nether attempting in fight, nether entrapping in treason the Englishemenn, never more sendinge for freshe soldiers owt of Denmarcke into the Ilonde. Somm there are which write, that accordinge to their agreement all the Danes did againe fleete into their contrie; which, as it is falselie affirmed of the writers, soe was it never done of the Danes. This was the vth yeare of the reigne of Aluredus, in the which the Danes, as they weare accustomed, passed the winter at London.

But now I muste somewhat declare as towchinge the comminge of Rollo into Englond, and afterward into Fraunce, of whome the Dukes of Normandie hadde their originall (whoe afterwarde possessed this realme), that the historie may proceade in dewe ordre. Rollo beinge a Dane, borne abowte the DCCCLXXXVIJ. yeare of our Salvation, arrived in Englond with noe small rowte of lustie yownge menne which serched new habitations, mindinge to joyne in aide with his contriemenn, and bie that conjunction cleane to abolishe the Englishe name; but when hee perceaved them weried and spente with longe warres to bee joyned in league with Englond, hee toke it verie heavelie, yet thinckinge it not beste to absteine eni longer from warre, for the more provocation of his ennemies to geeve him battayle, he consumed all thinges with sword and fier, bie the which thinge Aluredus conceaved noe lesse feare then greefe, whoe hoped a while to have ceased from the terrible clattering of armes; yeat, wayinge with himselfe that in the arrivall of a new adversarie there cowlde bee nothinge more safe then celeritee, hee forthewith determined to countergarde and withstande there attempts; wherefore comming spedelie to handestrokes, manie menn on bothe sides loste there lives, but the greater losse beefell unto the Danes. After these thinges, when as Rollo betooke himselfe to reste and sleape (as it is a thinge which moste of all vigethe the weried persons) it is reported that hee seemed to see over him and his armie a swarme of bees flienge in great noyse over the sea unto the next firme lande, and there feadinge on the sweete bloomes of the trees, didde wander throwghe the shore of the Frenche ocean, there heapinge all their flowres together which they hadd gathered; and that hee awakinge owt of his vision beeganne to ponder and examen this thinge with himselfe, accountinge it as an unfeyned divination, as whoe shoulde saye that it did prognosticat nothinge els but that he showlde have fælicitee, finishinge all his travayles in Fraunce. There are som others which make an other manner of relation as concerning this dreame, affirminge, that it appeared to himm that hee was sicke of a certaine swellinge lepraye, and beinge wasshed in the fountaine of a certaine hille was soone healed thereof, and that afterwarde in safetie hee ascendid to the toppe of the same hille. The which swiven or vision a certaine sowthesayer thus interprited, that the lepray signified the vaine relligion of the hethen goddes, wherein hee was from his cradel entangeled, and that the fowntaine beetokened the salutiferus water of baptisme, wherin being owtebathed he showlde obteyne his purpose and soe climbe to the toppe of the mowntaine, that is to saye, the highe and heavenlie glorie; wherefore Rollo beinge now replete with goodd hope and of muche lesse ranckoure and malice towards the Christians, havinge a watcheword thereof in his vision, hee hoysed uppe his sayles and passed over in to Fraunce, and first spoyling the parte Celtique therof which bowndethe on the Frenche ocean on this side the river Seyin or Sequana, possessed the same, and after using of the ministrie of Sequana, went forward againste the streeme unto Roan, and gave assaulte to the cittee, which at the lengthe the citizens dispairenge in them selves, and frustrate in there expectation for succours, didd voluntarilie yealde unto himme. This citte, as Cæsar wittenessethe, was som time in the dominion of the people named Aulecci. As sone as Rollo had subdewed this cittey, hee was fullie resolved to sett uppon the borderinge places, thinckinge it greatlie to availe his entente that he might use the commoditee of three navigable flooddes, Sequana, Liger, Garunna, which are usuallie called Seyne, Loyre, and Geronde; wherefore compasinge the greatest armie that hee cowlde, and furnishinge allso a navie, the jornieng partelie on the river Loyre, and partelie on londe, dismayde all Fraunce with noe lesse terrowre then slaughter. Rollo, that bie this meanes hee mighte annoye his adversaries, havinge daylie greater retinew of the borderers which ranne unto him, hee sent forthe armed menn into all costes; villages and howses were eche wheare sette on fire; great bootie was carried owt of all corners, untill Charles the kinge of Fraunce, surnamed Simplex, (a manne more to be redowted for the sincerite of life then renowned for warlike knowledge,) thinckinge he mighte rather mitigate his feerce enemie with goodd advertisements then sharpe strokes, sente ambassadowres to require of Rollo trewce for iij. monethes: which thinge, biecause it was noe lesse expedient for the Danes, whoe desiered releefe after soe longe labowres, it was not denied himme. But the time being once accomplished, Rollo, leadinge forthe his garrisons, didd invade the people called Caruntes, or Charters, and prepared to assaulte their towne; which when he hadde beeseeged, Richard duke of the highe Burgonians, (who in auncient time wear called Seguani,) with a great bande, camme to the reskewse of them that weare beeseeged, and incontinentlie assayled his enemies; which thinge when the townes menn once perceaved, taking good corage, burste forthe on their adversaries, their bishoppe goinge before in the place of a standerd-bearer, carrienge, as menn saye, the inner garment of the Virgine Marie, and imploringe the divine favor and assistance. The Danes weare not able to abide this vehement irruption, but, being driven away with noe small losse of their companie, they repayred to a place not farre off, and there enkendelinge one another with wrathe and rage, they gathered together all the dissevered multitude, and withowte delaye running hedlonge on eche side, thei molested and annoyed all the places of their enemies, and what for hope of praye, what for their conceaved hatred, with sleeinge and rifelinge they didde crewellie plague the miserable Frenchemen, neither sparinge age nor kinde, but consuminge with fier as well the tempells of Godde as the privat howses of menne; thus the barbarus people, withowte respecte, polluted bothe thinggs divine and humaine. In the meane space the Frenchemen spake muche disworshippe of their sufferain Lorde, alleginge that hee was bothe slowe and foolishe, of noe consideration to repell hostilitee, whearas, indead, king Charles didde muche more repose his comforte in the helpe of all-mightie Godd, then in his armoure; for he foreseeinge that the puissance of his adversarie daylie more increased then with safetie he might resiste, hee rather endevored to traine this nation, as well fierce of nature as in demaynor boysterus, to the embracing of the trewthe, and desier of his frindeshippe; wherfore agayne hee sente Legats unto Rollo, which showlde exhorte him to acknowlege the Christian pietie, and enfourme him that with large dowrie hee would geeve himm in mariage his dowghter Aegidia, a mayden of noe lesse demure beehavior then comlie countenaunce, if in the waye of sownde faythe hee wowlde receave her. Francio, bisshop of Roane, was cheefe of this embassage, a mann well knowne and accepted of Rollo. Wherfore hee, which now beganne to bee werie of the continuall broyles of warre, and of more civile disposition, bie his continuall entiercowrse with the Frenchemen, didd the more willinglie geeve eare to the embassage, and did perticipate with his frindes suche thinges in the waye of consultation as weare proposed. All men condiscended in this, that the conditions of peace weare not to bee refused; but to the Legates was made nother aunswere but that Rollo was desierus to conferre and commune with Charles himselfe. The embassadours in haste retourninge, made relation of their rejonder: wherfore, thei speedelie calling in cownsell, Charles and Rollo mett togethers, to whome hee gave his doughter, and for the dowrie that parte of Cæltica or Lions which at that time was called Neustria, and appertayned to the nearer Brittaine; which contree, as soone as Rollo hadde receaved, hee termed it Northmannia, because that menn cominge owte of the northe partes possessed the same, for northe and manne sownde in the Danishe speeche as thei doe in ours. But in time it camm to passe that levinge oute t. and h. for the more pleasaunte pronowncinge, it was called Normania. These things have I glened owte of the Norman writers curiuslie, but I knowe not how trewlie, considering that they agree not with other authors, which write more formallie; and allso seing that it is evident that beefore the comminge of Rollo, Gothofredus and Sigifredus being kinges, the Normans entered together with the Danes, and after peace made with Carolus Crassus, of himme they receaved a parte of Newstria to inhabite; wherfore they affirme that Rollo joyned with the Normans, there confirminge theire abode, when as Carolus Simplex reigned: and that Aegidia was not the doughter of Simplex, but of kinge Lotharius, and that Crassus himselfe bestowed her on Gothofredus kinge of the Normans: which thing trewlie was an occasion ef error, insomutche that writers surmised that she maried with Rollo, whoe no doubt espowsed Opes, the doughter of Berengarius earle of Beavoise. I thowght goodd to putt in sumwhat of thease thinges, sithe I have promised to write a most sincere historie, that, bie recitinge the opinions of writers, the reader shall have noe scrupulus dowbtes in the moste obscure matters. But let us retire.

Rollo getting suche dominion in the contrie of his enemie, beecam daylie lesse troublesom to all menn; yea, in shorte time hee waxed so full of clemencie and godlines, that, nothing at defiance with the trew relligion, of his owne accorde he was baptized of Francio bisshop of Roane, and named Robert, throwghe Robert earle of Poyters, whome hee desiered as a fatherlie witnesse of the receaving this sacrament. Sum write that the Normans weare commanded to paye a yearlie tribute to the kinges of Fraunce as lordes of Newstria, that it showlde not bee reported to bee gotten bie warrs, but bie the francke graunte of Carolus. Thus this Rollo was the first duke of Normandie, of whome the other dukes of Normandie hadde their originall; and duke William the bastard, whoe obtained the kingdom of England, as hereafter shall bee shewed in place conveniente. When as maturitee of yeares hadd brought Rollo, as time dothe all things, to his fatall ende, William, his first begotten sonne of his wife Opis, succeeded, of whome more in time to comm, as occasion shall serve. Now will I resume the discourse of Aluredus.

The Danes persisted a while in their league with the Englishemenn, but at the laste, breakinge their vowe, they sodainelie and unwars settinge uppon the horsemen of Aluredus, who lay securelie in their fortresses aboute the borders of the contrie, slewe them everie one. The kinge, as a mann stirred with juste indignation, chased these recreauntes unto Excitre; but for as muche as they weare readie to resiste at his verie entrie into the citee, hee wiselie paused and delibered in the case, and once againe taking hostages, graunted them peace, rather that hee mighte advise himme how to withstande this harde fortune, then that hee gave enie faythe to their unfaythefulnes. But the Danes, after the truce covenanted, was not one moment in quietnes, as the extreeme enemie of tranquillitee. The kinge, who was greatlie aggreaved at the continuall motion of the warres, being bie noe meanes able to chastise or deale with soe unreasonable creatures, commaunding newe musters of soldiers eche wheare to be taken, and with a demisse and sorofull harte, in the meane space, convayed himselfe with a fewe of his menn into certaine fenns and marishe growndes in the countie of Somersett, whear being overwhelmed and wrapped in great anxietee, while he earnestlie beeseeched Godd of succoure, and passinge certaine dayse in takinge advisement what weare beste to bee donne, beehowld hee mette with a poore man, as it seemed, who humblie requiered a peece of breade, and the kinge forthewith in humble wise perfowrmed. The nexte day hee is reported in his sleepe to have seene Sainct Cuthbert, standing preste bie himme, whoe assuredlie enfourmed himme that hee was the indigent creature on whome hee beestowed the shiver of breade, and bedde himme bee of goodd cheare. With thease thinggs the spirits of Aluredus weare so greatlie recreated that immediatlie hee repayred to his soldiars, and, accitinge ayde from all costes, hee tooke in hande the battayle againe; thus the godlie prince, beinge ere whiles anoyed with so manie perills, was quicklie as it weare owte of the maine sea into the haven, reduced into his owlde estate. Where-fore with exceadinge diligence he multiplieth his armie; hee reco-vereth the citties which forsooke himme, ether bie menacinge sternelie, or rewardinge bownteuslie; hee storethe himselfe with armowre, darts, engines, and all thinge requisite for the conflicte; hee riggethe his shippes, hee placethe them in convenient rode, hee mindethe as well to intercepte the hawnte of the Danes, which continuallie cam into the riollme, and to hinder their returne, which weare all readie nooseled in the sweetenesse of the soyle; and in the meane space, with a bowlde and presente corage, disguised in the attire of a servant, hee ventured into the tents of his enemies; hee espiethe out a meete time for the invadinge of theim, and finallie, with princelie animositee, settethe on them whilest they strayed dissolutelie. The Danes at the firste, like vagabunds, weare sharplie afflicted, yeat bie litell and litell they soe drew together that not onlie thei feared not, but on noe side they wowlde geeve backe. Thus oftentimes they skirmished bothe on sea and on lande, with variable fortune, till at the lengthe Ro-chester, London, and Chestre, beinge delivered from beeseeginge, the Englishe peple so plagued the Danes, bothe with strokes in field, and grappelinge in their navies, that of those which skaped deathe somme wente from whence they camm; somme, for feare of death, becamme Christians, emonge which number was their king, Gormo; whome the kinge embracing with fatherlie loove, made him cheefetaine over the North Humbrians. Somme tes-tifie that the kinge gave him allso the province of the Easte Angles, that is to weete Norffolke and Suffolke. But they noe doubte weare deceaved, for at that time Ericus, a Dane, was governor thereof, whome afterwarde Edwarde didd expell owt of his dominion. This Gormo being feerce, accordinge to the guise of his contrie didd crewellie governe the North Humbrians xii. years, after whome ensewed his sonne Sithricus, and his nephews, whoe weare deprived bie Adelstanus of their imperie, as it shallbee mentioned in processe. Aluredus, bie this time, having overcommed kinge Cevolphus, enjoyed the kingdom of Mercia; which exploytes and admirable travayles accomplished, he wholie bente himselfe, firste, to deserve well of the Christian relligion; secondarilie, of learninge, and all liberall sciences; thirdelie, of the common welthe; finallie, of the good demainor of all menn, for hee noe doubte was mindefull of the divine oracle of Sainct Cuthebertus, which I spake of beefore, when he was in noe lesse distresse then distruste; and for the same cause hee gave manie riche giftes to the churche at Chester, wheare the relliques of Sainct Cuthbertus weare reserved, encreased allso the possessions of the busshoppe, gevinge unto himm the teritorie of Durrham, which liethe betwine the rivers Tine and Theis, to use and possesse as his righte and jurisdiction. For at that time, which was abowte the yeare of our Lord DCCCLXXXIIJ., the Hollie Ilond being dispopulate bie the aliens, the see of the bisshop was translated to the towne which lieth next unto Deyrham, aboute vj. miles of; but within xlij. years after it was finallie transposed to Deirham; cclxxxv. after that Aydanus beganne his residence in the Hollie Ilande. Durrham is a citte neare to the sea coste, bownding northwarde uppon the river of Weeire. This river hathe his channell in a steepe stonie place, abowte a mile from the cittee, soe that there apeere great stones on ether side, which never are covered with water, excepte the raynie brookes ministre occasion of swellinge. But there chaunceth a thing wonderus to bee spoken in that place; if bie fortune a littell water bee powred on the stones, and there a littell tempered, it forthewith beecommeth salte, weare it beefore never soe sweete; the like in the whole river beesides cowlde never bee tried. Butt trewle it semethe soe to comm to passe, ether bie cause the nature of those stones is suche, or els bie cause the upper parte being parched, and brent with the vehemencie of the soonne and winde, it engenderethe the verdure and taste of salte; but now I will returne to mie matter. Aluredus beesides this ædified iij. relligius howses with excellent furniture, adowrning the one at Winchester, which is called the Newe monasterie; an other in the village named Shaftesburie, in the diocese of Sarisburie, apoyntinge noonnes to bee therin, and his dowghter Ethelgera, or Elgina, to bee the governesse; the thirde to bee in that place where, as beinge distracte with gnawing sorowse, hee was reported to have hadd consolation of Saincte Cuthbertus. He willed the relligius people of this howse to bee of the order of Sainct Benedicte, gevinge to the same, and the other two monasteries, large giftes and ample possessions. This place is som what eminent and higher then the grownde abowte it, in the fourme of an Ilonde within a great fenne, which wilbee commonlie drie in sommer, and standethe eastwarde, harde uppon the river Tanus, which, receavinge the sourge of the sea, flowethe with salte water even unto that place. This Ile in owld time was called Ethelingea, and now Athelnea, and liethe v. miles from the towne named Tawnton. This towne is indifferentlie well knowne; it bowndethe westewarde, beinge in the uttermost parte of the countie of Sommarsett, bie the which allso runnethe the river Tanus, who hathe his springe xij. miles aboove it. Of this river the towne seemethe to have derived the name. Aluredus didd these goddlie [acts] the xxi. yeare of his reigne, and the DCCCXCIIJ. of our Salvation.

This prince, when he was xx. yeares of age, gave him selfe studiuslie to learninge, and in shorte space becam verie well lettered, insomuche that the dialogues of Saincte Gregorie, Boethius' pamphlet of the comforts of philosophie, and the Psalmes of David he translated owte of Latine into his native speeche, that they might be understoode of all menn. Howbeit som menn suppose that Werefredus, busshop of Worciter, toorned bothe the dialogs of Sainct Gregorie, and the woorcke of Boethius, at his intercession, with whome I do not agree, sithe that hee was of suche reasonable literature and knowlege that justlie it maye bee thowght to bee his owne woorcke; but all the Psalmes hee cowlde not finishe, beinge prevented bie deathe. Hee studied moste ernestlie at suche time as learninge was verie rare emonge the westerne men, that bie all meanes hee might teache his people the way to live well, and generallie to instructe the mindes of everi degree with goodde letters, and in that respecte hee favored sharpe and pregnante wittes. Hee muche esteemed the dignitee of all estates; hee embraced the nobles, hee was affable and milde to the vulgares, hee looved all those in whome appeared enie sparke of vertewe. It is lefte in memorie that hee was wonte to permitte noe manne to entere noe college of preestes, excepte hee wear of approved honestie, of sufficient knowledge, of lowlie beehaviour, knowing the owld sayde sawe, that preestes weare the spectacle and looking-glasse of the whole worlde, and, therefore, the trade of other men's life to be easelie chaunged bie them, and for bie cause hee perceaved within himselfe how fewe suche menne there weare, hee sente owte of all costes for menne noe lesse devowte then scilfull, which showlde take on them this regall function, as the prince of the apostels termethe it; and, aboove all others, hee didde entierlie loove Neotus for his incredible learning, a moste hollie father of monasticall profession, at whose entretie and sollicitinge he founded the common Schooles or Universitee of Oxford, assigning stipend and rewarde for all suche as wowlde professe goodde artes, soe that thether repayred manie profounde learned menn to instructe and teache surelie, fro the time that Sigibertus, kinge of the Easte Angles, had erected scholes within the limits of his riolme, who, as the pleasaunt stremes of knowlege continuallie runninge owte of that plenteus fowntayne, did not onlie moyste and water all Englond, but Fraunce allso, with the delicious licoure of heavenlie discipline, for (as it is ells wheare declared) when as Offa, kinge of the Mercians, hadde sent Albinus or Alchuinus to Charles le Maine in the way of amitee and league, hee perceavinge suche exceadinge learninge in himme, as well deserved great reverence, he now intreated him, not as a legate, but an honorable gueste, and consequentlie not as a gueste but as his reader and instructer; followinge, I suppose, the auncient example of the Athenienses, whoe retayned still with them Gorgias, beinge sent on embassage to them in publique affayres from the Leontines, beeing greatlie enflamed and entangeled with his eloquence. Thus Alchuinus, an Englishe mann remaininge in Fraunce, beeganne at Parris to proffesse letterature and sciences, and bie his procurement, not longe after, Charles himme selfe didde first of all others erecte there an universitee, and likewise at Ticinum an other, which is now called Papia; this was abowte the yeare of our Lord DCCXCIJ. at the which time the brute goeth that oute of Irelonde, or as somm surmise Scotlonde, there camme two monachs into Fraunce with lowde voyce avowchinge that they hadde wisdom to sell, ownly desieringe meate and clothinge for their rewarde, and that the one of them named Clemens, was bie Charles still kept at Lutetia, to whose tuition and enfourming weare committed yownge menn of all sortes; but thother passed into Italie, teachinge and training upp yowth at Ticinum. Manie there are which ascribe this to the fower disciples of Beda, namelie, to Rabanus, Alchuinus, Claudius, and Jhoannes Scotus; but howesoever the case standethe, it is moste evidente that the Englishemenn weare the firste which toughte openly liberall sciences at Parris, for as muche as Alchuinus and Jhoannes Scotus weare for learninge menn of greatest fame in Englonde. But againe to the Universitee of Oxforde, which even from the originall, bothe for the studies of divine and humayne knowlege, and for the multitude of suche as buselie employed all goodlie faculties, it soe flourished in processe of time that in worthines and renowne it might cowntervayle enie universitee in the worlde; for the skollers thereof from the verie beginninge being instituted as it were in a certaine relligius reverence and observation of all degreese, doe noe lesse nurture their mindes with civile behavior, then adorne the same with learninge; they have howses byleded with princelie furniture, enriched as well with the divers giftes of kings, noble menn, and busshops, as of moste sincere and godlie woomen. These howses thei usuallie call Colleges, bie cause they are ther colliged in felawship and ministerie. The maisters and cheefe governers of them are selected as approved and honest menn, leadinge there lives commonlie at home with the whole boddie of their howses, having sufficiencie in livelod soe to maintayne them; and daylie in the morneing ether they them selves execute the divine function, or at the leaste wayse are preasent at the hollie service beefore they enter on their studies; above all things yealdinge due reverence to Godd; then livinge in union of chaste life, and enuring them selves with all laudable artes and sciences; soe that from thence, as from one of the moste learned theaters of the erthe, there commethe forthe bothe skilfull and goddelie menn, who, partlie bie their livelie instructinge, partelie bie there profownde writinge, doe marveluslie supporte, honor, and defend Christianitie. Som peradventure there have ben which were nothinge ægregius in these poinctes; but there delicatelie runninge the race of there life, bie ther evell ensample somtimes have muche hendered the tender yowthe of others which like wax is flexible into vice. Trulie for this sore might soone bee fownde a salve, if they which daylie geeve instructions and ordinances to colliges, wold prescribe certayne determinate yeares for schollers, that at their juste time they might procede as learned menne, or els beinge rejected from thence as asses from the harpe (accordinge to the owld saienge) thei mighte leave their roomes to other which might doe muche goodd therin. With this universitee of Oxforde (not withowte good cause) the moste noble and flourishinge universitee of Cambrige contendethe in renowned fame and famus antiquitee, which albeit, in number of schollers and magnificentie of colliges, it is not superior, yeat in the affluence of goodde artes and liberall sciences noe doubte it is æquall; nether trulie is that of noe moment wherin, as the trewe mother of sinceritee, it is woont to vaunte itselfe, namelie, that it never broughte foorthe enie child which was of erroneus judgement as towchinge relligion. What showlde I speake of the antiquitee wherein it farre surmountethe, for from the fowndation of the universitee of Cambridge to the erection of that which is at Oxforde CCXXV. yeare weare complete; for this laste was fownded bie Aluredus abowte the xxiii. yere of his reigne, which was the DCCCXCV. of our Salvation: the other was bielded of Sigibertus in the yeare of our Lorde DCXXX. But if wee will beeleeve the commentaries of an unknowne writer, the originall, as well of the towne as of the universitee, is farre more auncient, for it is reported that the owlde towne named Caergraunt in times paste was situat at the foote of an hill nott farre of called Withyll, and that in the time of Gurguntius, sonne of Bellinus, a certayne Cantabrian named Bartholomeus cam thether to teache and interprite, and havinge consequentlie in mariage the king's dowghter, called Chembrigia, bilded the towne Cantabrigia, alludinge to his wives name, and first of all others tought there himselfe. But I wil retorne to the historie.

After that Aluredus hadde sowed the precius seades of learninge in his region, as a mann fulley bent to the encreasinge of all vertewus, and behavior, and humanitee, hee promulged most sincere and sacred lawse, which I have fownde written in a moste auncient booke. But for as muche as emonge Englishe men they were longe since drowned with darcke oblivion, I thoughte it to noe purpose to make recorde of them. To be short, hee was a mann shininge in all kinde of vertewse, for to all menn, especiallie to the neadie, he wowlde willing geeve of his private substance: hee was verie uprighte in the execution of justice, for as hee didd allwayse geeve dewe chastisement to the offender, so with fatherlie loove hee didd mayntaine the innocent. In the warlike sciens it appeareth that hee was moste excellent of all other kinges, for as muche as noe one of them was conqueror of soe manie and divers battayles. He engendered bie his wife Ethelvitha two sonnes, Edward, surnamed Elder, and Adelwoldus, and three dowghters, Elfreda, Ethelgera or Elgina, and Etheluitha. Elfreda was maried to a certaine noble manne emonge the Mercians, named Ethelredus, havinge a parte of Mercia to her dowrie. This woman shewed a moste notorius example of despisinge the venereus and fleshlie pleasures, for, beinge impregned bie her husbande, after the time of travayle and deliverie of her childe, rememberinge her great tormentes and payne, woulde never more comm in bedde with enie mann, alleging that it was the veriest follee in the worlde to esteeme and employe suche voluptuus venerie as wolde bringe so muche sighenge and sorrowe. Aluredus beinge now striken in great years, and somwhat allso attynted with sickenes, made his will and testament, in the which he solemnelie assignes and made heyre apparent his sonne Edwarde; and, to the ende hee might cause manie menn to have him in remembrance, he francklie bestowed large giftes on his soldiers, familiers, servauntes, schollers of Oxforde, and as well to the byledinge as repayringe of churches. Afterwarde, beinge sore diseased, his finall daye drewe on, and at Winchester hee yealded uppe his spirite to allmightie Godde. His boddie was interred in the new abbay which hee fownded. Hee reygned xxviij. yeares. In that abbay there was afterwards instituted a college of seculer priestes, and after that againe of monachs, as we will declare hereafter.

THE SIXTH BOOKE

OF POLIDOR VERGILL ON THE ENGLISHE HISTORIE.

WEE have indifferentlie declared in owre two former bookes bie what stirringe and endinge of warres the imperie of the Englishe nation bothe sprange in Brittaine, which at this daye is Englonde, and howe bie littell and littell it grewe (as one woulde saye) to the full ripe yeares of a manne; for even as a man at his birthe hathe onlie the meere life vegetative; then he growethe to greene yowthe; consequentlie hee enterethe the beautifull flower of man's state; finallie he commethe to horie age; even so likewise kingedommes beeginne; they encrease, they flourishe, and, finallie, they comm to theyre fatall fall and distruction. The firste age, that is to weete the infancie of their kingdom, beeganne under the reigne of Engistus, the CCCL. yeare of our Salvation. From that time ensued the adolescentie, or yowthe thereof, under the jurisdiction of vij., sometimes viij. kinges (as beefore is sufficientlie declared), unto Egbertus, the xvij. westerne kinge, whoe, obteyning the kingdoms of Kente, Northe Humberlande, and Est Saxons, didde first nayme Brittayne Englond, and the whole nation Englishemenn, as elswheare it is notified. This age had his enduering space, leysurelie gathering increase, abowt cccl. years, beinge then moste puissant, bothe in menne and in armes. From the dayse of Egbertus the mature and mannlie yeares beeganne, which enduered more then clxxv. yeares, even unto Sainct Edwarde the martire; at the which time approched soroful owlde age, which, as it is accustomed in mann to bee accompanied with infinite diseases, soe in all humayne affayres if slewtheful idelnes bee disturbed and sollicited, it bringethe a thousande discommoditees. In that season firste the Danes, then the Normans, possessed the Englishe imperie; yeat at the last this croked and decrepite age, contrarie to the expectation of all men, was agayne renewed into yowthe, for the Normane name, bie continuance, beinge towrned into the Englishe, as more plainelie hereafter shall bee mentioned, the people weare universallie callede Englishmenne. Now, as concerninge the exploytes committed bie the Englishe people, in these malie yeares, and owlde age of the riolme, wee will prosecute, Godd willinge, bothe in this booke and the nexte.

Nexte unto Aluredus succeeded his sonne Edward, as xxiij. in the order of kings, being crowned with the rioll diadem, accordinge to the custom of his predecessors, of Athelredus archebisshopp of Cantuarburie, the DCCCCJ. yeare after the birthe of Christe. Wee made mention above, in the forthe booke of this woorcke, that Brithowaldus, the viij. busshop from Augustine, in the rome of Theodorus, beinge deade, was the firste Englishe Archebusshop of Canturberie, after whome, in the space of cxx. yeares, unto Athelredus, there ensewed ix. archebusshops; first, Tadwinus, who was resident iij. yeares; Notelius, v. yeare; Cuthebertus, beefore busshopp of Hereford, xviij. yeare; Brethwinus, iij. yeare; Lambertus, the abbot of Saincte Augustines, xxvij.; Adelardus, xiij.; Wilfredus, (who was asigned bie the Romaine busshopp,) xxxviij.; Theogildas, or Pleogildus, iij.; Chelnatus, or Celnotus, x.; after whome succeded Athelredus, as xviij. from Augustinus, being then busshopp of Winchester, and of noe lesse auctoritee then vertewe. But wee most returne to owre purpose. Edward, at the verie beginninge of his governinge, thinckinge that all things showlde bee especiallie considered which weare for the avayle of the weale publique, didd furnishe everie place with garrisons, diligentlie visitinge all suche cities as weare moste commodius to his enemies, and noysom to him. Hee gave vigilante attendance as well to the attemptes of his adversaries as his propre affayres; hee labored with infatigable industrie to prevent the guiles of barbarous people, that, accustominge his menne continuallie to martiall feates, partelie they might the easlier persiste in their loyall dewtie, partelie leste they beinge voyde of all feare, livinge dayntelie and securelie, might bee sodainelie over runne of their enemies, and cheefelie that all occasion and oportunitee of warrs might bee withdrawne from the Danes, whoe at that time weare cheefe lordes of Northe Humberland and East Angles. Yeat above all thease thinges hee thoughte expedient to prevente the Scottishe warrs for as muche as kinge Constantine did, withowte ceasing or intermission, vexe and waste the Englishe borders; wherfore Edwarde, in all expedition, gave him battayle, wherin there was great bloodde shedd on bothe sides: but, forasmuche as the greater calamitee didd redownde to his Scottes, hee was nothinge unwillinge to dismisse the warriors, obteyninge bie entreatie peace of the Englishe people. After this Edwarde reduced to conformitee the waveringe Wallshemenn, and retayned againe all Mercia, as shall bee shewed in processe, after the deathe of his sister Elfreda. Yet not bie all thease meanes cowlde hee eschewe the fraude and deceite of his adversaries, or have the fruition of quietnes, for the Danes, whoe then laye swellinge in Northe Humberlande, and dispituslie malingned the happie encrease of the Englishe prosperitee, wente abowte to sowe discorde betweene the two brothers, hopinge with other men's weapons to satisfie theyr hatred; wherefore they wente to Adelwoldus privelie, a younge manne of his owne nature, marveluslie desierus of rule. They stirred him uppe bie all wayse possible; thei towlde him that undowbtedlie this was the time, that if he wowlde he might enjoy the whole monarchie, bie the expulsion of his brother, sithe that hee at that presence was hated of all, as well his owne vassayles as neighbours, for as muche as, contrarie to all manns lawe, and Godd's lawe, hee didd owtragiuslie distende his owne dominion, and injuriuslie enchroche on other men's. For the speedie perfowrmance of soe goodd a matter they promised voluntarilie their assistance, and farther, that all perills and trowbles that mighte arise theyre bie showlde lie on their owne neckes. Bie thease traynes and allurementes thei browghte this springehole into suche a Mahomite's paradise that forthwithe, dotinge on his brother's kingedom, he prepared unnaturallie an armie, and invaded the same with straunge hostilitee. But when as the kinge camm in poste to withstande this injurie, then strayghte, as voyde of witte and cowncell, and striken with feare, as one which hadde wrowght rashelie, hee minded to flie unto the Danes in Northe Humberlande, that bie there helpe hee mighte bee assisted in this conflicte. Whereof when the kinge was donne to understande, hee pursewed with suche swiftnes that this yowthefull impe was fayne to forsake his pretended voyage, and, dechininge to the sea, was compelled to rove into the parties beyonde the sea, wheare remaininge skarcelie one whole yeare, he returned againe to the Northe Humbrians to renewe his warrs. The Danes, whoe greatlie feared kinge Edwarde, entertayned him jentellie, and made him capitaine of their battayles. Adelwoldus, being now in auctoritee, burned with ire against his brother, and bie force of armes invaded the bowndes of his kingdom, geevinge oportunitee to the Danes to consume all things with weapon and fire. Then he bente his power towardes Mercia, and did prostitute all thinggs to spoyle and wastinge, and finallie, costenge yet another waye, he passed the river Thames, and moste crewellie destroyd all the contrie unto the towne named Basyngstoch. On the other side the kinge with an armie meatethe his raging enemie, and sett on him whilst hee cam on with a dissolute companie. On ether parte they maynteyned the fight to the uttermost of their power, which was a great while no lesse feerce then doubtfull, so that mani one bothe sides hadde their balefull and deadlie wowndes. Adelwoldus at the first, joyninge coragiuslie skirmishinge emonge his enemies, was slayne; notwithstandinge whose deathe the Danes nothinge ceased or intermitted the battayle, as menn that hadd capitains of their owne, to whose valiaunce they trustinge, committed the shaddowe of the imperie to Adelwoldus, that the Englishe mann mighte rove himselfe throughe with his owne weapon. When a whiles they had thus sharpelie skirmished, the kinges soldiers, being putte to the worse, turned their backes; and the Danes, beinge weried with their longe travaile, didd not onlie easlie leave the pursewte, but allso, notwithstandinge they were superior for that presence, yet thinckinge beste awhiles to absteyne from battayle, thei requiered peace of the king; to whome kinge Edwarde, that he mighte seme the more terrible unto them, wolde in noe wise condiscende unto peace, but onlie graunted them trewse. In the meane season, throughe a great drowghte, there chaunced extreeme skarcitee of corne, which was the onlie cause whie the truce was not immediatlie broken of the Danes; yet, as they whome nature hadd not forged to bee alltogether quiet, they egged their confines to make commotion, continuallie conspiering and conferringe with them. This impendent daunger the kinge holdinge wisdome to foresee, made woonderful expedition into Northe Humberlande, and skourged them with so infinite damage that from thenceforthe they willinglie persevered in obeysaunce. Ther was an other warlike fier enkendelinge bie them which were cheefe menn emonge the Easte Angles, whose kinge was one Ericus, whoe, mortallie hatinge the Englishe name, indevored secretlie to suborne and ione other Danes in his societie, that, unitinge there power, they mighte at once cleane adnihilate the Englishe gooddes and puissance: but, for as muche as he administred all thinges with hedlonge temeritee, his endevoure was not unknowne to kinge Edwarde, whoe, preventinge his male engine, invaded his bowndes and spoiled the contrie, exceading pituuslie. The Dane, which hadd his menne all readie harnised, and partelie inflamed with wrathe, partelie burning in the desier of revenginge, buckeled hastelie with his adversarie: they fowght at the first with great feercenes; but the fighte on Danishe side, rashlie beegonne,

Note, allwayse that bie the Est Angles is mente Norffolcke and Sowthfolke, as is shewed in the second booke, and well agreeth with all auncient writers.

hadd a miserable ende, so that Ericus himselfe was easelie vanquished, and putte to flighte, after the filthie foyle and overthrowe of his soldiers. Yeat what for this odius and lamentable plague, what for that, governed with more extreemitee then hee was accustomed, the Easte Angles toke the paines to slea himme: nether yet was that deade so great a pleasure to them as they surmised, for in shorte time, theire force being not a littell apayred, they weare driven to com under the yoke of kinge Edwarde: and this was the finall fall of the mightie kingdom of the Easte Angles.

Kinge Edwarde havinge conquered this kingdom, now called Norffolk and Suffolke, didd allso bring all Mercia under his jurisdiction; for after the decease of Ethelredus, governer of the Mercians, without heires, his wife Elfreda didde noe lesse upprightlie then wiselie administer the regiment a few yeares; bie this meanes this prince soe enlarged the limites of his kingdom, that besides Scotlande hee hadde the imperie of the whole Ilonde. Albeeit as yet in Northe Humberlande the Danes hadde som dominion. Yet som write that hee, ejecting the Danes, possessed Northe Humberlande allso; but as menn nothinge warie in their doings in other places, they as contrarie to them selves, sayenge that this kinges dowghter, named Edithe, not long after her father's deathe, maried with a certaine Dane called Sithericus, cheefe ruler of Northe Humberland, whoe, as it is moste evident, died in the reigne of Adelstanus; wherfore, while Sithricus ruled, and kinge Edward lived, it is not to bee thowghte that the Northe Humbrians yealded fealtie and homage to himme, as shall bee plainelie declared in the life of Adelstanus. At the laste kinge Edwarde, havinge garded his riollme with tranquillitee, and greatelie studied the promulgation of lawes, which allbeit they weare verie goodde, yet of his posteritee they weare easlie ether owte of use or abolished. He byleded a castell at Bedforde, in times paste a walled towne, and now a famus village, standinge in a marveluslie well fensed grownde; therof at this daie is nether tracte nor token. Bie Edgina, a mayden of woonderus beawtie, hee hadd a sone

Mercia is all the middell partes of Englond; loke for it in the beginning of the second booke.

named Adelstanus, whoe was his successor. It shall nott bee labor loste (sithe somtimes wee delighte to satisfie the vulgares and common people, which is greatlie in loove with miracles,) if wee shall reherce a presagition and token, wherebie this Edgina conceaved hope to bringe forthe a childe, which in tyme to comme showlde reigne. She dreamed that there arose owte of her wombe a moone, which gave lighte to all Englonde with the brightnes thereof, which thinge when on a time she uttered to a certaine matrone, she not lightelie regardinge suche a vision as mighte have prodigius and strange effecte, caused the virgin, discended but of base ligneage, to bee fostered in goodd manners; whome, when she was ripe for the companie of manne, it fortuned the kinge to espie, as he repayred on a time to a mansion of his, and being enravished with her bewtie lay bie her, and on her begatt Adelstanus, as erste we mencioned; beesides this, by his wife Elfreda, hee hadde afterwarde these children, Etheluardus and Edwinus, whoe died streyght after his decease, then Elfreda, Edgina, or Elgina, Edburge, Ethilda, Editha, and Elgida; of these Elfreda and Edburga, for there noble virginitee, weare made noonnes, Edgina or Elgina was maried to Carolus Simplex, kinge of Fraunce, and Edith to Sithricus king of Northhumberland. Hee hadd allso bie another wife named Edgina two sonnes, Edmundus and Eldredus, who reygned after Adelstanus. At this time the Christian faythe waxed verie cowlde emonge the westerne menn, bie cause there was noe busshoppe there to instructe the people; the defaulte was in the prince, whoe more intendinge warrs then divine service, preestes weare hindered in their hollie functions; wherfor Ihon the x^{t}. busshop of Rome, being greatlie moved, didd correpte and chide king Edwarde in his letters, menacinge that hee wowlde denownce bothe him and his people enemies to relligion, onlesse he wowlde speedelie send for busshoppes, which might procurethe trew discipline of our Lorde to bee preserved; which thinges when the king hadd well digested, endevoring to recompense his forepassed negligence, hee soe debated the matter with Pleimundus archebusshop of Caunterbury, who succeaded Athelredus after the xviij. yeare of his residence, that hee immediatlie callinge a congregation didd consecrate manie busshopps for the better governinge of the dioceses. Afterward Pleimundus went to Rome to make his purgation, and appeased the bisshop. This Edward was a prince of exceadinge commlie favor, verie decent in everie degree of his age; allbeit the dignitee thereof in his later dayse was sore defloured with the multitude of diseases, of the which he was finallie consumed the xxiiij. yeare of his reigne, and DCCCCXXV. of our Salvation, and lieth interred at Winchester.

Abowte the verie same time died Rollo or Robert duke of Normandie, for that was his Christian name, a manne noe dowbte of great valiance in martiall prowesse, for no man living after him cowlde conquire in a lande of hostilitee a more goodlie kingdom for him and his posteritee, who beginninge with suche small principles, (as hereafter shalbe declared,) so encreased, that afterwarde it becamme æquall to the moste mightie and renowned kingdomes. Rollo lefte behinde himm a sonne named William, nether in wisdom nor in warlike affaires inferior to himselfe, and suche one as was of great authoritee emonge the Frenchemenn, wherof to make plaine and evident demonstration, wee must repete this matter more deepelie. Carolus Simplex kinge of Fraunce tooke in mariage, as was saide, Edgina or Elgina, the dowghter of kinge Edwarde, bie whome he hadd a sonne named Ludovicus, who bie cause hee hadd confedered in amitee with Rollo hee was greatlie hated of his own nation, soe that a good companie of the nobles slipped from him, insomutche that consequentlie there beefell suche strife beetwene them, that the nobles, fearinge the ruine of their commonwealthe, reconciled them to their prince, and joyninge together against Robert duke of Aquitaine, whoc maintayned wars againste Carolus, they destroyed him and all his armie: which thing Robert earle of Vermandois taking hevelie, as one verie desierus to revenge the quarell of his frinds, met with Carolus,

Viromandiu. as appeareth bie

Cæsars Comment. is a people of Picardie.

retiering from his victorie, as it weare in the way of gratulation; and at there firste meatinge this subtile foxe, mindinge the beter to glose this fainte greetinge, with his gentil cowntenance, (wherein lurcketh all dissimulation,) with smilinge visage and continuall entreatie sollicited so the kinge, that he broughte him into a towne of his named Perona, and there kaste him into prison; which thing being once knowne, Edgina the wife of Carolus, with her sonne Ludovicus, fled to here brother Adelstanus kinge of Englonde. In the meane season the Frenche menne, leaste theye showlde wante a governour, they pronownced as kinge Rodolphe, the sonne of Richard duke of Burgundie, whoe departinge oute of this mortal life, after the xij. yeare of his reigne, and Carolus allso abowte the same time dienge in prison, William duke of Normandie didde cause the peeres of Fraunce to sende for Ludovicus the sonne of Carolus owte of Englonde, and to proclaime him kinge at his cominge; but scarcelie v. yeares weare passed, but that allmost all the cheef men of the reame didde mislike Ludovicus, whoe, beinge thus destitute of his frindes, persuaded with Henrie, or his sonne Otho (as somm thincke,) to currie favor with the kinge of Germanie, which thing he browght to passe, bie the onlie meanes and counsell of duke William; which thinges, when the nobles perceaved, of their owne accorde they desiered the good will of their prince: thus the fame of this William beecam notable emonge all men, for, as a man borne onlie to doe goodde, hee gave especiall endevore to the preferring of his frindes, he succowred the miserable, hee redressed injuries; finallie, hee was to all men withowte respecte frindlie; wherbie it camm to passe that Herlowinus, a noble manne, beinge dejected bie Arnulphus prince of Flaunders, owt of the possession of his castell of Monasteril, hee betoke himselfe plaintife to duke William, as the commune revenger of injuries, whoe heringe the whole discourse, soe treated that the castell was restored to the yownge manne, and preserved him from all wrongs; which turned himself to noe small displeasure, all beit nothing of his deserte, for

Arnulphus, being aggreeved at the duke, appoynted with him selfe to entrappe him bie som treason, whome baselie hee beeguiled under the pretexte of love and amitee; for in shorte time it camm to passe that Arnulphus, at Pinciniacum, hadd brought the duke to private talke, and at their departure, when he wolde have entered into his barcke, mindinge to passe the streame (for all this was donne in an Ilonde compased abowte with the river of Seine), he was sodaynelie revoked bie the officers of Arnulphus, as whoe showlde say they hadde somwhat to tell that there trayterus prince hadd forgotten, and there, at his reversinge, hee was horriblie murthered. The Normans, whoe stode showtinge and crieing on the other bancke, bie reason of the depthe of the channell, cowlde not helpe their lorde; but afterwarde, nevertheles, thei gatte his corps, and at Roane they intumbed it with funerall pompe. This William hadd a son named Richarde, beinge a verie childe; the tuition of whome, and of all Normandie, Rodolphe and Barnard didd take on them, as the most famus and authorized emonge the Normains. But we will speake of them hereafter convenientlie. Now wee will returne thither from whence wee made digression.

Adelstanus the xxiiij. from Cerdicius, and son of Edwarde bie his concubine, was saluted kinge of the people, and of Athelmus archebusshop of Canturburie, accordinge to the custome of his predecessors, crowned at a towne named Kingston uppon Thamis, which even at this daye is a famus village. This Athelmus was xx. in the order of the archebusshops of Caunterburie, and successor to Pleimundus, the yere of our Lord DCCCCXXVJ. It was greatlie bruted and noysed in the beginninge of Adelstanus, that the Scottishe kinge Constantinus was allreadie in armes, assemblinge his people owt of all costes, and the Welchemen allso readie to rebell, for beefore all thinges hee addressed him to withstande thease evels hangenge over his hedde, and with noe small power he marched speedelie towards them bothe, and with like goodd fortune didde dawnte and overcom them bothe. But he thus used Constantinus after his overthrowe: hee made him sweare unto thease wordes; that in time to comme he showlde acknowlege the fruicion of his life and kingdom to bee bie his permission, and noe otherwise. The same trade was allso taken with other kinges of Scotland succeadinge, as somme menn write, howbeit there late writers make muche alltercation in that pointe, which wee take noe parte of our dewtie, for as muche as an historie is a declaration of thingges that have benn donne, not a contention or disceptation abowte them, and therefore have wee browght to lighte those thingges which the moste cronicles of England doe testifie, to the end that, with owte the offence of enie nation, wee maye absolutelie finishe this imparfaict woorcke; this I thowght good to say at the beginninge, leste enie mann showlde require the office of a judge in an historiographer of this donne longe beefore. But to our matter againe.

In this season Sithricus, kinge of Northe Humberland, died, which ministered opportunitee to Adelstanus to conquere it, for Analaphus and Gothofredus, the sonnes of Sithricus, like yonge men over desierus of rule, beganne to conspire and communicate in treason againste the Englishe prince; they groped the mindes of their borderers, there letters flew hether and thither, which being intercepted didd beewray their haynus entente, wherfore the kinge, being preevie to the councell of his enemies, didd immediatlie, with greate ire, invade Northe Humberlande; but the younge menn, as thei weare lighte in consultation, soe nothing stedfaste in their purpose, didde not looke for himme, but forthewith avoydinge, the one chaunsed into Irelond, the other in Scotland, whome the Englishe prince pursewinge in vayne, seased of and reaceaved to his grace the teritorie of North Humberlande, being destitute of a guide. Thus Adelstanus, wiselie foreseeing the casualtie of things, was necessarilie driven to deprive his nephewes, bie his sister Edithe, of there dominion.

While these affayres weare in contrivinge, Gothofredus hadde procured noe small succours in Scotlond, bie whose assistance of a sodayne he beseged Deirham, bie all meanes allueringe the inhabitants to rebell, whoe albeit of there owne minde desiered to receive their native prince, yet seinge himme to bee of suche small force, that well he cowlde nether defende himselfe nor the cittey, leaste there slipperie dealinge mighte turne them to displesure, they persevered still in loyaltie, albeit on other side they weare striken with great feare. This facte made Adelstanus not a littell offended with Constantinus, kinge of Scotts, in that hee hadde succoured his enemie, yeat bie purginge himme selfe hee camm soone againe into favor. Analaphus, the other brother, mindinge to revenge the shamefull losse of his imperie, with somme great mischeefe, chaunged his attire, and camm into the Englishe tents with a few confederats, to espie how he might oppresse his adversarie unwares, and wrought his feate soe closelie that hee hadde neare hande slaine the kinge; for in the nighte he ranne into the kinges tabernacle, but soe hastie he was and boysterus in his doings that he awaked him owte of his sleape, whoe understandinge that he was assaulted and in danger, hee sodainelie cried oute to armes, to armes, and woulde have drawne forthe his sworde, and when he could not finde it, beinge amazed with feare (which is wonte to distracte the wittes and councell of menn), he pawsed a whiles, as dowbtfull what to doe, and thinckinge him selfe destitute of manns helpe, beeganne alowde to expostulate the assistance of Godde, and at that verie instant layde his hande againe on his skaberd, and findinge his swoorde, hee assayled his enemies, and slayenge som of them putt the rest to flighte. Somm menne have lefte in memorie that Constantinus, the Scottishe kinge, was there, and slaine in that tumulte; but as they have sayde that nothinge credeblie, soe have thei written verie untrewlie that Analaphus was kinge of Irelonde, noe dowbte beinge deceaved in that poincte, for that hee beefore fledd thither, as aboove wee mentioned; and that sworde was longe reserved in the kinges armorie, as a testimoniall of the divine benefit. Adelstanus after this in all costes, havinge the better of his adversaries, obteyned a large dominion. This was the mature and manlie age of the Imperie then especiallie flowringe in menne, in valiaunce, and vertewe. For at this time ther florished menn no lesse renowned for the sanctimonie of their life then famus in learninge, as Ferthestanus bishop of Winchester, after whome succeaded Bristanus, allso Wilfemus or Wilselmus bisshop of Wells, and Wulstanus archebusshopp of Yorcke, whome Adelstanus did singulerlie loove for his pietie and sincere livinge; for his sake greatlie enriching the archebusshopricke of Yorcke; but there weare manie moe which excelled bothe in the warlike science and martiall prowesse, allthowghe there names are unknown throwghe the negligence of writers. At that time died Athelmus, busshop of Canterburie, in whose roome succeaded Wilfemus busshopp of Wells, and in the steade of Wilfemus, whoe died the xth yeare of his residence, Odo was substitute, an exceadinge wise mann, and xxij. in the ordre of busshopps. Laste of all, when as Adelstanus hadde gotten great imperie, he fullie disposed himselfe to the mayntenance of relligion, the preservation of peace, and augmentinge the commoditee of all menne, for he ædified to relligious howses of monckes Benedictines, the one at a village named Melton in the dioces of Saresburie, the other at Micelnie, a village in Somersettsheir, standinge in a fennie grownde, that the monckes showld not raunge abrode, at the least in the winter season, contrary to ther order; for in winter noe man can have accesse thereunto, excepte it be bie boate. He gave ample possessions to them bothe. He corrected divers owlde austere and sharpe lawes, and made newe ordinances, verie profitable for the common welthe, which was the laste of his noble deades; for immediatlie after hee died withoute issewe, the xvi. yeare of his reygne. His brother Edmundus, as xxv. in the order of kinges, was his successor, reigning onlie vi., whose prayses (which otherwise wolde have extolled him unto the heavens) weare obscuered bie the shortenes of his life; but whatsoever expectation and opinion hee hadd raysed emonge the people, his sonne Edgarus didd throughelie accomplishe. Som writers affirme that Edmundus overcamme the Scotts and Northe Humbrians, which wee have beefore ascribed to Aedelstanus, folowinge suche authors as are of goodd estimation; in verie deede he made lawse verie commodius to the riollme, but time didd adnihilate them all. Of his death there are divers assertions; som thincke that on a time, while he succored a servaunte of his who was assayled of his enemies, hee was sodaynlie thrust throwghe the boddie; others affirme that hee espienge a notorius theefe, whome of longe season hee detested, sodainlie sette on him and threwe himme on the grounde, geevinge him manie sore strokes; who, feelinge himselfe aggreeved, not remembringe the perill that wowlde ensewe, but desierus to eskape the presente harmes, didd peerce his side with a knife, for the which he was presentlie torne in peeces. Hee hadde beegotten bie his wife Elgida Edwinus and Edgarus, whoe reygned after Eldredus. This Eldredus succeded his brother Edmundus, as xxvi. from Cerdicius, who, in the yeare of our Lord DCCCCXLVI. was consecrate of Odo archebusshop of Canterburie, at Kingeston, whoe forthewith hadd a singuler regard of all estates. He was cheeflie a favorer of innocentie, and contrariewise a sharpe adversarie to all hurtefull persons; in the knowledge of the politique feats of warr he was accounted most coonning of all menn, soe that withoute weapons hee kepte the Scottes in obeysaunce, whome his brother Adelstanus hadde beefore receaved into allegiaunce. This place requiereth us somwhat to speake of the estate of the Scottishe affayres.

Next unto Constantine (who, as we sayde, sware feawltie unto Adelstanus,) succeaded Malcolmus, after whome ensewed thease kinges: Indulphus, Duffus, Culenus, Chennethus the thirde, and Constantinus Calvus, who obteyned the crowne bie violence; whearbie the people tooke occasion of sedition, which cowlde hardlie afterwarde bee extinguished. Constantine was slaine in this tumulte, and one Grimus succeaded, a partetaker of the same faction. After him folowed Malcolmus the seconde, who overthrew him in playne fighte. Then ensewed Duncanus and Maccabœus, a manne notorius for his wiccadnes and bowldnes, who bie plaine force entred on the kingdom; but, after this littel excourse, I will agayne drawe backe to mie purpose.

When Eldredus hadd appeased all broyles in everie place, he bente himselfe wholie to devotion, and to thende hee mighte bothe please Godd, and allso binde to him by benefitte one Ethelwoldus, a mooncke Benedictine, at the instance of his mother Edgina, hee restored the awncient abbay of Abyndon, beinge longe since erected bie kinge Ina, and now spoyled and defaced. Thus perseveringe a whiles in goodd deades, he dyed, after he had reygned ix. yeares. Menn didd speake muche shame of him for banishinge Wulstane archbusshop of Yorcke, notwithstandinge that within a yeare after hee was called againe into his contrie, and departed this mortall life beefore two yeares weare fullie complete and ended; after whome succeaded Oscitellus, Adelwaldus, and Oswaldus, an hollie father, and xix. in the ordre of those archbusshops, of whome we will make more full rehersall in an other place. After the decease of Eldredus ensewed Edwinus, the other sonn of Edmundus, being the elder, as xxvij[t]. in the ordre of the kinges, in the DCCCCIV. of our Salvation; and was with sollemme service crowned at Kyngston, bye the bisshop Odo, accordinge to the institucion of his awnceters, of whose life, thoughe it weare verie shorte, beefore we make enie tretise, it seemethe expedient to retire to Richard Duke of Normandie, that wee maye allsoe treate of them in theyr ordre.

This Richard being a child and pupill (as before wee mentioned) in the tuition of Rodulphe and Barnarde, to cheefe menn emonge the Normans, Ludovicus the Frenche kinge burned in desier, under the pretence and simulation of frindship, to defrawde the yonge impe of the Dukedome; for, hearing that William was slaine, he thought bie and bie uppon somm meanes to bringe his purpose to passe, and drewe unto Roane, wheare hee pretended to revenge the death of his frinde, when indeade his headd was encombred with other matters. The tutors or gardens of the childe mervayled muche at the pietie and jentilnes of the kinge, in consideracion whearof they entertayned him lovinglie. When the kinge perceavid his crafte and subtiltee to bee unspied of the Normans, he was then in full hope to have his purpose, and immediallie required to have the yonge Richard to bee fostered in his pallace; but forasmuche as in conclusion hee was fayne to use menaces and thretens in the case, (as it is harde by one meanes or other not to bewraye falshoode,) hee beegan sumwhat to fawle in suspicion with the people, who murmured that hee camm not so muche to assiste the yonge prince as to bringe Normandie under his subjection, as indeade his meaninge was. Hereof arose an exceadinge uprore emonge them, and they prepared treason for the kinge, for indeade they weare all readie preste in armes to defende theyr liberties, if enie mann showld goe abowte to abridge them theirof. The kinge, supposinge it necessarie to prevente this daunger, for the quietinge of this generall evil and displeasure, commawnded the childe to bee browght foorthe; and when the multitude was allmost now enraged, hee sayde to them, 'Goodd people, heere is youre lorde and duke, whose charge and governance I take on mee, in no other respect but that hee may bee fostered in good manners.' With this fayre speeche hee perverted their former opinion, minedinge neverthelesse to goe forward in his owlde attempte, and consequentlie treted with everie lorde in loving language that it mighte bee lawfull to leade yonge Richard with him into Fraunce; still keeping in his herte full intente to bee avenged of suche injuries as hee had receaved of the Normans, awayting his time for the purpose; which thinge leaste it showlde comm to lyght, hee browght upp the childe verie well and princelie. Arnulphus earl of Flawnders was not a littell dismayde with thease doengs, who not longe before hadd slayne bie treason the father of Richarde, thinckinge now that in that deade hee hadd deceaved him selfe; wherfore with all celeritee hee toke his voyage towards the Frenche kinge, to make his purgation; and with a large somm of monnie hee made, or at the leastwise dissembled, satisfaction of his crime unto him who was as false a foxe as himselfe. After this, the kinge having his wicked devices in his hedd, somtimes privelie, somtimes in open audience, spake verie evel and opprobriuslie of yonge Richard, that bie suche continewall revylinge hee might lavishe owte his conceaved mallice, and cawse him therbie as one of nowghtie nature to be odius to all the Normans; that if afterwarde it shoulde chawnce him to bee slaine bie eni fortune they might take the matter the more easelye: and in this politike tawntinge hee wente so farre that hee openlie cawled him bastard, threatening to dispossesse him of all his honors and goodds. Thus, in conclusion, the matter semed to drawe to extremitee and rigoure, in so muche that Osmundus the instructor of Richarde, detesting the intollerable creweltie of the kinge, whearas before hee hadd vertuuslie trayned him uppe, hee now cawsed him like a poppet to be dressed in sege and reedes, and secretlie to bee convayed to Laudunum, and consequentlie declared the whole circumstance to Barnard earle of Sylvanectum, who loved the yonge jentilman entierlie; whearuppon hee adjoyned to him Hughe the greate earle of Parris, and forthwith assemblinge divers legions, hee browght Richard unto Sylvanectum. Ludovicus in the meane space, hearinge that the yonge duke was stowllen away, commawnded Hughe to make restitucion. He signified bie his letters that it was not in his power so to doe. The kinge breeflie willed him to apeare, and, to bee shorte, at there meatinge and conference promised to geeve him sondrie townes in Normandie to take parte with him. Hughe was soone invegeled with fayre promises, and held with the kinge, and joyninge bothe their force together, they toke the waye to Normandie. Barnard earle of Sylvanectum thowght it more avaylable to deale with them politikelie then rigoruslie, and thereuppon treated with Barnard the Dane, presidente of Normandie, to sende legates unto kinge Lowis, who showlde say in the beehowfe of all the contrie that Normandie, the people, their boddies and goodds, weare all at his pleasure, and therefore thei beseeched him to com unto his owne menn withowte weapons, sithe it was their minde to bee pliante and obeysante. This greatlie delighted the king, being more then hee looked for at their hands, so that immediatlie hee wente unto Roane, wheare, bringinge all things to passe as hee wisshed, (or at the leaste wise as hee thowght in him selfe,) hee departed to Laudunum.

Barnard the Dane, to thende hee might keepe the Normans in their fayth towards Richard, bie his letters hee signified to Haraldus the v^{t}. kinge of Denmarcke, (who a littell beefore was driven owt of his contrie bie his soonn Sweno, and camm into Normandie, and as then sojornied abowte the borders of the Constantiens,) that now was comm the time when the kinges garrison mighte safelie bee beaten away, and therefore hee requiered him, ether by and bie to assiste him, or to sende thither his sowldiers, for bie that meanes hee sayde it wowld comm to passe that hee showlde fawle in communication with the Frenshe kinge; neither didd his expectation deceave him, for when as Haraldus was comm, Ludovicus, beinge certified of his sodaine comminge, wente to meate with him; they mett abowte the bancke of the river Sequana, wheare, whiles the two kinges commoned towchinge the murtheringe of William, and that everie mann helde their handes, it chaunced a certayne Dane to espie Herlowinus, and sodainelie to thruste him throwghe, for that William was slayne for his sake, whearof arose a crüell skirmishe, wherin the Frenchemen weare ether killed or putt to flighte. Ludovicus was taken prisoner, howbeit in the end the Normans restored him to the Frenchemen, taking his sonne Lotharius in pledge. Now was Richard of sufficiencie to beare rule, and forthwith proclaimed duke. I muste not lette passe to shewe that certaine historiens have fallslie affirmed that this Danishe prince who succored the Normans was called Aygholdus or Ligrotus, when indead there never reyned enie kinge in Denmarcke of that name, as well appeareth bie the historie of Saxo, who shewethe evidentlie that Haraldus the vth. as I sayde, was then expelled owte of his riolme bie his sonne Sweno (as allso the selfe same awthors doe grawnte), notwithstandinge that Saxo makethe no relation of this conflicte

with the Frenchemen. The kinge of Frawnce verie desierus to bee avenged was not afterwarde quiet; but, being bowlstered up by Otho kinge of Germanie, hee, tried manie thinges in vayne, and loste muche labor, for when as they bothe joynctlie wente into Roane and didd muche harme to the cittie, neverthelesse they weare fayne to geeve over in the ende, not withowte the destruction of their menn and their own infamie. In this yeare, beinge the DCCCCVI. of Christes nativitee, died the Frenche king, after whome succeaded his soonne Lotharius, who bie the procurement
Carnutes. of Theobaldus earle of Chartres beegann to professe mervaylus hostilitee towards duke Richard, bothe to mayntaine the owlde mallice of his father, and also for that the duke waxed so puissaunte that hee beecamme dreadefull to all the contries adjoyninge; whearfor firste of all hee assayled him bie traines of treason, which for that they framed not accordinge to his minde hee fell to open warre, whearin they both turmoyled with variable fortune; in fine they agreede of peace, at the instance of divers noble jentilmen. This Richard encreased bothe in the renowne of martiall valiance and allso vertuus qualities, for, employenge himselfe to sett forth Godds honor, hee bylded manie goodlie cherches, garnishinge them with sondrie giftes. Hee hadd but two onlie children that I knowe, Richard, and Emma who maried Etheldredus. Hee lefte his mortall boddie in the yeare of our Lorde DCCCCXCVI. After him succeaded his soonn Richard, of whome elsewheare I make rehersal as opportunitee shall serve. But now lett us com backe unto Edwinus.

It lothethe mee to write enie thing of this kinge, bothe for the shortnes of his reygne and allso for the filthines of his life, but that the dewe ordre driveth mee therto, for the verie daye whearin hee was denownced kinge hee defyled his owne coosin, the wife of a certaine noble mann, not onlie againste her will, but allmoste openlie like a brute beaste, insomuche that the rumor of the horrible crime ranne throwgheowte all the riolme. Wherfore, when as Dunstanus, who was latelie made abbot of Glastonburie, reprehended in fatherlie talke, admonishinge him heareafter to withhowlde himselfe from suche abhominable vice, hee was so farre from abyding his hollie admonitions, that heaping one evel deade on an other, hee banished this hollie father; which torned him to mutche displeasure, for the Northumbrians and Mercians cleane foorsooke him, and proclamed king his brother Edgarus, in wonderful showtes wisshing him all fælicitee. This was such a corsie to the herte of Edwinus, that shortlie after hee died in the iiij. yeare of his reygne. Thus obteyned Edgarus the kingdom, beinge a moste valient person bothe in boddie and minde, and was crowned at Bathe, or as somm thinck at Kingston, bie Odo the archebisshop, in the yeare of our Lord DCCCCLIX. In the beginninge of his government hee contemned all worldlie thinges in comparison of peace, knowing it to bee a thinge most delectable, which when hee hadd gotten, leste hee showlde bee molested bie foreyne nations, hee prepared a great navie, and placed it in three sondrie coastes, to keepe of suche strawngers as continuallie annoyed the contrie. Hee allso kepte the Scottes and Wallshemen in obeysawnce. I finde in verie oulde monumentes that the Wallshe people, who ever unwillinglie obeyed the Englishemen, didd ordayne them a prince of their owne nation, and that in the time of kinge Edgarus they hadd a lorde named Ludovallus, whoe payed tribute to the kinge of Englond, which their ordre as well of princes as also of paymente continewed certayne yeares after: howbeit, it is not to bee seene at what time they gotte this benefite of the Englishe kinges, nether is it specified that ever I cowld learne of enie grave author. Edgarus demawnded of Ludovallus for his yearelie rentes XXX. wolves, to thentent that that kinde of hurtfull bestes abownding in that parte of the Ilond, and verie mischevus to the greate flockes of sheepe, might utterlie bee destroyed; if it fortuned him to wante in his præscribed nombre of woolves, then in the steede of them hee showlde pay I knowe not well what sommes of monnie. Thus the wise kinge thowght beste to keepe his adversaries under, and to show himselfe in all times and places a mann borne into this worlde to do goodd; whearfore, settinge all delay aparte, hee called Dunstanus owte of banishemente, and cawsed him to bee consecrate busshop of Worcestre; and for as muche as there was great skarcitee of goodd governers, hee annexed thereunto the bishoppricke of London, which the sage prelate toke on him more for the commoditee of the peeple then his owne peculier gayne, for in those dayse the bisshopps hadd no more riches or welthe then other menn, but more learninge, sinceritee, and wisdom.

The queene Elfreda in the meane time departed this transitorie life, bie whome the kinge hadde a soonne named Edwarde, whose deathe cawsed the kinge to commit a moste detestable crime, for at that presence it was commonlie noysed that Horgerius duke of Cornwall hadd a dowghter called Alfreda, of most excellente bewtie, whome the kinge thinckinge to marrie, in all haste assigned his familier frinde Ethelwoldus to take veewe of the virgin, and in his name to require her in mariage of the Duke if it weare so that she was as fayre as she was reported. Ethelwoldus departed into Cornewall, and assone as hee caste his eye on the mayden, hee was neare madde in loove, insomuche that, forgettinge the kinges commaundement, hee desiered her for himselfe, and obteined; which doonne, he retorned to his prince and sayde that she was of no suche bewtie as was reported, or as beeseemed his maiestie; whearbie perceavinge the king's minde to bee somwhat alienated from loove, hee began bie littel and littel to entreate him to grawnte him his good will that hee might marie with her himselfe, which thing the king consented the more easlie unto, for that hee uppon his worde he seemed to contemne her. Thus Ethelwoldus obteyned the mariage of Alfreda, which in processe must needes breede his destruction, for the fame of her comlines daylie more and more encreased, beinge now more frequente in the ies of all men, in so muche that the kinge, beinge exceadinge desierus to have a syghte of her, purposlie wente on huntinge to a certayne manneir of Ethelwoldus, who assone as hee hadd once espied Alfreda, it is wonderus to bee towlde how extreemelie he burned in loove, in that hee bothe imagened how to slea her howsband, and to have her himselfe. The temptinge wooman enkendeled the brands of loove, whearin the kinge boorned, that hee attempted this horrible facte; for when her husband herde of the kinges comminge, hee is reported to have uttered the whole matter to his wife, praying her, for the savegard of them bothe, to shewe herselfe more dissolute and uncomlie then shee was accustomed to this yonge amoros knighte; but the woman forgettinge her howsbondes loove, contemninge his children, persisting still like herselfe, that is to say, light, covetus, and prowde, decked and picked herselfe in the hartiest manner, and like a pecocke, meetinge with the kinge, like a beaste undoed the bandes of chastitee. This deed mervayluslie dishonested the kinge emonge all estates, for the which hee was greatlie reproved of Dunstanus, and allbeit hee was ashamed and penitent for his misdeade, yeat cowlde hee not forgett his loove; but as for Alfreda, she not onlie not repented her doenge, but was exceadingelie wroth with Dunstanus for his well advising the kinge. Edgarus hadd bie Alfreda two sonnes, Edmunde, who lived but a fewe dayes, and Ethelredus, who when hee was christened polluted the fownte with the excrementes and ordure of his boddie, wheare uppon Dunstanus is reported to have sayde, that it wowld comm to passe that hee in time showlde procure the greate hurte and dishonor of his contrie. Edgarus besides this looved a certayne noonne named Wilfreda, or rather, as somm suppose, she hadd taken no vowe, but was kepte emonge noonnes for feare of defloweringe; of her hee ingendered a dowghter called Editha, who for her hollie livinge (as it is committed to memorie) was afterward canonized. Thease weare the vices of Edgarus in his blinde yowthe, which in time hee cleane overshadowed with the vertewse bothe of his boddie and minde, for in rydinge and armes hee was verie experte, in noble corage second to no mann, in labor and travailes aboove measure; his owne subjectes hee allwayse kept in their dewe homage; foreyners and strawngers, who weare woonte to annoye the

Ilond with incursions, hee so dawnted in the beginninge of his kingdom, that never after thei durste comm owte of the bowndes of their owne dunghill. Hee was a sharpe sercher and punisher of fawltes, yeat withowte ire and creweltie, for at small matters hee was often contented to wincke, that hee might rather show him selfe a proffitable then an ambitius prince. Beesides thease vertewse hee exceadinglie embraced godlines, esteeminge nothinge in respecte of relligion, enhauncinge the wise, learned, and hollie men, making them of his senat and cowncell, sufferinge no other to bee rewlers over the people. Whearfore next unto Dunstanus he favored one Ethewoldus, a manne of singuler witte and learninge, whome firste hee made abbot of Abyngdon, then bisshop of Winchestre. Bie his benefite allso was Oswalde the mooncke promoted to the bishopricke of Worciter, and, consequentlie, to the archebisshopricke of Yorcke, after whome Dunstanus was the next bisshop of Worcestre.

This prince attributed so much to the learninge and hollie lyfe of thease iij bisshops, wherein they seemed to excell (as mooncke are not to learne howe to showe a fayre glosse in that matter), that beinge entised and mooved with their prayers and intercession, yea somwhat angrie that the cheefe prelates showlde still keepe their wives, contrarie to the decree of hollie fathers, hee earnestlie treated with Pope Jhon the xiij. that uppon goodd consideracions which the mooncke hadd fownde owte for their proffet, hee wowlde vowchsafe to graunte bie his apostolike authoritee, that they mighte expell all preestes called seculer chanons owte of the colliges of Winchestre and Worcestre, and to bringe in their mooncke, which in fine hee obteyned; moreover, bie the instigation of Ethelwoldus and Dunstanus, in the newe college or abbay of Winchestre, latelie fownded by Alured, and in that allso which was at Schireburne, a village in Saresburie diocesse, the preestes weare kaste foorthe and monckes theire placed; and the one of them was intituled the abbay of Hide, the other of Schireburne, for eeven there consisted the cheefe See of the Weste

Saxon bisshops, of which diocesse Saincte Aldelmus was one of the firste governors.

Dueringe this season moonckes engroched on manie other places, and beegann to hourde upp riches unmeasurable in all parties, which turned their successors to muche damage; for whiles thei onlie employed the Divine service and avoyded the entercourse of menn, embracing solitarie dwellinges, wherof they hadd the first name of monasticall life, thei seemed ful wel to perfowrme their profession, but contrarie when they hawnted companie, despised the sole livinge, and thirsted after riches, it is incredible how muche they didd degenerate from their awnciters, consideringe that, mawgre their hedd, they weare fayne to care for worldlie matters, which no dowbte encomberethe the greater parte of a mannes yeares. What that the selfe same covetise, as a generall and infectuus pestelence, didd so enter into the hertes of all other priestes, that a greate nomber torned from their owlde devotion unto tyrranie, not knowing how to avoyde that which is forbidden bie the prophet, sayenge, Yf afflwence of riches chawnce unto the, sette not thine herte thereon. Their predecessors honored the ordre of priesthoode with the holines of their life, and sealed it with their bloodde; they disworshiped the samewith their riot and licentius livinge; the other receaved promotion slacklie and with shamefacednes, and bestowed dignitees onlie on goodd persons; these sewed for them impudentlie and used them as prowdelie; the others exercised liberalitee and shewed innocentie; thease weare assoted in avarice and used nowghtines; the others weare satisfied with litel and lived temperatelie; but theas, having too muche welthe, cowlde not live accordinge to their owne rightes, while they weare constreyned to geeve hospitalitee to others, which humainitee no dowte (for so is commonlie termed) is so farre indeade from the nature of humanitee, that it commethe nearer unto follie and slaverie, sithe therin they are often constreyned to offende: for what manne is there whose senses are not stirred uppe, after that hee hathe filled himselfe with divers meates and drinck, as of necessitee those priestes are enforced to doe, while bie mannes lawe they are driven to keepe plentifull howses, and to geeve deyntie interteinment to all commers; but I will nowe retorne to mie purpose.

Obscurior hic textus. Now died Odo, archebisshop of Canterburie, after hee hadde been resident xix yeares, or (as som suppose) but xiij. In whose see succeaded Dunstanus, as xxiij. from Augustinus. This Odo, with Oswaldus, archbisshop of Yorck, did solemnlie crowne kinge Edgare, which thinge, throughe the negligence of writers, is attributed unto Dunstanus, who, as beefore wee specified, was in banishement at his coronation, and shortlie after released. Kinge Edgarus, havinge now tranquillitee throughe owte his riolme, and being himselfe wholie bente unto godlie woorckes, ether restored or newlie bylded manie abbayes, or otherwise beestowed large giftes on them; emong all others, hee especiallie fownded a relligius howse of noonnes Benedictines in the village of Wilton, neare to the cittie of Saresburie, whereof his dowghter Editha was abbesse certaine years, untill it pleased Godd to dissever her soule and boddie.

This Saresburie liethe sowthward on level grownde, havinge divers pleasawnte brookes within it, and hath running bie it the river Nadder, which being encreased with the river Wyle and Havine, which glawnceth bie the village Wersminster, it floweth sowthward into the ocean. Butt to bee short, this Edgarus, to thende hee mighte traine his people to vertewus life, hee made verie profitable lawes, which time turned into nowghte; and finallie, in the xxxvij. of his age, and xvi. yeare of his reygne, hee departed owte of this worlde. After whome succeaded Edward the second, a sonne worthie of so noble a father, and xxxi. in the ordre of the kinges. In this yeare, being the DCCCCLXXV. of our Salvation, Dunstanus, archebisshop of Canterburie, called a congregation of the spiritualitee for the reformacion of relligion, and the betteringe thereof. Deweringe thease affayres certayne yonckers, who weare in dispaire of good loocke while all things weare so quiet, and hoped for a fayre day if somm commotion weare made, beeganne to stirre coles, being thereto provoked bie suche priestes as weare latelie dispossessed bie mooncкes, and thought one day to chalenge there owlde righte. The matter was browght beefore certayne judges, who, in open concurse debatinge the case, and the more parte agreing that the preestes owghte to bee restored to their former estate, a voyce was sodainlie heard, saienge, 'They are not well in their wittes that beare so muche with priestes;' as who showld say, the lawe didd beare more with the mooncкes in defeatinge of other men then with priestes in layeng clayme to their owne. Neverthelesse, forasmuche as an ymage of Christe standing beefore them seemed to have spoken those woordes, it was taken as a most certaine oracle; the poore prelates loste their sewte, and all the broyle was appeased. Thus the mooncкes bie divine helpe, or rather humaine subtiltee, withheld still thease gotten gooddes, for eeven at those dayse there weare divers who rather surmised it to bee the oracle of Phebus then Godd, that is to saye, rather craftelie cowntrefayted bie menn then uttered of the Lorde. Edward was proclaymed kinge, full sore againste the will of his steppe mother, Alfreda; and in his regall function hee shewed him selfe a devowte and moderate yonge prince, whearbie hee beecam beloved of all sortes, as one that directlie folowed the steppes of his father; which thinge muche agreeved the herte of Alfreda, who hoped to have borne the sway herselfe, and to have convayed the governement to her sonne Ethelredus, after the decease of Edwarde; but, forasmuche as now shee dispayred in the case, like a right stepmother, she ymagened to slea her sonne-in-lawe; and, to thende it mighte the more speedelie bee browghte to passe, shee invented an occasion of her purpose. It fortuned the kinge on a time to goe on huntinge unto the New Forreste, wheare, followinge ernestlie the deare and dogges, hee loste his companie, and theruppon drewe towards the howse of Alfreda, being harde bie, ether to drincke or to visite his halfe brother Etheldredus. In that place at this day standithe the castell called Corphe. When this wicked wooman see him comminge, she called one of her servants aside, and bidde him awayte his time and to slea him unwares. And bie cause the goodd prince showld misdowbte nothinge, shee mett with him and gave him drincke, (as hee desiered,) with all reverence and curtesie; and as hee satte on his horsse with the cupp at his mowth the villayne thruste him throwghe the boddie. The kinge fealing himselfe wownded, turned his horsse and galloped towards his menn; but the verie torment of his wownde caused him to fawle downe starcke deade. The develishe woman, leaste the crewell facte showlde bee open, cawsed the corpes of this innocent impe to bee browght in and to bee buried, wheare in shorte space his memoriall waxed famus, for the seyenge is that bie the providence of Godd it chawnced a blind woman to comm thither, and in great watchinge and prayer to have beeseched the hollie martir, that bie his meanes she mighte bee restowred to her sight, which incontinentlie she receaved. Divers miracles weare there shewed, (as antiquitees specifieth,) for the which Edward seemed not unworthie to bee accownted a sancte. His boddie was afterward translated from that vile place unto Glastenburie Abbaye, and theare honorablie enterred. Alfreda in the meane space beewayled her misdeade, afflictinge her frayle fleshe with stripes and fastinge, bestowinge all her goodes ether on poore people or relligius howses, for shee is thought to have fownded two noonries, one at Amisburie, a village in the diocesse of Sarisburie, another at Wherwel, in Winchestre diocesse, whearin she passed her life. Kinge Edward reyned iij. yeares, and thereunto somm writers have annexed vj. monethes After the deathe of this prince the rype yeares, and, as one wowlde say, manne's age of the kingdom decayed, for even as hee himselfe in the flowre of his yowthe, his sences being fresshe and lustie, hadd a sodaine fawle, even so all the strengthe of the monarchie beeganne to apaire, so that in the time of Etheldredus the owlde age and extreeme infirmitee thereof ensewed, as wee shall sygnifie in our next booke.

Ordinis Cluniacensis et ordinis divi Benedicti.

THE SEVENTH BOOKE

OF POLIDOR VERGILL ON THE ENGLISHE HISTORIE.

Etheldredus was the next enoynted king after the decease of this Edwarde, and xxx[tie] in nombre from Cerdicius; bie whose sloggishnes and follie the wele publique declined into soche disorder that justlie yt might be thought that the crooked and olde age of the kingdom beganne, for these three afflictions forthewythe ensewed, famine, pestilence, and battell, which evells weare signified and tolde before bie the godlie archebisshoppe Dunstanus, insomuche that he impungned ernestlie and resisted to consecrate Etheldredus, in that he aspiered to the emperie throughe the murthering of his brother; yeat beinge driven therunto bie compulsion, as an infallible deviner, hee pronownced and sayd yt wolde shortlie cŏmme to passe that the Englishe people, besides the losse of there liberties, sholde generallie sustaine sharpe punishmentes. Etheldredus hadde no knowledge in martiall affayrs, as a man alltogether hartlesse, and enveleyed with the delicius poyson of ease and riotinge, which thinges made him have evell reporte of his owne nation, nothinge feared of his borderers, and finallie despised of the barbarus people and forriners; wherfore certayn pirates of Denmarke, trustinge muche in there owne hautie coorage, in great tumultes entred the Ilond, not withoute greate slaughter, rawnginge everie wheare; and wheras the sea costes weare not fortified with anie garrison, theye did first of all toorne them to there use and

Ethelredus an Inglis kyng.

praye. The Danes beinge then encoraged bie this successe, ranne into all corners, spoylinge and distroyinge all thinges; with whome the kinge not daringe to encounter, didde of force geve unto them a great somme of golde, to the end theye wolde imediatlie depart into there cuntrie; which condition of peace dyd greatlie deceyve him, for he did not so much therebie dispatche his contrie of this present mischief, as he did bringe uppon it a greater; for the Danes, beinge the more entised with the swete savor of the golde, in shorte tyme breakinge there truse, didd agayne sett uppon the Ilonde, and that nether cowardlie nor rashlie, but administeringe all thinges with an huge armie and a well furnished navie. This fresh brute of newe warres astonied and appalled the kinge, who hoped that his ennemies would not have enie more enterprisede enie thinge after the recepte of this gifte, and therfore was nothinge readie to doe battayle. Neverthelesse, as sone as he colde, he prepared in good order his shippes, and ordayned as chefe ruler one Elfricus, a manne no lesse stronge in bodie then of valiant corage, yeat, as yt fell owte, nothinge faythfull or trustie. But I knowe not bie what reason it camme to passe, for when as the Danes aproched, hee, cownterfitinge great expedition to fighte, slipped awaye unto his adversaries; which thinges so dismayed the hartes of the counterparte, because yt happened contrarie to the expectation of them all, that almoste there was never a stroke striken; but in a small season somme shipps skowred awaye, some were taken, and the gretest parte overwhelmed in the middest of the fludde. The Danes being consequentlie broughte to the Ile with a prosperus wynde, betooke them selves to all kinde of botie. Howe be it, soche of them as entred the teritorie of Northe Humberlande, whilest over muche they endevorede the spoyle of the savage people, they were ether slayne or put to flight. Then soche as marched towardes London to assault yt, notwithstandinge they hadde on all sydes beeseged the same, yeat weare they fayne to geve over ther attempt, for that there oppugnation nothinge prevaylede, where the citizens cleved together licke burrs; yeat, notwithstanding all these discommodities, they plaged, vexed, and opressed the Englishemenn, and finallie gatheringe together in dew warlike order, not like pelferers, eche where they assaulted them; whome when Etheldredus, as a mann of muche lesse puissance, colde in no wyse resist, being all together daunted, he sent letters as concerninge treatie of pease, which was concluded on this condition, that Inglande sholde paye tribute to the Danes, which albeit yt weare ignominius and shamfull, yeat accordinge to the necessitie of tyme yt was marvelos convenient. Elfricus after this, who was made admirall of the kinges navie, beinge destitute of all hope emonge his enemies, retowrned agayne to Etheldredus, trusting to obteyne pardon of his premised offence, to whome the kinge francklie graunted life, but yeat for his offence hee caused his ieys to bee pulled owte. This peace was scarselie on all parties so soone confirmed as the kinge beganne to abuse the same, for while he ledde his life in this tranquillitee hee beecam more noysom and crewell to his owne liege people, for daylie ether hee beereved the richer sorte of their gooddes, ether hee slaunderuslie dishonested them, or for verie trifelinge defaultes hee ammerced them with bannishemente; more over promoters and abbettowrs hadd libertie to deceave whome they lusted, to whose leasinges and accusations his eares weare soe readie and open that no manne allmoste cowlde warrante himselfe as voyde fromme trespasse. With these pillages and extorcions the mindes of his subjectes weare soe wownded that generallie they shamefullie inveyed againste him. When the Danes hadd an inkelinge hereof, they beeganne agayne to kaste with themselves the invasion of the riolme, supposinge the commonaltie to bee sufficientlie provoked to rebellion throughe the vices of their prince, and soe mutche the more prone to yealde themselves to aliens. Wherfore their kinge Sweno the Firste immediatlie composed himselfe to warre with Etheldredus, assemblinge bie littell and littell a convenable armie: but beefore wee make enie farther declaration hereof, it is requisite that heare we make mention of Richard the Seconde duke of Normandie, as wee promised in our former booke, to the ende wee may observe the dewe ordre of those dukes.

This Richard was a manne of verie temperate livinge, of greate experience in warfare, and in all respectes well worthie the princelie hereditee of his father, which hee soberlie governed; for hee made open decree emonge his soldiers, that whiles hee was busied in warlike affayres that none of themme showlde bee soe hardie as to annoye his frindes, or once to intermedle with the hollie and sacred iewells, or to make prophane thinges that weare divine, so that as well in domesticall as martiall affayres hee referred all thinges to honestie, justice, and relligion. Robert king of Fraunce, and sonne of kinge Hugo Capetus, hadde especiall triall of his valiaunce in battaile, whoe when he was awayted and endaungered throwghe the treason of divers his nobles, hee finallie avoyded themm bie the onlie assistance and pollicie of this Richarde; yeat emonge thease soe great verteus weare enterlaced not a fewe vices, for greatlie hee was noted of luxurie, in that hee looved manie woomen, and emonge the reste one of obscure lineage, from whose companie, beinge admonished of his nobilitee, hee would not onlie not abstayne, but allso contrarie to their persuasion joyned with her in matrimonie, of whome hee beegotte iij. sonnes, Richard and Robert, whoe afterwarde rewled Normandie, and William, whoe beetooke himselfe to the monasticall life; and as manie dowghters, wherof Alice the eldeste was espowsed to Reginaldus, an earle of the Brittons, Elinore the seconde to Baldwinus earle of Flaunder, and the thirde to the kinge of Navarra. In processe of time this Richarde, being of goodd yeares, deceased, and after him succeded Richard the Thirde, his soonne, a moste noble and princelie person, whoe died after iij. yeares, not withowte suspicion of empoysoninge, in whose place was substitute his brother Roberte, of whose actes shallbee declared in an other place more convenient. Now let us make retrayte to Sweno king of Denmarcke.

Richard duke of Normandies 3 sonns by the obscure woman.

Sweno king of Denmarcke arrived in Englonde.

Hee arrived with a great fleete in that coste of Englonde which bowndethe estewarde, wheare, sendinge abrode his sowldiers, as soone as hee was donne to understande bie his espialls that the inhabiters of these quarters weare in nothing appoincted for warrs, leavinge a small garrison in his shippes, hee overthrewe their villages, hee burned howses, hee made spoyle of menn and cattayle; then bendinge his power northwarde, and provoked to straye farther throwghe the sweetenes of the bootie, withowte resistance hee invaded North Humberlande. The North Humbrians, partlie amazed with the present perill, partelie remembringe that beefore this time they hadd obeyed the Danes, and therfore imagininge that they retorned not to their enemies but rather to their natives, yealded themselves of their owne accorde. After these exploytes hee sette on the Mercians, whome with great facilitee hee subdewed; then towrninge southeward, hee there overcamme all the borderers. This Dane being daylie more animated and prowde through this fortunate successe, minded to geeve assaulte unto London, whether he harde say that Etheldredus withdrewe himmselfe bie reason of this trooblesom commotion. Whearfore, havinge all thinges requisite for suche an attempte, hee goethe forwarde, in minde to sett uppon the cittey, and sodaynlie beeseeged the same, that in this laste perill as it seemed hee might ether utterlie distroye his adversarie, or at leaste wise hee mighte perceave of what force hee weare. On the other side, the citizens, allbeit they weare astonied with the sodaine terror, yeat ponderinge within themselves that the desolation of the whole contrie was joyned with their calamitee and distresse, for as much as theirs was the cheefe and principall citte, thei bestirred and defended themselves manfullie, for somm made haste to meete with their enemies, somm threwe them from the walls, somm kepte them off with stones, and finallie eche mann, accordinge to his habilitee, endevored coragiuslie to withstande their violence. In this conflicte, albeit the Danes weare feerce and eger, yeat the Englishemenn, mindinge to the uttermost to garde their kinge, shrincked not one whit in these sharpe broyles, in soe muche that in greate thronge they russhed foorthe of the gates, and stoutelie dealed with hande strokes emonge the thickest of their adversaries. The Danish prince, whilest he coveted to succoure his companie, and to maynetane the victorie which he reckened to bee allreadie in his handdes, was environed of his enemies, bothe on the right hande and on the lefte, not withowte greate occision of his menne, soe that necessitee urged him to breake forthe in the middest of his enimies weapons, and bothe daye and nighte, for the space of two dayse, hee tooke his jornie toward Bathe. This certis was a singuler and notable fighte, wheerin the Englishe people didd well specifie their manwhode and valiance, who havinge Etheldredus to their capitan, a mann of small corage and lesse wisdom, didd repell so mightie hostillitee from the assault of the cittee. While Sweno sojornied at Bathe hee was soe molested with the penurie of corne, that he was constrayned to suffer the Englishemen to redime of him the tribute wherwith the realme tofore was levied, after the which receipte of this monnie he retiered into Denmarck, mindinge with a great number in all speede to returne againe into this londe.

Etheldredus in the meane whiles supposed that this release or rather sale of the annuitee camme to this pointe, that the Danes for ever hereafter showlde be quiet; but the nobilitee did not soe unadvisedlie misconster so covert a traine, but, easlie foreseeinge that soe great a mischeefe cowlde not easlie bee shunned, exhorted himme that with all celeritee hee wowlde furnishe an armie; and in deade Sweno (as the nobles wiselie adjudged) made small tarienge, but in fewe dayse dispatched himme selfe into Englonde. Nether was there muche protractinge on the Englishe parte, but with æquall ranckoure and stomacke thei ranne together on bothe sides. The contention was harde in the beginninge on ether parte, but shortlie it camm so lamentable throwghe the slippinge away of certaine Englishemenn to the adverse parte, that at the lengthe Etheldredus, perceaving how hee was browght to extreeme miserie, after his overthrowe, called his cheefe men together and spake in this wise: 'I mighte safelie use continuall silence, O mi nobles and frindes, if ether I hadde the sage wisdom of an auncient father in giving councell and administration of mie kingdom, or els our warriers sufficient puissaunce and faythe for the defence and munition of their contrie. Trewlie I acknowlege how glorius a thinge deathe is in the beehoofe of our contrie, and here mie selfe am preste and readie ether to prostitute mie bodie as a sacrifice for mie realme, or to throwe mie selfe into the middeste of mine enemies; for here presentlie I see beefore mine ies the ruine of mie lond, and of all Englishemen, except with maturitee provision bee hadd in this great sea of evvels. Wee are vanquished of the Danes, and howe? not bie there weapons, but bie owre owne malicius treason wee are wasted. In the first raginge of these broyles I prepared an exceading goodlie navie, which the perfidius traytor Elfricus surrendered to our adversaries; then ful often have wee skirmished, but throwghe the unfaythful dealinge of our owne feeres and confederates wee have ended unhappelie and shamefullie; wherebie wee weare constreined to make that fowle and unseemelie league with foriners, in extreme necessitee, which surelie onlie Godde may overcome; yeat was it concluded to our utter undooinge, for asmuche as wee dealed with suche wicked and miscreant creatures, with owte ether honestie or godlines, as weare not afrayde or ashamed, contrarie to divine and humaine lawse, and contrarie to our expectation, to infringe all covenantes and promises; and thus are wee comm to the passe that onlie wee maye not feare the losse of our imperie, but allso that thenglishe name for ever bee not extinguished. Wherfore, sithe even now our foes are over our heddes, deere frendes, whoe all wayse I knowe have regarded mie demandes and peticions, vowchsafe yee to provide, consulte, and releeve yowre contrie, which is at the poynct to fall and beecomm waste.' At these woordes all menn beecamm more intentive to the common helthe and utilitee, and callinge a cowncell, they delibered what was moste for their avayle; but sodaynlie thei fell into great dowbtes and pensivenes, as menn which (according to the Greek proverbe) didde howlde the woolfe bie the eare; for if thei showlde addresse them selves to fightinge, they didde plainlie perceave that they hadd more cause to feare there owne fellowse then their adversaries, whoe allwayse bent themselves to shrinckinge awaye as soone as cause of terror was objected; againe, if they showlde geeve place or relente, they reckened how filthie and opprobrius it weare to yealde them selves; yet that they accounted to bee the lesse evell, thincking that manie therebie mighte bee preserved from slaughter, whoe in time to comm mighte healpe to recover the fraunchise and fredom of their contrie. This verdite pleased all sortes; wherfore the kinge purposed to commit himselfe and his goodds to the safe conduite of Richarde the Second duke of Normandie, whose sister named Emma he hadd espowsed in mariage; and leste hee showlde seem over rashelie to attempte it, hee sente beefore Emma, with his two sonnes, Alfredus and Edwarde, to trie how the duke was affected. This Richard curteuslie enterteyned his sister and her children, and promised that her husband Etheldredus showlde lacke noe succours for the defence of his kingdom. In the meane while Sweno possessed the greatest parte of Englond, and bie littell and littell receaved the rest into his jurisdiction, for the people voluntarilie yealded themselves; soe that Etheldredus, thinckinge it highe time to geeve roome to his enemie, after XXXV. yeare of his reigne fledd to Richard duke of Normandie, and Sweno consequentlie obteyned the whole dominion over Englonde. Thus the Danes weare the next straungers which, after the Englishe menn, gatte a kingdom in the Ilonde, which was the MXIIIJ. yeare of our Salvation. Sweno used his victorie verie rigoruslie toward the Englishemenn, to the ende that, theye beinge weakened, hee might from thenceforthe bee the more voyde from all daunger; but hee was insatiable bothe in the exercising of his severite and also in the spoyling of theyr substance, insomutche that he withhelde not his incontinent hande from relligius persons and thinggs sacred; for this hethen dogge, mindinge no lesse to extirpe the Englishe name then the

King Etheldredus fled to Normandie with his ij. sonns Alfredus and Edward.

Sweno possesseth the kingdom very rigoruslie, being the first of the Danys prinses that ruled in Englond.

Christian relligion owte of the hartes of all menn, after he hadde pilled the nobles of the Ilond, and sacked manie cherches of their jewels, he raced allso the abbay of Burie, wherein lieth the boddie of Saincte Edmund, kinge and martyr, with all the territoris adjoyninge. Not longe after Sweno suffered dewe punishemente, as the moonks made reporte, whoe weare to muche assoted on miracles, for hee, say they, whilest hee bosted emonge his soldiors of the conqueringe of his kingdom, was sodaynlie pricked as it weare with the poyncte of a dagger fallinge from aboove, wherwith hee fell to the growde, crienge owtragiusli that hee was slaine, and forthewith gave upp the ghoste; in soe muche that the standers bie beinge wonderuslie agaste at the soodaine chaunce, and seeinge no mann likelie to geeve the stroke, didde thincke it to be donne bie the wrathe and indignation of our Lorde. Moreover, the fame wente even unto theyr posteritee that hee was slayne with the verie same weapon which saincte Edmunde ware in his life time. Howbeit, accordinge to the assertion of Saxo Grammaticus, Sweno hadde a muche more happie ende of his life, whoe affirmeth that this prince, after divers his memorable feates, conquirred the Englishemenne, granting on this condition peace unto Etheldredus, (whome he falselie nameth Adelstanus,) that after his decease the inheritance of rioll diademe showde be divoluted unto him, and that Sweno in fine beecam Christian, purginge his offences with muche godlines and pietee. These thinges are not alltogether dissident from the trewthe: namely, that Sweno died a Christian; secondarilie, that Etheldredus reygned throughe intercession, sithe it is evident that he died in Englond; and this maye seeme a suer argument as towchinge the godlines of Sweno, that under his reygne the Danes embraced the Christian faythe: but let us prosecute owre matter.

Not longe after that Sweno was departed owte of this mortall life the Danes proclamed as their kinge Canutus his sonne, a yownge man of gooddlie disposition, and well affected towardes the relligion of Christe. The Englishemenn, whoe greatlie longed

Canutus kyng, sone to Sweno.

to rejecte the servile yoke of the Danes, when the rumor of the deathe of Sweno was eche wheare bruted weare exceading gladde, and immediatlie bie there letters certified Etheldredus of the death of his enemie, exhorting him with all expedition to com and deliver his riolme owte of the handds of straungers, and therin thei profered their assistance, boddies and gooddes. These tidinges recoumforted the spirits of the kinge, whoe, beinge propense to revenge, made noe delayse in this offered oportunitee; yet misdowtinge the fickle unstedfastenes of the vulgare people, accordinge to the arbitrement of his menne, premised Edwarde, his elder sonne, into England, to feele and assaye the mindes of the comminaltie. This yownge manne used noe trifelinge procrastination in the case, but with singuler prudence severallie undermined the sentences of all estates, and returned with æquall celeritee into Normandie, makinge relation to his father that all thinggs weare in saftie if hee woolde woorcke speadelie. With this messenger of trust Etheldredus conceaved soe good hope that indeade hee minieded to assaye his fortune: wherefore, partlie trustinge to the fidelite of his nation, partlie to the succours which he receaved of Duke Richarde, he quickelie sayled into Englonde. His comminge was verie acceptable to the people, emonge whome the Danishe governement beganne longe beefore to bee verie tedius and hatefull, as a thinge moste exitiall and pestilent to the Englishe name and stemme, notwithstandinge that Canutus with all jentilnes and liberallitie greatlie endevored to preserve them still in there obeysaunce and loyaltie; whoe, to the ende hee mighte have the better successe in his regiment, is reported to have appeased Saincte Edmunde in his wrathe conceaved towards his father Sweno. The common people fabled that emonge the giftes which hee offered for his mitigation to have been a crowne of gowlde, which afterwarde shoulde bee redimed, if it soe liked himm, for a great somme of monie; wherebie didd springe a custom that kinges succeading shoulde doe the same, but sewerlie it was not long observed, or rather never, for (as Persius sayth) what entercourse hathe gowlde with hollie things? Allso hee adorned the temple with manie giftes, and gratified the relligius with ample possessions. Within a fewe dayse after the arrivall of Etheldredus in Englonde, with a well appointed armie, hee marched towardes Canutus, who withhelde himselfe at Lincolne, and putte himme fromme his place, spoylinge all the provence with fier and sworde, and sleaing a great compenie of thinhabitants. This cittie is of goodd renowne, and situate eastwarde, the one parte thereof standing on an hill, and garnished with the princelie cherche of the divine Virgin our ladie, and supported with a stronge tower: the other parte consisting on a levil grounde sowthewarde, havinge hard bie it the river Witham (for soe it is vulgarlie termed), and goodd feeldes, of noe lesse fertilitee then pleasaunce. Canutus, who gave grownde in that he was not of semblable power, enteringe his shippe, which was redie at the entri of Humber, retiered to the havin of Sandwiche and the Kentishe coeste, where his navie stoode at anchor, and there kutte of the noses and handes of certaine of the Englishe nobilitee geeven in hostage to his father Sweno; and leavinge a garrison for the munition of the porte hee hasted into Denmarcke, in minde to returne and acquite thease injuries and scathes as soone as his busines wowlde suffer. In the mean time, being forced to have more care of dissention at home then of the warres in England, he suppressed the rebellius Sclavens, which thinge when hee hadd woorthelie acchieved, he kastinge greater matters in his hedde (for so often it chauncethe that the luckie endinge of one thinge is the beginninge of an other,) hee appointed to assayle the Norvegians, of whome a littel beefore hee was defrauded of the kingdom of his aunciters; yeat, remembringe that it was not goodd to comprise so manie battayles at once, hee referred it to an other season; notwithstanding that the Norvegians hearing of the death of Sweno, least they shoulde enie more becom vassayles to a forreyne prince, pronownced one Olavus as their lorde and kinge;

Ethelredus returne into his kyngdom and Canutus fled.

yeat hee, beeing alltogether intentive to the Englishe warrs, did studeiuslie sollicite all thinges expedient thereto.

At that verie time divers prodigius wonders weare shewed, whearebie men openlie avowched that the chaunge of the kingdom was prognosticate and signified; emonge other thingges, the unaccustomed sowrge of the ocean was especiallie noted, which withowte enie apparent cause (which might seeme to abate the admiration therof) didd flowe into suche great heyght, that it drowned manie menne and theyre villages. In the meane time Etheldredus, as one that was drowsie and slacke in the execution of all things, didd not assemble an hoste for the comminge of his adversarie, neither prepare suche things as weare necessarie for the warrs, but, like a wooman desierus to revenge, he didde so oppresse the Danes whoe hadde begotten children on Englishe wives, and hadd all their treasures in the Ilonde, that, after great effusion of theyre bloodd, manie weare apprehended, and after crewell tormentes miserablie slayne; emonge which number Sigifredus and Morgandus, two moste noble menn of the Danes, weare falslie accused to the kinge bie one Edricus Stratonius, a mann verie stoute and likelie bothe of boddie and minde, but skarslie of goodd witt and forecaste; bie the which mischeefe there was an other evell heaped on, for emonge the captives was the wife of Sigifredus, a wooman of noe lesse singuler chastitie then excellent beutie, whome the kinges sonn Edmundus hadd longe since luxuriuslie deflowred, albeit that afterwarde hee maried her when her howsbond was decesed; which thinges, as sone as they weare revealed to Canutus, they soe enchafed himm, that, speedelie finishinge all his busines in Denmarcke, hee retowrned in poste cheefelie to revenge the injuries of his menne, and, leaving convenient garrison in his shippes, he entered in Kent, and wastinge on all sides, hee peerced unto the Weast Saxons, leavinge nothing inviolate that mighte bee defaced ether with fier or sworde. Etheldredus was then in a feaver, and therbie hindered for that season. Whearfor hee gave in precepte to his sonne Edmundus to furnishe forthe with an armie, and to encounter with his enemie. Edmundus was a manne as wel stronge of limbes as hawte of corage, and therefore was surnamed Ironsides, whome Etheldredus didd beeget, not of his wife Emma, but of an other named Ethelgina, discended of obscure and base stocke; this manne, bie his valiant harte and prowesse, wanne bothe glorie to his father and nobilitee to his mother. Edmundus, havinge knowlege of his enimies voyage, prepared as ample a bande of menn as hee cowlde devise, and throwghe preevie pathes and cliffes he was gotten beefore them, mindinge on a sodayne to sette uppon them. Edricus Stratonius was fellow and partetaker of all his devises, who repining and maligning at the woorthines of the yonge impe, counseled him in noe wise to geeve the onsette. Edmundus gave credit to his follie, awaytinge better oportunitee to assaulte. Edricus in the meane time busilie sought occasion willinglie to beetray him to his adversarie, which when he perceaved would take noe effecte, thinckinge it to noe purpose enie longer to dissemble, did now openlie take parte with Canutus; whearbie it camme to passe that a great multitude, surrenderinge hostages of their free will, cam in league, yea, in jurisdiction, under the Danes. Onlie the Mercians continued in their allegiaunce, affirminge that to the deathe they would not shrincke soe that they hadd a capitain. While thease thinges weare in dooenge, Etheldredus, being a littell recovered, marched towards his enemies, and, hearinge sodainlie of thease mischaunces, hee was so afflicted with the doloure and pensivenes of his unquiet and unluckie life, that hee toorned towardes London, and beeganne to bee sicke more vehementlie then ever beefore. But Edmundus, in soe great confusion of thinges reteininge his manlie and noble corage, thought best in time to recover certaine citties which weare slipped away for feare; whearfore, preferringe that woorcke beefore the pursuit of his foes, hee assayled divers places; somme hee conquered, som he made playne with the earthe: he extreemelie punished the rebells, that others might conceave the more terroure bie suche terrible execution, or bee more preste to persevere still in their deutie. Canutus, on the other side, knew that the pollicie of his adversarie wolde muche disadvayntage him except hee should anticipate it, and therfore parte of his soldiers hee sent into North Humberland to spoyle and waste the patrimonie of Uthredus, whoe was made the firste Earle therof bie Etheldredus, as a moste valiaunte capitain, and one whome Edmundus hadd ordeyned lodesman of his armie. This practise was devised that he necessarilie mighte bee drawne homewarde for the tuicion of his privat goodds: nether was this devise frustrate, for Utredus, hearinge tidinges of thease pretensed damages, hasted into Northe Humberlande, where, albeit for a season hee manfullie defended himme selfe, yeat at the last, despayring in his safetie, hee yielded himme selfe and all the cowntrie; yet in shorte time moste dispituoslie, and contrarie to the lawe of armes, was hee strangeled. Edmundus, in this season, for that hee was destitute of the assistaunce of Utredus, hee went to London unto his father; which thinge when Canutus understoode, fortifieng North Humberland with a sufficient bande, hee tooke shippinge, and returned to his navie at the Kentishe coste. In this year Etheldredus departed from his mortall life, partelye throughe the continuance of his diseas, partli throughe the languishinge vexation of his minde, in that all things thrived preposteruslie with him, whoe was more geven to idelnes then warfare, more to the pleasures of the boddie then the vertewse of the minde; yeat beinge somwhat bettered with the tracte and processe of time, he laboured earnestlie, albeit in vaine, to prohibite and withstande the ruine of his contrie. He was buried at London in great pompe, in the churche of Sainct Paule. Hee hadde bie his first wife Ethelgina, or, as somm affirme, his concubine, iij. sonnes, Edmundus, Edwinus, and Adelstanus, and one dowghter, called Edgina, and bie his wife Emma ij., Edwarde, a moste hollie

Uthredus the firste Erle of Northumberland.

Ethelredus dieth, and his sone Edmundus kyng.

Alfredus and Edward, sones to Ethelred by Emma, his ij wyfe, both kyngs her after.

mann, Alfredus, or Aluredus. Hee made exceadinge goodlie lawse. This was the xxxviij[th] yeare of his reigne, and third after his fleete into Normandie, and MXVI. of our Salvation.

There weare at that time menn of singuler wisdom and noe lesse godlines, and emonge the rest one Ethelwoldus, of monasticall profession, elected busshop of Winchester for his highe knowlege, of whose devocion there weare manie monuments extant, and especiallie ij notable relligius howses, the one of noones at Winchester, the other of mooninckes at Peeterboroughe, (soe termed bie cause it was dedicated to Sainct Peter; it standeth estward in the cowntie of Northantoune, in the dioces of Lincolne,) whoe for his mervaylus good life was after his death ascribed emonge the sainctes. Next unto him succeaded Elphegius, a man moste excellent in all respectes, whoe was created in shorte space archebusshop of Canterburie; in soe mutche that the cittie beinge taken bie the Danes and sacked, whilest with preachinge and alleaging examples he endevored to plante the divine relligion in the grosse and barberus adversaries, hee loste his life, and wonne the noble victorie of martirdom. Dunstanus allso lived at this time, who bie good cowncell, wise advertisements, and godlie instructions, did noe lesse merite towards his contrie then in relligion, whose pietee bothe towards Godd and menn caused that his memoriall was perpetuall as freshe in the mindes of men as if presentlie he hadd wroughte miraculus wonders. Throughe all the degrees of promotion hee aspiered to the archbusshoprick, beinge first abbot of Glastenburie, then busshop of Woorceter and London, as one worthie of manie honors at once; at the last archebusshop of Canterburie. He did consecrat Kinge Edward and Etheldredus; and finallie dyed the xxviij. yeare of his residence, and was canonized for his sinceritee. These archbusshops ensewed, Ethelgarus, Siricius, and Aluricius, which weare abowte xviij. yeares reulers of that diocess. Then folowed Elphigius, as xxvij. in the order of the archebisshops of Canterburie, of some menne reckened in the dayse of Etheldredus, which indeade breaketh square if the yeares have hadd juste accounte in the beginninge, for there wear xiiij. yeares betweene the death of Dunstanus and the decease of Etheldredus, in the which space Aluricius was resident; wherefore it muste neades bee after that time that Elphegius governed the dioces of Canterburie, and was martired even muche abowte the season that bye the murtherynge of Edmundus the whole imperie of Englonde was revowlted unto Canutus. And abowte the yeare of oure Lorde DCCCCLXXIX. died Oswaldus, archebusshop of Yorcke, after the xxiij. yeare of his residence, and for the pure and sownde life which hee ledd hee was accounted in number of sainctes. The relligius howse of Benedictines, which he bylded at Ramsie, a village in the dioces of Lincoln, is a plaine argument of his goodd meaning and devotion. After him ensued Adulphus, Wulstanus, Alfredus, Chiusius, and Aldredus, the xxiiij. in the order of the arche prelates, whoe, accompanied with Aluredus, archebusshop of Canterburie, did consecrate the kinge named Haraldus, of whome more ample discowrs shall bee made in the life of King William, who conquered himme.

In those dayes the pontificall see, which than was in the Hollie Ilond, was translated to Deirham, and thether was transposed the corps of Sainct Cuthberte, as elswhere we have made mention.

Edmundus, after the decease of his father, was proclaimed kinge bie the citizens of London, but other counties, partlie for beastlie feare, partlie for the fanatike desier of fonde novelties, didd denominate Canutus as their lord and maister. But Edmundus, beinge the more feerce in corage and stomacke, immediatlie reclaimed his soldiers owt of their wintering colonies, and in hoope to receive againe divers places, in greate jornies, and with a swifte bande of menn, he marched westwarde, and for the more terroure of his adversaries with a well furnished armie hee gave assaulte to Glocester and Bristowe; and with noe lesse stowtenes then pollicie he caused the Danes, which weare lefte in garrison and victualled but for a daye, to comm forthe to hande strokes. For feare of beeseeging they susteyned for a season the broonte of this skirmishe, notwithstandinge that they weare amazed with the sodaines thereof; but in shorte time beinge put to flighte, whilst eche manne hyed to places of saftie, manie of them weare slayne in the chase, with the which thinge divers of the places adjoyninge, as all astonied, yealded themselves, and plyghted pledges of theyr faythe. In the meane while not a fewe of the Danes which escaped the terrible flame of the late overthrowe camme to Canutus into Kente, and declared the effecte of their repulse. Hee, as who showld saye hee hadd herde of noe such matter, assembled lustilie his aydes, tooke his jornie to London, and, commaundinge his shipps to comm thither bie Thamis, hee beeseeged the citie; but the citizens, who weare verie faytheful and well purvayed, bothe of men and armowre, didd not onlie not adread of the comminge of their enemies, that, settinge their gates wide open, they hurteled forth emonge them, in so mutch that they, beinge not able to abide there irruption, forthe with avoyded. There was not mutche bloddshedde, for as mutche as they bickered but a littell, while suche haste made Canutus to cope with Edmundus, whome hee understoode to bee retoorned to Andover, a towne within xv. miles of Sarisburie, whether as soone as hee approched hee planted his tentes on a plaine grownde, within the sight of his enemies, and brought his soldiers forthe in good araye. Edmundus refused not the profer, as soone as hee espied the standerdes of his adversaries to bee hoysed. They continued the fight from iij. of the clocke until verie night, and nether partie on the better hande; at the lengthe Edricus, mindinge to appall and kill the hartes of the Englishe menn, wente uppe into a certaine watch tower, and there, crieng with an highe voice that Edmundus was slaine, showed foorth a swoorde droppinge full of blodd, whome, while he thus yelled and showted, the Englishe archers hadd neer hand slayne. This deceytfull trayne was a small pleasure to the devisers, for the kinge, now being accended with woonderus indignation, encoraginge his noble warriers, soe furiuslie assayled them that firste hee caused them to geeve grownde, and consequentlie,

The batte of Andove &c. verye valyent.

as alltogether enraged, hee putt them all to flighte, and hadde committed woonderfull slaughter if they hadd not been verie swifte and the nighte verie darcke and farre spente. Canutus, being thus foyled, travayled all the night toward Winchester, and harborowed himselfe in a safe place. Edmundus, as I finde in summ writers, didd not pursewe his adversarie, but deflected towardes Sarisburie, mindinge to succoure his people there, beinge in distresse through an other rowte of the Danes. Not longe after Canutus was there himselfe in presence, soe that, addressing their companis, they fought not farre from the cittie. The conflicte was crewell to behowlde while their stomacks and boddies weare freshe and continued in æquall proportion, untill the nighte departed them. The nexte daye, from the verie risinge of the sonne, the Englishemenn stode in araye, untill that Canutus camm unto the fight, which was mayntained noblie and with like ende on both sides; with much slaughter and semblable conclusion the eveninge dissevered them. The day ensewenge ether armie tooke reste, refreshinge themselves with meate, and, heapinge all the deade carkases together they boorned them; nether yeat in the meane whiles didde they lay their weapons from them, for on bothe sides they wanted xx. thowsand. The nighte followinge Canutus privilie bie stelthe removed his tentes and wente towards London, which cittie was allmoste beeseeged with his navie. Edmundus, assone as the daylight discried the departure of his adversaries, followed their steppes, and with finall conflictes raysed the seege; wherefore in greate pompe and triumphe hee entered the cittie. Canutus, being frustrat of his expectation, gathering bootie owte of the places adjoyninge, hasted to visit his shipps, which a littall beefore entered the river ronninge bie Rochester, in times paste called Medegware and nowe Medeweye, whear Canutus sojornied a fewe dayse, partlie to enlarge and fortifie his armie, partlie to knowe the councells of the cownter parte, which easlie hee was donne to understonde, for Edmundus, as impacient of all delay, assemblinge in all haste more ample succours, pitched his abode not farre from his adversaries there, in manie woordes advertisinge his warriers to bee mindefull of their former battailes, and nowe finallie from the uttermost of their power to contende and sweate to represse and abate the whole pride of their adversaries, that bie the vehement and urgent contention of this one battayle they might make an ende of all their laboure and travayles. The soldiers, being wonderfullie animated with these exhortations, and not a little irked with the arrogancie of their enemies, which daylie provoked them, issued forthe with great ranckowre. Canutus allso lingered not, who daylie and howerlie commaunded his Danes to bee in redines for the encounter. They bickered bie the space of iiij. howers, till the Danes beganne to shrincke, which thing assone as Canutus perceaved he commaunded his light horssmen to enter into the fore froonte; but while the other ranne tremblinge away they camm slacklie into their roomes, the whole armie was disturbed, for that finallie, when shame overcamm feare, thei beetooke themselves to flight. Three thowsande and five hundred Danes weare slayne, and emonge them cheefe capitaines of the nobilitee. Of the Englishe menn but vi. hundred at the uttermoste, and they all footemenn. Edmundus wowlde have used the commoditee of his victorie, that is to say, pursewed his enemies, that in that daye hee might have brought them all to extremitee, which no doubte hee hadde donne if fatall destenie hadde not withstoode him, for after the honorable achievinge of that battayle, takinge deliberation whether hee showlde chase his foes or not, it was putt into his hedd that it showlde bee muche for his avayle if hee woold contrive the remnante of the day and night in the reposinge and relaxation of himselfe and his weried soldiers, soe that it was justlie thought that that daye was to the Danes a goodd releef, but not to the Englishemenn. At the springe of the next daye Edmundus caused his vassayles to gather spoyles, and the residew to make expedition in the prosecutinge of his adversaries. Wherfore, hearing that they who weare disperpeled wear now gathered together, and passinge the Thames invaded the East Angles, hee dispatched himselfe thether for the succours of his people, and, sowndinge a trompet, fell on his enemies, whoe, allbeit they wear buffeted and assayled on all hands, yeat didd thei not once geeve grownde; echė mann encoraged his feeres, and Edmundus, noblie fightinge in the forewarde, gave watche worde to his centuriens still to kepe his menne in ther araye, crieng aloude that this daye shoulde ether establishe and ratifie all their victories and laboures, if awhile they wolde urge instantelie their enemies, or els bee the beginninge of all calamitees if never so littel thei showld recule. With these wordes the fight becamm soe crewell that forthewith the Danes gave grownde, which thinge as soon as Canutus espied, he, immediatlie pressinge towards the lefte winge, where the greatest daunger was, wonderuslie succored his menn, and with greate deades of armes hee overthrew all suche as didd withstande, wherbie it chaunsed that a great troupe of Englishe warriers which weare sore traveled in this longe contention, hearinge the rumor of this terrible occision, as all afraide, beegann to flie; but Edmundus, thrustinge him selfe into the formost frontiers, didd awhiles valiantlie recrayte them, yeat, for as muche as the aray was once broken, hee cowlde not well restore and renewe the order, insomutche that, nether being of sufficiencie to resiste, nor havinge enie hope in flieng, bie reason that the passages weare straghtlie awarded bie there enemies, they were allmoste everie one browght to confusion, soe that the verie flowre of their cheevalrie was there destroyed. Edmundus, accompanied with a fewe soldiers, ceased not to jornie till he camm into the weste contrie to Glocestre, whome Canutus within the space of two howres folowed, but hee was not able to overtake him.

This horrible over throwe, albeit it had daunted the heartes, appalled the corage, and debilitate the strengthe of the Engleshe warriors, especiallie sithe that London and manie other renowned places now at the lengthe quakinge shrincked in the Danishe dominion, yeat Edmundus neverthelesse furnished speedelie an armie, and bie great jornies approched to his adversarie, notwithstandinge that right well hee understode that if thie showlde skirmishe once againe the uttermost of all affayres lay in the casualtee of that battayle; and, indead, hee was now fullie resolved to have fowght his laste fighte. Wherfore bothe the armies stode in sighte not farre from the bancke of Severne redie to bicker, and hoysinge uppe their ensignes of hostilitee as menn fullie bente to deale sharpe strokes, Edricus (as somm affirme) procured that the kinges might commone together beefore they fowght, knowinge certainlie that it was noe lesse conducible to the Englishe parte then to the Danes. Hee which didd all things in fore time moste villanuslie, begann nowe to dissemble honestie in sollicitinge of peace beetwene the two most puissent capitaines, whoe thincking as that time his cowncell not to be contemned, albeit they feared all wolde bee in vayne, yet they mette together, and conferred awhile beetweene them selves, not with owte mervaylus expectation of all menne. As towchinge their composition and determination their remainethe some dowbte. Somme menn have lefte in memorie that peace was concluded, and Mercia allotted to Canutus, and the weste partes to Edmundus. Other writers have made minde that the matter was thus ordered: one of the capitaines, not knowne whether hee weere Dane or Englishe, requiringe licence to speake, uttered these woordes before the two kinges: 'Most redowbted and worthie princes, ye have fought sufficientlie on bothe sides, yee have dolefullie shedd the blodd of manie noble menn, yee have hadd sufficient triall in the valiaunse of youre warriers, yeat canne yee suffer nether goodd nor eevell fortune, for whoe soe vanquishethe hee crewelli persecuteth him that is vanquished, and whoesoe is vanquished hee repayrethe his harmes, hee licketh his wondes, and freshelie assayleth him that vanquisheth. Now what in the devels name meaneth this willfulnes? Doe you preferre the horrible tortures of warre beefore tranquillitee? Whie doe yow soe greatlie luste after imperie and thirste after honors? If you contende for the kingdom, divide yow twaine this riche and opulente riolme which in times paste hathe suffised vij. kinges. If the desier of glorie have driven you to this uncertaine marte of imperie and servilitee, finde somm meane waye bie the which, with owte great slaughter or much bloodshed of ether nation, it may bee easlie decerned who is the better manne.' Thus hee made an ende, whose conclusion nothing misliked Edmundus. It was not disalowed of Canutus, who founde great favor assuredlie of the destinies. Whearfore this ordre was taken, that the kinges shoulde trie it owte at the weapon; and whosoever was conquirer, the other showlde geeve him place, and yealde to him the totall possession of the kingdom.

The two valient kynges agreed to try the vyctory in their owne persons.

Within a littell space there was a littell island enveroned with the river Severne, called Olvea, and now termed Olanegea, into the which bothe the kinges alited in armes, their armies standinge rownde aboute them on the banckes with hevie hertes, as they whoe being suspense and full of anxietee behelde a sorowfull and lamentable sighte. The baleful blaste of the terrible trumpett sownded, and the too puissant princes, with hatefull hartes and armes, rushed to gether, as menn in minde knightlie to accomplish this perticuler fighte. Edmundus, whose boddie was no lesse notable for the largnes of his limbes than his stomacke, frawghte with greate corage, much surmountinge the other in quantitie, addressinge his shilde on his lefte arme to receave the strokes of his adversarie, gave unto him with his weapon soe mightie a stroke, that with huge noyse the dinte thereof greatlie resownded. Canutus, a man of meane stature, yeat of highe and noble corage, thoughe hee somwhat rebated throwghe the boysterus stripe, yeat sone hee gathered in againe to his enemie. Thus longe they fought, hande to hande, dealinge manie sore blowes on ether side, when the matter continuing in æquall balance and doubteful hope on bothe partes, the Dane, as one that in deade was farr unequall in strengthe, beganne bie and bie to bee afrayde, and with lowde voyce cried, 'What bootethe or needethe it, moste puissant prince, that ether of us shoulde die an untymelie deathe for a kingdome? Trulie me thincke it weare better for us, laying aside all ranck-

The yealding of Canutus to peas, and

oure and malice with our weapons, to treate of peace. Use thow at thie pleasure thine owne Canutus, whoe is preste and at commandement to benefite thee.' The roughe and fierce yonge mann was mollified with these milde woordes, and incontinent throwinge awaye his weapon, gave his right hande to his enemie. So didd allso the two armies, whoe looked for the like fortune and successe in their contrie, as martiall chaunce showld have ministered to their kinges. Finallie they, confederinge peace and amitee for ever, devided the kingdom betweene them. All the weast contrie was assigned to Edmundus, and all the residew to Canutus: but see how frayle and slipperie are all humaine affayres.

hit curtuously accepted.

The realm was devyded.

Whilest the Danes sojornied at London, Edmundus, hoping to have the fruition of quietnes after the accomplishinge of soe manie battayles, sodaynelie departed owte of this mortall worlde. Trulie the deathe of this prince was piteus and lamentable, bothe for that it beerefte the floure of his age, and allso browght hedlonge to confusion the whole riolme. I showlde use too muche curius circumstance if I showlde make rehersall of all those things wherin authors varie as concerninge the death of Edmundus. Certayne of them affirme (whome mie minde geeveth mee are to bee folowed) that the son of Edricus (his name is not mentioned that I knowe) at the instance of his father, watched him as hee was at the preevie, and there, with a weapon, thrust him throughe the bellie and bowells. Another sorte, whoese fonde mindes more sweetelie fede on phantasies, assever that himselfe, Edricus, at his howse didd soe artificiallie, with a vice, put a sworde in the hande of an ymage, that as often as hee lusted it shoulde with the point strike such as approched; and, immediatlie biddinge Edmundus to a supper, he caused it to thruste him throwghe while intentivelie hee behelde it. Finallie, som others surmise that he died of a disease: but surelye, how soe ever it was, a constante reporte went throughe the heddes of all menn, that this bocherlie and fellonus deade was committed bie Edricus, who immediatlie after the murthering of Edmundus

Edmundus dieth by treason.

saluted Canutus as the monarche of all Englonde, offeringe to hime the hedd of his new frinde, and owlde enemie: but the Danishe prince abhorred this develishe deade, and regrated with conding punishment the trator Edricus. Yet som saye that hee exceedinglie loved him, advancing himme unto great promotions, bie cause that finallie throughe his meanes hee hadde obteined the whole dominion. But now let us reherse suche thinges as Saxo Grammaticus hathe written hereof. Hee makethe mention as towching the division of the English kingdom betweene them, and of the slainge of Edmundus: but hee feynethe his Danes to have been superiors in that conflicte, for the two kinges, sayethe hee, fought hand to hande, and the Danishe armie, beinge putt into the woorse, was renewed and becam conquiror throwghe the valiaunce of one Thuno, a standerd bearer, in soe mutch that Edmundus, being in dispayre, made Canutus copartener of the riolme; and that vij. yeares after the deathe of Edmundus certayne bowlde yonckers in jeste sayde to Canutus, that he was king of England bie subtiltee, not bie prowesse; and, in conclusion, in earneste bruted and reported that the kinge was slayne bie his advise. Wherwith, hee beinge greatlie angered, didd sharpelie chastise the sclaunderers; and, least so fowle a blemishe might perhaps bee to him in time to comm imputed, hee allwayse utterlie denied that hee was previe to the deathe of Edmundus. All this we purposlie and featlie recited, that bie the rehersall of divers testimonialls the historie might bee the plainer. Let us comm againe to our purpose. Edmundus reigned one onlie yeare, and riollie was interred in the monasterie of Glastenburie. The whole maiestie of the imperie didd fall with this prince, being allways after like to the boddie of manne withered and crooked with owlde age, that is to weete, tossed and turmoyled with the Danes bie the space of xxvi. yeares ensewenge; and somwhat revived againe under the governemente of King Edwarde, the sonne of Etheldredus; yeat readie to perishe againe, as ells whear shalbe mentioned.

Canutus having obteined soe mightie a kingdom, with all maturitee called an assemblee of his nobles, and, accordinge to the owld custom of his aunciters, was consecrated kinge bie Aluredus archbusshop of Canterburie, which was the MXVIJ. yeare of our Salvation. After this his coronation hee forthwith chose himm a domesticall senate of sages, bie whose cowncell all the affayres of the riolme showlde bee administred. The first thinge bie them hee practised was to exile and banishe Edmundus and Edwarde, the two sonnes of kinge Edmunde Ironside. Whearfore, they takinge their jornie into Pannomia, and there well intreated, ledde there lifes as proscribed owtelawes. This Edwarde lefte beehinde him two sonnes, Edmundus and Edgarus, and as manie dowghters, Margarite and Christine, of whome aptlie wee will make discowrs in the life of kinge William of Normandie. The kinge havinge thus disposed all things at home, bie cause hee hadde onlie two illegitimate sonnes, Haraldus and Sweno, bie his concubine Alvina, desierus to have one rightlie and lawfullie beegotten, which accordinge to the lawe mighte bee his successor, hee espowsed in matrimonie Emma, the former wife of kinge Etheldredus, whoe lived in exile in Normandie with her brother Richerd, and her sonnes Edward and Alfredus, unto the whiche duke Richarde hee on the other side hadd geeven in mariage his sister Hestritha. Moreover in this convocation he pleted and browghte to passe that as well the nobles as the whole comminaltie showld sweare unto his will. Then hee ordeyned Hircius earle of Northumberland, and Thrug of East Angles, bothe of Danishe progenie, and, as somm menn saye, Edricus earle of Marches. Finallie, hee made and promulged manie goodlie and howlsom lawse, which the Normanian perversite, with manie others, didd cleane deface and disannull. After the dissolvinge of this assemble, hee immediatlie purposinge to garnishe the kingdom with civile beehavior, to instructe the nobilite with all clemencie and jentell demaynor, to polishe eche condition, and finallie to doe goodd unto all menne, he was certified of the irruption of the Norways into Denmarcke,

Canutus kynge, and so the kingdom termoyled with the Danes the space of 26 years.

and earnestlie requiered foorthwithe that hee wold comm to the succowrs of his subjectes. This matter seemed of noe small moment, for Olavus kinge of Norway heeringe that the power of Canutus daylie encreased, thought it muche for his owne saftie and avayle to interupte and disturbe his conquestes, fearinge that hee wowlde againe recover from himme the realme of his aunciters: whearfore, accompanied with his brother Haraldus, he invaded Denmarcke, hee wasted their teritories, he bickered with suche garrisons as weare lefte in the fortrises, hee seemed allmoste at the poincte to bee lorde of all, excepte redresse weare fownde in suche imminent perill. Wherfore Canutus immediatlie toke muster bothe of Englishe and Danishe soldiers, and enteringe with propice and fortunate wether with incredible celeritee arrived in Denmarcke, wheare hee sawe his enemies stand readie in armowre freshe and breathinge from the late spoylinge of his contrie; wherfore he gave commandement to advance his standerdes and pursewe his adversaries. All thease thinges weare spedelie executed, while the Englishe men contended with som ægregius deade to shew there manwhode, hopinge therebie to bee in more favor with their prince. The battayle was beegon strayghtwaye with suche corage and dispite that the clamor and noyse peerced the heavens; the contention hanged longe in doubte; but finallie throwghe the feercenes of the Englisemenn the advers parte was cleane overthrowne. The nexte day Canutus chased his enemie, takinge his voyage towards Norvegia; whether, as sone as hee camme, hee mette with embessadowrs with humble submission treating for peace, whome hee mildelie hearde, and receaving hostages didd lovinglie pardon and remitt whatsoever they hadd trespased; and thus Norway was retayned; and Olavus, being in despaire after this discomfiture, beetooke himselfe to his father in lawe named Gerithaslaus, a duke of the Esterlings,* that there he might safelie passe his voluntarie banishemente; whoe, while hee minded

* Orientalium.

to disturbe that which was other mennes, hee loste his owne : yeat in verie deade this innocent loste nothinge ; for, beeing fownde to bee verie sincere and honest in these calamitees, bie all menns judgement hee was accounted a moste hollie parson. This Norvegia, wherof wee have mentioned, is an halfe Ile northewarde, within the Germanian ocean, havinge verie unfruitfull grownde, echewhere stonie and full of briars. In the same tracte and discours of the sea is allso Swetia or Swicherlande, bowndinge weastwarde on Denmarcke and Norwaye. These som men suppose to bee those which our menne call Glessariæ, and the Greekes Elec trides, for the abowndance of awmber. The king of Denmarcke at this daye withhowldethe them bothe. Canutus in shorte time quenched this conspiracie confedered againste him bie Olavus and the great prince Ulvo, wherwith noe doubte hee hadde ben entrapped but that quicklie hee bothe perceaved the originall therof, and repressed the same bie putting the authors to deathe. But now againe to our pretensed matter.

In this fight Canutus hadd proofe bothe of the fidelitee and allso especiallie in the valiaunce of Englishe menne, whome afterward for the same hee exceadinglie looved and rewarded with bownteus liberallitee; which exploytes beinge achieved in Denmarcke, not longe after the kinge retiered into Englond, wheare, honorablie dealing with all his nobilitee, regratinge themm with munificentie, rather diminishinge then increasing the yearlie pensions and subsidies, hee ministered to noe mann cause of repininge or commotion, he restored everie cittee in allegiaunce towards him, and amitee beetweene them selves, and consequentlie, kastinge his minde to the service and maintenance of the Divine pietee, thincking bie somme meanes to deserve well thereof, hee erected two abbays, one in Englond, in Norfolke, within the fennes, termed sainct Benedicts, wheare beefore stoode an heremitage, being vij. miles distant from Norwiche ; and an other in Norvegia ; but, forasmuche as wee have made mention of Norwich, peradventure it shall seeme expedient that wee declare the situation thereof. It is a cittie in the countie of Norffolke, which is in that coste which liethe eastward, within xij. miles of the sea, standing on two hills dissevered with the river, vulgarlie termed Wensdon, which, runninge throwghe vales into the Frenche ocean, makethe an haven at the village named Hiermuthe. But yeat againe to our purpose.

In conclusion, the yeare of our Lord MXXX., and xiij. of his reygne, for the accomplishinge of his vowe hee wente to Rome, where hee was curteuslie intertayned of Ihon, the xx[ti]. bisshop of Rome; and after the performance of his vowe, hee shortelie retiered safelie to Englande. Manie dayse weare nott passed but that of necessitee hee was enforced to moove warre against Richard Duke of Normandie, whoe, contrarie to the lawe, for a verie trifelinge cause, hadd divorced his wife Hestritha, the sister of Canutus, as wee shewed beefore, of the which injurie hee mindinge to bee revenged, hee fournished a great navie, and sayled into Normandie, wheare hee hadd scarslie so sone pitched his pavilions, but hee was certified of the deathe of his sonne Sweno, cheefe rewler of Norwaye, whome hee looved entierlie; which thinge so griped his harte with sorowe that hee fell into a fever and died. O worldlie welthe and pompe, allwayse fickle and unstable, and ofte comminge to ruine in the middest of the race; at what time Canutus seemed most blessed, beehowlde the inevitable power of fatalitee didd quite dispatche him an other waye! wherefore his sowldiers, covenauntinge with the Normans for free pasporte, after they hadd riallie solemnized the funerall ceremonies for the kinge at Roane, they departed thither from whence they camm. Of this quarrell in Normandie the Englishe Chronicles make noe mention, nether that Canutus there deceased, as hereafter wee shall showe. Howbeit I doe not greatlie force wheare hee ether died or was buried, whose life is not unknowne.

This verteus prince a littell beefore his deathe didd nothinge more abandon then utterwardelie to be in suspense and ambiguitee beetweene goodd and evill livinge; as one that wholie depended and was affianced on vertewe and sinceritee, which is evidentlie manifested bie this his facte worthie perpetuall memorie. Trewlie it chaunced him in the waye of recreation to walke bie the shore of the sea, not farre from the haven of Sutheantonne, wheare of a flatteringe servitor of his, who thought to tickell him in the eare, it fortuned himm to bee saluted as the moste puissaunt kinge of all kinges which bare rule ether over menne, ether on the erthe, or on the Sea; at the which greeting hee, howldinge his peace, sodainelie converted his minde to the contemplation of the infinite power of Godde, desierus to reprove the vayne assentation and flatterie of his men bie som sensuall argument, putt of his garmentes, and, windinge them upp together, he satte him downe on them as neare the water as was possible, and, perceavinge the maine flowe greatlie to arise, he sayde, 'O water, I commaunde the that once thowe towche not mie feete;' which as soone as hee hadde spoken, whiles all menn mervayled to what ende hee didd it, the sowrge of the sea comminge on didd wonderuslie wette him. Then hee geevinge backe sayde, 'Beehowlde, mie lordes, yee call mee kinge, which with all mie imperie and commaundement cannot staye or assage this littell water; wite yee for suretie that noe mortall manne is worthie that name; there is one onelie kinge, soothelie, the father of our Lord Jesus Christe, with whome hee reygneth, and at whose becke all thinges are governed, heavenlie and terrestriall. Mie nobles, let us then woorshipp him. Lett us call him kinge; let himme have the title to bee master and lorde of all nations; lett us not onlie acknowlege but professe allso that hee is emperour of heaven, earthe, and sea, and none other besides him.' This beeinge finished hee wente unto Winchester, and there with his owne handes toke the regall crowne from his hedd, and sett it on the hedd of the crucifix of Christe, which was in the churche of the Apostles Peter and Paule, and never after wowlde weare enie suche notable ornament on his hedde. He died the xx. yeare of his reygne, and was buried at Winchestre. Hee begat of his wife Emma a sonne named Canutus, whome the Englishe coronographers call Hardi Canutus, and a doughter

Canutus dieth.

named Gonnilda, who maried the emperowre called Henrie. There flourished at that time men of singuler sanctimonie, as Alphegius, of whome wee made mention beefore; whoe aboute the ix[t]. yeare of this kinge, at the invasion of Canterburie, the vj. yeare of his residence, was martired, and noe doubt purchased heaven; allso Livingus archebusshop of Canterburie; and Athelnotus, as xxix from Augustinus, whoe was dearlie beeloved of Canutus, as one whose helpe and pollicee hee used in his administration. There flowred allsoe warriers of noe lesse politique prudence then prowesse in chevalrie, as Edulphus and Hircius earles of Northumberlande, and Trugillus of Este Angles; that is to saye, Norffolk and Suffolk.

THE EIGHTH BOOKE

OF POLIDOR VIRGILL ON THE ENGLISH HISTORIE.

IN the yeare of our Lorde Godde MXXXVI. the nobles weare assembled at Oxforde, abowte the election of a kinge, wherin their was great altercation. Som thought goodd to chose Haraldus, whome his father didde substitute as cheefe governer of the lond, at such time as hee tooke his voyage into Normandie; others minded to preferre Canutus, begotten of Emma, as the heyre-apparrent of his father, whoe at that season governed Denmarcke. Finallie, the greater parte condiscendinge in one sentence, Haraldus, as xxxiij. in the order of the kinges, was pronownced the sole monarche. The deathe of Canutus did noe lesse disquiet all thinges in foraine contries, for the Norvegians, slippinge sodainlie the coller, didd ordaine as their sufferaine prince Magnus, the sonne of Olavus, and the Danes Canutus the Thirde, to whome, bie right of inheritance, beelonged the whole imperie. And thus the ample dominion of the Danes was sodainlie appayred at this time, for as muche as the regall stemme and pedegree was allmost utterlie extinguished. The Englishe people weare not a littel carefull for the succession of their kinges. With this cogitation was especiallie sollicited one Brithovaldus, a monck of Glastonburie, whoe was afterwarde busshoppe of Winchester, or rather of Worciter, as I find in somm authors. It was crediblie reported that duringe this anxietee, at his reste, hee seemed to see Peeter the

Harold, whom Canutus his father left chefe governer over this land at his going into Normandye, is chosen kyng by the Dayns.

Apostle consecrate kinge Edwarde, the sonne of Ethelredus, at that time exiled in Normandie; and, demaundinge who showlde succead after him, the Apostle made aunswere, 'Force thow nott on suche thingges, for the Englishe kingdom is the kingdom of Godd;' the which thinge in ernest didde so fall owte, for, notwithstandinge the Englishe nation of all thinges dothe least make accompte of the common wealthe, but are to muche assoted on the bellie, notwithstandinge it hathe susteyned soe maniefowlde scathes and direptions, beinge firste spoyled and raced of the Danes, secondarilie of the Normans, a moste feerce nation; and not onlie contented to bereave them of their imperie but allso cleane to stripe them from their stocke. Notwithstandinge that this evel disposed people did for the moste parte abandon, disanull, and treade under their feete the most hollie lawse, promulged and sacred bie the former kinges, bringinge in their owne rigorus and unequall statutes, as thei who like a viper detested the Englishe name, as consequentlie shall be declared; yeat (thanckes bee to Godd) the Englishe imperie consistethe on sewer pillers, nether seemethe it likelie to fall, as that which our Lorde not a littell regardethe, for it is surelie to be thowght for, that therin the studie of godlie relligion dothe noe lesse daylie waxe hotte and fervente, then in other places it waxeth cowlde and faynte. Hetherto have wee sufficientlie strayed.

Haralldus succeaded into his father's kingdom, but not as heyre of his good demaynor, for hee beeganne his governement with the injurius handelinge of the people. He banished his stepp mother Emma; his subjectes hee nether hadd in ennie reputation, and wonderuslie hee oppressed them, having himselfe notable vices and defaultes; but the shortenes of his life muche avayled his name, for hee died after the iiijt. yere of his reygne; and in the selfe same yeare Athelnotus, archbusshop of Canterburie, deceased, after whome succeaded Edsinus, as xxx. in that ordre.

The deathe of Harold.

His brother Canutus raynethe.

In the meane season, Hardie Canutus, beinge donne to understande of the death of Haraldus, forthwith taking muster of his soldiers, and furnishinge a navie, toke his jornie towards England, and arriving in the Kentishe coste throwghe a prosperus winde vj. dayse after his setting forthe, marched towards London, wheare, being joyfullie receaved, bie the commune consent was proclaymed kinge, whoe, counterfaytinge his brother Haraldus, beeganne his rayne with creweltie; for remembringe the wronges donne to himme and his mother Emma, commaunded the boddie of the late buried Haraldus to bee taken owte of the grownde at Westeminster, and cuttinge of the hedd to caste it in the river, which beinge shortlie after fownde owt bie the fishermenn was againe interred. Moreover, hee severallie ammerced and punished the nobles, for that they hadd beestowed the riolme which was dew unto himm. Hee levied the commonaltie with intollerable taxes and subsidies, which procuered unto him great hatred. Then, revertinge a littell to pietee, hee called home his mother Emma, leadinge as then her life in Flaunders, bie whose cowncell, with the assistance of Godwinus earle of Kente, a verie wittee, or rather wilie, man, hee was alltogether rewled. Edwarde camme this same yeare owte of Normandie, to visite and salute his mother, and his brother Canutus; and tarieng but a small time hee retiered againe from whence hee cam. Som saye that at the commandement of the kinge bothe hee and his Normans that camm with him weare evel entreated, and that with muche adoe hee escaped. But moe there are which doe affirme that Canutus lovinglie enterteyned his brother, which I thincke to bee lesse dissident from the trewth, for hee was a mann of his owne nature, noe lesse jentil then liberall, and especiallie in banquette, for allwayse hee gave his guestes noe lesse bownteus then trim and fine intertaynement, oftentimes feasting of the people, and suche as wowlde eate, three sondrie times in the daye.

Hee allso was accustomed oftentimes to suppe with others, whearfor at the lengthe, beinge invited to the mariage of a certaine noble manne, at suche time as he satt at the banquet, on the other side of Thamis, right over against Westminster, in the village called Lamehithe, as hee was drincking, sodaynlie he died, not

Canutus dyeth the last kinge here of the Danes.

withowte suspicion of empoysoninge, ij. yeares after the beginninge of his raygne. But Saxo Grammaticus, whose credite is of som force, dothe farre otherwise contrive the storie of this time, whoe hathe lefte in memorie that Haraldus, the sonne of Canutus, was made cheevetaine over the Englishemenn, who dienge before the decease of his father, Sweno, the sonne of Hestritha, succeaded him in his office; for this Hestritha, who in her widohoode maried Richard Duke of Normandie, was first espowsed to one Ulvo, a Swetian, bie whome shee hadde this sonne, and thus hee specifieth that Haraldus never reygned, but that Hardi Canutus, the son of Canutus, didde succeade in the kingdom, and that hee, goinge into Englond, when, throwghe the industrie of Sweno, the cheefe rewler, hee gave uppe the emperie to his brother Edward, on the side of his mother Emma, and begotten of Etheldredus. But for as muche as Edwarde, thowghe hee weare a towarde younge manne, yeat voyde of experience, and unripe for administration, hee therefore didd appoincte for his depute Sweno, which showlde accompanie Edwarde in the regiment. Then Canutus dieng within ij. yeares after, Sweno committinge the charge of the riolme partlie to Edward, partlie to the sones of Edwinus earle of Kente, beinge his kinsmen, as wee shewed beefore, hee retowrned into Denmarcke to clayme his dew inheritaunce, which Magnus, the sonne of Olavus, didde possesse, beinge fittinge to him no lesse bie the righte of league and composicion then accordinge to the testament of Canutus; and thus Saxo declareth how the Danish affaires camm into controversie, wherof hereafter more at large; but now lett us retire home.

The deathe of Canutus beinge divulged and knowne, the piers of this region, desieringe ether to sett them selves throughlie at libertie, or at the leaste wise to have an Englishe name to their kinge, didd assemble together and delibered what showlde seme moste for the. avayle of the contrie. Finallie, havinge especiall consideracion that under the Danishe prince as well the nobilitee as ruralls and common people weare evel regarded, owte of favor and owte of authoritee, soe that all men seemed happie in comparison of them, and perceaving now or never was the time whearin they mighte rejecte the yoke of foriners, they decreed to make Alfredus, the valiant son of Etheldredus, their kinge, and to persecute the Danes unto the deathe. Wherfore, prevelie sendinge for Alfredus, in violent wise eche weare they assayled the Danes. The multitude was soone stirred upp, partelie throwghe their former severitee, partlie throughe the hope and occasion of recoveringe their freedom. The Danes, albeit they weare overcharged with the sodaine assaulte, and astonied at this strange mutation, yet, sometimes bie fightinge, somtimes bie flieng, they indevored to repell these injuries; but in fine they weare all ether slaine, ether driven into the next continent, soe that bie the commune consente a decree was made, that never hereafter enie Dane showlde bee elected kinge of England. Bie this meanes ceased in England the Danishe imperie, the xxviij. yeare after that Sweno, the firste of the Danishe princes that rewled in Englond, obteined the whole monarchie, in the which space Etheldredus, returninge into his contrie after the decease of Sweno, reygned ij. years, and Edmundus but one, wherebie it appeareth that the imperie of the Danes surmownted not xxv. yeares in this lond. The deathe of Canutus didd noe lesse turne all thinges topsie-turvie in Denmarcke; for when as noe man survived to whome of verie righte the regall hereditee was apperteininge, Sweno, the sonne of Hestritha, beegotten of Ulvo the Swetian, currieng favor with certaine of the nobilitee, endevored to obteine the same. Wherefore Magnus, kinge of Norvegians, agreinge well with his name in verteus and pollicie, toke great indignation hereat, avowchinge that this kingdom was dew unto him. Hee allewred the Danes with giftes and renowne of his valiance from faveringe of Sweno, and therebie causinge him to desiste from his enterprise he obteyned the kingdom of Denmarcke. Sweno being thus injuriuslie dealte with, gatheringe aides and succours with all expedition, and confederinge with the Sweuians, his native contrimen, marched in

Alfredus a Englisheman, and the imperi of the Danes pas not xxv. years in this lond.

good ordre towards Magnus, who with noe lesse celeritee camm into the fielde. The fight was continued from the morninge to eventide; but in conclusion Magnus, discomfiting his adversaries, beecam superior, and duringe his whole life governed bothe Danes and Norways withowte enie broyles and uprores; yeat, the terme of his life being expired, Sweno possessed the Danishe riolme: but Haroldus, the brother of that Olavus which after his decease was accownted a saincte, obteyned Norvegia after the deathe of Magnus. This Haroldus, puttinge to flight his brother Olavius, as wee saide before, fledde into Byzantium, where of the barbarus people beinge falslie accused of manslaughter hee was kaste unto a lyon, whome as a valiaunt mann hee slewe, contrarie to the expectation of all men, which was the occasion that bothe hee obtained remission of punishemente and allso licence to departe; whearfore at his returne hee easlie obteined the kingdom, which as yeat was possessed of noo manne. This place requireth that wee showlde make somme mention of Robert Duke of Normandie and his sonn William before wee accomplishe our treatise touchinge Alfredus and Edward.

After Richard the iij. Duke of Normandie, as wee sayde aboove, succeaded his brother Roberte, a pleasaunt jentilman, liberall, grave, yet noe lesse stowte then prudent, whoe kepte noblie his subjectes from all injurius skathes, aydinge oftentimes his cousines and neighbours, releevinge the neadie with his substaunce, and usinge munificente dealinge towardes all menne. But hee especiallie defended Henry kinge of Fraunce, imploringe his frindelie assistaunce againste the attemptes of his mother Constantia, which a littell beefore hadd nott a littell disquieted her sonne. Of a certaine beautifull virgin, his concubine, hee begatte his sonne William. I will heere, in the way of mirthe, declare a prettie dog tricke or gibe as concerninge this mayden, not biecause it is ether exceadinge honeste or verie worthie the memoriall, but biecause there is noe lawe limited to an historie that it should kepe enie deede secret. The first night that ever she lay with the duke

William Conquerors mother.

for shamefacednes she would not putt of her smocke, but when he made haste to his busines, of cowncell she forthwith slitte the upper parte thereof, and, being demaunded of himme whie she soe didd, shee made aunswer that it didd not become her to toorne upp the skirtes thereof, which weltered aboute her legges, unto the mouthe of her lorde. She is reported moreover beefore her deliverie to have dreamed that her bowells wear caried on hyghe, and unfoulded abrode throughe the whole circuite of Englonde and Normandie, wherbie she beeganne to conceave great hope in the puissaunce to comm of her sonn William. In fine, Robert beinge penitente that hee hadd with poyson destroyed his brother, and, mindinge to goe to Hierusalem for the performance of his vowe, hee commended his sonne to Henrie kinge of Fraunce, gevinge him in charge that if it fortuned him to die in his voyage hee shoulde bee next Duke of Normandie: wherefore firste he went to Rome to obteine leave of Benedictus the ix. busshop, as the usage is, wheare he shewed his large and bowntеus magnificencie, for he revestred the statue of the emperoure Constantine with a golden cloke, arguinge the Romaines of ingratitude, for that thei wowld not yearlie beestow a vesture on so worthie a prince: hee allso adorned their temples with francke giftes. Thus departinge from thence it chaunced him to stray asyde from his companie, and, fallinge into reasoninge and so to altercation with a stronge stubberne clomperton, he was shrowdlie beaten of him, yeat hee kepte him from beinge hurte of his menne, grauntinge that hee hadd well deserved those stripes. From thence takinge his jornie to Constantinople and was curteuslie interteyned of the emperowre Constantinus Duca, whoe, havinge hearde beefore that the duke was full of civilitee and prettie conceytes, hee didd of purpose commaunde his servitors in no wise to geeve unto them to sitt on at dinner enie stooles that weare aboove one foote and an halfe in heyght. The duke, whoe hadd a pregnant and present witte, putte of bye and bie his upper garment, and, windinge it rounde together, sat doune thereon, likewise didde the reste of the Normans; and when dinner was ended they removed from thence and lefte their garments behinde them. The emperowre, smileinge, bidd them take awaye that which was their owne boldelie. 'Noe,' quod the duke, 'and it lyke you the Normans use not to carrie their cheres or seates with them.' Within a few days the duke goeng forward in his jornie was attainted with such a diseas as hindered his ridinge, whearbie hee was of necessitee constreined to hyer the rurals and clownes to carrie him on theyr showlders. In the mean whiles it fortuned that one of his earles, having gotten libertie to retire into his contrie, required what hee shoulde say of him to his Normans. To whome hee made this pitthie and merie aunswere: 'Tell them that thou haste sene devells carrienge Duke Robert to heaven.' Bie the devels hee meaned the rude, savage, and ungodlie rusticalls; bie heaven, hee signified Hierusalem; biecause that from thence camme our salvation. And assone as hee camm thether he used suche liberalitee towards all menn, that the keaper of the temple, moved with humanitee, restored a greate peece of the monnie customable payde for the entringe into the churche, which hee wowlde in noe wise receave, but willed it bee distributed to the neadie. After the accomplishinge of his vowe he departed from thence, and camm into Bithinia, a region of the lesser Asia, right against Thracia, wheare is situate the famus Constantinople, wheare hee departed this mortall life the MXL. yeare after the nativitee of Christe. William, his base sonn, succeaded in the dukedom, a man no lesse prudente then manlie, with whome Alfredus and Edwarde longe lived in theyre banishement. But now wee muste returne thether from whence wee made digression.

Alfredus, hearinge tidings towchinge the death of Canutus, camm speedelie into Englonde. In this space the nobles hadd assembled in consultation whoe shoulde bee kinge. Emonge whome Godwinus, bie all meanes, procuered to marie his dowghter Editha to the kinge, or otherwise minded to disturbe all things, to the ende that his sonne, Haraldus, might finallie obteyne

Non sine ratione textum apposite immutavimus.

the kingdom, for all thease weare his children, Haraldus, Edithe, Biorno, Tosto, and Thira, the wife of Canutus. Yeat, fearinge the sharpe witte of Alfredus, and partlie distrustinge to obteine his purpose, hee beeganne grevuslie to discommend him unto all menn, affirminge that hee hadd browght with him a greate bande of the Normans, to whome hee hadd promised the gooddes and substaunce of his citizens, whome in his minde hee hadd allreadie wounded and destined to the deathe. Thease things, whether they weare trew or false which hee spread abrode, they soe moved the mindes of noble men, that eche manne beegann to feare for his owne parte, wishinge secretlie that somm such adversitee wowlde happen as might frustrate the reigne of Alfredus. Which things when Godwinus understode, with expedition hee minded to dispatch Alfredus owte of his life. Wherfore he marched towards him with a great rowte of armed men, and, comming on him unwares, slewe him and all his companie. He toke the Normans captives, and killed them from the firste to the laste. Godwinus, after this haynus facte, torninge towardes London, went streyght abowte newe treason. For first hee endevored bie manie arguments to wipe awaye the crime of the sleainge Alfredus. Then hee perswaded the people to sende legates into Normandie to cowncell the vertuus mann, Edwarde, the brother of Alfredus, to keepe him away. Hee didde not this, ether for that he zelouslie loved Edward, or minded the preservation of the realme: but hereof sprange his coloured charitee; bie cause this Edwarde was a manne of jentil disposition, nothing nimble or subtile of witte, hating warre above all thinges, insomutche that, being in exile, hee was wont to saye, that he had rather continuallie leade a private life, than bie the slaughter of mann to purchase a kingdom. Whearefore hee hoped ether at his pleasure to rule such a one as was ignorant in the administringe the common wealthe, or, at the leaste wise, finallie to destroye himme. Nevertheles, Edwarde, feelinge the desire of his menne, and being assisted with the ayde and goods of Duke William, camm luckelie into Englonde, and

Godwyn's treson.

Edward crowned kynge. with suche ineffable gladnes was crowned kinge that all estates hartelie prayed for his prosperus reigne; and so muche the more bie cause hee set their hertes on fire towardes him with his singuler clemencie. In which thinge Godwinus havinge noe small confidence (after hee hadd once felte his pulses and perceaved his diet) wente unto him, and bie all meanes purged him as concerninge his brother's deathe, whome, in that hee semed to have compunction of penitence, the king francklie released his crime, and consequentlie didd, of all others, most use his advice and helpe Emma. againste his mother, Emma, with whome, for manie causes, hee was sore agreeved. For, firste, her marriage with Canutus, the enemie of the contrie, was objected against her; then, that she spared to succoure and releeve her banished children; and, finallie, that it was bruted how she imagined their utter destruction: for the which false criminations this verie hollie matrone was spoyled of all her substaunce, at the instigation of Godwinus, unto the which calamitee was annected that which was worse, weetlie, the losse of her goodd name, for she was accused of uncleane livinge with Adwinus bisshop of Winchester, for the which thei weare bothe their committed to prison, wheare ether of them with other piteuslie lamented and sorowed for the mischaunce and infamie of the other, but especiallie the indignitee and false allegation so doloruslie pricked and tormented Emma, that, trusting to her innocencie, shee openlie offered that the verie flame and fier showlde trie her continent chastitee. Whearunto the kinge, as one leaning more to other menn's devises than his owne, was som what bent; and the daye was appoynted for the crewell punishing of his mother; who, being guiltie of nothinge but goodde, (for trewthe was on her side) and havinge admonishment (as menne saye) in the night season, while she tooke her reste, bie Saincte Swithine, at her time assigned goeng on coulters made redd whotte with fier was nothinge hurte, acquited her good name and chastitee (as the owlde saienge is) with fier and water; with the which miracle the kinge being moved, didd ever after, with great reverence, loove and honor his mother. This was done in the vth yeare of the reigne of Edwarde. In the which year certayne Danishe pyrats, arrivinge in Sandwiche, robbed and wasted all the sea costes; yeat shortelie they weare all withoute difficultie either slaine or putt to flighte. After which time, bie the space of xix yeares whearin Edward governed, there was noe warrs within the riolme, but that ether it was extinguished with small slaughter, or with owte enie notable eande chaunged into peace, which trewlie I maye bowldlie saye was doonn bie the divine providence, for it seemethe that God was willinge that the prince, which from his beginninge determined noe lesse to deserve well of relligion then of men, who was norished, delighted, and fostered in these studies, shoulde bee voide and free from all suche fanaticke cares and travailes as everie wise mann accounted frayle and slipperie, to thend he mighte the more securelie use the contemplation of things celestiall.

In this season Godwinus espowsed his dowhter Editha, beegotten of Thira the sister of Canutus, not of his, otherwise as somme menn falslie conjecture, to kinge Edwarde, and was in wonderus authoritee with him untill suche time as great discorde arose betweene them. The cause thereof was Ewstachius, earle of Bononia, who had married the kinges sister longe beefore, whoe, as soone as hee sette foote on the Kentishe shore, hee toke the streyght way to Canterburie, in minde to visite the king. Whereas chauncing a fraye or skirmishee to bee made beetweene the citizens and his menn, in soe muche that one of the inhabitants was slayne. Wherewith the townesmenn. being generallie aggreaved, toke their weapons in hande and invaded the band of Eustacius, and slewe manie thereof. Then Eustachius, as one all enraged, sett furiuslie on the citizens, so that on ether parte they skermished sharplie: but Eustachius, being sore addread, for that his menn fell downe deade on all hands, ceasinge littell and littell to fight, fledde to London to the kinge, and declared the injurie donne unto himme in the breache of the rightes of hospitalitee.

The kinge toke the matter in verie evell parte, and commaunded the transgressours to be severlie punished. The Kentishe menne repayred to their Earle Godwinus, beseechinge his assistaunce againste the Frenche menn, the mortall enemies of the Englishe name and nation, makinge huge clamor that they offred the first wronge in sleange the citizen of Canterburie, alleginge that they made noe tumulte, but onlie according to lawe in the waye of repellinge force bie violence. Godwinus, being somewhat stirred upp with this unseamlie dealinge, thought not goodd to obeye the kinges proclamation; but, immediatlie furnishinge an armie, was fullie bent to garde his menn from all harmes. The kinge, on the other side, more and more stricken with indignation, sente a rowte of soldiers against Godwinus, beinge proclaymed a traytor, with all his familie. But fewe dayse beefore they camm to the verie poincte to deale hande strokes, Godwinus, all dismayde with the king's puissaunce, dispayring to have the upper hande, fledd with his sonnes into Flaunders. Then Edward, punishinge the guiltie parsons, dispatched away the dowghter of Godwin, publishing and makinge confiscation of her gooddes. Godwinus, in the meane while, throughe the ayde of Baldwinus earle of Flaunders, whose dowghter was maried to his son Tosto, prepared a navie, and forthwith infested all the sea costes of the Ilonde, with whome bie and bie the king's shipps grapeled. Howbeit, beefore they bickered, bie the instillation of Godde, as it is well to be thought, the capitaines advertised one the other how fowle a thinge it weare that one so noble a nation showlde comm to confusion throughe their owne power. So that reconciliation and concorde forthwith ensewed; and Godwinus, restored to his former condition, renderinge to the kinge his sones Biorno and Tosto as hostages of his fidelitee; and this noble prince humblie againe receaved his wife. But Godwinus, notwithstandinge, cowlde bie noe humaine pollicie escape his well deserved penaltie: for in fewe dayse after it happened that his sonne Heraldus, ministring drincke to the kinge at his dinner, slipped with the one foote and hadd almoste fallen, and yet so recovered himselfe and stayed it with the other that hee saved the wine from spillinge. Then his father, which sette with the kinge, sayde, 'Loe now how one brother helped another.' This worde, thowghe it were spoken in jeste, yeat it soe troobled the kinges minde, that, remembringe his brother Alfredus, hie tourned towards Godwinus, and sayd, 'If it hadde not beene for thee, even soe hadde mie brother succoured mee.' This evil disposed mann, fearing the kinges ire, beganne to excuse him selfe, and to appeyle to the deite in the witnessinge of his innocentie, adjoining thereto a solemne othe, as thowghe he hadd debated the matter with an ignorant creature, protestinge in this wise: 'Most redowbted prince, if ever I wrought enie thinge, ether in the death of thie brother or againste thee I praye our Lorde this peece of breade may choke and stranguil mee.' Which as soone as hee hadd spoken, and putt it in his mouthe, his gawes closed, and he was throteled, with such terrible and sodaine deathe recompencinge his willful murther. This was thend of Godwines life, whoe, accordinge to the ghospel, which biddethe us aske and have, didd aske and receaved not the pardon of his sinnes as he oughte, but deathe, meate for his offence. I wolde God in our time manie woulde bee stricken with this example, which knowe not how to steppe one foote excepte perjurie leade the waye. At this time deceased Emma the king's mother, and William duke of Normandie, at the king's requeste, camm to England; for Edwarde was verie desierus to seeme to gratifie the duke for his owlde hospitalitee and interteinement, as one not unmindefull of goodd toornes; wherfore he receaved him princelie, and bowntefullie rewarding him with many presents, beesides all thease deades of humanitee, as I finde in somme authors, kinge Edwarde promised to make him his heyre if it showlde chaunce him to die withowte issewe of his boddie, and that noe lesse he signified to himm while he sojornied with him in Normandie; which thinge was a mayme to his contrie, as in an other place shall bee specified.

A miserable end of Godwyn.

King Edwards promise to Wylliam duke of Normandy to make him his heyr, yf he dyed without issewe, which some thyncke was done ether scarse advisedly in his necessety, or rather not made at all.

King Edwarde delivered unto duke William at his departure Biorno and Tosto, the pledges of Godwinus, that they mighte bee kepte in Normandie. Here it is expedient that I geeve the reader warninge that certayne writers, nothinge skilled in antiquitees, doe call thease the sonnes of Godwinus, and manie others bie straunge names, pervertinge the historie, and causinge it to bee of more obscuritee.

Kinge Edwardes lawes, afterwards termed the common lawes.

In the xij. yeare of the reigne of kinge Edwarde, hee having gotten peace and quietnes both on sea and on lande, and foreseeinge noe lesse the saftie of his people then himselfe, as a mann naturallie bente to the lovinge of all menn, which is the verie grownde of right and foundation of the lawe, hee minded aboove all things to make such lawes as hee thowghte good and expedient at that time, surelie weare manie lost in ure, made firste of the Britons, then of the Saxons, and last of all of the Danes; soe that manie menn measuring all things accordinge to their private commoditee oftentimes applied for thear purpose iniquitee in the steade of justice. Wherfore king Edwarde, owte of the abowndance of lawse, picked forthe everie moste holsom and necessarie decree, ordeinenge onlie certayne selected to bee used as indifferent rules and prescripts of good life unto all degrees, which bie the posteritee weare termed common lawes; and whereas they greatlye complayned and muttered at the takeinge away of them bie the Normans, whoe assigned others in theyr roomes, they proceeded allso to reclaime them againe with weapon as the better parte of their life, often plaguenge suche kings as denied to ratifie them with their pristinate power, thinckinge them to bee unfruitfull, as hereafter shallbe made declaration. This foundacion of justice being laide, to the ende that the ensample of charitee, liberalitee, and devotion mighte from him to others flowe as from a fowntaine, the kinge with great diligence beganne to releeve the poore, to have relligion in more syncere reverence, to deserve well of all sortes, by the which vertewse hee beecamme soe acceptable unto Godd, that throughe the assistance of him he wrought so wonderuslie that, if I shoulde mention all his miraculous doings, time woulde soner fayle then matter; yeat will I recite certayne verie worthie the memoriall. When as on a time the collectors and gatherers of pensions hadd exacted a great somme of monnie of the people, and browghte a marveylous heape their of beefore his face for to delight and make hime merie, hee seemed of a sodaine to see the devill plaieng and skippinge aboute it, and therefore as a moste execrable thinge detestinge it, hee commanded it forth with to bee carried owte of his sighte and to bee restored to his subjectes. Farder more, hee is reported at the divine service, in the eucharistiall sacrament, to have seen the Lorde Jhesus in the fowrme of a childe (whome allso a verie hollie man, named Leofredus, earle of Mercia, didde beehoulde a goodd season); and the kinge immediatlie burst forthe in great laughter, and beinge requiered to utter the occasion thereof, he made aunswere that hee sawe the Danes hastinge to invade Englonde, but for that their cheefe and mayne shippe was drenched they retired againe into Denmarcke. This thinge in verie deade consequentlie ensewed, which was a manifest argument that Godd hadde especiall regarde of the realme. Moreover, as one foreseene in thinges to comm, hee divined that in fewe yeares the Normans wowlde bie violence enjoy the kingdom, for Haraldus at the same time ernestlie seweng unto himme for licence to goe into Normandie to visite his brethrene, whoe as wee saide weare geaven in hostage to the duke (albeit perchaunce hee conceaved som other thinge in his hedd), the kinge made this aunswere, 'Goe thie waye, seinge I cannott withhowlde thee, butt, beeleeve mee, thou attemptest a thing noe lesse hurtfull to thie selfe then thie contrie.' Haraldus departed, and when a whiles hee hadde desiered the duke to render his pledges, whom he required not as alltogether his peticion weare unknowne to kinge Edwarde, hee tooke juste occasion to open his purpose unto himme, for the duke, whoe a good season hadd lived in hope to attayne the Englishe realme, shewed to Haraldus how that often times the kinge hadd promised to make himme his

His meracles.

Harolds promes to Wyl. of Normandy to solyset for him to kyng Edward to make him his heyre.

heyre if hee never begatte children; and, for as muche as hee was now paste hope of procreation, hee entreatid him in enie case earnestlie to sollicite the matter with him, which if he cowld bringe to passe. then shoulde hee have juste cause to looke for great rewardes and highe honors at his hande. Haroldus bounde him selfe bie othe to farther thease matters to the uttermoste of his power, and obtayninge one of his brothers, named Tosto, he retowrned into Englond, and in goodd ordre expressed all thinges to kinge Edwarde which hee hadd communicated with the duke: whereunto the kinge, as it is reported, aunswered thus, 'Didd not I shewe thee beefore that thease mischeeves thow woldest bringe into this contrie if thow showldest goe unto duke William; but Lorde, I praye thee, graunte that this eevell chaunce not, or if it doe chaunce that it beefall not in owre time.' Whearbie wee maye easlie gather that ether king Edwarde kepte not his promise, which peradventure in the beginninge he skarce advisedlie made to the duke concerninge the hereditee of the kingdom, accordinge to the guise and fasshion of banished parsons, whoe francklie promisse seas of silver and mountaines of goulde, least theye showlde bee destitute and forsaken of theyr frindes: or rather that hee made noe promisse at all, as it is more credible and likelie.

Helyng of the kynges evell.

This goodd kinge was accustomed with onlie towchinge, bie the divine power of Godde, to heale the swellinge in the throte, called in Latin struma, in Italion scrophula, in Englishe usuallie now termed the kings eavell; this disease beinge like littell acornes, and commonlie creapethe throughe the throate and breste. This immortall gifte, as it weare bie lineall propagation, discended to the kinges succeadinge: for eeven presentlie the English kinges bie towchinge, and recitinge of certaine himnes and ceremonies, doe heale thease lothesom swellings. Bie thease heavenlie tokens kinge Edwarde was declared to bee verie leefe and deare unto Godde, and now beeinge in the xxiiij. yeare of his reygne, as of credible reporte hee was enfowrmed that a ringe was browghte unto him bie certaine poore menn from Hyerusalem, which hee beefore hadd geven secretlie to a neadie creature for the loove of Sainct Jhon the Evangelist, bie thease divine admonitions the kinges deathe was signified, for not muche after, being sore diseased, hee was therof in his sleape assertayned of our Savior Christe, to whome shortelie after hee yealded his innocent ghoste, after the xxiiij. yeare of his reigne. Hee was buried in the churche at Westminster, and successivelie for his demerits ascribed emonge the saincts. His foresayd ringe was with greate veneration longe preserved in the same churche, bie cause it was medicinalle againste starke and deade limmes and the fallinge sickenes, if the parties weare towched therewith that weare attainted with suche passions; bie meanes whearof it camm in ure that kinges of Englonde weare woonte on Good Frydaie to hallow ringges with muche ceremoniall solemnitee, which these that weare never were molested with enie suche sicknes. This hollie king hadd noe issew of his boddie. In his time flowrished divers notable menn, as Edsinus archebusshop of Canterburie, whoe was resident xi. years, and in his rome succeaded Robert bisshop of London, borne in Normandie. Hee at the first was greatlie beeloved and reverenced of kinge Edward; but afterward, where as he perswaded that his mother Emma, who was falslie appeached of uncleanes, showlde acquite her selfe bie that fierie triail, and that shee was escaped that perill, as beefore wee mentioned, hee repentinge and fearinge fledde into the next continent, and theare, after the second yeare of his residence, with the verie languor of his minde was quickelie consumed. Next unto himme ensewed Stigandus, xxxij. in the ordre of the archebussopps. Wulstanus allso, bisshop of Worciter, was notable for his hollie life and inestimable learninge, and therefore, after the finishinge of the shorte race of hie godlie life, hee was canonized.

King Edwards death.

Halowed rynges.

Suardus earle of Northumberland, and Northumbrian borne, then flowred as prince of chevalrie, whoe havinge terrible fluxe of the wombe, and feelinge his strengthe bie littel and littel to ap-

Swardus earle of Northumberland governed.

paire, and his life draw to the ordinarie date, hee armed himselfe at all poincte, and stode upp lustilie in his armowre, that (as Vergilius sayth) hee seemed preste to gripe with his enemie; sainge that it beeseemed not a valiant manne to die lyenge a longe like a beaste, and soe departed his life, counterfayetenge in that poyncte the usage of the Nasamones, a people of Libia, which wee have sufficientlie expressed in owre booke intituled, "De rerum inventoribus."

After Swardus Tostus governed, after him Morcatus.

In the place of Swardus, who was deade, was substitute Tostus bie kinge Edwarde, whome Morcatus followed. The deathe of kinge Edwarde didd keepe the nobles verie suspense and doubtfull on whome they showlde bestowe that princelie function, for there was not one manne meate for the governement of them which hadde enie right or intereste therto, allbeit that one Edgarus, surnamed Ethelingius, begotten of Edward the sonne of Edmunde Ironside, abowte that time camme owte of Pannonia, whear he was borne, with his mother and sisters into Englonde; yet being a childe of soe small yeares hee was not feate for soe highe a regimente: furthermore, beinge put in greate feare with manie oracles, which they imagined shoulde portende the chaunge of the kingedome, they hadd allsoe in greate jelowsie duke William, bothe for that hee was a Norman, and allsoe bie cause hee affirmed that the riolme was dewe unto him as the heyre lawfullie instituted bie kinge Edwarde, and soe muche the more bie cause he was adjoyned to him in kinred in the seconde and thirde degree. For Richarde the firste duke of Normandie begat Richard the second, and Emma, who, by Etheldredus kinge of Englond, hadd Edwarde, which Edward ingendered Richarde the thirde and Roberte, whoe beegate duke William of his concubine. While they tossed theese thinges uppe and downe in their heads,

Harold usurped, and was crowned.

Haraldus, the sonne of Godwinus bie the sister of Canutus, trustinge to his strengthe and kinred, pronownced himselfe as kinge. This deade alltogether misliked not the people, whoe hadde goodd affiance in his valiantnes; wherefore, accordinge to ordre of his predecessors, hee was consecrate kinge bie Aldredus archebusshop of Yorcke, or, as som saye, with owte all ceremoniall circumstances, hee putt the crowne on his owne heade, which was don in the year of our Lord MLXVJ. Hee, in the firste beginninge of his dominion, callinge to minde that violentlie hee possessed the diademe, for the better deservinge of all mens benevolence, he omitted noe occasion to exhibite und shew his liberalitee, jentilnes, and affabilitee, for the great taxes of his people ether he diminished or quite toke them awaye, hee enhaunsed the stipend of his soldiers and wages of his servauntes, not forgettinge his diligent endevoure in the beehalfe of Goddes trewe relligion. Whiles hee shewed this popularitee and mildenes to all sortes, sodainlie camm embassadours from duke William of Normandie, who well understoode the whole estate of administringe the commonwealthe, whose embassage grated muche on this poyncte, that hee wowld call to minde the othe which he sware to the duke, and stande to his covenaunt, as reason requiered; whereunto Haraldus made aunswere, "Bie all meanes possible I wolde bee glad to pleesure the duke, but yeat soe I minde to gratifie him that hee shall not desier the kingdom which I all readie doe possess." William of Normandie hearing this aunswere, as one that minded firste to assay all thinges bie wisdom beefore the clatteringe of armes, bie legats yet agayne sollicited himme, that if soe bee that in all other thinges hee wowde flie towche, yeat that hee wowld not fayle as towchinge the mariage of his dowghter, whoe, allbeit she was not ripe for wedlocke, yeat, as somme menn constantlie affirme, hee made full espowsall promisse of her at his abode in Normandie. The name of this virgin, that ever I cowld learne, is not rehersed of enie mann, I thincke bie cause she lived not long. But Haraldus, who I weene was enticed therto bie his evel spirite, staringe on the embassadowrs with prowde and sterne cowntenance, sayed he wowlde perfowrme nether of them, and sent them packinge with that cuttid aunswere, and, leaste he showld bee taken unprovided, hee prepared his shippes and warriors for the sea, mindinge bothe by water

W. of Normandy demaunded that Harold sholde kepe his othe and promes made in Normandy which was denayed by Harold, wherupon W. made his warres in Inglond.

and lande to repell the Normans from his borders, if they camm to bee revenged. The duke, when bie his legats he understode the haute answere of the kinge, hee called his men to councell, and diligentlie conferred concerninge warre to bee made in Englonde. Haraldus in the meane while beganne to be infested with domesticall dissention throughe the meanes of his brother Tosto. But in the ende wee may make all thinges playne, here must I recognise som things more deepelie. There was in Haraldus, from his verie childehoode, manie trimme giftes bothe of boddie and minde, excellent beawtie in all his yeares, wheare-in was noe lesse dignitee then favore, great strengthe, docilite and towardnes in all artes, marvaylous knowlege bothe in ridinge and in armes, which thinges enkendeled the love of all menn towards himm, and especiallie of kinge Edwarde. On the other side his yonger brother named Tosto (whoe as wee shewed beefore camm with himme out of Normandie) soe maligned and envied at these his manifowlde commendable qualitees, that on a time, in the king's presence, he strake at the hedde of Haraldus, and awhiles skirmished with himme; and, beinge for the same unseemelie facte blamed of his prince, hee departed to Hereforde, wheare, for that hee evell intreated the companie and bande of Haraldus, the kinge banished him; and hee toke his voyage into Fraunce: whearfore, as soone as hee hearde of the deathe of kinge Edwarde, hee gathered shipps on all sydes, hee proclaymed open warrs againste Haraldus, and, takinge the Isle of Wyghte, hee spoyled the same. Then, bendinge towards Kent, hee annoyed that whole coste with robberies, which thinge fell owte merveluslie eevell for Haraldus: for he was constrayned to revoke his armie and navie, lately addressid towards Normandie, for the repelling of this distres, which thinge beinge once blowne abrode, Tosto, for feare, marched towardes North Humberland, and theare landinge his garrisons, made greete slaughter of people. Yeat partelie of the inhabitants, who hated himme as a common theefe and rover, partelie of the kinges shipps, hee was driven into Scotland, with noe lesse detrement of his navie then of his menne.

This broyle was skarcelie so soone quenched as an other more daungerus evell insewed in the necke thereof: for Tosto, when hee sawe small hope of succours in Scotlonde, he hoysed his sayles and went into Norvegia, havinge goodd hope to be releeved bie the goods and puissauce of the kinge thereof, named Haraldus, whoe was of renowned fame as then in all contries. Hee earnestlie requested him that hee wowlde vowchsafe to ayde him in soe a profitable a quarrell; and with manie gowlden promisses drave himm soe farre in to the blinde desire of purchasinge a kingdome, emong these flambes of domesticall sedition, that he entred the Sease, and with prosperus wind was driven to the Englishe shore, even to the entrie of the river Tine, which runnethe bie Newcastle, a fayre towne within the territorie of Deirham. I cann in noe wise condiscende to those coronographers which make mention that the Norwegian kinge, after hee understode the dissention of the two brothers, of his owne accorde, and meere desire of imperie, attempted these warrs, which is indeed soe far distante from all truthe that unethes it hathe enie face or likelihoode of veritee: for who is soe unwise to beleeve that Haraldus, a grave and prudent prince, unscilful bothe of the menn and places (for neether hadd hee intercourse with the Englishe nation, nether cowlde he claime enie righte in them), wolde enterprise soe longe and uncertaine a voyage, nether knoweng what daungers lurcked therein, nor cowlde well perceave emolument or proffetts ensewinge. Wherfore it is likelie that hee was called forthe of Tosto, as Saxo witnessethe, whoose credite must nott all together be frustrate, especiallie in relacion of his owne contries affaires. Wherfore Heraldus and Tosto, a fewe dayse abydinge at Tinemowthe for the relaxation of their sowldiers, and the better preparaunce of theire battayle, in fine toke on their waye, settinge their menn in ordre, with whom the two brothers Edwinus and Morcatus, earles of Mercia and North Humberland, didd encounter with a reasonable armie. The onsett was sounded on bothe sides, and the fight beganne, and a good while endewered doubtfull: but at

The Norvegians brought in by Tosto, brother to Harold, who proceded from Newcastell to Stanford, wher they were bothe slayne.

the lengthe the Englishemenn beinge encompased with too huge a multitude of enemies was overcommed, and yealded themselves, perfourminge hostages. Kinge Haraldus, whoe hasted to succoure his subjectes, beinge certified in his jornie of the evel adventure, was nothinge dismaid, but with more expedition after iiij. dayse cam to Staunford, wheare the Norvegians weare encamped a litell beyonde the river Derwente, and kepte the bridge, least their enemies should sodainlie passe over. The next day, puttinge there armies in araye, the kinge aproched nearer that he mighte conducte his men over the bridge, wheare a great parte of the daye hee was hindered of his passege bie the onlie manlie feates of one of the Norvegians, whoe, being assigned his standinge on the bridge for the defence therof, when he sawe the Englishemen hastelie russhinge thitherwarde, hee wente to the formost steppe therof, and rowlinge his ieys ruthefullie abowte his hedde, hee first slewe one and then another, and afterward manie of them hee ether put abacke or killed them forthe righte, while they strived to winne the bridge; with this marvelus fortitude hee soe amazed his adversaries, for as muche as alone hee withstoode suche a multitude, that with one consent they ymagened to slay bie some deceyte. The bridge was then all of woodde, and the middell pere therof was full of chinckes and riftes; whearbie, while certaine helde him taske in fightinge, one goenge privelie underneathe him with a boate perced his bowells with a darte, and soe bie that sleighte this mann, whose name deserved immortalitee, fell downe deade after greate slaughter, not voyde of memorie and fame. Haraldus, after the winninge of the bridge, camm on backe of their enemies while they wandered at pleasure, slayinge at the firste onsett the Norvegian kinge and his brother Tosto, which beinge once knowne, all the reste beetooke themselves to flighte. The occision of this pursuite and chace redownded to the utter distruction of the Norwegian parte, as there wheare we more pricked them forwarde then valiance; nether weare the Englishemenne free from detrement, or cleare from blood shedd.

The valyentnes of on of the Norvegians.

The remainders of Norvegians whoe weare lefte for the preservation of the shippes, as soone as they harde of the deathe of the kinge bie suche as fledde to them, they loosed their shipps, and sodaynlie beinge caried owte of the sighte of the lande they directed their race into theyr contrie, whether as soone as they camme, they replenished all sortes with dolorus mourning for this soe great a plague. All Norway beecam lamentable, and beeinge berefte of such a noble prince it shortlie beecamm servile to the Danes. It lothes mee in this place to note the grosse negligence of certaine Englishe writers whoe contende that this warre was begonne of the Danes, not of the Norwayes, under the reygne of Harvicus, whearas, indeade, none of their kings was soe named. For Sweno, who indeade at that season was kinge of Denmarcke, was soe busied at home that hee cowlde not entend foreine wars; whearfore I wowld say, that Tosto was not so fonde as to requeste him of ayde; but trewlie even of the verie Englishe affayers those writers (whose names I willinglie forbare) doe ofte times write all things soe diverslie that a man wold thincke they hadd never sene the cronicles of that nation, which is most manifestlie proved bie there varienge bothe in places and menns names. This I thought good to advertise, partlie that this one admonition mighte suffise, partelie that their incurie may not be a blemishe to our historie, when the readers of suche matters shall perceave the diversitee of it: but lette us prosecute the reste. Kinge Haraldus, greatlie rejoycing in this victorie, went unto Yorcke, that he mighte refowrme and appease the province, being tossed in the waters of soe manie battayles.

Norway servile to the Danes.

In the meane season William duke of Normandie was certified bie espialls that the Englishe menne weare busied in the Norvegian warrs, and that the sowthe costes weare kept with noe garrison, wheare hee minded to sett his shippes at rode; wherfore chosinge forthe the flowre of the yowthefull parsons, hee fraught his shipps, and, with the good hope of all his fiers, hee speedelie sayled into Englond with xxx. shippes and above, and landed at

W. Conquerors arryvall at Hastings, in Sussex.

the village named Hastings, and there assemblinge his companie he pitched his tents. Even there he is reported to have hadde a token and ominus prognostication of this imperie to comm, for at his first stepping owte of his shippe he slipped with the one legge, and, stayeng on the other, didd thruste it verie deape in the sondes, which being espied, a certayne citizen rejoycinge for gladdnes, skipping, sayde, 'O duke, thow howldest Englond on sewer foote.' But the inhabitants of the places adjoyninge, being astonied at the sodaine arrivall of soe great an armie, spedelie certified the kinge of all thinges bie their letters, who was mervalus pensife for this sodaine and unminded affaires. Moreover, in the battayle of the Norways hee allmoste loste the cheefe puissaunce and flowre of his soldiers: yea, and manie of them which as yeat weare extant weare verie maliciuslie bente, for that the late bootie was unæquallie distributed, whome for goodd reason he hadd in ielowsie. With which things allbeitt Haraldus weare pricked, yeat as he was of noble corage, soe at the first tidings hee chaunged his pretensed jornie, and bie and bie assemblinge his people, hee was compelled to repayre towards London, and soe to his adversarie, indifferentlie augmentinge his armie, while all suche resortede unto him as regarded the healthe of their contrie. Wherfore, traveling x. miles farder, he pitched his pavilions neare unto his enemie. The Norman allso moved his tentes and drew into sighte of the counterparte, as all in readines to doe battayle. Here have I mine authors affirminge that manie conditions weare offered on bothe sides, that the matter mighte bee pacified without bloodshedde; howbeit ether of them made refusall as they who minded to assaye the chaunce of battayle, and therfore earnestlie admonished and stirred up their enemie to the fighte. But Haraldus firste callinge his companie together made this oration: 'Yow have hearde eftsones (I dare saye, mie noble warriors,) that our aunciters and forefathers obteyned this rioll kingdom at the firste not without great travayle, deadlie wars, and piteus effusion of bloodde; yow are not ignoraunt howe perpetuallie they have acc-

[...]e oration [of] Harold.

quited and clensed the same from the vexation and incursions of their borderers; yow know assuredlie that bie their vertew and prowes they have soe enlarged the same that now at this presence some nations feare our wealthe and power, somm regions envie and repine at the same; owr confines and neighbours are adreade, whoe daylie fall at our feete for peace and tranquillitee; the barbarus alienes and foriners malignethe therat, who being pressed and griped at home with the streyghtnes and exilitee of all things, keepe there teethe watering at other mens goods, and, for verie hunger stervinge, are feyne more like roges and villans then accordinge to the right martial lawes to take their weapons in hand and in forayne contries desperatly to endaunger themselves to a thowsand perills. This was the verie reason whie the Danes soe manie years annoyed us; this was the cause that the Norvegians (ceasinge to reherse enie more) didd invade this our awncient monarchie, whome yowe bie youre worthie valiance have putt to flight and utterance: finallie, there is noe other quarel indeade whie the Norman dothe now desier to have adoe with us, surelie a kinde of people descended from the Danes, whome we have often vanquished, whome wee accounte our vassayles, and have yoked with servilitee. Nevertheles this William, the base sonne of an whorishe concubine, gathering a bande of theeves, dothe nowe intende to robbe us of our goods, to pollute this our excellent riolme, to extirpe and destroy the nobilitee; whearefore I lovinglie advertise yow to bee of trustie and present corage, and wheras, bie the helpe of Godd, yow shall enter on this battayle, call to minde that in youre right hands consisteth the saftie and healthe noe lesse of youre selfe then of the whole Englishe nation. If wee shall overcomm we shall for ever deliver our contrie from the injuries of our adversaries; if wee ourselves bee vanquished (which Godde forbedd) we shall die in the behoofe of our common wealthe, which is the goodliest thing in the worlde.' When hee hadd thus sayde, with great showtes eche mann made a signe that withowte all feare they wowld ronne on their adversaries. On the other parte, the Duke encoraging his men sayde thus: 'Whethersoever I turne mine ieys (mie moste faytheful and valiant subjects,) I see yow all full of corage and strengthe; I beehowlde allsoe yow, mie feeres and confederats, not withowte a gladde herte, howe noblie, beesides yowr faythfulnes, yow agree with Rollo, the beginner of our line and nation, in vertew and valiance; trulie the verie same imperie which hee with unspeakable toyle comprised in a land of hostilitee, owre predecessors bie there manwhood have worthelie amplified, and yow yowre selves have princelie supported and made moste flowrishinge; whereunto nowe bie Godds favor and permission yow shall adjoyne Englonde, which indeade is owres bie the promisse and gifte of that worthie prince our kinsmanne kinge Edwarde; whearfore wite ye well, mie lordes, that wee make noe warrs against the londe, but againste Haraldus, the sonne of the traytor Godwinus, wrongfullie withholdinge it, mindinge bie all meanes to dispossesse himme, and rewarde him with deserved penaltie for the breache of his othe, as one in whome is noe credite, noe estimation of synceritee, noe feare of the divine Power, who with thease intollerable offences (as it is justlie to bee thoughte) hath wonderuslie provoked Gods wrath and indignation; wherfore the victorie shall bee owres, whearof the greater the hope is, soe mutche the more ernestlie addresse yowre selves herto, as menn that shall fighte for an assewered and present rewarde.'

With these advertisementes the mindes of eche parte beinge enflamed, the day beefore the Ides of Octobre, bringinge foorthe their armies, and hoysing theire standerds, and according to the auncient guise sowndinge the blooddie onsett in great showtes and malicius ranckowre, they rann together, yeat first spending their shotte and dartes, and after takinge theire brighte swordes in their handes. The Englishemenn, as mindefull of their owld worthines, waxed verie hotte and coragius; the Normans manfullie resisted, as voyde of all feare; the combate was mainteyned with great rigor. Thus the battayle a whyle endeweringe on æquall condition, Haraldus with his light horsmen entered the vawarde and souccered the travayled persons and restored freshe in the roowme of the maymed. In the meane season the Norman capitaine seinge the Englishemenn enforced them selves to doe feates of armes, hee commanded his horssemen to russhe into the middest of the cownter parte to breake their aray; but perceavinge them nether able one foote to drive backe the Englishe men and to bee stryken doune on all sides, as a politique governor hee thowghte beste to dissemble flienge awaye, and privelie commanded his menn to abate their violence, and to retrayte a littell, that their enemies folowinge might loose their ordre, for the Englishe people, which weare fewer in numbre, hadd pitched themselves orderlie together againste the multitude, wherfore the Normann, seinge his menne geeve grownde, and the enemie beginne intentivelie the chase, he forthwith placed a portion of his horsmenn and freshe footemenn privilie in a place not farre from the maine battaile, sodainlie to sett uppon their adversaries. Thus the broyle waxed greate, bie reason they fayned to torne their backes, they gave yeat a littell more grounde. Then the Englishe parte beinge triumphant, as they whoe reckened the victorie allreadie in their right handds, lefte their aray, and skatteringe them selves in the persewte, alyghted on the place wheare the trayne and ambushement laye. The Normans thronged owte in sharpe assawte on the Englishe; thus beinge dissevered, and running abowte them in a ringe, hindered their passage and made great slawghter. It is wonderus to be towlde with how presente spirits and bowlde harte, with what force the Englishe menne, beinge cleane owte of ordre and encompassed of theire enemies, didd resiste, nothing abating the fight, whilest noblie theyr kinge encoraged them, fowght in presence, and worthelie assisted them. But after they saw his braines roved throwghe with a darte, and him fallinge deade from his horsse, then they piteuslie quayled, som saving themselves bie flighte, and the reste beinge slayne. Duke William after this victorie rejoiced more then cann bee ex-

W. Conqueror's victory. The dethe of Haroide, and he

buried at Waltham Crose, being the very laste of the English line who had contynued after the coming in under Hengestus, 618 years.

pressed, and is reported the nighte enseuing to have hard a voyce from above, sayinge, 'O! William, thow haste nowe vanquished, thow and thine offspring shall heare reygne.' Thus it commethe to passe that of those thinges wee dreame which wee earnestlie desier. The nexte day was dedicated to the gatheringe of spoyle and refresshinge of their werie bodies, which beinge done, the duke desieringe to use the oportunitee of his victorie, toke his voyage towardes London, and from all coste the people mette with himme, and for feare yealded to his mercie: but a more convenient place in the nexte booke shall make relacion herof.

After this discomfiture the earles Edowinus and Morcatus, which escaped in this great overthrowe, fledd to London, in minde to deliberat what weare beste to bee donn; but there a mann cowlde have hearde nothinge but dolefull lamentacion, neather seane enie thinge but sorowfull visages.

This was a most noble fighte, and supported with the exceading occision of ether parte, to the nombre of more then xx. thowsand menne, wherin the whole Englishe puissance and imperie camm to ruine, which was portended bie a comete, or blasing starre, of woonderfull bignesse, which appeared manie dayes. Haraldus was fownde emonge the deadd carkasses of his soldiers, and his corps was restored to his mother Thira bie his enemie. It was buried in the churche of the hollie crosse at the village named Waltham, which hee beegann to bylde, or rather restored, as appeareth bie the shortenes of his life. There was an abbay of secular chanons, and is distante from London abowt xii. miles, wherunto hee gave fayer possessions. The river Lea ronnethe bie Waltham, which dividethe Essex from Hertfordshier.

Haraldus was xxxvj. in the ordre of the kinges from Cerdicius, whoe, beinge the verie laste of the Englishe line, at one verie instance of time was within the revolution of a yeare berefte bothe of his life and kingdom, in the yeare of our Lorde Godd MLXVIJ., and the DCXVIJ. yeare after the comminge of the Englishe people into Brittaine, under the conducte of Hengestus, in the which space the reignes and dominions greatlie altered. The first was the Kentishe kingdom, which hadd originall the CCCCL. yeare of our Salvation; and after that vj. other kingdoms hadd their beginninges at other times, as aboove wee have convenientlie specified; which all for that in conclusion thei weare resolved into the Westerne kingdom, wee must neades speake somwhat towchinge the duracion therof. The reigne of the West Saxons, Cerdicius being the firste fownder therof, beganne DXXI. yeare after the nativitee of Christe, and LXXI. after the arrivall of the Englishe men, and there unto, within the space of ccccxvij. yeares ensewinge, wear annected the other realmes, which was in the DCCCCXXXVIIJ. yeare of our Salvation, at the which time Adelstanus, the sonn of Edwarde the elder, after the xiij. yeare of his reigne, receaved into allegiance and homage the Northumbrians, putting to flighte Analaphus and Gothofredus, the sonnes of the Dane Sithricus, as wee beefore made mention in owre vj. booke: bie meanes whearof hee was the first of the Englishe kinges that attained the whole monarchie, which endeured abowte an cxxviij. yeares after, unto the deathe of Haraldus, whoe was vanquished bie the Normans, yet not alltogether sownde and inviolate, for in this discours xxi. yeares weare spente in Danishe dominion and reygne; whearfore the Westerne regiment, bie dewe computation, ceased the DXLVJ. yeare after that Cerdicius, their firste prince, obteined jurisdiction in the Ilonde, and the DCXVIJ. after the comminge in of the Englishemen, and finallie the MLXVIJ. yeare of our Salvation, at the which time William duke of Normandi, bie the overcomminge of Haraldus, gotte the kingdom. And thus doe all humaine affairs ebbe and flowe, soe that nothinge is so certaine as incertayntee it selfe, and continuall chaunge ether into better or into woorse.

FINIS.

INDEX.

B.

C.

J. B. Nichols and Son, 25, Parliament Street, Westminster.